THOMSON'S FAMILY LAW IN SCOTLAND

THOMSON'S FAMILY LAW IN SCOTLAND

Eighth Edition

Katy Macfarlane
Lecturer in Law at the University of Edinburgh

Bloomsbury Professional

LONDON • DUBLIN • EDINBURGH • NEW YORK • NEW DELHI • SYDNEY

BLOOMSBURY PROFESSIONAL
Bloomsbury Publishing Plc
50 Bedford Square, London, WC1B 3DP, UK
1385 Broadway, New York, 10018, USA
29 Earlsfort Terrace, Dublin 2, Ireland

BLOOMSBURY and the Diana logo are trademarks of Bloomsbury Publishing Plc

First published in Great Britain 2022

Reprinted 2022

British Library Cataloguing-in-Publication Data

A catalogue record for this book is available from the British Library.

ISBN:	PB:	978-1-52651-387-8
	Epdf:	978-1-52651-389-2
	Epub:	978-1-52651-388-5

Typeset by Evolution Design and Digital (Kent)
Printed and bound by CPI Group (UK) Ltd, Croydon, CR0 4YY

To find out more about our authors and books visit www.bloomsburyprofessional.com. Here you will find extracts, author information, details of forthcoming events and the option to sign up for our newsletters

For James and Lizz
with love

Contents

Preface

Professor Joe Thomson was one of the very best and it has been my honour to update *Thomson's Family Law in Scotland.*

There have been many significant changes to family and child law in Scotland in the eight years since the previous update of this book. In that time, legislation has reflected the different forms of family and lifestyles that are prevalent in Scotland and the growing respect for the legal rights of children and their involvement in decisions that affect them. There is still a way to go.

I would like to thank all those who gave me advice, support and practical help throughout my work on the Eighth edition of this book. In particular, I am deeply indebted to Andrew Steven, John Fotheringham and Sarah Trainer all of whom have contributed their substantial legal expertise. I would like to thank my research assistants: Morag McEwan, Molly Little and Gabriella Lipschitz whose input was invaluable and who helped shape this edition for a new generation of lawyers.

Thanks also to Bloomsbury Professional for their patience in allowing me additional time to produce the new edition during the pandemic lockdown.

Finally, Bloomsbury Professional and I would like to thank Annie Thomson for her understanding of the importance of producing a new edition of Joe's work for Scots law students and professionals alike.

Katy Macfarlane

August 2022

Table of Statutes

References are to paragraph number

Table of Statutory Instruments

References are to paragraph number

Table of Conventions

References are to paragraph number

Table of Cases

References are to paragraph number

D

H

N

Introduction

In this short introduction it is proposed to explain the selection of subjects chosen for extended treatment and to discuss the policies underlying some of the most important features of contemporary Scots family law.

From the end of the eighteenth century the nuclear family became the essential family unit in Scotland.[1] This comprised a man and a woman, who have a sexual relationship, and their children. Before their relationship gave rise to mutual legal rights and obligations, as a general rule the couple had to marry. More importantly, it was only when a couple married that the law regulated their income and capital when their relationship broke down, in the form of financial provision on divorce. Similarly, a spouse had important legal rights in respect of succession to a proportion of the deceased spouse's estate.[2]

It was a fundamental principle of the law that to be eligible to marry the parties had to be of the opposite sex, *viz*, only men could marry women and only women could marry men. With the increasing acceptance of gay and lesbian relationships in the latter part of the twentieth century, the Civil Partnership Act 2004 enabled parties of the same sex to register a civil partnership which gave them similar legal rights and obligations as spouses. In 2014, just ten years later, the Scottish Parliament accepted that it was wrong to continue to prevent persons from marrying on grounds of their sexual orientation. And so, under the Marriage and Civil Partnership (Scotland) Act 2014, marriage is now open to same sex as well as different sex couples.[3] The Civil Partnership (Scotland) Act 2020 amended the CPA 2004 to allow different sex couples to register a civil partnership.[4] Thus, in contemporary Scots Law, marriage means 'marriage between persons of different sexes and marriage between persons of the same sex'.[5] References to the word 'marriage' (and related expressions) in any enactment, passed or to be passed, or in any document, is to be interpreted to include marriages between persons of the same sex as well as persons of different sex.[6] In so far as being married is relevant for the operation of any rule of law,[7] the rule of law applies equally to different sex and same sex marriages.[8]

Over the last years of the twentieth century, the law began to recognise that a large number of couples were living in different sex relationships outside marriage and that non-married different sex cohabitants faced similar problems to married couples, especially when their relationships broke down. To address this, the legislature began to provide cohabitants with certain rights in relation to particular matters, for example the occupation of the home in which they were, or had been, living.[9] These rights were extended by the Family Law (Scotland) Act 2006 to include the right to financial provision when the cohabiting couple separates or the relationship ends on the death of one of the parties and the deceased died without a will, ie intestate. These statutory provisions apply to same sex as well as different sex cohabitants.

Thus, Scots law has responded to the different forms of lifestyle which are prevalent in Scotland in the twenty-first century by providing three legal regimes, *viz*, marriage, civil partnership and cohabitation. This study of Scots family law attempts to examine these regimes.

Although marriage and civil partnership are central institutions in Scots family law, it should be noted that they are of very little legal significance for the spouses or civil partners *during* the marriage or civil partnership. Until the later years of the nineteenth century, a woman lost many important rights on marriage, for example in relation to her property. Since then, the law has endeavoured to achieve legal equality between the spouses by enacting that for various purposes, for example contract, delict and property, the spouses should be treated as though they were unmarried.[10] Similarly, for many legal purposes, civil partners are treated as though they have not registered their partnership. But while legal equality may have been achieved, the application of rules which ignore the fact that the persons concerned are married or have registered a civil partnership, leads, particularly in relation to property matters, to results which are both artificial and unjust. Consequently, legislation has introduced special rules for spouses, civil partners and, to a lesser extent, cohabitants which take into account the fact that they are living together.[11]

Of course, marriage and civil partnership do give rise to rights and obligations for the spouses and civil partners. Spouses and civil partners, but not cohabitants, owe a duty to aliment (ie maintain) each other during the marriage or civil partnership.[12] Moreover, when parents are married at the date of a child's conception or subsequently, the father will automatically have parental responsibilities and parental rights in relation to the child;[13] if the couple never marry, only the child's mother will have parental responsibilities and parental rights unless the man has been registered as the child's father, or until he obtains them as a consequence of a court order or agreement with the mother. But the most important legal consequence of marriage and civil partnership is that a court can award financial provision for the spouses or civil partners if their relationship ends in divorce or dissolution.[14]

Judicial divorce has been possible in Scots law since the Reformation in 1560, but divorce was not a prevalent feature of Scottish society until the twentieth century. The reasons for this are complex. While the grounds for divorce were restricted to the defender's adultery or desertion until the Divorce (Scotland) Act 1938, religious disapproval of divorce must also have acted as a considerable restraint. As a result of the increasing secularisation of Scottish society in the twentieth century, the social upheavals of two world wars and the emphasis on personal fulfilment in sexual relationships, divorce has become an accepted part of contemporary Scottish society. The law has responded to the demand for easier divorce with the introduction of a system based, theoretically at least, on the no fault principle of irretrievable breakdown of marriage.[15] It is estimated that in Scotland at least one in three marriages now ends in divorce and a divorced person will often enter a second marriage. There is no reason why the dissolution of civil partnership should prove to be less common.

Given this high incidence of breakdown, it is crucial that the law provides a system of financial provision which will enable the income and capital of the spouses or civil partners to be redistributed in a fair manner on divorce or dissolution. Until 1964, divorce was treated as judicial death: financial provision took the form of treating the defender as though dead and awarding the pursuer the legal rights to which a spouse would have been entitled from the defender's estate. That system was replaced[16] by one which gave the judge who was hearing the claim discretion to make financial provision which appeared just in the circumstances. Any advantages of flexibility which this system may have had were outweighed by the uncertainty that ensued. A much more sophisticated system was introduced by the Family Law (Scotland) Act 1985. This provides a set of principles to be used in determining the financial provision that should be awarded in the circumstances of a particular marriage or civil partnership.[17] This gives greater certainty on the outcome of possible litigation and so enables spouses and civil partners – and their legal advisers – to negotiate a settlement without recourse to the courts.

The law on divorce and dissolution can be criticised on the ground of its complexity which inhibits the parties from being able to end their marriage or civil partnership with the minimum of legal intervention. On the other hand, the reform of the law on financial provision has, because of the increase in certainty as to the outcome of litigation, enabled the parties or their legal advisers to reach a settlement more frequently than in the past. It is generally accepted that modern family law should encourage spouses and civil partners to settle, between themselves, the property and other issues which arise when their relationship breaks down without recourse to litigation. At present, Scots law only does this to a limited extent. The opportunity was not taken in the Family Law (Scotland) Act 2006 to introduce an even more simplified form of divorce and dissolution under which the parties simply give notice of an intention to do so:[18] and more support could then be given to family mediation services to help spouses and civil partners reach agreement on such issues as property, financial provision and looking after their children.

Children have always had rights in Scots law. They are born as rights holders. Most of these rights were, and are, exigible against their parents. The difficulty, of course, is that children will not be in a position to exercise these rights when they are too young to have the required capacity to do so. Scotland is committed to the full acknowledgement and respect of children's rights and, to this end, is currently progressing with incorporation of the UN Convention on the Rights of the Child (UNCRC) into its domestic law.[19]

Scots law has always recognised that parents owe duties towards their children, albeit that the parents never married. For centuries, however, the extent of a child's rights which were exigible from his or her parents – and remoter relatives – depended upon whether or not the child was legitimate. A child was legitimate if he or she was conceived or born during the parents' marriage. During the twentieth century, piecemeal reforms alleviated the legal position of the illegitimate child. As a result of the Law Reform (Parent and Child) (Scotland) Act 1986,[20] the legal position of an illegitimate child was, for all but a few minor purposes, equated with that of a legitimate child. The status of illegitimacy was finally abolished by the Family Law (Scotland) Act 2006, s 21. Nevertheless, it remains the case that when a child is a member of a one-parent family, he or she will more often suffer social disadvantages stemming from impoverished economic circumstances than a child who is brought up by two adults.

While parents owe responsibilities and obligations towards their children, for example the duty of aliment, they also enjoy important rights in respect of the care and upbringing of their child. The nature and extent of these parental responsibilities and parental rights has been one of the most controversial aspects of modern family law – in particular finding the balance between the gradual relinquishing of parental authority and control to allow for the growing autonomy and decision-making of the child, for example, on such important matters as medical treatment or contraception. Here the views of the child are at the centre of the decision-making process and should be adequately represented.

Given the prevalence of the breakdown of adult relationships, an important issue for modern family law is to attempt to ensure that the children of the family are well looked after when the parents or carers separate. Scots law applies the welfare principle as the criterion for the determination of such issues.[21] In practice, however, the courts are generally reluctant to disturb the arrangements which have *de facto* been operative prior to the breakdown, thus preserving the *status quo ante*: this is generally thought to be in the best interests of the child. Thus, the law merely underpins the self-regulation by the parents or carers themselves of how the children of the family should be looked after when their relationship breaks down. It remains the case that, in relationship breakdown, the mother will *de facto* be looking after any children, so the preservation of the *status quo* which is generally endorsed by the courts when applying the welfare principle unintentionally reinforces the traditional view that the care of a child is primarily the responsibility of the mother. However, the law stresses that children need both parents and that parental responsibilities and parental rights continue where the child no longer lives with the parent concerned.

In a modern society, the state has a crucial role in supporting children who are at risk when their families have become dysfunctional. State agencies have certain powers and duties to help in this situation.[22] Scots law also has a system of children's hearings which can provide compulsory supervision orders for children in need of care and protection.[23] The danger of any welfare-based system is, of course, that a parent's *prima facie* right to bring up a child and the child's *prima facie* right to be brought up in his or her family environment may be given insufficient weight when it is thought that the removal of the child from the family is desirable for the child's welfare. Therefore, a delicate balance has to be found and procedural safeguards must exist so that the rights of parents and children towards each other are given proper consideration. At the same time, the procedures must be compatible with the European Convention on Human Rights, most of which has been incorporated into domestic Scots law.[24]

One of the most remarkable features of contemporary Scots family law is that much of the law is of recent origin. As well as the introduction of civil partnerships.[25] and same sex marriage,[26] the last forty years have, for example, seen the full-scale reform of financial provision on divorce,[27] illegitimacy,[28] parental responsibilities and parental rights[29] and financial provision for cohabitants on separation and death.[30] These reforms are the result of the work of the Scottish Law Commission which has played an important role in providing Scotland with a system of family law that is capable of meeting the needs of contemporary Scottish society.

1 Before that time the extended family in the form of clans was important, at least in the Highlands of Scotland.

2 On the spouses' rights to succession, see **Ch 3**.

3 Civil partnerships continue and, ironically perhaps, only same sex couples can register a partnership.

4 Civil Partnership Act 2004, s 1.

5 Marriage (Scotland) Act 1977, s 26(2).

6 Marriage and Civil Partnership (Scotland) Act 2014, ss 4(1), (5), (11), (12) and (13). This does not apply if the enactment or document otherwise provides.

7 For example the rules on marriage by cohabitation with habit and repute discussed at paras 1.14ff above.

8 MCP(S)A 2014, s 4(6).

9 See **Ch 9**.

10 On contract and delict, see **Ch 3**; on property, see **Chs 4** and **5**.

11 See, for example, the Family Law (Scotland) Act 1985, s 25: discussed in **Ch 4** and the Family Law (Scotland) Act 2006, s 26: discussed in **Ch 9**.
12 On aliment, see **Ch 3**.
13 Children (Scotland) Act 1995, s 3(1)(b): discussed in **Ch 10**.
14 On financial division on divorce and dissolution, see **Ch 7**.
15 Divorce and dissolution are discussed in **Ch 6**.
16 Succession (Scotland) Act 1964, Part V; later replaced by the Divorce (Scotland) Act 1976, s 5.
17 Family Law (Scotland) Act 1985, ss 8–17; discussed in **Ch 7**.
18 See the Divorce, Dissolution and Separation Act 2020 which amends the Matrimonial Causes Act 1973, s 1 and Civil Partnership Act 2004, s 44 for the reform of divorce and dissolution law in England and Wales.
19 See: United Nations Convention on the Rights of the Child (Incorporation) (Scotland) Bill.
20 The Law Reform (Parent and Child) (Scotland) Act 1986 is discussed in detail in **Chs 9** and **10**.
21 See **Ch 12**.
22 See **Ch 14**.
23 See **Ch 15**.
24 Convention for the Protection of Human Rights and Fundamental Freedoms (Rome, 4 November 1950; 213 UNTS 221; TS 71 (1953); Cmd 8969). Most, but not all, of the 1950 Convention has been incorporated into United Kingdom law, as Sch 1 to the Human Rights Act 1998.
25 Civil Partnership Act 2004.
26 Marriage and Civil Partnership (Scotland) Act 2014.
27 See the Family Law (Scotland) Act 1985: discussed in **Ch 7**.
28 See the Law Reform (Parent and Child) (Scotland) Act 1986: discussed in **Ch 9**.
29 See the Children (Scotland) Act 1995, Pt I: discussed in **Ch 11**.
30 Family Law (Scotland) Act 2006, ss 28 and 29: discussed in **Ch 8**.

Chapter 1

Getting married and registering a civil partnership

PART I: GETTING MARRIED

INTRODUCTION

1.1 Article 12 of the European Convention on Human Rights[1] provides:

> 'Men and women of marriageable age have the right to marry and to found a family, according to the national laws governing the exercise of this right.'

Scots law goes further and recognises the right of men to marry men and women to marry women.[2] In this part we shall discuss how persons can marry under Scots law.

---

1 Convention for the Protection of Human Rights and Fundamental Freedoms (Rome, 4 November 1950; 213 UNTS 221; TS 71 (1953); Cmd 8969). Most, but not all, of the 1950 Convention has been incorporated into United Kingdom law as Sch 1 to the Human Rights Act 1998.

2 Marriage (Scotland) Act 1977, s 26(2) See: Kenneth Norrie, *Now the dust has settled; The Marriage and Civil Partnership (Scotland) Act* 2014 JR 135; and *Converting civil partnerships into marriages* Fam LB 2015, 133(Jan), 4–7.

ENGAGEMENTS

1.2 It is customary for a couple to become engaged for a period before they marry. At common law an engagement was a contract and wrongful failure to implement the promise to marry gave rise to an action in damages. These damages included not only compensation for pecuniary loss arising from the breach, for example the cost of preparations for the wedding, but also for solatium to compensate the innocent party's injured feelings and wounded pride.[1] The Scottish Law Commission took the view that actions for breach of promise had become anachronistic in the late twentieth century and recommended abolition.[2]

By s 1(1) of the Law Reform (Husband and Wife) (Scotland) Act 1984, it is declared that:

> 'No promise of marriage or agreement between two persons to marry one another shall have effect under the law of Scotland to create any rights or obligations; and no action for breach of any such promise or agreement may be brought in any court in Scotland, whatever the law applicable to the promise or agreement.'[3]

The extent of this provision is wide. First, an engagement is no longer a legally enforceable contract; therefore any contractual remedies for breach of promise are no longer competent in Scottish courts.[4] Secondly, by stipulating that a promise or agreement to marry does not create any rights or obligations in Scots law, it would appear that the section excludes any delictual liability which might arise from a breach of promise. For example, if A deliberately lied by promising to marry B, B would appear to have no right to sue A in delict on the ground of A's fraudulent misrepresentation.[5] Thus unlike the parallel English legislation[6] which only prevents agreements to marry operating as contracts, the Law Reform (Husband and Wife) (Scotland) Act 1984 prohibits delictual, as well as contractual, remedies.

The 1984 Act does not address itself to any of the property issues which can arise between engaged couples. Where the marriage does not take place, any property dispute, for example over the ownership of a house which was bought with a view to marriage, will be governed by the general principles of the law of property.[7] The law of unjustified enrichment may also be relevant. In *Shilliday v Smith*,[8] a woman provided her fiancé with funds so that he could improve the house in which they intended to live after they were married. When the marriage did not take place she obtained recompense for the expenditure since it was clear that she had not intended the money to be a gift and that the payment was conditional on the marriage taking place.[9]

Where the couple does marry, any property acquired during the engagement for use as a family home, or to be used in the home, will be regarded as matrimonial property for the purpose of financial provision on divorce.[10]

There are no special property rules in relation to gifts between engaged couples. If the gift is intended to be outright, for example a birthday present, it need not be returned if the engagement is broken off. Where a gift is made expressly or impliedly[11] conditional on the marriage taking place, it must be returned if the condition fails: and the donor may use the *condictio causa data causa non secuta*[12] to recover the property.

Unlike the position in England,[13] under Scots law, there are no specific provisions in respect of gifts of engagement rings. In one sheriff court case it was held that the gift of an engagement ring is made unconditionally[14] but in another[15] it was thought that the ring was returnable if the marriage did not take place – unless the donor had unjustifiably broken off the engagement. A third possibility is that the ring is given on the implied condition that it should be returned if the marriage does not take place for any reason. Given that engagements give rise to no legal rights or obligations between the parties, it is thought that it would be consistent with the policy of the Law Reform (Husband and Wife) (Scotland) Act 1984 if engagement rings were presumed to be outright gifts; but that this presumption should be able to be rebutted on proof that the gift was intended to be subject to the condition that it should be returned if the marriage did not take place. Where the engagement ring is of sentimental value or is a family heirloom of the giver, then its return would be implied if the engagement is called off.

Where a couple receives engagement presents from third parties, it is thought that these are returnable if the marriage does not take place.[16]

Note that s 128 of the Civil Partnership Act 2004 mirrors s 1(1) of the Law Reform (Husband and Wife) (Scotland) Act 1984:

> 'No promise or agreement to enter into a civil partnership creates any rights or obligations under the law of Scotland; and no action for breach of such a promise or agreement may be brought in any court in Scotland, whatever the law applicable to the promise or agreement.'

1 *Hogg v Gow* 27 May 1812 FC.
2 Report of the Scottish Law Commission on Outdated Rules in the Law of Husband and Wife (1983) (Scot Law Com No 76).
3 By the Law Reform (Husband and Wife) (Scotland) Act 1984, s 1(2), the provision is expressly made retrospective.

4 This is so, whatever the proper law of the promise or agreement.
5 Similarly, there would be no right to sue in negligence if the promise was made carelessly: for example, if without taking reasonable care to discover whether he had the capacity to marry the promisee, a man gives a promise to marry which he cannot fulfil.
6 Law Reform (Miscellaneous Provisions) Act 1970, s 1(1).
7 In *Grieve v Morrison* 1993 SLT 852, an engaged couple bought a house, title to which was taken in joint names. Part of the price was the free proceeds from the sale of the woman's previous house. When the marriage did not take place, the woman failed to recover the proceeds because she had not established that the transfer of the proceeds to purchase the new house was made in consideration that the marriage would take place. Instead, the court ordered a division and sale under which both parties obtained half the free proceeds from the sale of the new house. On actions for division and sale, see **Ch 5**.
8 1998 SC 725.
9 For discussion on the law of unjustified enrichment in relation to cohabitation, see **Ch 8**.
10 Family Law (Scotland) Act 1985, s 10(4): discussed in **Ch 7**. Similarly, moveable property obtained in prospect of the marriage is subject to the presumption of equal shares in household goods: Family Law (Scotland) Act 1985, s 25: discussed in **Ch 4**.
11 For example, the gift of family jewellery.
12 Stair *The Institutions of the Law of Scotland* (6th edn, 1981) I 7.7. The *condictio* provides that, where payment or performance has been given and the counterpart consideration has failed, the money paid or the value of the performance should be restored under principles of unjustified enrichment. Before the *condictio* is applicable, it must be clear that the transfer of the property was subject to a mutually agreed understanding that it was made in consideration that the marriage would take place: *Grieve v Morrison* 1993 SLT 852. See also *Shilliday v Smith* 1998 SC 725. The obligation to make restitution arises when the marriage will no longer take place, ie when the condition has failed, and not when the property was originally transferred.
13 See the Law Reform (Miscellaneous Provisions) Act 1970, s 3(2), where there is a rebuttable presumption that the gift of the ring is made unconditionally.
14 *Gold v Hume* (1950) 66 Sh Ct Rep 85.
15 *Savage v M'Allister* (1952) 68 Sh Ct Rep 11.
16 Stair I 7.7.

THE FORMALITIES OF MARRIAGE

1.3 A marriage will not be valid unless the parties have capacity to marry and the marriage conforms to the formalities required by the law of the place where the marriage is celebrated. In this section, the formal requirements of a valid marriage celebrated in Scotland are discussed.

Scots law recognises two possible methods of marrying, ie regular or formal marriages and irregular or informal marriages.

Regular marriages: formal marriages

1.4 The law on the formalities of regular marriages is to be found in the Marriage (Scotland) Act 1977.[1] No person domiciled in Scotland may marry before he or she attains the age of 16.[2] Where a marriage in Scotland between two person either of whom is under the age of 16, the marriage shall be void.[3]

There are two types of regular marriage in Scotland: a civil marriage and a religious or belief marriage. However, before either can take place, the parties must follow certain civil preliminaries.[4]

---

1 As amended, particularly by the Marriage and Civil Partnership (Scotland) Act 2014.

2 Marriage (Scotland) Act 1977, s 1(1). Note that the minimum age for marriage or registering a civil partnership in England and Wales is to be increased to 18 years old. See the Marriage and Civil Partnership (Minimum Age) Act 2022, s 1 (marriage); s 3 (civil partnerships) (not in force at time of writing (June 2022)). Will Scotland follow suit?

3 M(S)A 1977, s 1(2).

4 Accordingly, the proclamation of banns has no legal significance in Scots law.

Civil preliminaries

Marriage notices

1.5 Each of the parties to a marriage which is intended to be solemnised in Scotland, whether it is to be a civil, religious or belief ceremony, must submit a notice of intention to marry – a marriage notice – to the district registrar for the registration district in which the marriage is to be solemnised.[1] There is no need for either party to be resident in that registration district, nor, indeed, in Scotland; but as one of the parties must appear to finalise arrangements for a civil ceremony or, alternatively, collect the marriage schedule for a religious or belief ceremony, in practice one of the parties must be present in Scotland before the date of the ceremony.

The marriage notice is accompanied by the prescribed fee and the birth certificate of the party submitting it. If either party has been married before and the marriage has been dissolved, a copy of the decree of divorce or declarator of nullity must be included. Similarly, if either party is a person who had been married before and that marriage ended on the death of the previous spouse, the death certificate of the former spouse must be submitted.[2] If one of the parties is domiciled abroad,[3] he or she must 'if practicable' submit a certificate issued by a competent authority in the state in which the party is domiciled that he or she 'is not known to be subject to any legal incapacity (in terms of the law of that state) which would prevent his marrying':[4] this is known as a certificate of capacity.[5] There is no need to submit a certificate if no certificate has been issued only by reason of the fact that the parties to the intended marriage are of the same sex.[6]

On receipt of the marriage notice, the registrar enters the following prescribed particulars (of the person who has submitted the notice) in a marriage notice book: the party's name, address, marital or civil partnership status, date of birth and the proposed date of the marriage.[7] The names – but not the addresses – of the parties and the proposed date of the marriage are then displayed in a 'conspicuous' place at the registration office.

Any person claiming to have reason to submit an objection to an intended marriage can inspect any entry relating to the marriage in the marriage notice book. The objection to the marriage must be submitted in writing to the district registrar.[8] Where the objection is concerned with a trivial matter, for example an inaccuracy as to the age of the parties, the district registrar can, after notifying the parties, make the correction.[9] However, if the objection goes to the capacity of either party to marry,[10] for example if it is alleged that one of them is already a party to a subsisting marriage or a civil partnership that is not a 'qualifying civil partnership',[11] then the district registrar must notify the Registrar General and the completion or issue of the marriage schedule is suspended until the matter has been considered by the Registrar General.[12] If after consideration the Registrar General is satisfied that there is no legal impediment, he or she will inform the district registrar and the marriage can go ahead. If there is a legal impediment, the Registrar General must direct the district registrar to take all reasonable steps to ensure that the marriage does not take place.[12]

It will be obvious that there must be sufficient time for objections to be made and any subsequent investigations to be carried out. As a general rule, there is a minimum waiting period of 28 days from the receipt of the marriage notice and a civil ceremony[14] or the issue of a marriage schedule for a religious or belief ceremony.[15] However, the Registrar General has a dispensing power to allow a marriage to be celebrated within a shorter period if the circumstances justify doing so. This power is used sparingly.

1 Marriage (Scotland) Act 1977, s 3(1).
2 M(S)A 1977, s 3(1)(a) and (b). An extract of an entry in the Register of Divorces is sufficient evidence of the decree of divorce or declarator of nullity: see the Registration of Births, Deaths and Marriages (Scotland) Act 1965, s 28A(5).
3 And has not been resident in the UK for more than two years. (M(S)A 1977, s 3(5)(ii)(a)).
4 M(S)A 1977, s 3(5).
5 M(S)A 1977, s 3(5). Where the *lex domicilii* does not recognise the party's divorce, but the divorce would be recognised in Scotland, a marriage can go ahead without a certificate of capacity: M(S)A 1977, s 3(5)(ii)(b). See also the Family Law Act 1986, s 50.
6 M(S)A 1977, s 3(5)(ii)(c).
7 M(S)A 1977, s 4: the particulars are prescribed in the Marriage (Prescription of Forms) (Scotland) Regulations 1997, SI 1997/2349, reg 5.
8 M(S)A 1977, s 5(1).
9 M(S)A 1977, s 5(2)(a).
10 M(S)A 1977, s 5(4).
11 M(S)A 1977, s 5(6). See para **1.19** below.
12 M(S)A 1977, s 5(2)(b).
13 M(S)A 1977, s 5(3)(a).
14 M(S)A 1977, s 6(4)(a).
15 M(S)A 1977, s 19(1).

Marriage schedule

1.6 After the usual waiting period has expired and the district registrar is satisfied that the parties have capacity to marry, the district registrar makes up the marriage schedule. The schedule contains the details of the parties and serves as an initial record of the marriage for registration purposes. Where there is to be a religious or belief ceremony, in addition the marriage schedule acts as a licence authorising the celebrant to proceed. If more than three months have elapsed since the receipt of a marriage notice, the Registrar General has discretion to direct the district registrar not to complete the marriage schedule unless a new marriage notice is submitted.[1] A marriage schedule for a religious or belief ceremony will not be issued to the parties earlier than seven days before the ceremony unless the district registrar has been authorised to do so by the Registrar General.[2]

1 Marriage (Scotland) Act 1977, s 6(2).
2 M(S)A 1977, s 6(4)(b).

Civil marriage

Different sex and same sex marriages

1.7 If there is to be a civil ceremony, the district registrar retains the marriage schedule until the date of the marriage. The ceremony is conducted by the district registrar (or assistant registrar)[1] and takes place in his or her office. There is no restriction on the time when the ceremony must take place but in practice it will be during the registrar's normal office hours. In addition, the registrar may conduct a civil ceremony in an 'appropriate place'. It is for the district registrar to determine in each case whether the proposed place is appropriate for a civil wedding, for example, the bride's home or a local hotel.[2] It is expressly enacted that religious premises cannot be an appropriate place for a civil ceremony.[3]

Both parties must be present with two witnesses professing to be aged 16 or over.[4] The marriage schedule must be completed in accordance with the Marriage (Scotland) Act 1977 and the district registrar explains to the parties the nature of marriage in Scots law. The parties declare there are no legal impediments and are then asked if they take each other as spouses. The registrar declares them to be married and the marriage schedule is signed by both parties, the witnesses and the registrar. The marriage is then registered. A registrar cannot refuse to marry a couple on the ground that they are of the same sex, ie there is no conscientious exemption for registrars.

1 M(S)A 1977, ss 8 (1) (b) and (1B)(b).
2 M(S)A 1977, s 18(1).
3 M(S)A 1977, s 18(1A).
4 M(S)A 1977, s 19(2)(c).

Religious or belief marriage

1.8 If there is to be a religious or belief ceremony, the district registrar issues the marriage schedule *to the parties*. This is because the schedule acts as a licence to the celebrant to solemnise the marriage. A religious or belief ceremony can be carried out at any time, for example, in the evening, and at any place, for example, in a hotel. The date and place chosen must be specified in the marriage schedule. If, for any reason, the marriage cannot be solemnised on the date and at the place stipulated, another marriage schedule must be issued or substituted specifying the new date and place.[1]

Different sex marriage

The authorised celebrant is a person who is:[2]

(i) A minister or deacon of the Church of Scotland;

(ii) A minister, clergyman, pastor, priest or other celebrant of a religious or belief body prescribed in regulations made by Scottish Ministers. A religious or belief body is an organised group of people: (a) which meets regularly for religious worship; or (b) the principal object (or one of the principal objects) of which is to uphold or promote philosophical beliefs and which meets regularly for that purpose.[3] Religious bodies will include the major Christian churches and denominations and non-Christian religions such as Islam and Hinduism. Belief bodies will include non-religious organisations such as Humanists. However Scottish Ministers can only prescribe a body if that body requests them to do so and the Ministers are satisfied that the body meets the qualifying requirements.[4] The qualifying requirements will be made in regulations but will be designed to ensure, *inter alia*, that marriages are not conducted as a profit-making business and that the celebrants are aware of the risk of sham and forced marriages.

(iii) A person nominated to solemnise different sex marriages by a religious or belief body which is not prescribed under (2) above. The nominee is registered as a marriage celebrant by the Registrar General under s 9(1) of the Marriage (Scotland) Act 1977. The

Registrar General can reject the nomination if the nominating body does not meet the qualifying requirements. The nominee is authorised for three years in the first instance.

(iv) A member of a religious or belief body temporarily authorised by the Registrar General under s 12 of the Marriage (Scotland) Act 1977 to solemnise different sex marriages. The religious or belief body must meet the qualifying requirements. These would include celebrants who are registered under s 9(1) but whose area of operation does not extend to the place where the marriage is to be celebrated, ministers from outside Scotland who have been asked to solemnise a marriage in Scotland, or ministers who are in Scotland on pulpit exchange. The authorisation must be in writing and is limited either to the marriage specified in the authorisation or for a specified period.

The celebrant must follow the form of ceremony approved by the Church of Scotland or the religious or belief body. The ceremony must be in an appropriate form which includes and is not inconsistent with: (a) a declaration of the parties, in the presence of each other, the celebrant and two witnesses, that they accept each other as husband and wife or spouses; and (b) a declaration thereafter by the celebrant that they are husband and wife or spouses.[5]

Same sex marriages

The authorised celebrant is a person who is:[6]

(a) A minister, clergyman, pastor, priest or other celebrant of a religious or belief body prescribed by regulations made by Scottish Ministers, or who, not being of the foregoing, is recognised by a religious or belief body so prescribed as entitled to solemnise marriage between persons of the same sex on its behalf. Again, Scottish Ministers can only prescribe a body if that body requests them to do so and the Ministers are satisfied that the body meets the qualifying requirements.[7]

(b) A person nominated to solemnise same sex marriages by a religious or belief body which is not prescribed under (1) above. The nominee is registered by the Registrar General under s 9(1A) of the Marriage (Scotland) Act 1977. The Registrar General can reject the nomination if the nominating body does not meet the qualifying requirements. So, for example, the Church of Scotland could nominate a particular minister who was prepared to conduct same sex marriages.

(c) A member of a religious or belief body temporarily authorised by the Registrar General under s 12 of the Marriage (Scotland) Act 1977 to solemnise same sex marriages. The religious or belief body must meet the qualifying requirements. An authorisation for a specified period can only be made if the person is a member of a religious or belief body which has been prescribed under (1) above or has nominated celebrants under (2) above.[8]

Section 8(1D) of the Marriage (Scotland) Act 1977 provides for the avoidance of doubt that no religious or belief body is obliged to seek to become a prescribed body or to nominate any member to be registered as empowered to solemnise same sex marriages. So a religious or belief body may request to be authorised to solemnise different sex marriages while not seeking authority to solemnise same sex marriages. Similarly, no person is obliged to apply for temporary authorisation to solemnise such marriages. Moreover, where a person is an approved celebrant to conduct same sex marriages he or she is not obliged to do so. Accordingly, even where a religious or belief body has been prescribed to solemnise same sex marriages, any member of that body can still refuse to participate by relying on this conscientious exemption and need not secede from the body.[9]

The ceremony must be in an appropriate form which includes and is in no way inconsistent with: (a) a declaration by the parties, in the presence of each other, the celebrant and two witnesses, that they accept each other in marriage; and (b) a declaration thereafter by the celebrant that the parties are then married.

In all marriages, the approved celebrant must not proceed unless:

(a) the parties produce a marriage schedule issued in accordance with the Marriage (Scotland) Act 1977;

(b) *both* parties are present; and

(c) there are two witnesses professing to be aged 16 or over.[10]

After the ceremony the marriage schedule is signed by both parties, the witnesses and the celebrant. The schedule must be returned to the district registration office for registration within three days of the ceremony.[11] This was traditionally the task of the best man who paid the registration fee as part of his wedding gift!

1 Marriage (Scotland) Act 1977, s 6(5).
2 M(S)A 1977, s 8(1).
3 M(S)A 1977, s 26(2).
4 M(S)A 1977, s 8 (1A).
5 M(S)A 1977, s 9(3).
6 M(S)A 1977, s 8(1B).
7 NB: At the time of writing (May 2022), members of the General Assembly of the Church of Scotland voted in favour of changing the Law of the Church of Scotland to allow ministers and deacons to apply to become celebrants who can marry same sex couples (before May 2022, ministers and deacons could marry only opposite sex couples). No minister or deacon will require to take part in the solemnisation of a same sex marriage unless he or she explicitly seeks to do so. It is thought that this will also extend to the solemnisation of same sex marriage in religious premises. See: Kenneth Norrie, *Authorising marriage celebrants: Scotland's Rococo legislation*, Fam LB 2022, 178.
8 M(S)A 1977, s 12(1C).
9 The Equality Act 2010 cannot be used to challenge the individual's decision not to conduct same sex marriages. See n 7 (above).
10 M(S)A 1977, s 13(1).
11 M(S)A 1977, s 15(2).

Effect of irregularities

1.9 By virtue of s 23A, a marriage solemnised under the Marriage (Scotland) Act 1977 will not be invalidated by non-compliance with these formalities provided both parties were present at the ceremony and the marriage was duly registered.[1] There must be some form of ceremony but otherwise the marriage will not be invalidated by formal defects.

The scope of s 23A of the 1977 Act was considered in *Saleh v Saleh*.[2] The pursuer sought a declarator of nullity. The parties had originally intended to be married by a Church of Scotland minister in Grangemouth. Marriage notices were lodged but the registrar was unable to issue a marriage schedule as there was doubt as to the defender's freedom to marry. Faced with this difficulty, the couple decided to be married in a mosque in Edinburgh. No marriage notices were lodged with the appropriate district registrar nor was any marriage schedule made up, far less issued. Nevertheless, the ceremony took place and the matour (said to be equivalent to a minister) issued a certificate recording the ceremony; but because of the absence of a completed marriage schedule, the marriage could not be, and was not, registered. In granting the declarator, the Lord Ordinary (Clyde) held that this was not a case where s 23A of the 1977 Act was applicable because, although the parties were present at the ceremony, there was no registration. Lord Clyde thought that s 23A could save a marriage when, for example, the schedule had been issued prior to the time limits, or if the person who conducted the ceremony was not an approved celebrant, or a marriage schedule was not produced at the ceremony, always provided that the parties were present and the schedule had been issued, signed and registered.

In *Sohrab v Khan*[3] the Lord Ordinary (McEwan) held that s 23A of the 1977 Act could not save a marriage where a marriage schedule had not been issued at the time of the ceremony. It was irrelevant that a marriage schedule was issued and registered at a later date. In other words, there must be a marriage schedule which can be produced at the solemnisation of the marriage.

Even if the marriage can be saved by the Marriage (Scotland) Act 1977, s 23A, the parties and the celebrant may be liable to criminal sanctions for breach of the 1977 Act, for example if a person falsifies or forges a marriage schedule.[4]

1 However, if the registrar refuses to register the schedule because he or she believes that there has been non-compliance with the formalities, s 23A is not triggered and the marriage is not valid.

2 1987 SLT 633.

3 2002 SLT 1255; see also, *A v K* [2011] CSOH 101 (marriage by telephone).

4 See the M(S)A 1977, s 24 for a full list of offences.

Conclusion

1.10 The purpose of legal preliminaries to the solemnisation of marriage is to ensure that the parties to a marriage have legal capacity to marry. As a result of the Marriage (Scotland) Act 1977, all persons who wish to enter into a regular marriage in Scotland must follow the same preliminary procedure whether or not they intend to have a civil or a religious or belief ceremony. This makes for simplicity and uniformity. Moreover, it is submitted that the current rules give sufficient time for objections to be made and appropriate investigations to take place. The procedure itself is admirably simple without the complexities of residence requirements for the parties.

Irregular marriages

Introduction

1.11 Before the Reformation in 1560, Scots law recognised the validity of irregular marriages.[1] These involved no ecclesiastical formalities whatsoever. There were three kinds:

(1) A declaration by the parties that they took each other as husband and wife: marriage *per verba de praesenti*. The consent of the parties was sufficient to constitute the marriage and there was no need for the presence of an episcopally ordained priest or witnesses.

(2) A promise to marry at some future date followed by sexual intercourse on the faith of that promise: marriage *per verba de futuro subsequente copula*. The sexual intercourse on the faith of the promise was deemed to be agreement to marry. Not surprisingly, perhaps, there was no need for the presence of an episcopally ordained priest or witnesses.

(3) Marriage constituted by the tacit agreement of the parties to marry presumed from a period of cohabitation with habit and repute that they were husband and wife: marriage by cohabitation with habit and repute.

After the Reformation these forms of irregular marriage continued to be recognised as constituting valid marriages in Scots law. The first two forms of irregular marriage were abolished by s 5 of the Marriage (Scotland) Act 1939 which came into force on 1 July 1940.[2] However, the third form, marriage by cohabitation with habit and repute, remained a valid method of constituting marriage in Scotland until it was abolished by s 3 of the Family Law (Scotland) Act 2006. Note that any marriage constituted by cohabitation with habit and repute that began before the abolition and continues shall still have effect.

Because many of the older cases involved irregular marriages, it is proposed to outline the salient features of *de praesenti* and *de futuro* marriages and then to consider marriage by cohabitation with habit and repute in some detail.

---

1 For full discussion see E M Clive *The Law of Husband and Wife in Scotland* (4th edn, 1997, W Green/Sweet & Maxwell), Ch 5.
2 The section was not retrospective.

Marriage by declaration de praesenti

1.12 The essence of this form of marriage was that the parties seriously and genuinely exchanged present consent to marriage. The couple was married as soon as consents were exchanged. Consummation was not required: *consensus non concubitus facit matrimonium*. Because there was no need for witnesses, there could be formidable problems of proof, particularly where one of the alleged spouses had died and the issue arose in a claim by the other for rights of succession.[1]

The exchange of consents had to take place in Scotland.[2] This explains the popularity of elopements from England to marry at Gretna Green. Eventually, a residence requirement of at least 21 days was introduced by the Marriage (Scotland) Act 1856. The *de praesenti* marriage has not been a competent form of contracting a marriage since 1 July 1940.[3]

---

1 See, for example, *Dunn v Dunn's Trustees* 1930 SC 131.
2 *Macdonald v Macdonald* (1863) 1 M 854.
3 See the Marriage (Scotland) Act 1939, s 5.

Marriage by promise subsequente copula

1.13 In this form of irregular marriage, if a promise was made of marriage at some date in the future and sexual intercourse took place on the faith of the promise, the couple was taken to be married at the date of the intercourse. The theory was that while mutual consent was essential to marriage, where a woman permitted sexual intercourse in reliance on a man's promise to marry her, it was to be presumed that there and then the parties had exchanged consents to present marriage and, if this presumption was not rebutted, a marriage was constituted by promise *subsequente copula*.[1] Both the promise and the sexual intercourse had to take place in Scotland.

In time, this form of marriage was treated with scepticism. As Lord Sands explained in *N v C*:[2]

> 'According to the theory of the law, when two persons who are engaged to be married indulge in sexual intercourse, presumably they there and then exchange matrimonial consent and become married persons. But, according to the view which prevails in those sections of the community in which antenuptial fornication is most apt to occur, they do nothing of the kind. They yield to desire and indulge in immoral intercourse, robbed doubtless of some of its danger by the prospect of future marriage ... Parents, employers and clergymen in rural Scotland have often had occasion to deal sorrowfully with a girl whose betrothed had got her in the family way. I much doubt if it has ever happened that the girl advanced the plea in excuse that she was a married woman ... Marriage by promise *cum subsequente copula* is a plant nourished by the law which has never taken root in the understanding or the conscience of the common people.'

It is therefore not surprising that this has not been a competent form of contracting a marriage since 1 July 1940.[3]

1 See *N v C* 1933 SC 492.
2 1933 SC 492 at 501.
3 Marriage (Scotland) Act 1939, s 5.

Marriage by cohabitation with habit and repute

1.14 The Marriage (Scotland) Act 1939 did not abolish the third form of irregular marriage, marriage by cohabitation with habit and repute. The theoretical basis of the doctrine has been the subject of controversy.[1] It is not simply a matter of evidence. Although there is a presumption from long cohabitation as husband and wife that a couple have been married,[2] this is rebuttable by evidence that the alleged ceremony did not take place.

However, marriage by cohabitation with habit and repute is not merely a rule of evidence that the parties are *prima facie* to be presumed to have married by declaration *de praesenti* or promise *cum subsequente copula*, for if that were so, marriage by cohabitation with habit and repute would have been impliedly abolished by the Marriage (Scotland) Act 1939. Instead, the basis of the doctrine is that the parties' tacit consent to marry, inferred from, and combined with, cohabitation with habit and repute constitutes marriage: a legitimate enunciation by the parties to themselves and others of their matrimonial consent which has never expressly been put into words.[3] Because of their cohabitation with habit and repute that they are married, the law presumes that the parties have tacitly agreed to be married, with the result that they are married unless evidence is led that they never intended to take each other as husband and wife.

1 See, for example, Ashton-Cross 'Cohabitation with Habit and Repute' 1961 JR 21.
2 Or before 1 July 1940, that the couple had married by *de praesenti* consents or promise *cum subsequente copula*.
3 *Campbell v Campbell* (1866) 4 M 867 at 924–925.

The requirements

1.15

(1) There must be cohabitation, ie the couple must live together: merely to have sexual intercourse is not enough.[1]

(2) The cohabitation must be as husband and wife. However, cohabitation which began on an indeterminate footing can develop into such a marriage if the couple later cohabit as

husband and wife.[2] Where a couple live together with the intention that they will marry at a future date, since they are not cohabiting as husband and wife, they cannot become married as a result of the doctrine of marriage by cohabitation with habit and repute.[3] *A fortiori* the doctrine does not apply when a couple live together without any intention of ever marrying.[4]

(3) The cohabitation must take place in Scotland.[5]

(4) The cohabitation must be sufficiently long for the court to infer that the parties tacitly agreed to marry. At one time it was thought that this must be at least a year,[6] but in *Shaw v Henderson*[7] it was emphasised that there was no hard and fast rule: all that is required is that the evidence of cohabitation is sufficient for an inference of tacit agreement to be drawn. An eleven-month cohabitation was enough in that case. It is ultimately a question of fact.[8]

(5) The parties must be reputed to be husband and wife and this reputation must be 'uniform and undivided'. But it is not fatal if some persons know that the couple is not married provided they are generally thought by friends and society in general to be husband and wife.[9] But if a substantial number of relatives and friends do know that the couple is not married[10] or are merely contemplating marriage, the doctrine will not apply.[11]

(6) The parties must have legal capacity to marry.[12] If, for example, one of the parties is already married to a third party, the doctrine cannot apply; but once the impediment is removed by the death or divorce of the existing spouse then, as the party will now have capacity to marry, the doctrine is applicable.[13] However, the parties can only rely upon the cohabitation with habit and repute which occurs after the impediment has been removed.[14] Thus if A who is married to B begins to cohabit with C in 2000 and B dies in 2002, the period of relevant cohabitation only begins with B's death in 2002: the period of cohabitation – albeit with habit and repute – between 2000 and 2002 is irrelevant except as background material.[15] Where a relationship begins illicitly, it may, of course, be difficult to establish the necessary repute that the couple are living as husband and wife. But the doctrine will still be applicable once the parties are aware that the impediment

has been removed.[16] No weight is now given to the old idea that a relationship which begins illicitly should *prima facie* be presumed to continue illicitly. As Lord Caplan observed in *Gow v Lord Advocate*:[17]

> 'if the parties clearly showed an inclination to adopt the married state before they became free to marry, this could reflect on their attitude to the relationship if cohabitation continues when freedom to marry arises'.

Whether a man and a woman have cohabited as husband and wife with the necessary repute to draw the inference of tacit consent is essentially a question of fact.[18]

---

1 *Quaere* whether a couple can cohabit for this purpose if they do not have sexual intercourse.

2 See, for example, *Nicol v Bell* 1954 SLT 314 (woman began as man's housekeeper, became his mistress, but on the birth of his child was treated as his wife: they were married as a result of 20 years' cohabitation as husband and wife); *Vosilius v Vosilius* 2000 SCLR 679.

3 See, for example, *Low v Gorman* 1970 SLT 356; *Mackenzie v Scott* 1980 SLT (Notes) 9.

4 See, for example, *Gow v Lord Advocate* 1993 SLT 275 at 276, per Lord Caplan: 'The case must be viewed against the background of modern social conditions where it is not at all uncommon for a man and woman to live together openly in an intimate relationship while retaining a distinct disinclination to enter the marriage state.'

5 *Dysart Peerage Case* (1881) 6 App Cas 489; *Walker v Roberts* 1998 SLT 1133.

6 See, for example, *Campbell v Campbell* (1866) 4 M 867; *Wallace v Fife Coal Co Ltd* 1909 SC 682.

7 1982 SLT 211.

8 *Kamperman v MacIver* 1994 SLT 763 (a period of six-and-a-half months not necessarily insufficient).

9 *Shaw v Henderson* 1982 SLT 211; *Vosilius v Vosilius* 2000 SCLR 679. Nor is it fatal that the woman continued to use her maiden name: *Donnelly v Donnelly's Executor* 1992 SLT 13.

10 *Low v Gorman* 1970 SLT 356; *Walker v Roberts* 1998 SLT 1133.

11 *Mackenzie v Scott* 1980 SLT (Notes) 9.

12 A couple who were parties to a regular marriage and then divorced have capacity to marry again as a result of the doctrine of cohabitation with habit and repute: *Mullen v Mullen* 1991 SLT 205.

13 *S v S* 2006 SLT 471. But if the parties are not free to marry when they first begin cohabiting, once they gain capacity to marry there must be a change in the nature of their relationship and how it is regarded by the rest of the world.

14 *Low v Gorman* 1970 SLT 356; *Vosilius v Vosilius* 2000 SCLR 679. In *Kamperman v MacIver* 1994 SLT 763, the Second Division held that pre-removal cohabitation is not wholly irrelevant as it is part of the background material which could colour the nature of the cohabitation after the impediment is removed.
15 *Kamperman v MacIver* 1994 SLT 763.
16 *Campbell v Campbell* (1866) 4 M 867. The case proceeded on the assumption that the parties knew of the death of the first husband. Thus, it would appear that the presumption of tacit consent would be rebutted if the parties continued to believe that the impediment existed.
17 1993 SLT 275 at 276.
18 *Kamperman v MacIver* 1994 SLT 763.

Procedure

1.16 A party to the alleged marriage by cohabitation with habit and repute will raise an action in the Court of Session for declarator of marriage. But it should be emphasised that the couple is married by virtue of the doctrine: there is no need for a declarator to establish the marriage. A declarator has been granted where the couple was married by cohabitation with habit and repute albeit that they had separated before the husband's death.[1] By the nature of the doctrine it will be difficult to establish exactly when the couple was married. While the matter is not free from difficulty, there is force in Professor Eric Clive's view that the date should be when there was sufficient relevant cohabitation with habit and repute for the inference of tacit consent to be drawn.[2] When a declarator has been granted, the Principal Clerk of Session will intimate the relevant details to the Registrar General to enable the marriage to be registered.[3]

1 *Morris v Morris* 1987 GWD 39-1437.
2 See E M Clive *The Law of Husband and Wife in Scotland* (4th edn, 1997, W Green/Sweet & Maxwell) at pp 57 ff.
3 Marriage (Scotland) Act 1977, s 21.

The 'abolition' of marriage by cohabitation with habit and repute

1.17 There was no doubt that marriage by cohabitation with habit and repute was anomalous. The doctrine only applied when a couple who had legal capacity to marry *pretended* to be married. Where it was useful, however, was the case where a couple believed that they were regularly married but the marriage was void because of a temporary impediment: once the impediment was removed, they could become married by cohabitation with habit and repute. On the other hand, many couples were under the impression that they were validly married by virtue of marriage by cohabitation with habit and repute when the doctrine was inapplicable to them either because they lacked capacity to marry or, more commonly, because they had made no pretence of being married and therefore lacked the requisite repute that they were husband and wife. In these circumstances both the Scottish Law Commission[1] and the Scottish Executive took the view that the doctrine should be abolished.

Section 3(1) of the Family Law (Scotland) Act 2006 provides that: 'The rule of law by which marriage may be constituted by cohabitation with habit and repute shall cease to have effect.' Nevertheless, a couple may still become married by cohabitation with habit and repute: (i) if the cohabitation began and ended before the commencement of the Act,[2] ie when they have already become married by cohabitation with habit and repute; and (ii) if the cohabitation began before but continues after that date.[3] In other words, a couple can still become married by cohabitation with habit and repute even though post-Act cohabitation as well as pre-Act cohabitation has to be used to infer that they have done so. It will be evident that the rule has only been abolished in respect of couples whose cohabitation with habit and repute *begins* after the commencement of the 2006 Act. Therefore, knowledge of the law on marriage by cohabitation with habit and repute will still be needed for many years.

Indeed, there is one exceptional situation when a couple can still be married by cohabitation with habit and repute even though the cohabitation began after the commencement of the Act. This is when A and B go through a ceremony of marriage abroad. They believe that they are validly married but, in fact, the marriage is invalid under the law of the place where the wedding took place. A is, or becomes, domiciled in Scotland and they live here with the repute that they are married. If B dies domiciled in Scotland, a declarator that they were married by cohabitation and repute can be obtained if A became aware that the purported marriage was invalid after B had died.[4] It does not matter that the cohabitation with habit and repute began after the commencement of the 2006 Act. But the exception applies only when the invalid marriage took place abroad. If A and B went through a ceremony of marriage in Scotland which, unknown to them, was void they cannot become married by post-commencement cohabitation with habit and repute. And B must have died before A discovered that their marriage is invalid. If B was still alive when A made the discovery, the exception does not apply and A and B would have to go through a new regular marriage.[5] This is very strange because if the discovery was not made until B had died, A can get a declarator that they had become married by cohabitation with habit and repute long before B had passed away!

In so far as the law of marriage by cohabitation with habit and repute remains relevant it applies to same sex as well as opposite sex marriages.[6]

1 Report on Family Law (Scot Law Com No 135) rec 42.
2 4 May 2006.
3 Family Law (Scotland) Act 2006, s 3(2).
4 FL(S)A 2006, s 3(3) and (4).
5 This could be difficult if, for example, B then lacked capacity to marry because of mental impairment.
6 Marriage and Civil Partnership (Scotland) Act 2014, s 4(6).

PART II: REGISTERING A CIVIL PARTNERSHIP

1.18 Section 1 of the Civil Partnership (Scotland) Act 2020 amends s 1 of the Civil Partnership Act 2004 thus enabling persons of different sexes to enter a civil partnership in Scotland.[1] Each of the intended civil partners must submit to the district registrar a notice of their intention to enter a civil partnership.[2] This is known as a notice of proposed civil partnership. Particulars from the notice are entered into the civil partnership book.[3] The names of the parties and the date on which the registration is to take place are then publicised.[4] The registration can only take place 28 days after these details have been publicised.[5] This gives persons the opportunity to raise an objection as to why the registration should not go ahead and the registrar the chance to make appropriate investigations. Once satisfied that there are no legal impediments, after the 28-day period has expired the registrar can complete a civil partnership schedule.[6]

The civil partnership is formed by registration. The district registrar asks the intended civil partners to confirm that the particulars set out in the civil partnership schedule are correct.[7] Each of the partners then signs the civil partnership schedule in the presence of each other, two witnesses (both of whom have attained the age of 16) and the authorised registrar.[8] The schedule is then signed by the witnesses and the registrar in the presence of the civil partners and each other.[9] The registrar will then enter the details of the schedule into the civil partnership register.[10]

Part 2 of the Marriage and Civil Partnership (Scotland) Act 2014 introduces religious and belief registration of civil partnerships. The rules for the authorisation of non-registrar civil partnership celebrants are the same as those for the authorisation of religious or belief celebrants of same sex marriages.[11]

Several points should be noted. Unlike a marriage, where the couple is married by mutual consent and the active involvement of a registrar or religious celebrant, a civil partnership is created by the partners registering as civil partners. It is the registration *per se* that creates a civil partnership. The parties do not register their partnership whereas a married couple do register their marriage. The registrar or religious or belief celebrant does not declare the parties to be civil partners; his or her function is simply to register them as civil partners. In contrast to marriage where the witnesses need only profess to be aged 16 or over, witnesses to a civil partnership registration must have attained the age of 16.[12]

A civil registration can take place in a registration office or any appropriate place that the registration authority agrees can be the place of registration· However, civil registration cannot take place in religious premises, ie premises which are used solely for religious purposes or have been used for such and have not subsequently been used solely or mainly for other purposes.[13] Thus, for example, a civil registration of a civil partnership cannot be carried out in a university or college chapel but could be done in a restaurant or bar that had been a former church. It does not matter that the religious body endorses same sex marriage. A religious or belief civil partnership may be registered only on the date and at the place specified in the civil partnership schedule; the specified place can be religious premises.[14] The civil partnership schedule cannot be issued to one or both parties earlier than seven days before the date of the intended registration.[15]

By s 95A, once the civil partnership schedule has been registered under the Civil Partnership Act 2004, the civil partnership cannot be held to be invalid on the ground of failure to comply with the formalities of registration.[16] So, for example, a civil partnership which has been registered would not be invalid if it was later discovered that one of the witnesses was not 16 or over.

A civil partnership can only be created by registration. Therefore, there is not, and never has been, any possibility of a civil partnership arising by cohabitation with habit and repute of civil partnership.

1 See *R (on the application of Steinfeld) and Keidan v Secretary of State for International Development* [2018] UKSC 32.
2 Civil Partnership Act 2004, s 88.
3 CPA 2004, s 89. Each of the intended civil partners must submit their birth certificate and if previously married or civil partnered, a decree of divorce or dissolution or, where the former spouse or civil partner has died, the death certificate of the former spouse or civil partner.
4 CPA 2004, s 90.
5 CPA 2004, s 90(2)(b). There are provisions for early registration: CPA 2004, s 91.
6 CPA 2004, s 94.
7 CPA 2004, s 95(1).
8 CPA 2004, s 85(1).
9 CPA 2004, s 85(4). But the parties are civil partners by virtue of s 86(1) even though this does not take place: s 85(3).
10 CPA 2004, s 95(1).
11 CPA 2004, ss 94A–94E. See para **1.8** above.
12 CPA 2004, s 85(1)(b).
13 CPA 2004, s 93(1A).
14 CPA 2004, s 93A.
15 CPA 2004, ss 94(2) and (3).
16 The parties and the registrar may, however, be guilty of an offence: CPA 2004, s 100.

Conversion of civil partnership into same sex marriage

1.19 The Marriage and Civil Partnership (Scotland) Act 2014 provides two methods under which the parties can convert their civil partnership into a same sex marriage. First there is to be an administrative process which will be contained in regulations made by the Scottish Ministers.[1] Secondly, the civil partners may simply marry in accordance with the rules under the Marriage (Scotland) Act 1977.[2] The civil partnership must be a 'qualifying civil partnership'. This is a civil partnership which was registered in Scotland and has not been dissolved, annulled or ended by death.[3] Scottish Ministers have the power to modify the definition to include civil partnerships registered abroad.[4] While there is a legal impediment to marriage where one or both of the persons are already married or in a civil partnership, this impediment to marry does not apply where the couple are parties to a qualifying civil partnership.[5] Once the civil partnership has been converted into a same sex marriage, the civil partnership is brought to an end[6] and the couple is treated as having been married for all purposes from the date of registration of the civil partnership.[7] For the avoidance of doubt any decree of aliment under s 3 of the Family Law (Scotland) Act 1985 continues after the civil partnership has been dissolved by marriage and any orders relating to the occupation of the family home under s 103(3) or (4) of the Civil Partnership Act 2004 are to be treated as having been made under the Matrimonial Homes (Family Protection) (Scotland) Act 1981.[8]

There are no provisions enabling a couple to a same sex marriage to convert it into a civil partnership.

1 Marriage and Civil Partnership (Scotland) Act 2014, s 10.
2 MCP(S)A 2014, s 11(1)(a).
3 Marriage (Scotland) Act 1977, s 5(6).
4 MCP(S)A 2014, s 9(1).
5 M(S)A 1977, s 5(4)(b).
6 CPA 2004, s 1(3)(c).
7 MCP(S)A 2014, s 11(2)(a) and (b).
8 MCP(S)A 2014, s 11(7) and (8) On aliment, see para **3.8** ff below. On occupation of the matrimonial and family home, see para **5.8**ff below.

Chapter 2

Legal impediments to marriage and civil partnership

INTRODUCTION

2.1 As we saw in the last chapter,[1] as a result of s 23A of the Marriage (Scotland) Act 1977 and s 95A of the Civil Partnership Act 2004, non-compliance with the formalities for regular marriages or registered civil partnerships will not normally affect the validity of the marriage or the civil partnership. But in addition, both a marriage and a civil partnership may be defective if the parties lack legal capacity to marry or are not eligible to enter into a civil partnership or if there is not true consent. An opposite sex marriage, but not a same sex marriage or civil partnership, is also legally defective if it cannot be consummated as a result of the incurable impotency of one or both of the parties. In this chapter we shall examine the impediments to marriage and civil partnership that exist in Scots law.

1 See paras **1.9** and **1.18**.

VOID MARRIAGES AND CIVIL PARTNERSHIPS

2.2 As a general rule, where such impediments as described above exist a marriage will be void in Scots law, ie it is treated as never having existed. There is one exception to this principle, namely where an opposite sex marriage has not been consummated as a result of the incurable impotency of one or both of the parties. In this case, the marriage is voidable, ie it remains valid until a court action is raised, resulting in a declaration that the marriage is ended. Non-consummation by reason of impotence 'has effect only in relation to a marriage between persons of a different sex'.[1] A civil partnership is void if the parties were not eligible to register a civil partnership or either of them did not consent to the formation of the civil partnership.[2]

Where a marriage or civil partnership is void, *prima facie*, it has no legal effect whatsoever. There is no need for the parties to obtain a declarator of nullity. However, any person who has a legitimate interest may seek a declarator of nullity on the ground that a marriage or civil partnership was void. In certain circumstances, a void or voidable marriage or a void or voidable civil partnership may have legal consequences. For example, a man will be presumed to be the father of a child if he was married to, or in a civil partnership with, the child's mother at any time in the period beginning with the conception and ending with the birth of the child, or if not married to or in a civil partnership with the mother, if he and the mother acknowledge that he is the father and he has been registered as such.[3] The husband or male civil partner will have parental responsibilities and parental rights over the child if he and the mother entered into the marriage or civil partnership believing in good faith at that time that the marriage or civil partnership was valid.[4] Moreover, if a declarator of nullity is obtained by one of the parties, the court has the same powers to award financial provision for the parties as it does in actions of divorce or the dissolution of a civil partnership.[5]

1 Marriage and Civil Partnership (Scotland) Act 2014, s 5(1).
2 Civil Partnership Act 2004, s 123.
3 Law Reform (Parent and Child) (Scotland) Act 1986, s 5(1) and (2); discussed in **Ch 9**.
4 Children (Scotland) Act 1995, s 3(1), (2); discussed in **Ch 11**.
5 Family Law (Scotland) Act 1985, s 17(1). Financial provision on divorce and dissolution is discussed in detail in **Ch 7**.

VOIDABLE MARRIAGES

2.3 In the case of a voidable marriage, the marriage subsists unless and until a declarator of nullity of marriage is obtained. Only a party to the marriage can seek declarator and, unlike the case of a void marriage, declarator cannot be obtained if one of the parties is dead. However, the effect of the decree is to declare that the marriage has never existed, ie it has retroactive effect. Nevertheless, the court can award the parties financial provision in the same way as in an action of divorce.[1] Nor does the retroactive effect of the decree affect the status of any children of the marriage.[2] Given that the sole ground of a voidable marriage[3] is the incurable impotency of one or both of the parties, the number of children is likely to be small, but with modern reproductive techniques, the existence of children of a voidable marriage is not impossible.

1 FL(S)A 1985, s 17(1).
2 Law Reform (Miscellaneous Provisions) Act 1949, s 4.
3 Incurable impotency is not a ground on which a mixed civil partnership can be voidable.

CAPACITY TO MARRY AND ELIGIBILITY TO ENTER A CIVIL PARTNERSHIP

2.4 We shall now consider the grounds on which a marriage or civil partnership is void in Scots law as a result of the parties' lack of legal capacity to marry or ineligibility to register a civil partnership.

Nonage

2.5 By s 1(1) of the Marriage (Scotland) Act 1977, no person domiciled[1] in Scotland may marry before he or she attains the age of 16.[2] Thus, for example, a 15-year-old girl who is domiciled in Scotland has no legal capacity to contract a marriage in Scotland or any other country in the world even if the law of the foreign country allows its domiciliaries to marry below the age of 16. Where a Scottish domiciliary is aged 16 or over, he or she has legal capacity to marry a foreign domiciliary who is under the age of 16, provided the ceremony takes place abroad and the foreign party has capacity under his or her *lex domicilii* and the law of the country where the ceremony takes place (the *lex loci celebrationis*).[3] By s 1(2) of the Marriage (Scotland) Act 1977, a marriage solemnised between persons either of whom is under the age of 16 is void. Consequently, even if one or both of the parties have capacity to marry under the age of 16 under their *lex domicilii*, the marriage is void if the ceremony takes place in Scotland.

Two people are not eligible to register in Scotland as civil partners of each other if either has not attained the age of 16.[4]

1 Domicile is a complex legal concept: its essence is a person having his or her permanent home in Scotland or having a Scottish domicile of dependence as a result of his or her parent being domiciled in Scotland.
2 Marriage (Scotland) Act 1977, s 1(1). Note that the minimum age for marriage or registering a civil partnership in England and Wales is to be increased to 18 years old. See the Marriage and Civil Partnership (Minimum Age) Act 2022, s 1 (marriage); s 3 (civil partnerships) (not in force at time of writing (June 2022). Will Scotland follow suit?
3 Family Law (Scotland) Act 2006, s 37.
4 Civil Partnership Act 2004, s 86(1)(c).

Forbidden degrees of relationship

Marriage

2.6 By s 2(1) of the Marriage (Scotland) Act 1977,[1] a marriage between persons who are related to each other in a forbidden degree is void if solemnised: (a) in Scotland; or (b) at a time when either party is domiciled in Scotland. A person is related to another in a forbidden degree if related to that person in a degree specified in Schedule 1 to the 1977 Act.[2] The list is exclusive in the sense that where the relationship is not mentioned in the Schedule, the parties may validly marry[3] unless it would be contrary to their *lex domicilii* or the *lex loci celebrationis* for them to do so. The list is as follows:

1 – Relationships by consanguinity

Parent	Aunt or uncle
Child	Niece or nephew
Grandparent	Great-grandparent
Grandchild	Great-grandchild
Sibling	

2 – Relationships by affinity

Child of former spouse	Former spouse of grandparent
Child of former civil partner	Former civil partner of grandparent
Former spouse of parent	Grandchild of former spouse
Former civil partner of parent	Grandchild of former civil partner

3 – Relationships by adoption

Adoptive parent or former adoptive parent	Adopted child or former adopted child

The prohibited relationships arise from: (1) blood ties (consanguinity); (2) marriage or civil partnerships (affinity); and (3) adoption.

1 As amended by the Marriage and Civil Partnership (Scotland) Act 2014, s 1.

2 Marriage (Scotland) Act 1977, s 2(1ZA). For the purposes of para 2 of the Schedule – relationships by affinity – 'spouse' means in the case of opposite sex marriages a husband in relation to his wife and a wife in relation to her husband and in the case of same sex marriages, one of the parties to the marriage in relation to the other: M(S)A 1977, s 2 (1C)).

3 M(S)A 1977, s 2(3). Similar principles apply to marriages by cohabitation with habit and repute: see E M Clive *The Law of Husband and Wife in Scotland* (4th edn, 1997, W Green/Sweet & Maxwell), p 76.

(1) Consanguinity

2.7 Prima facie we are concerned with persons who are genetically related. However, where a woman gives birth to a child as a result of a fertilised ovum donated by another woman, she is to be treated as the child's mother and not the woman who donated the egg.[1] Therefore the child cannot marry the woman who gave birth to him or her even though she is not genetically related to the child; but the child could marry the donor who is genetically related as she is not the mother for any legal purpose. Similarly, where a spouse agrees to the artificial insemination of his or her spouse using a donor's sperm (AID) or a civil partner agrees to her partner having a child by AID, the spouse or the civil partner is treated as the parent of the child for all legal purposes and not the donor.[2] And so, for example, even although she is not genetically related, an AID child cannot marry her mother's former spouse nor can she register a civil partnership with her mother's former civil partner; but she could marry the donor, who is genetically related to her, as he is not her father for any legal purpose.[3] Such children will also be deemed to be genetically related to the other members of the family, for example grandparents or siblings.

For the purpose of consanguinity, half-blood is treated as full blood[4] and illegitimacy is irrelevant.[5] For example, a man cannot marry his half-sister, ie his mother's daughter by a man who was not his father or his father's daughter by a woman who was not his mother. Also, it is irrelevant whether or not a child is born to married or unmarried parents. It should be noted that first cousins are free to marry.

1 Human Fertilisation and Embryology Act 1990, ss 27(1) and 29 and the Human Fertilisation and Embryology Act 2008, ss 33(1) and 48.
2 HFEA 1990, ss 28(2), (4) and 29: HFEA 2008, ss 35(1), 42(1) and 48; Marriage (Scotland) Act 1977, s 2(7A).
3 Similar prohibitions apply when a man is the child's father or a woman is the child's second female parent under HFEA 2008, ss 36 and 43. For further discussion of these provisions see **Ch 9.**
4 Marriage (Scotland) Act 1977, s 2(2)(a).
5 M(S)A 1977, s 2(4). See: Law Reform (Parent and Child) (Scotland) Act 1986, Sch 1, para 17.

(2) Affinity

2.8 A degree of affinity is created by marriage or civil partnership and not merely by the fact that sexual intercourse or other forms of sexual relations have taken place between the persons concerned. And so, for example, a man cannot *prima facie* marry his father's former wife, but he can marry his father's cohabitant even if she has lived with his father for many years and borne him children. Stepbrothers and stepsisters are free to marry.

In certain circumstances a marriage between persons related by affinity is not prohibited. Persons who are related within the degrees of affinity may marry provided that both parties have attained the age of 21 at the time of the marriage and the younger party has not at any time before attaining the age of 18 lived in the same household as the other party and been treated by the other party as a child of the family.[1] For example, a man may marry his father's former wife provided both are over the age of 21 and, if he is the younger party, he has not lived in the same household as his stepmother and been treated by her as a child of the family before he had reached the age of 18. If he has been so treated, the parties cannot marry. In other words, provided the parties related within the specified degrees of affinity have never assumed, in effect, the roles of parent and child, they are free to marry if both are over the age of 21.

For these purposes, if one of the parties (the relevant person) has had sex reassignment surgery and whose 'changed' gender has become the acquired gender under the Gender Recognition Act 2004,[2] then any reference to former wife or former husband of the relevant person includes (respectively) any former husband or former wife of the relevant person. For example, H and W are married. W has a son, S, from a previous marriage. H acquires a female gender. W divorces H. H cannot avoid the impediment to marrying S by arguing that at the time of the purported marriage, he is not the former husband of S's mother, W.

---

1 Marriage (Scotland) Act 1977, s 2(1A). Either party can petition the Court of Session for declarator that the conditions are satisfied which enable them to marry: see M(S) A 1977, s 2(5).

2 Discussed below at para **2.12**.

---

(3) Adoption

2.9 The Marriage (Scotland) Act 1977 only prohibits marriage between adoptive parents and their adopted children.[1] Thus, if H and W adopt A, A cannot marry W, his adoptive mother, or H his adopted father; but if H and W then adopt B, A can marry B unless they are genetically siblings.[2]

---

1 Adoption and Children (Scotland) Act 2007, s 41(2). Where a couple who have commissioned a surrogate child obtain parental rights and parental responsibilities by virtue of a parental order under the Human Fertilisation and Embryology Act 2008, s 54, they are treated as being adopted for the purpose of the law on prohibited degrees of marriage: HFEA 2008, s 55.

2 Adoption and parental rights orders do not affect the prohibitions on the grounds of consanguinity; so an adopted child cannot marry his or her genetic mother or father etc: AC(S) Act 2007, s 41(1).

Conclusion

2.10 There are policy reasons behind the prohibited degrees of relationship. It is believed that marriage to a close relative greatly increases the risk of conceiving a physically or mentally disabled child; yet marriage between first cousins is permitted, and that marriage between closely related persons can give rise to disruption within the family. The law permits adopted siblings to marry even if for many years they believed they were siblings by blood. Moreover, restrictions on marriage between persons who are related only by affinity have been held to be a breach of Article 8 (right to respect for private and family life) and Article 12 (the right to marry) of the European Convention of Human Rights.[1] This has led to the removal of restrictions on parents-in-law marrying their former children-in-law.[2]

1 *B and L v UK* [2006] 1 FLR 35.
2 Family Law (Scotland) Act 2006, s 1.

Civil partnership

2.11 In June 2021, s 1 of the Civil Partnership (Scotland) Act 2020 came into force. This Act enables persons of different sexes to register a civil partnership in Scotland.[1] By s 86(1)(b) of the Civil Partnership Act 2004,[2] two people are not eligible to register in Scotland as civil partners of each other if they are related in a forbidden degree. The forbidden degrees are the same as for marriage.[3] Thus, for example, a person cannot register a civil partnership with his or her parent or sibling or child (consanguinity). Nor can a person register a civil partnership with his or her parent's former spouse (step parent) or his or her parent's former civil partner or the child of his or her former spouse (step child) or his or her former civil partner's child (affinity).[4] However, in the case of affinity the prohibition is disapplied if: (a) both persons have reached the age of 21; and (b) the younger has not at any time before the age of 18 lived in the same household as the elder and been treated by the elder as a child of his or her family.[5] An adopted child cannot enter into a civil partnership with his or her adoptive parent. and an adoptive mother cannot enter into a civil partnership with her adopted daughter.[6]

1 See: *R (on the application of Steinfeld) v Secretary of State for International Development* [2018] UKSC 32.
2 As amended by the Marriage and Civil Partnership Act 2014, s 24(3).
3 Civil Partnership Act 2004, Sch 10. A reference to mother includes a woman who is a parent of the child by virtue of the Human and Embryology Act 2008, ss 42 and 43: CPA 2004, s 86(5A).

4 When the relevant party's gender has become the acquired gender under the Gender Recognition Act 2004, former husband includes former wife (and vice versa): CPA 2004, s 86(4) and (5).

5 Civil Partnership Act 2004, s 86(3). The prohibition on persons entering into civil partnerships with their former children in law or the children of their former civil partners (and vice versa) has been abolished: Family Law (Scotland) Act 2006, s 33 and Sch 1, para 2.

6 Adoption and Children (Scotland) Act 2007, s 41(2).

The sex of the parties

Marriage

2.12 For centuries marriage in Scots law was regarded as a union between a man and a woman.[1] A marriage was therefore void if the parties purporting to marry were of the same sex. Section 5(4)(e) of the Marriage (Scotland) Act 1977 expressly stipulated that there was an impediment to a marriage if 'both parties were of the same sex'. The Marriage and Civil Partnership (Scotland) Act 2014 repealed this restriction and opened marriage to same sex couples.[2] Marriage means 'marriage between persons of different sexes and marriage between persons of the same sex'.[3]

Even though marriage between persons of the same sex is permitted in Scotland, there remain differences in the formalities between different sex and same sex marriages. It is still necessary to consider how a person's sex is to be determined for the purposes of family law. There is an interesting background to this area of family law. In the 2003 case of *Bellinger v Bellinger,*[4] the House of Lords held that biological criteria only should continue to be used:[5] these are genital, gonadal and chromosomal.[6] In a case of genuine intersex, a choice must be made on the basis of the preponderance of biological criteria.[7] If later developments, including psychological factors, suggest that the original assignment of the child's sex was wrong, then it can be changed. But when all the criteria are congruent at birth, a child's sex is established and could not be changed.[8]

This raised acute problems for transgender persons whose psychological sex is the opposite of their biological sex. Even after gender reassignment surgery, their sex did not change for the purpose of the law of marriage. The House of Lords in *Bellinger* accepted that this constituted a breach of

Articles 8 and 12[9] of the European Convention of Human Rights as they could not marry in their reassigned gender.

This led to the Gender Recognition Act 2004.[10] The law at the time of writing (May 2022) is that a person of either gender who is aged 18 or over can apply for a gender recognition certificate on the basis that he or she is living in the other gender (the acquired gender).[11] The application is determined by the Gender Recognition Panel.[12] If the Panel is satisfied that the applicant (a) has or has had gender dysphoria; (b) has lived in the acquired gender; and (c) intends to live in the acquired gender until death,[13] then the Panel must grant the application for a certificate and issue a full gender recognition certificate.[14]

If the applicant is a party to a 'protected Scottish marriage'[15] and the application includes both a declaration that the applicant wishes the marriage to continue after the issue of a full gender recognition certificate, and a declaration by the applicant's spouse that he or she wishes the marriage to continue after the issue of a full gender recognition certificate, then the Gender Recognition Panel will issue a full gender recognition certificate.[16] However, where the applicant is a party to a 'protected Scottish marriage' and the other spouse does not consent to the marriage continuing after the issue of a full gender recognition certificate then the Gender Recognition Panel will grant an interim gender recognition certificate.[17]

The applicant can then apply to a sheriff for a full gender recognition certificate which if the application is made within six months of the issue of the interim recognition certificate, the sheriff must grant the application.[18] While the marriage continues, the interests of the non-consenting spouse are protected as that spouse, and indeed the applicant, retains the right to obtain a divorce on the ground in s 1(1)(b) of the Divorce (Scotland) Act 1976[19] as that ground which arose when the interim gender recognition certificate was issued does not lapse when the full gender certificate is granted.[20]

It should be noted that, at the time of writing (May 2022), the Gender Recognition Reform (Scotland) Bill is in draft form and remains at Stage 1.[21]

1 Stair *The Institutions of the Law of Scotland* (6th edn, 1981), I 4.1–I 4.6.

2 Marriage and Civil Partnership (Scotland) Act 2014, s 2 (a).
3 Marriage Scotland) Act 1977, s 26(2) as inserted by MCP(S)A 2014, s 4(14).
4 [2003] HL 21.
5 This was the approach taken by Ormrod J in *Corbett v Corbett* [1971] P 83.
6 In the cells of biological males, Y as well as X chromosomes are present; no Y chromosomes are present in the cells of a biological female.
7 This appears to be the approach that was taken by the Lord Ordinary (Hunter) in the mysterious case of *Forbes-Sempill* (unreported). This case proceeded on the basis that the person concerned was a true hermaphrodite. See A I L Campbell 'Successful sex in succession: sex in dispute – the *Forbes Sempill* case and possible implications' 1998 JR 257 and 325.
8 *X, Petitioner* 1957 SLT (Sh Ct) 61.
9 The European Court of Human Rights had finally reached the same conclusion in *Goodwin v UK* and *I v UK* (2002) 35 EHHR 18.
10 At the time of writing (May 2022) the Gender Recognition Reform (Scotland) Bill is currently at Stage 1 of the parliamentary process.
11 Gender Recognition Act 2004, s 1(1)(a).
12 GRA 2004, s 1(3).
13 GRA 2004, ss 2 and 3.
14 GRA 2004, s 4(1) (2).
15 GRA 2004, s 25(1). These definitions were inserted by Civil Partnership (Scotland) Act 2020. See also: Marriage and Civil Partnership (Scotland) Act 2014, Sch 2.
16 GRA 2004, s 3(6) to (6E).
17 GRA 2004, s 4(3)(a).
18 GRA 2004, s 4E. But note that the Gender Recognition Reform (Scotland) Bill (as introduced) intends to repeal s 4E of GRA 2004.
19 See para **6.11**.
20 D(S)A 1976, s 1(3B)(b).
21 The Gender Recognition Reform (Scotland) Bill (as introduced) seeks to change the process of acquiring a gender recognition certificate (GRC). The GRC certifies that the holder's gender is not that assigned at birth, but is their 'acquired gender'.

Civil partnership

2.13 Section 86(1) of the Civil Partnership Act 2004 empowers two people of the same or different sex to register in Scotland as civil partners of each other.[1]

The rules in relation to the application for a gender recognition certificate that apply to marriage also apply to civil partnerships. This means that if the applicant for a gender recognition certificate is a party to a 'protected Scottish civil partnership'[2] and the application includes both a declaration that the applicant wishes the civil partnership to continue after the issue of a full gender recognition certificate, and an application by the applicant's civil partner that he or she wishes the civil partnership to continue after the issue of a full gender recognition certificate, then the Gender Recognition Panel will issue a full gender recognition certificate.[3] Where the applicant's civil partner does not consent to the civil partnership continuing, after the issue of a full gender recognition certificate, then the Gender Recognition Panel will issue an interim gender recognition certificate.[4]

Again, similar to the process for marriage, the applicant can apply to the sheriff for a full gender recognition certificate which, if the application is made within six months of the issue of the interim gender recognition certificate, the sheriff must grant the application.[5] While the civil partnership continues, the applicant civil partner and the non-consenting civil partner retain the right to obtain a dissolution on the ground in s 117(2)(b) of the Civil Partnership Act 2004 as that ground does not lapse as a result of the granting of a full gender recognition certificate.[6]

1 Note that Civil Partnership Act 2004, s 86(1)(a) (necessity that both parties were of the same sex) was repealed by s 6(2) of the Civil Partnership (Scotland) Act 2020. In England and Wales, different sex couples can register a civil partnership. See: *R (on the application of Steinfeld) v Secretary of State for International Development* [2018] UKSC 32; [2020] AC 1. See also: CPA 2004, s 1 (as amended by the Civil Partnership (Opposite-sex Couples) Regulations 2019 (SI 2019/1458).
2 Gender Recognition Act 2004, s 25(1).
3 GRA 2004, s 3(6)–(6E).
4 GRA 2004, s 4(3)(c).
5 GRA 2004, s 4E.
6 CPA 2004, s 117(3A).

Prior subsisting marriage or civil partnership

2.14 A person who is already a party to a valid marriage or civil partnership lacks legal capacity to enter into a subsequent marriage or civil partnership while the first marriage or civil partnership continues to subsist.[1] The exception to this is where the parties are in a 'qualifying civil partnership' and wish to change it to a marriage.[2] There is no legal impediment if the first marriage or civil partnership is void. If, however, a marriage is only voidable, it will operate as a bar to a second marriage or civil partnership unless and until a declarator of nullity of marriage has been obtained.[3]

Even though the parties entered into a marriage or a civil partnership with the belief held in good faith that any prior marriage or civil partnership had ended as a result of the death of the spouse or civil partner or divorce or dissolution, the marriage or civil partnership will still be void if *in fact* the prior marriage or civil partnership was subsisting at the time of the ceremony or registration. However, if a decree or declarator of nullity were obtained, financial provision for the spouses or the civil partners would be available.[4] Moreover, once the prior marriage was dissolved and the impediment to marriage thereby removed, the parties could have become married as a result of subsequent cohabitation with habit and repute.[5]

Where one of the parties is aware of this impediment, the innocent party may obtain damages for fraud. This was illustrated in *Burke v Burke*.[6] In this case the husband was living with his first wife. He went through a ceremony of marriage with the pursuer (his second wife). He told her that he was divorced from his first wife. He also informed the pursuer that he was working night shifts but he spent his evenings with his first wife. When the pursuer discovered that no divorce had taken place, she sought declarator of nullity and aliment for her child who had been conceived during the 'marriage'. The court held that the pursuer did not have to prove the validity of the first marriage: she could rely on the doctrine *omnia praesumuntur rite et solemniter acta esse*.[7] The onus lay on the defender to establish which, in the circumstances, he could not, that the first marriage was void. Accordingly, the pursuer obtained declarator and aliment for the child. In addition, the court held that the pursuer was entitled to damages in delict as a result of the defender's fraud and awarded her £2,500.[8]

A marriage or civil partnership will be void even though the parties believed, in good faith, that a prior marriage or civil partnership had been dissolved as a result of the death of the spouse or civil partner. This can raise difficulties for a person whose spouse or civil partner has disappeared and who wishes to enter a second marriage or civil partnership. At common law, there was a very strong presumption of life and a person who had disappeared was presumed to live to a ripe old age.[9] This presumption could be rebutted by evidence establishing beyond reasonable doubt that a spouse was dead but even so, a subsequent marriage was void if the spouse was in fact still alive.

This unsatisfactory position was resolved as a result of the Presumption of Death (Scotland) Act 1977. Under this statute, any person with sufficient interest may petition the Court of Session or the sheriff court for a declarator of death. The court may grant decree if satisfied on a balance of probabilities that either:

(a) the missing person is dead – including the date and time of death; or

(b) the missing person has not been known to be alive for a period of at least seven years: in this case, the court will declare the missing person to have died at the end of the day occurring seven years after the date on which he was last known to be alive.[10]

The Presumption of Death (Scotland) Act 1977 therefore covers two situations. In the first, a person has disappeared in circumstances which point to his or her death at a particular time, for example if a person was travelling in an aeroplane which disappeared. Here there is no need to wait seven years before bringing the action. In the second, a person has simply gone missing and there are no circumstances to suggest that he or she is dead. Here no action can be raised until seven years have elapsed during which there is no evidence that the missing person is alive.

A declarator of death is effective 'for all purposes including dissolution of a marriage or of a civil partnership to which the missing person is a party'.[11] Once a marriage or civil partnership has been dissolved as a result of a decree, 'the dissolution of the marriage or civil partnership shall not be invalidated by the circumstance that the missing person was in fact alive at the date specified in the decree'.[12] Thus if, for example, a person has obtained a declarator of death of a missing spouse or civil partner, that person will have capacity to enter a subsequent marriage or civil partnership and this later marriage or civil partnership is not affected even if the missing spouse was, in fact, alive at the date of the later ceremony.

Although there are provisions for the variation or recall of the declarator if the missing person is found to be alive within five years of the date of the decree, no variation or recall 'shall operate so as to revive a marriage of the missing person dissolved by virtue of a decree in an action of declarator'.[13] It should be noted that any person, for example a beneficiary under the missing person's will, may apply for declarator. If it is granted, it will have the effect of dissolving the missing person's marriage or civil partnership, even though the missing person's spouse or civil partner continues to entertain the belief that the missing person is still alive and does not wish the marriage to be dissolved.

It is a criminal offence to purport to enter into a marriage knowing that either or both parties are already married to, or in a civil partnership with, another person[14] and it is a criminal offence to purport to register a civil partnership knowing that either or both parties are already in a civil partnership with, or married to, another person.[15] However, by s 13 of the Presumption of Death (Scotland) Act 1977 it is a defence to these offences for the accused to prove that at no time within a period of seven years immediately preceding the date of a subsequent marriage or civil partnership had he or she any reason to believe that a prior spouse or civil partner was alive.

---

1 Marriage (Scotland) Act 1977, s 5(4)(b); Civil Partnership Act 2004, s 86(1)(d).

2 See M(S)A 1977, s 5(6) as amended by the Qualifying Civil Partnership Modification (Scotland) Order 2015, art 3.

3 Even though a declarator of nullity of marriage renders the marriage retrospectively null, it will probably not operate to validate a second marriage which was entered into before declarator was obtained.

4 See para **2.2**.

5 See para **1.15**; and Family Law (Scotland) Act 2006, s 3.

6 1983 SLT 331.

7 The Latin means that 'all things are presumed to have been solemnly done and with the usual ceremony'. This is a rebuttable presumption of compliance with the appropriate formalities.

8 It has been held that a woman in this position is not entitled to compensation from the Criminal Injuries Compensation Board as she has not been the victim of a crime of violence when she had sex with a man whom she believed was her husband – her remedy was to sue him for fraud: *Gray v Criminal Injuries Compensation Board* 1999 SC 137.

9 Stair IV 45.17. See, for example, *Muhammad v Robertson or Kettle or Muhammad* 1972 SLT (Notes) 69.

10 Presumption of Death (Scotland) Act 1977, s 2(1).

11 PD(S)A 1977, s 3(1).

12 PD(S)A 1977, s 3(3).
13 PD(S)A 1977, s 4(5). It does not appear that this section has been amended to prevent a civil partnership which has been dissolved from reviving if the missing person turns out to be alive. It can be assumed that the same provision would apply.
14 M(S)A 1977, s 24(A1). The common law offence of bigamy has been abolished: Marriage and Civil Partnership (Scotland) Act 2014, s 28(3).
15 Civil Partnership Act 2004, s 100(1).

DEFECTIVE CONSENT

Marriage

2.15 Marriage is a contract and like any other contract requires consent. At common law a marriage was null if the parties did not truly consent to take each other as husband and wife. The law has now been put on a statutory basis and is to be found in s 20A of the Marriage (Scotland) Act 1977. The provisions only apply to marriages which are solemnised in Scotland.

Incapacity

2.16 By s 20A(3) of the 1977 Act, a marriage is void if at the time of the ceremony a party to the marriage was incapable of understanding the nature of marriage or of consenting to the marriage. This could arise from mental illness or mental impairment. However, the fact that a person is suffering from a mental illness, for example depression, does not necessarily prevent the giving of valid consent, provided the necessary capacity is present at the time. Marriage is a simple contract and persons of limited intelligence can validly consent to marriage. It has long been established[1] that there is a very heavy burden on any person denying the validity of a marriage to establish that one or both parties were incapable of understanding the nature of marriage as a result of mental impairment or mental illness at the time of the ceremony. But if this burden can be discharged, the marriage will be void. A person may be of sound mind but physically or mentally weak, ie facile. As a result, such persons may easily be persuaded to act against their interests. In the absence of duress,[2] such a marriage is valid. Scots law has firmly rejected the contention that a marriage can be voidable on the grounds of facility and circumvention or undue influence.[3]

A party may lack capacity to consent as a result of drunkenness or abuse of drugs at the time of the ceremony. The effect of alcohol or drugs must be extreme before capacity is lost. In *Johnston v Brown*,[4] the pursuer, Mary Brown, obtained declarator of nullity of marriage on the ground that at the time of the ceremony, and for three days thereafter, she was so inebriated that she lacked capacity to consent to the marriage. Accordingly, the marriage was void.

1 *Long v Long* 1950 SLT (Notes) 32.
2 See para **2.18** ff.
3 *Scott v Kelly* 1992 SLT 915.
4 (1823) 25 495.

Error

2.17 By s 20A(2) of the 1977 Act a marriage is void if, at the time of the ceremony, a party who was capable of consenting to the marriage purported to give consent but did so under error. For this purpose, error is restricted to error as to the nature of the ceremony or the identity of the other party.[1]

An error as to the nature of the ceremony would arise if A goes through a ceremony of marriage with B, believing it to be merely a betrothal.[2] An error as to identity is only operative in cases of impersonation. An extreme example may occur in the case of identical twins where one twin impersonates the other twin at the ceremony and this goes unnoticed by the other party to the marriage. In *M'Leod v Adams*[3] no error as to identity arose. The defender had deserted from the army. Using a false name to avoid detection by the authorities, he told a widow that he was a sergeant in the Black Watch. The couple married by exchanging *de praesenti* consents whereupon the defender promptly deserted his wife taking her savings with him. Lord Sands held that there was no operative error as the widow clearly intended to marry the man before her and accordingly there was no error as to the identity of the parties to the marriage.[4] It is thought that the same result would be obtained under s 20A of the 1977 Act.

At common law it was settled that an error as to the qualities of a party to the marriage does not operate to vitiate consent. 'Errors in qualities or circumstances vitiate not.'[5] In the contract of marriage parties take each other 'for better or worse' and the Scottish courts refused to imply resolutive conditions into the contract which would be inconsistent with this fundamental principle.[6]

Moreover, in *Lang v Lang*,[7] the Inner House of the Court of Session held that it was irrelevant that an error as to qualities was induced by the fraudulent misrepresentation or concealment of facts by the spouse concerned. The pursuer in this case sought a declarator of nullity on the ground that he had been induced to marry the defender as a result of her representation that she was pregnant by him when, in fact, she was carrying another man's child. The court maintained that neither concealment of pregnancy *per alium*, nor a fraudulent misrepresentation of the true source of a disclosed pregnancy, was a ground of nullity in Scots law as these merely gave rise to errors as to qualities of the spouse and were therefore not sufficiently essential to vitiate consent. Again, it is submitted that the same result would be obtained under s 20A of the 1977 Act.

The limited scope of operative error in relation to marriage can be the cause of considerable injustice. Although a person in the position of the pursuer in *Lang v Lang*[8] could seek a divorce, he may well have to wait two years before he has a relevant ground.[9] The fraudulent misrepresentation cannot constitute grounds for divorce as behaviour as this purpose is restricted to the defender's conduct '*since the date of the marriage*'.[10]

---

1 Marriage (Scotland) Act 1977, s 20A(5).
2 A betrothal ceremony is a formal commitment by the parties to marry in the future. (An engagement is where the couple signifies their intention to marry in the future.)
3 1920 1 SLT 229.
4 Declarator of nullity was, however, granted on the grounds that the marriage was a sham: see para **2.20** ff.
5 Stair I 9.9.
6 There is one exception: the marriage is voidable if one or both of the parties are unable to consummate the marriage as a result of incurable impotency. See para **2.21** ff.
7 1921 SC 44, overruling *Stein v Stein* 1914 SC 903.
8 1921 SC 44.
9 That is two years' non-cohabitation: Divorce (Scotland) Act 1976, s 1(2)(e). See **Ch 6**.
10 Divorce (Scotland) Act 1976, s 1(2)(b): see **Ch 6.**

Duress

2.18 Section 20A(2) of the Marriage (Scotland) Act 1977 provides that a marriage is void if at the time of the marriage ceremony a party to a marriage who was capable of consenting to the marriage purported to give consent but did so only by reason of duress. However, duress is not defined.

At common law a marriage was void if the will of one of the parties was overcome as a result of force or fear. The test was subjective.[1] In other words, the question was 'Was this particular person overcome by force or fear?' not 'Would a person of reasonable fortitude have been terrified?'.

It was accepted that where a person marries out of deference to his or her parents' wishes, the marriage was not void. An example of this may be an arranged marriage whereby the parties comply with their parents' choice of spouse, and where consent to marry is given freely by the parties. But unremitting pressure intentionally sustained by the parents,[2] or the threat of being cut off from financial support and being sent to a foreign country,[3] goes beyond the limits of acceptable parental influence and could constitute duress.[4] It is submitted that duress for the purpose of s 20A of the 1977 Act should be construed in the same way.

As a matter of principle, duress may emanate from a third party, for example state authorities. In the leading English case of *Buckland v Buckland*,[5] the Court of Appeal held that before it is relevant the fear must have been unjustifiably imposed. Thus, for example, if a man is forced to marry a woman who is pregnant with his child because of the threat that paternity proceedings would be brought against him unless he did so, he could not rely on the fear as it would be argued that it was justly imposed. Professor Eric Clive has argued[6] that this distinction is hard to justify as the consent is no more free where the fear is justly imposed. This may well be a case where reasoning from legal principle must give way to considerations of public policy.

The concept of duress in Scots law is narrow. Even if a marriage is void as a result of duress, there will have been a ceremony and the victim may have been compelled to leave his or her family and live with his or her spouse. Put another way, while a marriage can be null because of duress, the law was slow to prevent the 'marriage' being performed in the first place. In order to alleviate public concern about forced marriages, the Forced Marriage etc. (Protection and Jurisdiction) (Scotland) Act 2011 enables a court to make a forced marriage protection order (FMPO).[7] The purpose of the order is to protect a person from being forced into a marriage or from any attempt to force the person into a marriage, or to protect a person who has been forced into a marriage. The order will require persons, for example the victim's family, to stop using violent, threatening or intimidating conduct to force the protected person to marry.[8] An application for an order can be made to the sheriff by the 'protected person',[9] a local authority or the Lord Advocate, or a person specified by Scottish ministers, for example, a representative from a women's support agency.[10] An application can also be made after the marriage, for example to prevent the protected person from being compelled to leave the country.[11] Breach of a protection order is a criminal offence. In *City of Edinburgh Council v S*,[12] the pursuer applied for a FMPO in respect of a 15-year-old girl. The application included claims that, as forced marriages had already taken place within the family, the girl required the FMPO to protect her from such a future marriage. In this case the application was refused, among other reasons, on the grounds that an FMPO can only be granted where a specific marriage is in prospect, not for general future protection. In *C v T*,[13] a local authority applied for a FMPO to protect a 17-year-old young woman from being taken from Scotland to Pakistan because of the risk that she would be forced to enter a marriage. The young woman's father had issued threats to her that he would take her to Pakistan and kill her.

---

1 *Mahmood v Mahmood* 1993 SLT 589; *Mahmud v Mahmud* 1994 SLT 599; *Sohrab v Khan* 2002 SLT 1255.

2 *Mahmud v Mahmud* 1994 SLT 599. The pursuer in this case was a young man. In *Sohrab v Khan* 2002 SLT 1255, part of the pressure was the threat by the pursuer's mother that she would kill herself unless her daughter (the pursuer) entered into a marriage.

3 *Mahmood v Mahmood* 1993 SLT 589. The disapproval of the parents' or the child's community is not *per se* enough.

4 While it may be easier to infer duress when, as in *Mahmud*, the 'marriage' was never consummated and the parties never lived together, in *Mahmood*, declarator was granted even though the marriage had been consummated.

5 [1967] 2 All ER 300; [1968] P 296.

6 E M Clive *The Law of Husband and Wife in Scotland* (4th edn, 1997, W Green/Sweet & Maxwell), p 86.

7 Forced Marriage etc (Protection and Jurisdiction) (Scotland) Act 2011, s 1(1)(a).
8 FM(PJ)(S)A 2011, s 2.
9 FM(PJ)(S)A 2011, s 1(1).
10 FM(PJ)(S)A 2011, s 3. See also Children's Hearings (Scotland) Act 2011, s 67(2)(q).
11 FM(PJ)(S)A 2011, s 1(1)(b).
12 2015 SLT (Sh Ct) 69.
13 2022 Fam LR 39. See also: *B v D* 2022 Fam LR 26 in which the 21-year-old protected person applied to the sheriff for a FMPO. The order was made for five years and ordained the parents of the young woman to refrain from attempting to take her out of the UK, to refrain from conspiring to force her into a marriage and to stop using violent, threatening and intimidating behaviour towards her.

Civil partnerships

2.19 By s 123(1) of the Civil Partnership Act 2004, a civil partnership is void if the parties are ineligible to register in Scotland as civil partners.[1] A person who is incapable of understanding the nature of civil partnership, or validly consenting to its formation, is not eligible to register.[2] A civil partnership is also void if at the time of registration one of the parties who was capable of consenting to the formation of the civil partnership purported to consent but did so by reason only of duress or error.[3] Error is restricted to error as to the nature of civil partnership or the identity of the other party.[4] The same issues which arise have been discussed in the context of marriage. Scottish Ministers have the power to apply the provisions of the Forced Marriage etc (Protection and Jurisdiction) Act 2011 to civil partnerships.[5]

1 Civil Partnership Act 2004, s 123(1)(a).
2 CPA 2004, s 86(1)(e).
3 CPA 2004, s 123(1)(b) and (c).
4 CPA 2004, s 123(2).
5 Forced Marriage etc (Protection and Jurisdiction) Act 2011, s 10. See also Children's Hearings (Scotland) Act 2011, s 67(2)(p).

Sham marriages

2.20 At common law it was recognised that a marriage was null if it could be established that one or both parties had, for religious or other reasons, intended not to become married at the time of the ceremony,[1] ie that at the time of the ceremony one or both of them had tacitly withheld consent to the marriage. Put another way they were saying 'yes' when they meant 'no'. This was known as the sham marriage doctrine. It became controversial because parties could go through a ceremony of marriage to obtain certain rights deriving from the status of matrimony, for example in relation to immigration, then later obtain a decree of declarator of nullity on the basis that their marriage was a sham.

Section 20A(4) of the Marriage (Scotland) Act 1977 provides:

> 'If a party to a marriage purported to give consent to marriage other than by reason only of duress or error, the marriage shall not be void by reason only of that party's having tacitly withheld consent to the marriage at the time when it was solemnised.'

'Sham marriage' and 'sham civil partnership' are defined in ss 24(5) and (6), and ss 24A(5) and (5A), respectively, of the Immigration and Asylum Act 1999. Section 3 of the Marriage (Scotland) Act 1977 and s 88 of the Civil Partnership Act 2004 extend the power of the district registrar to require 'specified nationality evidence' for both a marriage and a civil partnership.[2]

The matter of sham marriages is dealt with in Sch 1A of the Marriage (Scotland) Act 1977[3] and relates to a 'referred marriage', which is a 'proposed marriage' that has been referred to the Secretary of State for investigation.[4] While under investigation, the district registrar may not issue the Marriage Schedule (within the statutory 28 days). The reasons (or 'events') that may lead to a delay in completing the Marriage Schedule include: that the Secretary of State has given the district registrar a s 48 notice[5] and that notice states that the decision has been taken not to investigate whether the referred marriage is a sham; that a s 48 notice has been given to the district registrar and that notice states that the decision has been taken to investigate whether the referred marriage is a sham; or the 70-day period has elapsed and the Secretary of State has not given the district registrar a s 50 notice.[6]

The referral and investigation scheme has been extended to proposed marriages and civil partnerships under the law of Scotland and the same investigative and reporting procedures apply.[7]

1 See, for example, *Orlandi v Castelli* 1961 SC 113; *Mahmud v Mahmud* 1977 SLT (Notes) 17; *Akram v Akram* 1979 SLT (Notes) 87; *H v H* 2005 SLT 1025. A marriage could be void as a sham where only one party withheld consent: *McLeod v Adams* 1920 1 SLT 229.

2 Added by the Marriage and Civil Partnership (Scotland) Act 2014, ss 17 and 25.

3 Added by Referral and Investigation of Proposed Marriages and Civil Partnerships (Scotland) Order 2015 (SSI 2015/396) Sch 1, para 3.

4 Marriage (Scotland) Act 1977 s 6(4ZA).

5 Immigration Act 2014, s 48 (Decision whether to investigate).

6 Immigration Act 2014, s 50(7) (Notice of the decision taken by the Secretary of State).

7 Civil Partnership Act 2004, Sch 10A.

VOIDABLE MARRIAGES: INCURABLE IMPOTENCY

2.21 The parties' consent is the essential element of marriage in Scots law: *consensus non concubitus facit matrimonium*. However, a different sex marriage[1] is voidable if, and only if, one or both of the parties is at the time of the ceremony permanently and incurably impotent. As Lord President (Clyde) explained in *L v L*,[2] *potentia copulandi* is a resolutive condition of the contract of marriage: if it is not fulfilled the marriage is a nullity. But before the marriage will be treated as null, a party to the marriage must obtain a declarator of nullity of marriage whereupon the marriage is retrospectively void from the date of decree.[3] It has been recommended that incurable impotency should cease to be a ground on which a marriage is voidable.[4]

1 Section 5(1) of the Marriage and Civil Partnership (Scotland) Act 2014 provides that: 'For the avoidance of doubt, the rule of law which provides for a marriage to be voidable by reason of impotence has effect only in relation to a marriage between persons of different sexes.' Nor does the law affect civil partnerships.

2 *L v L* 1931 SC 477 at 481.

3 See para **2.2**.

4 Report on Family Law (Scot Law Com No 135) rec 49. There are few declarators of nullity each year and it is doubtful whether they are all concerned with incurable impotency. The numbers concerned are therefore very small. It is true that specific matrimonial relief on the ground of incurable impotency is anomalous: there is no specific relief, for example, if a spouse marries when suffering from sterility or an incurable or infectious disease. It is argued by the Scottish Law Commission that divorce on the ground of irretrievable breakdown should be a sufficient remedy in

cases of incurable impotency. This recommendation was not accepted by the Scottish Executive and the Family Law (Scotland) Act 2006 did not reform this area of the law apart from extending the jurisdiction to grant declarator to the sheriff court: FL(S) A 2006, s 4. The sheriff can grant declarator when the marriage is void as well as when it is voidable.

The meaning of incurable impotency

2.22 'Impotence' means incapacity to have sexual intercourse. The Scottish courts have taken the view that sexual intercourse involves full and complete sexual intercourse: *vera copula perfecta* accomplished *modo naturalis*. For the purposes of consummating a marriage, partial penetration by the husband of the wife is not enough.[1] However, once full penetration has been achieved, the marriage has been consummated. Moreover, impotence is incapacity for sexual intercourse not the capacity to procreate. Consequently, sterility does not amount to impotence. If a spouse is capable of sexual intercourse but refuses to consummate the marriage, that is not a ground of nullity in Scots law though it could give rise to grounds for divorce.[2]

The impotence may be the result of physical or psychological causes. It may exist only in relation to the other spouse: *quoad hanc* (*vis-à-vis* the wife) or *quoad hunc* (*vis-à-vis* the husband). Indeed, both spouses may be impotent in relation to each other: *quoad hanc et quoad hunc*. The impotency must exist at the date of the marriage and must be permanent and incurable at the date of the action for declarator of nullity. The courts have taken a realistic approach on the question of incurability and have held that the issue is whether the impotence is incurable in the context of the particular marriage. Thus, for example, in *M v W or M*,[3] the husband suffered from a nervous or psychological inability to consummate the marriage. He was advised by his doctor that the impotency was curable if he had hormone treatment and had the full support and help of his wife. After the hormone treatment was administered, his wife refused to have sexual intercourse with him. The Inner House held that the husband's impotence was incurable *quoad hanc* as the cure involved both the hormone treatment and the wife's help which had not been forthcoming.[4] While this decision illustrates the court's sympathy towards the pursuer, it must be restricted to its own special facts: a potent spouse cannot argue that he is impotent *quoad hanc* merely because his wife refuses to have sexual intercourse with him since this would, in effect, be recognising wilful refusal to consummate as a ground of nullity.

If the impotence is curable, where the action is brought by the potent spouse, a decree is not granted until the impotent spouse has had an opportunity to undergo the necessary treatment: if the defender refuses treatment, a decree will then be granted.[5] If the impotent spouse is the pursuer, the action will fail if reasonable steps could be taken to effect a cure. Where the treatment carries a risk to life or intolerable pain, the impotent spouse is not expected to undergo such an ordeal and the impotency will be regarded as incurable.

The potent spouse can obviously bring an action. But in *F v F*,[6] the Inner House held that because impotency was an involuntary condition, the impotent spouse can also seek a declarator of nullity on the ground of his or her own incurable impotency.

---

1 *J v J* 1978 SLT 128.
2 The behaviour of one party's refusal to consummate a marriage may contribute to the establishment of the ground of irretrievable breakdown. Divorce (Scotland) Act 1976, s 1(2)(b). See **Ch 6.**
3 1966 SLT 152.
4 But the Lord President (Clyde) thought that the question was whether the husband was impotent throughout the marriage rather than whether it was curable at the date of the action: *M v W or M* 1966 SLT 152 at 154.
5 *WY v AY* 1946 SC 27.
6 1945 SC 202.

Personal bar

2.23 A spouse may be personally barred from obtaining declarator of nullity on the ground of incurable impotency. Personal bar will arise if, with knowledge of the impotency and the availability of a legal remedy, the pursuer has either approbated the marriage or taken advantage of, or derived benefit from, the matrimonial relationship with the result that it would be unfair or inequitable to permit the pursuer to treat the marriage as null.[1]

Two points should be noticed. First, personal bar will arise only if the pursuer knows of the facts and the availability of a legal remedy. But knowledge of the law will *prima facie* be assumed and the onus should therefore be on the pursuer to show that he or she did not have knowledge of a legal remedy. Secondly, it is the pursuer's *conduct* which constitutes approbation or the taking of advantages, etc, which renders it unfair or inequitable to grant decree. Examples of this principle may include: (i) Delay that causes serious prejudice to the defender; or (ii) Knowledge of the incurable impotency. Where the pursuer entered the marriage with the knowledge of the defender's incurable impotency, this will result in a personal bar on the basis that the pursuer has homologated the defender's condition. Conversely, an impotent spouse who has allowed the potent spouse to enter the marriage with knowledge of the impotency is personally barred from seeking declarator on the ground of his or her own impotency; and (iii) Personal bar may also arise where the pursuer has homologated or adopted the voidable marriage by agreeing to adopt a child or have a child by artificial insemination.

---

1 *CB v AB* (1885) 12 R (HL) 36 at 38, per Lord Selborne.

Chapter 3

The legal consequences of marriage and civil partnership

PART I: GENERAL

INTRODUCTION

3.1 In this and the following two chapters, it is proposed to discuss the major legal consequences for the parties of marriage and civil partnership. This chapter is concerned with a diverse but not exhaustive range of subjects and certain important matters, for example bankruptcy, evidence, immigration and taxation, are not discussed. In Chapters 4 and 5 the implications of marriage and civil partnership on the law of property are treated in some detail.

The twentieth century saw a drastic decline in the legal consequences of marriage.[1] In the interests of equality between the spouses, many changes in the law have taken the form of regarding the spouses as though they were unmarried. Property is one such area. However, the perception that mothers have the primary responsibility for caring for and bringing up children has the consequence that, in a marriage, the wife often becomes economically dependent on her husband thus reducing her opportunities to acquire property during the marriage. On the other hand, under the system of financial provision on divorce, a wife can be compensated for economic disadvantages sustained by her as a result of her role within the marriage. Moreover, when a marriage is terminated by death, Scots law protects the surviving spouse by providing him or her with rights to a proportion of the deceased's estate which cannot be defeated by the deceased. It is perhaps not too cynical to observe that during the marriage the legal consequences of being married are, with some important exceptions, such as aliment[2] and the right to occupy the matrimonial home,[3] relatively insignificant compared with being married when the marriage is terminated by divorce or death.

Unless there is a child of the family, the economic disadvantages of being a same sex spouse or a civil partner are less acute. But the legal position of same sex spouses or civil partners *vis-à-vis* each other is the same as that of opposite sex spouses.

1 See generally, E M Clive *The Law of Husband and Wife in Scotland* (4th edn, 1997, W Green/Sweet & Maxwell), Part II.
2 Discussed at paras **3.8** ff.
3 See **Ch 5**.

PERSONAL EFFECTS

Domicile

3.2 At common law spouses had a duty to adhere to each other. If a spouse refused to adhere without reasonable cause, that spouse was in desertion.[1] Desertion is no longer a ground of divorce or dissolution,[2] so it would follow that the obligation of adherence no longer subsists. The right of a husband to choose where the spouses should live was abolished in 1984.[3] Because a wife had to live with her husband, the rule developed that a wife's domicile depended on that of her husband. Accordingly, while the marriage subsisted, a wife could not have a domicile which was different from her husband's. The wife's domicile of dependency was abolished by s 1 of the Domicile and Matrimonial Proceedings Act 1973 and a wife can now acquire an independent domicile.[4] Of course, these rules, and changes thereto, do not apply to same sex spouses or civil partners.

1 E M Clive *The Law of Husband and Wife in Scotland* (4th edn, 1997, W Green/Sweet & Maxwell), Ch 11.
2 Discussed below at para **6.7**.
3 Law Reform (Husband and Wife) (Scotland) Act 1984, s 4.
4 See the Domicile and Matrimonial Proceedings Act 1973, s 1(1): abolition of a wife's dependent domicile; s 1(2): a wife who had a domicile by dependence retains that domicile unless and until it is changed by acquisition or revival of another domicile on or after the 1973 Act came into force.

Sexual relations

3.3 If a spouse in a different sex marriage is unable to consummate the marriage as a result of incurable impotency, the marriage is voidable.[1]

If a spouse or civil partner wilfully refuses to have sexual relations, this could give rise to an action of divorce or dissolution on the ground of irretrievable breakdown established by the defender's behaviour.[2] If a spouse voluntarily has sexual intercourse with a third party during the subsistence of a different sex marriage, this can give rise to an action of divorce on the ground of irretrievable breakdown as established by adultery.[3] This is not the case for same sex marriage. Adultery retains its common law definition of sexual intercourse between a man and a woman. Therefore, in a same sex marriage, irretrievable breakdown can only be established by adultery where one spouse has sexual intercourse with a member of the opposite sex.[4] Irretrievable breakdown as a ground for dissolution of a civil partnership cannot be established by adultery. Where one civil partner has sexual intercourse with a third party, irretrievable breakdown may be established on the basis of unreasonable behaviour.[5]

At one time, it was thought that a husband could not be guilty of raping his wife if he had sexual intercourse with her without her consent. This was based on the view that, on marriage, a wife is *prima facie* deemed to have surrendered her person to her husband. Where there was evidence, for example, that the couple was *de facto* separated, then the husband could be prosecuted for rape and not merely indecent assault.[6] In 1989, the High Court of Justiciary held that these rules were anachronistic and that a husband could be guilty of raping his wife whether they were living together or not.[7] In the course of his judgment the Lord Justice-General (Emslie) said:[8]

> 'Nowadays it cannot seriously be maintained that by marriage a wife submits herself irrevocably to sexual intercourse in all circumstances. It cannot be affirmed nowadays, whatever the position may have been in earlier centuries, that it is an incident of modern marriage that a wife consents to intercourse obtained only by force. There is no doubt that a wife does not consent to assault upon her person and there is no plausible justification for saying today that she nevertheless is to be taken to consent to intercourse by assault.'

---

1 Discussed at paras **2.22** ff.

2 Divorce (Scotland) Act 1976, s 1(2)(b); and Civil Partnership Act 2004, s 117(3)(a). Also discussed below at para **6.6**.

3 Divorce (Scotland) Act 1976, s 1(2)(a), discussed at paras **6.3** ff.
4 Divorce (Scotland) Act 1976, s 1(3A).
5 Civil Partnership Act 2004, s 117(3).
6 *HM Advocate v Duffy* 1983 SLT 7; *HM Advocate v Paxton* 1985 SLT 96.
7 *S v HM Advocate* 1989 SLT 469.
8 1989 SLT 469 at 473.

Name

3.4 There is no legal requirement for a wife to take her husband's surname on marriage. It is, however, still common for a wife to use her husband's surname but this is mere usage. In formal legal documents a married woman may sign using her own surname and her husband's surname, for example, Mrs Elizabeth Smith (own surname) or Brown (husband's surname).[1] There is no similar usage in relation to same sex spouses or civil partners in legal documents. Some same sex couples and civil partners, if they wish, may double-barrel their surnames.

1 For the form of names used in court proceedings, see E M Clive *The Law of Husband and Wife in Scotland* (4th edn, 1997, W Green/Sweet & Maxwell), pp 149 ff.

OBLIGATIONS

Contract

3.5 At common law a wife had no contractual capacity. In time the courts recognised exceptions to the general rule and in a series of statutes culminating in the Married Women's Property (Scotland) Act 1920, a married woman was deemed to 'be capable of entering into contracts and incurring obligations … as if she were not married'.[1] There is, of course, no similar background in the context of same sex marriage or civil partnership. Nevertheless s 24(1)(b) of the Family Law (Scotland) Act 1985 reinforces that, subject to the provisions of any enactment, marriage or civil partnership does not of itself affect the legal capacity of the parties to the marriage or the partners in a civil partnership. Thus, marriage or registration of a civil partnership *per se* has no effect on the contractual capacity of the spouses or civil partners.

At common law a wife was presumed to have been placed by her husband in charge of his domestic affairs and consequently she could pledge his credit for household expenses, for example food and clothing. This was known as the wife's *praepositura*. The *praepositura* was thought to have become anachronistic and was abolished in 1984.[2]

It is, however, perfectly possible that spouses or civil partners may expressly agree that one will act as agent for the other in a particular transaction. Moreover, one spouse or civil partner may *impliedly* authorise the other spouse or civil partner to act as his or her agent by acquiescing in a series of transactions.

When a spouse, A, enters into an obligation with a third party which benefits the other spouse, B, for example the grant to a bank of a standard security over A's property to be used to guarantee B's debts, there is no *presumption* in Scots law that A acted under the undue influence of B. Where A has *in fact* acted under B's undue influence, or under error as a consequence of B's misrepresentation, the third party may be unable to enforce the obligation unless it can be shown that the third party acted in good faith towards A throughout the transaction.[3] For example this could involve the third party being under a duty to advise A of the nature of the transaction and suggest that A seeks independent legal advice.[4] In the absence of the third party fulfilling these duties, A can have the obligation with the third party reduced. This duty of good faith does not arise if A also received a benefit from the third party such as an increased borrowing facility at a bank.[5] While the case law has related to wives acting as guarantors for their husbands' business debts, the principles here are general and apply to similar transactions involving civil partners or cohabitants[6] as well as parents and children.

---

1 Married Women's Property (Scotland) Act 1920, s 1. For a full account of these developments, see E M Clive *The Law of Husband and Wife in Scotland* (4th edn, 1997, W Green/Sweet & Maxwell), pp 211 ff.

2 Law Reform (Husband and Wife) (Scotland) Act 1984, s 7.

3 *Smith v Bank of Scotland* 1997 SC (HL) 111. *Clydesdale Bank v Black* 2002 SLT 764, approving *Braithwaite v Bank of Scotland* 1999 SLT 25 and *Wright v Cotias Investments Inc* 2001 SLT 353. See also *Cooper v Bank of Scotland Plc* [2014] CSOH 16. The later cases narrowed the scope of the decision in *Smith* which had been described by Professor Thomson as 'a blatant example of judicial legislation'. His view was that 'the

policy considerations advanced by the House of Lords display a misplaced concern for the social and economic position of wives in contemporary Scottish society'. See J M Thomson, 'Good Faith in Contracting: A Sceptical View' in A D M Forte (ed), *Good Faith in Contract and Property Law* (Hart, 1999) 63–75.

4 When the wife has a solicitor who appears to represent her interests, the third party can assume that she was properly advised even though the solicitor was also acting for the husband: *Forsyth v Royal Bank of Scotland* 2000 SLT 1295; *Ahmed v Clydesdale Bank* 2001 SLT 423. The detailed duties under the analogous doctrine in English law laid down in *Royal Bank of Scotland v Etridge (No 2)* [2001] 4 All ER 449 do not apply in Scots law: *Clydesdale Bank v Black* 2002 SLT 764; *Thomson v Royal Bank of Scotland* 2002 GWD 18-591. See: G L Gretton and K G C Reid, *Conveyancing* (5th edn, Sweet & Maxwell, 2018) para 1-15.

5 *Royal Bank of Scotland v Wilson* 2003 SLT 25.

6 See Thomson in n 3 (above).

Delict[1]

3.6 At common law, spouses could not sue each other in delict. The anachronistic nature of this rule can be illustrated by the case where as a result of a husband's negligent driving, the wife was injured but could not sue her husband. This was indefensible, particularly as the loss would ultimately fall on her husband's insurance company. This position was modified by s 2(1) of the Law Reform (Husband and Wife) Act 1962, which provided that each of the spouses had 'the like rights' to bring proceedings against the other in respect of a delict 'as if they were not married'. If the action was brought during the subsistence of the marriage, the court had a discretion to dismiss the proceedings if it appeared that no substantial benefit would accrue to either party if the action continued.[2] The court's discretion was unlikely to be invoked as the action had to proceed if a benefit accrued to the *pursuer* even though the couple as a family unit did not benefit. The opportunity was taken in the Family Law (Scotland) Act 2006[3] to repeal the 1962 Act. The original common law rules do not, of course, revive.[4] The common law rules never applied to same sex spouses or civil partners.

Under the Damages (Scotland) Act 2011,[5] where a spouse or civil partner has died from personal injuries caused by a delict of a third party, the surviving spouse or civil partner[6] has a right to damages for loss of support, including a reasonable sum for loss of the deceased's personal services,[7] funeral expenses and compensation for grief, distress and the loss of the deceased's society.[8] As a general rule, it is presumed that loss of support amounts to 75% of the deceased's income.[9] A surviving *divorced* spouse or former civil partner can only obtain damages for loss of support and funeral expenses.[10] While it is not necessary that the deceased was under a legal obligation to aliment the claimant, the divorced spouse or former civil partner can only obtain compensation for the actual loss of support he or she was receiving from the deceased.[11] Where the person dies before the conclusion of the action, the deceased's executor may recover damages for any necessary services rendered to the deceased before he or she died.[12]

The Damages (Scotland) Act 2011 is concerned with the situation where the delict results in death. Where a person is injured, it was held at common law that the defender did not owe a duty of care to the victim's spouse or relatives if they suffered loss as a result of the delict. Accordingly, the family could not sue for damages.[13] Moreover, the victim could not sue for losses sustained by a relative, for example a spouse, who had given up his or her job to nurse the victim.[14] As a result of s 8 of the Administration of Justice Act 1982, where a person has sustained personal injuries, the injured person can now recover damages which amount to reasonable remuneration for necessary services rendered to him or her by a relative.[15] For these purposes, a relative includes a spouse, a divorced spouse, a civil partner or former civil partner.[16] The pursuer, ie the injured person, will then account to the relative for any damages recovered under this provision.[17]

When the victim is not earning, at common law he or she had no right to sue for loss of earnings. This was particularly unfair to wives who had given up their employment to look after the home or children. Section 9 of the Administration of Justice Act 1982 provides that an injured person who has been providing *unpaid* personal services to a relative can sue for damages if, as a result of the injuries, he or she is unable to continue to do so. Again, a relative includes a spouse, divorced spouse, civil partner or former civil partner.[18] The personal services must be services which:

(a) were or might have been expected to have been rendered by the injured person before the injury;

(b) were of a kind which when rendered by a person other than a relative would ordinarily be obtainable on payment; and

(c) the injured person, but for the injuries in question, might have been expected to render gratuitously to a relative.

These would include a spouse or civil partner's unpaid housekeeping and DIY services for the benefit of the other spouse or civil partner and their family.[19] Because the personal services must have been rendered gratuitously before s 9 applies, the 1982 Act recognises the fact that work at home is still *prima facie* unpaid but that its economic value to the community is such that justice demands that the injured person receive compensation even though he or she has not suffered patrimonial loss.[20]

---

1 See generally Thomson's *Delictual Liability* (6th edn, 2021, Bloomsbury Professional) Ch 13.

2 Law Reform (Husband and Wife) Act 1962, s 2(2).

3 Family Law (Scotland) Act 2006, s 45 and Sch 3.

4 Interpretation Act 1978, s 16.

5 Damages (Scotland) Act 2011, s 3.

6 D(S)A 2011, s 14(1).

7 D(S)A 2011, s 6 and Administration of Justice Act 1982, s 9. See, for example, *Ingham v John G Russell Transport Ltd* 1991 SCLR 596.

8 D(S)A 2011, s 4(1)(a), s 4(3)(b), s 4(5) and s 14. Compensation was not reduced where a wife married her husband knowing that he was suffering a fatal disease allegedly caused by the negligence of the defender: *Phillips v Grampian Health Board* 1989 SLT 538.

9 D(S)A 2011, s 7(1)(a).

10 D(S)A 2011, ss 4(1)(b),(3),(5) and 14.

11 D(S)A 2011, s 7(1)(b).

12 See: *McManus' Executrix v Babcock Energy Ltd* 1999 SC 569.

13 *Robertson v Turnbull* 1982 SLT 96.

14 *Edgar v Lord Advocate* 1965 SC 67.

15 Damages can also be awarded as reasonable remuneration for necessary services to be rendered by a relative after the date of the action: Administration of Justice Act 1982, s 8(3). This reverses the decision in *Forsyth's Curator Bonis v Govan Shipbuilders* 1988 SLT 321.

16 Administration of Justice Act 1982, s 13(1), definition of 'relative' in (a) and (aa).

17 AJA 1982, s 8(2). Damages will not be paid if the relative has expressly agreed that no payment should be made for these services: s 8(1) and (3). For an example of the operation of the provisions, see *Denheen v British Railways Board* 1986 SLT 249. There is no equivalent to s 8(2) in respect of recovery of damages for future services under s 8(3).

18 See above n 15 and AJA 1982, s 9(3).
19 See, for example, *Ingham v John G Russell Transport Ltd* 1991 SCLR 596.
20 Of course, if the victim was being paid for his or her services, they could recover damages for loss of wages in the usual way.

INCOME SUPPORT/UNIVERSAL CREDIT[1]

3.7 For the purpose of obtaining income support or applying for universal credit, it is necessary to aggregate the needs and resources of any couple who are living together. Spouses or civil partners who are members of the same household are a couple for this purpose. A couple is also defined as two people who are not married to, or civil partners of, each other, but are living together as if they were a married couple or civil partners.[2]

The relationship between the system of state support and the private law obligation of aliment is discussed in the next section.

1 It is no longer possible to make a new claim for income support. Claims made are for universal credit. Persons already claiming income support will continue to receive income support benefit while the system is being transferred to universal credit.
2 Social Security Contributions and Benefits Act 1992, s 137(1).

ALIMENT

The nature and extent of the obligation

3.8 A spouse has a duty to aliment, ie *maintain*, the other spouse and vice versa.[1] Similarly a partner in a civil partnership is under the same obligation to aliment the other partner and vice versa.[2]

A spouse or civil partner's duty of aliment is 'to provide such support as is reasonable in the circumstances', having regard to the matters which a court is required or entitled to consider in determining the amount of aliment awarded.[3] The effect of this provision is that a spouse or civil partner will always have a *prima facie* right to aliment from the other, but the extent of the defender's duty to aliment will depend on the same factors as govern quantification of an award.

The factors which must be considered are set out in the Family Law (Scotland) Act 1985, s 4(1). They are:

> '(a) the needs and resources of the parties;[4]
>
> (b) the earning capacities of the parties;[5]
>
> (c) generally, all the circumstances of the case.'

---

1 Family Law (Scotland) Act 1985, s 1(1)(a) and (b). Obligations of aliment exist between parents and children; these are discussed in **Ch 9.**

2 FL(S)A 1985, s 1(1)(bb).

3 FL(S)A 1985, s 1(2).

4 'Needs' means present and foreseeable needs; 'resources' means present and foreseeable resources: FL(S)A 1985, s 27.

5 The court is concerned with earning *capacity*, not merely a party's likely future earnings: consequently, a claimant cannot elect to be unemployed.

Family Law (Scotland) Act 1985, s 4(3)(a)

3.9 In relation to s 4(1)(c), s 4(3)(a) provides that the court, '*may*, if it thinks fit, take account of any support, financial or otherwise, given by the defender to any person whom he maintains as a dependant in his household, whether or not the defender owes an obligation of aliment to that person'. The effect of this provision can be illustrated by the following example: Spouse A separates from spouse B, who is unemployed. Spouse A sets up home with a cohabitant, C. Spouse A supports C financially. In an action for aliment brought by B against A, the court *may* take into account the fact that A is supporting C. If it does, there will be fewer resources available for B and consequently a smaller amount of aliment will be awarded. Section 4(3)(a) of the 1985 Act reverses the previous rule under which financial or other support *in fact* made by a defender to a third party was *not* taken into account unless he or she was under a legal obligation to aliment that person, for example his or her child.[1]

It is submitted that the courts should be prepared to exercise their discretion under s 4(3)(a), particularly where the defender is a low wage earner. If A in the example above was earning very little, then if the fact that he or she was supporting C was taken into account (under s 4(3)(a)), B may receive no aliment at all. If that were the case, then it would allow B to have full recourse to universal credit and other benefits. If it were not taken into account, the amount of aliment awarded would be small. Even if A paid regularly, B would be no better off financially since the aliment would merely reduce the amount payable in universal credit.

Where either spouse or civil partner is being financially or otherwise supported by a third party, this will be a relevant factor under s 4(1)(c) as it is clearly one of the circumstances of the case. For example, in an action for aliment by a spouse or civil partner, the court is entitled to take into account the fact that the defender spouse or civil partner's new cohabitant is contributing to their joint outlays; *but* the joint incomes of the defender spouse or civil partner and cohabitant could not simply be aggregated as that would subject the cohabitant to an obligation of aliment to the pursuer spouse or civil partner, which the cohabitant does not owe.

1 *Henry v Henry* 1972 SLT (Notes) 26. Moreover, a pursuer's entitlement to income support was ignored, with the result that defenders could be ordered to pay awards of aliment which they could not afford while continuing to support the third party: *McAuley v McAuley* 1968 SLT (Sh Ct) 81; *McCarrol v McCarrol* 1966 SLT (Sh Ct) 45.

Family Law (Scotland) Act 1985, s 4(3)(b)

3.10 In relation to s 4(1)(c), s 4(3)(b) provides that the court 'shall not take account of any conduct of a party unless it would be manifestly inequitable to leave it out of account'. The effect of this provision is that a spouse or civil partner has a *prima facie* right to aliment from the other, even though the pursuer has, for example, committed adultery,[1] has behaved in an intolerable way, or refuses to live with the defender. Moreover, in assessing the amount of aliment such conduct is to be ignored by the court unless it would be 'manifestly inequitable to leave it out of account'.[2] It is submitted that it should only be in very extreme circumstances that the pursuer's conduct should be taken into account to reduce the amount of aliment which would otherwise be awarded.[3] When a relationship is breaking down, there can be fault on both sides. Certainly, it is most unjust to penalise a spouse or civil partner financially for conduct which reflects a symptom rather than a cause of relationship breakdown.

Nor does this raise injustice to the defender. The purpose of aliment is to oblige spouses and civil partners to maintain each other *during the marriage or civil partnership*: the obligation to aliment ends on divorce or dissolution of the civil partnership. Consequently, if a defender feels aggrieved at being obliged to aliment a pursuer whose conduct has been the cause of the relationship breakdown, the remedy is to bring an action for divorce or dissoluton.[4] On divorce or dissolution, the obligation to aliment ceases and, instead, financial provision can be ordered which will result in a financial clean break between the parties.[5] This approach is consonant with current public policy which is to encourage marriages or civil partnerships that have irretrievably broken down to end, and to allow each party to move on in as independent a way as possible.

1 This issue is discussed in the context of divorce in **Ch 6**.
2 Family Law (Scotland) Act 1985, s 4(3)(b).
3 One example might be where the pursuer's conduct had reduced the defender's resources: for example, by injuring the defender so that his or her earning capacity was impaired. Another is illustrated by the facts of *Kyte v Kyte* [1987] 3 WLR 1114 where the wife had actively encouraged her husband's attempts at suicide! In *Walker v Walker* 1991 SLT 649, Lord Clyde stated that where the defender had lied as to his income and assets, this *was* conduct which it would be manifestly inequitable to leave out of account.
4 See **Ch 6.**
5 See **Ch 7**.

Defences

3.11 Section 2(8) of the Family Law (Scotland) Act 1985 gives a general defence to a claim for aliment[1] if the defender makes an offer to receive the pursuer into the defender's household and to fulfil the obligation of aliment *provided* it is reasonable to expect the pursuer to accept the offer. In considering whether it is reasonable for the pursuer to accept the defender's offer, s 2(9) enjoins the court to look at all the relevant circumstances including conduct and any decree, for example an interdict against violence,[2] which has been obtained.

So, for example, if a spouse or civil partner (A) has been the victim of domestic abuse by spouse or civil partner (B), then there can still be a good claim for aliment by A even where B makes an offer to A to receive A into B's household. It is submitted that, as a result of B's conduct, the offer is not one which it would be reasonable to expect A to accept.[3]

Where a couple has agreed to separate, s 2(9) of the Family Law (Scotland) Act 1985 provides that the mere fact that they have agreed to live apart does not of itself establish that it is unreasonable to expect the pursuer to accept the defender's offer. For example, if civil partners agree to part and one of them later seeks aliment; if the other makes him or her an offer to return to the household, this may constitute a s 2(8) defence because it is not unreasonable to expect the pursuer to accept such an offer merely because the parties have earlier agreed to part. Of course, other circumstances, for example, the defender's behaviour or abuse while they lived together, may make it unreasonable to expect the pursuer to accept the defender's offer.

---

1 Except where the claim is brought by or on behalf of a child under the age of 16: see **Ch 10.**
2 Discussed in **Ch 5.**
3 Family Law (Scotland) Act 1985, s 4(3)(b), discussed at para **3.10**.

Aliment where the parties are living together

3.12 At common law a spouse who was being inadequately maintained had to leave the matrimonial home before an action for aliment could be brought.[1] Section 2(6) of the Family Law (Scotland) Act 1985 provides that an action for aliment is competent notwithstanding that the pursuer is living in the same household as the defender. Such an arrangement may be agreed by the spouses or civil partners until they have made the necessary financial and other arrangements to facilitate one party moving out of the household. Where the parties continue to live in the same household, and the pursuer brings an action for aliment, the defender can raise the defence that he or she is already fulfilling the obligation of aliment (by financial or other means) and intends to continue doing so.[2]

---

1 *M'Donald v M'Donald* (1875) 2 R 705.
2 Family Law (Scotland) Act 1985, s 2(7).

The nature of an award

3.13 On granting a decree of aliment, s 3(1) of the Family Law (Scotland) Act 1985 provides that the court may, if it thinks fit:

(a) order the making of a periodical payment, whether for a definite or an indefinite period or until the happening of a specified event: but the court cannot substitute a lump sum for a periodical payment;[1]

(b) order the making of alimentary payments of an occasional or special nature, for example funeral or hospital expenses: these will usually be small amounts;

(c) backdate awards to the date of bringing the action or, on special cause shown, even earlier;

(d) award less than the amount claimed even if the claim is undisputed.[2]

The prohibition of lump sum payments and the continued insistence that an award takes the form of a periodical payment reflect the fact that aliment is an obligation which arises from, and continues throughout, a marriage or civil partnership. In contrast, on divorce or dissolution of a civil partnership it is envisaged that any financial provision will generally take the form of capital payments, ie lump sum payments, to encourage a financial clean break between the parties.[3]

On an application by either party, a decree of aliment can be varied or recalled if there has been a material change of circumstances since the date of decree.[4] If the value of the original award has been undermined by inflation, the decree may be varied upwards; conversely, if the defender has been made redundant since the date of the original award the decree can be varied downwards or indeed recalled. The mere fact that at the time of the original award the court proceeded upon a particular hypothesis which turned out to be incorrect is not a material change of circumstances.[5] In an action for variation, the court has the same powers, for example, to backdate awards, as in an original application for aliment.[6]

A decree of aliment comes to an end if the parties divorce or a civil partnership is dissolved. Where the couple is a qualifying civil partnership, a decree of aliment does not come to an end if the civil partnership is converted into marriage.[7]

1 Family Law (Scotland) Act 1985, s 3(2). A defender cannot be ordered to provide security for an alimentary payment: *MacDonald v MacDonald* 1995 SLT 72.

2 This overrules *Terry v Murray* 1947 SC 10 where it was held that the court was bound to grant decree for the amount claimed in an undefended action for aliment.

3 FL(S)A 1985, s 3(2) and see **Ch 7**.

4 FL(S)A 1985, s 5(1); See: *Ahmed v Ahmed* 2004 SCLR 247 where the Inner House agreed with the Lord Ordinary's decision that the amount of aliment should increase given the level of income of the children's father. See also: *Walker v Walker* 1991 SLT 649. An agreement to aliment a spouse can also be varied on a material change of circumstances: FL(S)A 1985, s 7(2). It cannot be varied after the parties have divorced: *Drummond v Drummond* 1995 SCLR 428, 1996 SLT 386. The court has the power to backdate the variation: FL(S)A 1985, ss 7(2ZA)–(2ZC).

5 *Walker v Walker* 1995 SLT 375.

6 FL(S)A 1985, s 5(2) impliedly incorporating s 3: see *Hannah v Hannah* 1988 SLT 82. However, there is authority that in a variation the court cannot backdate beyond the date of the decree sought to be varied: *Walker v Walker* 1991 SLT 649, *sed quaere*.

7 Marriage and Civil Partnership (Scotland) Act 2014, s 11(7). On qualifying civil partnerships and their conversion to marriage, see para **1.19**.

Procedural matters

3.14 A spouse or civil partner may bring a claim for aliment *simpliciter* in the Court of Session or the sheriff court.[1] In practice a claim for aliment is often brought along with other related proceedings. In addition, in an action for aliment or in an action for divorce or dissolution, separation, declarator of marriage or declarator of nullity of marriage or civil partnership, the court can order interim aliment until the final disposal of the action.[2]

When decree of divorce or dissolution has been granted, but a claim for financial provision is still pending, an award of interim aliment remains competent.[3] Because an action for interim aliment is not technically an action for aliment within the meaning of the Family Law (Scotland) Act 1985,[4] it has been held that the court does not have the power to vary or recall a decree of interim aliment with *retrospective* effect.[5] The factors in s 4 of the 1985 Act have also been held to be relevant to a claim for interim aliment.[6]

As interim aliment is awarded to a party to the proceedings, it does not matter that the proceedings finally establish that, for example, because the marriage or civil partnership was void, the parties did not owe an obligation to aliment each other because they were never spouses or civil partners. A pursuer in an action of declarator of nullity can apply for interim aliment, although denying the existence of the marriage or civil partnership.[7]

1 Family Law (Scotland) Act 1985, s 2(1).
2 FL(S)A 1985, s 6(1).
3 *Neill v Neill* 1987 SLT (Sh Ct) 143.
4 FL(S)A 1985, s 2(2) and (3) and s 27(1).
5 FL(S)A 1985, s 6(4) does not give a power to vary or recall an award of interim aliment retrospectively. *McColl v McColl* 1993 SLT 617. This can cause difficulties if the award of aliment is backdated to cover the period when the defender was obliged to pay an award of interim aliment. Because the decree of interim aliment cannot be recalled with retrospective effect, the defender would have to pay both the backdated award of aliment *plus* any arrears of interim aliment. See *Kirk v Kirk* 2003 Fam LR 50.
6 *McGeachie v McGeachie* 1989 SCLR 99: for the s 4 factors, see para **3.8** ff. An appeal from an award of interim aliment is possible with leave of the sheriff: *MacInnes v MacInnes* 1990 GWD 13-690; *Richardson v Richardson* 1991 SLT (Sh Ct) 7. See also: *Adams v Adams* 2002 SCLR 379.
7 FL(S)A 1985, s 17(2).

The relationship between aliment and Universal Credit

3.15 It will be clear that the guidelines in the Family Law (Scotland) Act 1985, s 4 are sufficiently wide to allow a court considerable discretion in assessing the amount of aliment. Apart from the *prima facie* exclusion of misconduct and the fact that the defender's financial or other support to a third party may be taken into account, there are few guidelines on how the court should exercise its discretion. Couples will often negotiate an appropriate figure with the advice of their lawyers. But where the couple is in the lower income bracket, there may not be enough money to aliment the family adequately when the relationship breaks down, particularly if the wage earner has become involved with another family. Consider the following examples.

Example

(1) Spouse or civil partner (A) separates from spouse or civil partner (B) and A, a low wage earner, cohabits with C and supports

C financially. If the court exercised its discretion[1] and took into account A's financial support of C, then B may receive no aliment. If B were unemployed, then B would be eligible to apply for universal credit.

(2) A and B have entered an agreement whereby A pays B £200 per month. If B then becomes unemployed and claims universal credit then the £200 will not be taken into account when calculating the universal credit *entitlement*. However, the £200 will be considered as 'unearned income' and the amount of universal credit *paid* to B will be reduced pound-for-pound accordingly. Aliment payments for a child or children will not reduce the amount of universal credit paid.

By s 78 of the Social Security Administration Act 1992, because they are 'couples'[2] for the purposes of the legislation,[3] spouses and civil partners are liable relatives. This means that when universal credit is paid to or on behalf of a person who is not being alimented by a liable relative, the Secretary of State can take proceedings against the liable relative to make a contribution towards the amount of support paid.[4] A sheriff having regard to all the circumstances, including the defender's resources, can order the defender to pay such sum, weekly or otherwise, as may be appropriate.[5] Thus, in the example of A and B (above) the Secretary of State could take proceedings against A (the liable relative) who has failed to aliment B (the dependent) for a contribution towards the amount of universal credit B can receive.[6] If B has a decree of aliment against A, the Secretary of State can enforce the decree.[7]

1 Family Law (Scotland) Act 1985, s 4(3)(a).
2 Social Security Contributions and Benefits Act 1992, s 137(1).
3 Social Security Administration Act 1992, s 78(6).
4 SSAA 1992, s 106(1).
5 The sheriff's discretion is very wide on the sum payable.
6 In our example, the court can order payments to be made to B rather than the Secretary of State; in other words, the Secretary of State, in effect, raises an action of aliment on behalf of B: SSAA 1992, s 106(4)(b) and (c).
7 SSAA 1992, s 108.

SUCCESSION

Introduction

3.16 As submitted at the outset, in modern family law it is important for a person to have been married or have registered a civil partnership for legal rights to be invoked. This is particularly true in relation to succession where Scots law gives a surviving spouse or civil partner certain rights to succeed to a proportion of the deceased spouse or civil partner's estate which cannot be defeated by testamentary deed. In this section it is proposed to give an outline of these rights. As they are closely related to similar rights enjoyed by the deceased's children, it is convenient to discuss these at this stage.

Legal rights

3.17 Since the Succession (Scotland) Act 1964, a surviving spouse is entitled to legal rights (*jus relicti* or *jus relictae*)[1] out of the deceased spouse's free moveable estate. A surviving civil partner also is entitled to legal rights out of the deceased civil partner's free moveable estate.[2] Children[3] are also entitled to legal rights (*legitim*) out of their deceased parent's moveable estate.

The surviving spouse or civil partner has a right to one-third of the deceased's free moveable estate if the deceased is survived by children or to one-half of the deceased's free moveable estate if there are no surviving children. Where the deceased is survived by children, then the children have legal rights to one-third of the deceased parent's free moveable estate if survived by a spouse or civil partner; or to one-half of the deceased's free moveable estate if there is no surviving spouse or civil partner. Moveable estate consists of money, shares, pictures, cars, etc, but excludes land, ie heritable property, of which the most important is likely to be the matrimonial or family home.

For example, if spouse or civil partner (A) dies survived by spouse or civil partner (B) and children, B is entitled to one third of A's free moveable estate as legal rights. The children are entitled to one-third of their deceased parent's free moveable estate, as legal rights, and the deceased can only effectively test (ie make testamentary provisions) on the remaining third.

But if the estate includes heritable property, for example the matrimonial home, A is free to dispose of the property as he or she wishes by testamentary deed, as legal rights are not exigible out of heritage. So, A could, by will, leave his or her house to a friend, or to a charity.

Legal rights may be discharged in the lifetime of the spouses or civil partners or parents. Similarly legal rights may be renounced after the death of a spouse, civil partner or parent. This can be done either expressly or impliedly by acceptance of testamentary provisions which were intended by the deceased to be in satisfaction of legal rights.[4] If, however, the surviving spouse, civil partner or children elect to take legal rights, they will forfeit any testamentary provisions in testamentary deeds executed after 1964, unless forfeiture is expressly excluded.[5]

1 The terms *jus relicti* and *jus relictae* were replaced with 'legal rights' by Sch 28, para 6 of the Civil Partnership Act 2004; see also Succession (Scotland) Act 1964, s 36(1).

2 CPA 2004, s 131.

3 Scots law makes no distinction between legitimate and illegitimate children in this context: Law Reform (Parent and Child) (Scotland) Act 1986, Sch 1, para 7(2), discussed in **Ch 8.**

4 By the Succession (Scotland) Act 1964, s 13, acceptance of a provision in a post-1964 testamentary disposition is, in the absence of express provision to the contrary, deemed to be an implied renunciation of legal rights in so far as they would conflict with the settlement.

5 S(S)A 1964, s 13; for deeds executed pre-1964, see *Ballantyne's Trustees v Ballantyne* 1993 SLT 1237.

Prior rights

3.18 Where a spouse or civil partner dies intestate,[1] ie without a will, the surviving spouse or civil partner enjoys substantial prior rights[2] out of the intestate estate. Prior rights rank above all other entitlements in a deceased's estate.

By s 8 of the Succession (Scotland) Act 1964, the surviving spouse or civil partner is entitled to the dwelling house (in which the intestate had a relevant interest) and in which he or she was ordinarily resident at the date of the death of the intestate.[3] If the value of the dwelling house does not exceed £473,000 then the surviving spouse shall be entitled to the house.[4]

In addition, the surviving spouse or civil partner is entitled to the furniture and plenishings (which were owned by the deceased) of a dwelling house[5] in which he or she was ordinarily resident at the date of the death of the intestate. However, if the value of the furniture or plenishings exceeds £29,000, the surviving spouse or civil partner is entitled to such parts of them as he or she may choose, to a value not exceeding £29,000.[6]

By s 9 of the Succession (Scotland) Act 1964 the surviving spouse or civil partner is entitled to financial provision out of the intestate's estate. If the intestate is survived by issue,[7] however remote, the surviving spouse or civil partner is entitled to £50,000; in other cases, the surviving spouse or civil partner is entitled to £89,000.[8] Where the net intestate estate is less than £50,000 or £89,000, as the case may be, the surviving spouse or civil partner is entitled to the whole of the intestate estate.[9] Where it is more, the surviving spouse or civil partner's financial provision is borne by the heritable and moveable parts of the estate in proportion to the respective amounts of those parts.[10]

After satisfaction of these prior rights, the surviving spouse or civil partner is entitled to claim legal rights from the remaining free moveable estate.[11] Only then is the remaining intestate estate distributed to the deceased's heirs.[12]

It will be obvious that the prior rights of a surviving spouse or civil partner will exhaust the value of most estates. Consequently, the surviving spouse or civil partner may well be better off if the deceased dies intestate rather than leave a testamentary deed bequeathing the estate to the surviving spouse or civil partner. For in this latter case, any surviving children will be entitled to claim legal rights; but on an intestacy, children can only succeed to the intestate estate after satisfaction of the surviving spouse or civil partner's prior rights.

---

1 For these purposes intestacy includes partial intestacy. See Succession (Scotland) Act 1964, s 36(1).

2 S(S)A 1964, s 36.

3 S(S)A 1964, s 8(1). If more than one house qualifies, the surviving spouse has six months to elect which house is to be subject to prior rights: s 8(2B)(a).

4 S(S)A 1964, s 8(1). The current amounts were set by the Prior Rights of Surviving Spouse and Civil Partner (Scotland) Order 2011, SSI 2011/436.

5 It does not matter if the dwelling house did not form part of the deceased's intestate estate.
6 S(S)A 1964, s 8(3)(b).
7 There is no distinction between legitimate and illegitimate issue: see S(S)A 1964, s 36(1).
8 The current amounts were set by the Prior Rights of Surviving Spouse and Civil Partner (Scotland) Order 2011, SSI 2011/436.
9 S(S)A 1964, s 9(2).
10 S(S)A 1964, s 9(3).
11 Discussed at para **3.17**.
12 These will in the first place be the deceased's children and their issue. No distinction is made between legitimate and illegitimate issue: see the S(S)A 1964, s 36(1). For a full list of heirs see S(S)A 1964, s 2; on representation see S(S)A 1964, s 5.

The effect of divorce, dissolution or annulment on a will

3.19 The Succession (Scotland) Act 2016 updated elements of succession law that were widely accepted to be out-of-date and did not reflect modern family life. One of these is the effect of divorce, annulment or dissolution of a civil partnership on a will. The Scottish Law Commission addressed this in 1990.[1] Prior to the 2016 Act coming into force (on 1 November 2016) divorce had no *automatic* effect on a will in Scotland. In its Report, the SLC stated: 'Usually, it may be supposed, a divorced testator would not wish his former spouse to continue to take under his will.' Section 1 of the 2016 Act addresses this matter. It states that, where a marriage ends by divorce or annulment,[2] or where a civil partnership is dissolved, this event will revoke those provisions of the will in favour of the testator's former spouse or former civil partner, even where the marriage or civil partnership did not occur until after the will was signed.[3] The surviving former spouse or former civil partner is simply treated as having died before the testator.[4]

Section 1(3) retains a provision whereby, if a will expressly provides that the former spouse or civil partner is to have benefit from the provisions of the will, this will stand even where the marriage or civil partnership is terminated.[5]

1 Report on Succession (HMSO, 1990) Scot Law Com No 24.
2 The s 1 revocation applies only to divorce, annulment or dissolution obtained from a

court of civil jurisdiction in the United Kingdom, Channel Islands or the Isle of Man or, if not so obtained, is recognised as valid in Scotland. See Succession (Scotland) Act 2016 2016, s 1(5).

3 S(S)A 2016, s 1(1)(b).

4 S(S)A 2016, s 1(2). See para **5.3**.

5 S(S)A 2016, s 1(3). See: Elizabeth Sparks, *Changes to the laws of succession – the importance for family lawyers*, Fam LB, 2017, 145, 1–4.

CONCLUSION

3.20 As a result of the system of prior rights, a surviving spouse or civil partner is generously treated on an intestacy. Where the deceased has left a will, the system of legal rights affords some degree of protection for the deceased's surviving spouse or civil partner and family. But there is nothing to stop the deceased from defeating claims to legal rights by converting all the property into heritage and disposing of it by testamentary deed to whomsoever he or she chooses.[1] The same result can be achieved if the deceased has transferred his or her moveable property to a third party during his or her lifetime. The *inter vivos* transfer must be genuine: a pretend or sham transaction will not suffice.

1 In these circumstances, the surviving spouse may have an equitable claim for continuing aliment from the deceased spouse's estate: see E M Clive *The Law of Husband and Wife in Scotland* (4th edn, 1997, W Green/Sweet & Maxwell), pp 604 ff. It does not appear that a surviving civil partner would have such a claim.

Chapter 4

The legal consequences of marriage and civil partnership

PART II: MOVEABLE PROPERTY

INTRODUCTION

4.1 Until the Married Women's Property (Scotland) Act 1881,[1] as a general rule, all moveable property – money, shares, furniture, etc – owned by a wife or subsequently acquired by her during marriage, for example by legacy, passed to her husband as a result of his *jus mariti*. The husband could do anything he wished with the property. There were limited exceptions to this rule such as alimentary provisions in favour of the wife under a marriage contract and the wife's *paraphernalia*, ie her clothes and jewellery including their receptacles. The 1881 Act abolished the *jus mariti*.[2] Where a wife owned heritable property, for example land or a house, it remained hers, but the property was administered by her husband as a result of his *jus administrationis*.[3] The *jus administrationis* was abolished by the Married Women's Property (Scotland) Act 1920.[4]

As a result of the Married Women's Property (Scotland) Acts of 1881 and 1920, Scots law accepted that marriage should have no effect on the property rights of spouses during marriage and that for this purpose they should be treated as strangers. Accordingly, in relation to the property of spouses, Scots law has a system of separate property. The common law rules did not apply to civil partners. Nevertheless, s 24 of the Family Law (Scotland) Act 1985 states:

> '... marriage or civil partnership shall not of itself affect—
>
> (a) the respective rights of the parties to the marriage or as the case may be the partners in the civil partnership in relation to their property'.

Scots law therefore proceeds on the basis that *prima facie* the ordinary rules of property law apply to spouses and civil partners as though they were unmarried or had not registered their civil partnership. The separate property system achieves legal equality between the spouses and civil partners in respect of their property. In practice this can lead to injustice as in our society women tend to bear the major responsibility of childcare, thus reducing their opportunity to acquire property, but this injustice may affect whichever spouse or civil partner has the major responsibility for childcare.[5]

Moreover, the separate property system ignores the fact that when spouses or civil partners acquire property, they do not regard themselves as strangers. Often they will pool their resources to purchase a matrimonial or family home and other domestic property. In addition, property is often bought not for the use and enjoyment of the purchasing spouse or civil partner but for the use and enjoyment of the family, for example furniture. In relation to such property, the application of the ordinary rules of the law of property is difficult and likely to lead to unrealistic results. Scots law recognises that the property rules relating to spouses and civil partners cannot ignore the 'family' element in their property transactions. Consequently, special property rules apply to spouses and civil partners and do not treat them as strangers.

Thus, while the basic property regime is still that of separate property, there are special property rules that recognise that the parties are married or in a civil partnership. These rules are designed to take into account the 'family' element in the parties' property dealings. To some extent, these rules have alleviated the injustices which in practice arise from a strict application of the separate property system.

The law as it relates to moveable property is examined in this chapter; the law in relation to the matrimonial and family home is considered in Chapter 5.

---

1 For the history of the law, see E M Clive *The Law of Husband and Wife in Scotland* (4th edn, 1997, W Green/Sweet & Maxwell), pp 219 ff.

2 Married Women's Property (Scotland) Act 1881, s 1(1).

3 Until 1881, income arising from her land, for example rents, belonged to the husband by virtue of his *jus mariti* as the rents were, of course, moveable property.

4 Married Women's Property (Scotland) Act 1920, s 1.

5 A spouse or civil partner can obtain compensation for any economic disadvantages suffered as a result of marriage or civil partnership in the form of financial provision on divorce or dissolution: see **Ch 7**.

WEDDING OR CIVIL PARTNERSHIP PRESENTS

4.2 The giving of presents in prospect of a marriage or civil partnership taking place is, generally, conditional on the ceremony going ahead. If the ceremony is cancelled, then it is implied that the presents will be returned to the donors.

The ownership of a wedding or civil partnership present depends on the intention of the donor. Did the donor intend the gift to be owned in common by the spouses or civil partners or only by one member of the couple? There is no difficulty if there is direct evidence of the donor's intention. But problems can arise if such evidence is not available.

In the established case of *McDonald v McDonald*,[1] the sheriff took the view that 'the practical rule which is normally applied is to regard as the owner of the present the spouse from whose friends or relatives the gift was received'.[2] The sheriff goes on to say that 'the real principle is to discover the intention of the donor and it might be that the nature of the gift – eg, a necklace – would supply the answer'. Applying this principle would help to inform the basis of resolving a conflict between spouses or civil partners in relation to contested ownership.

1 1953 SLT (Sh Ct) 36.
2 1953 SLT (Sh Ct) 36 at 36.

GIFTS BETWEEN SPOUSES AND CIVIL PARTNERS

4.3 The ordinary law of donation (ie, a gratuitous transfer of property) applies in relation to the transfer of corporeal moveable property between spouses and civil partners. Accordingly, the presumption *against* donation is *prima facie* applicable.[1] But as gifts between spouses and civil partners are not uncommon, the presumption is not difficult to rebut.[2]

For example, where a spouse or civil partner (A) transfers property as a gift to spouse or civil partner (B), then the onus is on B to show that A intended to make the gift. The presumption against donation can be easily rebutted if B can show that the donor intended to transfer ownership of the property as, for example, a birthday or anniversary gift. As well as the rebuttal of the presumption, there must also be delivery of the property to B before ownership of the property transfers from the donor to the donee. This can give rise to difficulties where the property is already in the matrimonial or family home before the gift is made.

It is an established principle in Scots law that the gift, itself, remains matrimonial or partnership property and, so, forms part of the net matrimonial property that may be subject to division on divorce or dissolution.[3]

The common law rule that gifts between spouses were revocable during the donor's lifetime has been abolished.[4]

---

1 *Jamieson v M'Leod* (1880) 7 R 1131; *Smith v Smith's Trustees* (1884) 12 R 186; *Beveridge v Beveridge* 1925 SLT 234 at 236.

2 There is no presumption against donation in transfers of property between parent and child: Stair *The Institutions of the Law of Scotland* (6th edn, 1981) I 8.2.

3 See **Ch 7**.

4 Married Women's Property (Scotland) Act 1920, s 5. The gift may be struck down as a gratuitous alienation if the donor becomes bankrupt.

CORPOREAL MOVEABLES BOUGHT BY THE SPOUSES OR CIVIL PARTNERS

4.4 It is a cardinal principle of a system of separate property that the spouse or civil partner who buys or otherwise acquires corporeal moveable property *prima facie* owns it; so if a spouse or civil partner buys a car, he or she is the owner. Where both spouses or civil partners contribute to the purchase price, they own the property in common in proportion to their contributions to the price. But in the absence of evidence of joint contribution to the price, the common law does not assume common ownership merely because the property is used by both spouses or civil partners or the family.[1]

Apart from the problems of proving which of the spouses or civil partners paid for the property, perhaps many years after the date of its purchase, the separate property system could give rise to injustices in the following situations.

(1) Where, in a marriage or civil partnership, spouse or civil partner (A) gives up his or her job for several years to look after the

children of the family, A will lose the opportunity to earn and, consequently, to acquire property. (Under the common law, if spouse A gave up work, then A would have no proprietary interest in the property acquired by the other spouse (B) during that period.)

(2) Where both spouses or civil partners (A and B) are working and they agree that, for example, A's earnings should be used to run the household while B uses his or her earnings to purchase, for example, antiques or items of interest, the common law gave A no proprietary interest in the property purchased by B.

The injustices of the application of the system of separate property in practice are obvious and the position has been alleviated to some extent by legislation.

1 *Harper v Adair* 1945 JC 21 at 28, per the Lord Justice-General (Normand); *Preston v Preston* 1950 SC 253 at 261, per Lord Keith.

Household goods

4.5 Where a couple, either in prospect of marriage or civil partnership or during the marriage or civil partnership, obtains items for 'joint domestic purposes', s 25 of the Family Law (Scotland) Act 1985 sets out a presumption about how these items, known as 'household goods', should be treated on the breakdown of the relationship.

Section 25(1) of the Family Law (Scotland) Act 1985 provides that:

> 'If any question arises (whether during or after a marriage or civil partnership) as to the respective rights of ownership of the parties to a marriage or the partners in a civil partnership in any household goods obtained in prospect of or during the marriage or civil partnership other than by gift or succession from a third party, it shall be presumed, unless the contrary is proved, that each has a right to an equal share in the goods in question.'

In other words, there is a presumption that the household goods are *owned* in common by the spouses or civil partners.[1]

Household goods are defined[2] as 'any goods (including decorative or ornamental goods) kept or used at any time during the marriage or civil partnership in any family home for the joint domestic purposes of the parties to the marriage or the partners', other than: (a) money or securities; (b) any motor car, caravan or other road vehicle;[3] and (c) any domestic animal. These items are expressly excluded from the definition of 'household goods' and, accordingly, are not subject to the presumption of equal shares.[4]

Consider the following examples:

(1) If A buys an antique painting for his collection before the registration of his civil partnership with B, the presumption of common ownership does not apply as the property was acquired before the civil partnership was registered and not in prospect of the civil partnership. But if before registration, A buys a rug with the intention that it is to be used in the family home after registration, the presumption of equal shares will apply as the goods were bought in prospect of civil partnership.

(2) If A inherits a grandfather clock during the marriage to B the presumption of common ownership will not apply as property acquired by gift or succession from a third party is excluded.[5]

(3) If A wins £10,000 on the lottery during the marriage to B and puts £5,000 in a bank account and uses the remainder to buy items for use in the family home, the presumption of equal shares does not apply to the money deposited with the bank as money and securities are expressly excluded,[6] but it will apply to the items as these are household goods.

(4) If A buys a car during the marriage which is used by B for work and leisure purposes, the presumption of common ownership does not apply as road vehicles are expressly excluded.[7]

It is important to stress that s 25 of the Family Law (Scotland) Act 1985, gives rise only to a *presumption* of equal shares in household goods. It is therefore open to the purchasing spouse or civil partner, if he or she alleges that the goods were not intended to be owned in common, to bring evidence to rebut the presumption and establish that they were to be owned outright by the purchasing spouse or civil partner. However, s 25(2) provides that the presumption of equal shares will not be rebutted merely by the fact that while the parties were married or in civil partnership *and living together* the goods in question were purchased from a third party by either party alone or by both in unequal shares. Consider the following examples:

(1) During the marriage and while the spouses or civil partners (A and B) were living together, A buys an antique bookcase. *Prima facie* the bookcase is household goods and the presumption of equal shares applies. The mere fact that A bought the bookcase from a third party using his own money is not in itself sufficient to rebut the presumption. Consequently, the bookcase is owned in common by A and B.

(2) During the marriage or civil partnership and while A and B were living together, A buys an antique bookcase. *Prima facie* the bookcase is household goods and the presumption of equal shares applies. A had collected antiques before the marriage or registration but not with the prospect of marriage or registration. This fact, combined with the fact that A bought the antique bookcase from a third party using his or her own money, could be sufficient to rebut the presumption and establish that the bookcase was intended to be part of A's antique collection and to be owned outright by A, along with other items in the collection.[8]

(3) During the marriage or civil partnership, but when A and B were not living together, A buys an antique bookcase. *Prima facie* the bookcase is household goods and the presumption of equal shares applies. But as the bookcase was bought when the couple was not living together, s 25(2) does not apply and the fact that A bought the bookcase from a third party using his or her own money may in itself be sufficient to rebut the presumption of common ownership and consequently establish that the antique bookcase is owned outright by A.

There may be difficulties in the interrelationship between s 25 of the Family Law (Scotland) Act 1985 and the law of gifts between spouses and civil partners.[9] If A purchases a painting during a marriage or civil partnership with B, *prima facie* s 25 applies as the painting is household goods and therefore there is a presumption of common ownership. If A transfers the painting to B on B's birthday, B may be able to rebut the presumption *against* donation and establish that A intended the painting to be an outright gift to B. It is submitted that if B can do so this would amount to a rebuttal of the presumption of equal shares in household goods in s 25.

The examples given are intended to show how s 25 of the Family Law (Scotland) Act 1985 may be applied and should not be thought to undermine its evident utility. In the vast majority of cases the presumption will not be capable of being rebutted and consequently spouses and civil partners will be taken to have equal shares in the normal contents of the family home, ie consumer durables such as furniture, carpets, televisions, fridges, cookers and kitchen utensils.

Moreover, the definition of household goods[10] demands that not only must the goods be kept or used in the family home, but also that they must be kept or used 'for joint domestic purposes'. Thus, corporeal moveables used exclusively for a spouse or civil partner's business (eg computer equipment) or hobby (eg sports equipment) will be excluded from the presumption where it is evidenced that the items were not acquired for 'joint domestic purposes'. But difficulties arise where property is bought both as a collector's item and for use by the spouses or civil partners as in the example of the bookcase (above): such property could be defined as household goods so giving rise to the problems outlined above.

The items listed in s 25(3)(a)–(c), namely, (a) money or securities, (b) any motor car, caravan or other road vehicle, or (c) any domestic animal, can present more difficulties to a separating couple as these items are subject to the separate property system and, as such, they are not 'household goods' so no presumption of equal shares applies.

For example, s 25(3)(a) of the 1985 Act relates to 'money or securities'. The fact that a bank, or other, account is held in the joint names of the parties is not conclusive proof of ownership of the monies therein. It is part of the agreement with the bank that both parties are entitled to draw on the account. The separate property rule applies to such accounts and securities, and the source of the deposits will be a relevant consideration when resolving a dispute over ownership. Where both spouses or civil partners have contributed to the funds held in a joint bank account, it is submitted that it may be inferred that there was an intention to create equal shares in the monies.

It should be noted that, where one spouse or civil partner is not earning because, for example, he or she has given up work to attend to caring duties and where the caring party relies solely on a 'housekeeping allowance' from the earning party, then any savings made by the caring party, or any property acquired by the caring party out of such money will be treated as belonging to each party in equal shares.[11]

Section 25(3)(b) refers to vehicles. It is more difficult to justify the exclusion of motor cars, caravans or other vehicles, as these are often bought as a result of a couple pooling their resources. Ownership of a vehicle, ie the party who paid for the car (as compared to the 'registered keeper' which is the name on the Vehicle Registration Document (V5C)), can be relatively easily proved by producing evidence of payment. Also, spouses and civil partners tend to consider cars to be owned by one or other spouse or partner.

The exclusion of domestic animals under s 25(3)(c) is, perhaps, more understandable. Without specific evidence to show ownership of a domestic animal, the parties will be expected to decide between themselves who will have the animal in the event of a relationship breakdown. In *Smith v Duncan*,[12] the parties both claimed to own the dog that they bought during their relationship. The place of residence of any children may have a persuasive effect on the outcome.

It should also be noted that, as common owners, either spouse or civil partner, can apply for an action of division and sale of the property.[13]

1 *Kinloch v Barclay's Bank* 1995 GWD 24-1316.
2 Family Law (Scotland) Act 1985, s 25(3).
3 For example, a bicycle.
4 FL(S)A 1985, s 25(3)(a), (b) and (c).
5 FL(S)A 1985, s 25(1)
6 FL(S)A 1985, s 25(3)(a).
7 FL(S)A 1985, s 25(3)(b).
8 If the bookcase was kept in an attic and never used, arguably it is not household goods as it has not been kept or used for joint domestic purposes.
9 See para **4.3**.

10 FL(S)A 1985, s 25(3).
11 FL(S)A 1985, s 26.
12 [2022] SAC (Civ) 16.
13 Actions for division and sale are discussed in the context of heritage: see para **5.11** ff.

Furniture and plenishings in the matrimonial or family home

4.6 The Matrimonial Homes (Family Protection) (Scotland) Act 1981 contains provisions which give rights to a spouse to continue living in a matrimonial home although the marriage or relationship is breaking down.[1] It was appreciated by Parliament that these rights would be of limited value if the spouse who owned the furniture and plenishings of the home could sell them leaving the house empty. Accordingly, a spouse who has a right to occupy the matrimonial home[2] can apply under s 3(2) of the 1981 Act for an order granting the applicant the 'possession or use in the matrimonial home of any of its furniture and plenishings' owned by the other.[3] Section 103(2) of the Civil Partnership Act 2004 provides a similar remedy for a civil partner in relation to the possession and use of furniture and plenishings in a family home.[4] 'Furniture and plenishings' mean any article situated in the matrimonial home or family home which is owned or hired by either spouse or civil partner[5] and 'is reasonably necessary to enable the home to be used as a family residence'.[6] It follows, therefore, that an order is not available when the spouses or civil partners own the property in common. As common owner of the property, a spouse or civil partner can apply for an interdict to stop the other spouse or civil partner preventing the applicant from using or possessing the property.[7]

The court[8] must first make an order declaring that the applicant has occupancy rights in respect of the matrimonial or family home.[9] The court can then make such an order as appears just and reasonable having regard to all the circumstances of the case including, *inter alia*:

(a) the conduct of the spouses or civil partners in relation to each other and otherwise;

(b) the needs and financial resources of the spouses or civil partners;

(c) the needs of any child of the family; and

(d) the extent, if any, to which the matrimonial or the family home, or any item of furniture and plenishings is used in connection with a trade, business or profession of either spouse or civil partner.[10]

An interim order may be made provided the non-applicant has been afforded an opportunity of being heard or represented before the court.[11] However, the court cannot make an order if the effect of the order would be to exclude the non-applicant spouse from the matrimonial or family home.

Where the furniture or plenishings are being paid up under a hire-purchase or a conditional sale agreement, an order does not prejudice the rights of the hirer or creditor to recover the property for non-performance of any obligations under the agreements.[12] But the spouse or civil partner in whose favour the order is made is entitled to make any payments under the agreements in lieu of the debtor.[13] Similarly, he or she can carry out any essential repairs to the furniture and plenishings.[14] On the application of either spouse or civil partner the court can apportion any such expenditure between the parties.[15]

The effect of an order is therefore to override the property rights of a spouse or civil partner in relation to the furniture and plenishings of the matrimonial or family home to the extent that the applicant is entitled to the use and possession of the relevant property for the duration of the order. It must be stressed that such an order regulates only the possession and use of the property. The ownership of the property is still determined by reference to s 25 of the Family Law (Scotland) Act 1985[16] and the common law rules. Moreover, the definition of furniture and plenishings in the 1981 and 2004 Acts is narrower than that of household goods for the purposes of s 25 since it is only furniture and plenishings which are *reasonably necessary* to enable the home to be used as a family residence which can be the subject of a s 3(2) or s 103(2) order.[17] The following examples illustrate the interrelationship between the two provisions.

(1) Spouse or civil partner (A) buys a bed during the marriage or civil partnership with B. The presumption of equal shares applies and is not rebutted. A and B therefore own the bed in common. Although a bed is an article reasonably necessary to enable the home to be used as a family residence, B cannot apply for a s 3(2) or s 103(2) order for the use and possession of the bed because the orders apply only where the furniture and plenishings are

owned *solely* by one of the spouses or civil partners. At common law, B as common owner would be entitled to seek an interdict preventing A from disposing of the bed.[18]

(2) During the marriage or civil partnership, A inherits a dining table and chairs from a grandparent. The presumption of equal shares does not apply[19] and the table and chairs are owned outright by A. But if they are the only table and chairs in the house, B can apply for a s 3(2) or s 103(2) order for their use and possession as they are articles reasonably necessary to enable the house to be used as a family residence.

(3) A inherits a painting during the marriage. The presumption of equal shares does not apply. A therefore owns the painting outright. But as the painting is not reasonably necessary to enable the home to be used as a family residence, B will be unable to obtain a s 3(2) or s 103(2) order for the use and possession of the painting.

Again, it should be emphasised that these theoretical difficulties should not be allowed to detract from the evident utility of these provisions. It is further recognition that the incidents of ownership of property may have to be overridden in the interests of the family for whose benefit the property was acquired. In particular, it should be noted that the needs of the children of the family will be an important factor in determining whether an order should be made.[20]

---

1 The Matrimonial Homes (Family Protection) (Scotland) Act 1981 is discussed in detail in **Ch 5**.

2 See Ch 5. For the definition of 'matrimonial home', see MH(FP)(S)A 1981, s 22.

3 MH(FP)(S)A 1981, s 3(2).

4 For the definition of 'family home', see the Civil Partnership Act 2004, s 135.

5 Or is being acquired by either spouse or civil partner under a hire-purchase agreement or conditional sale agreement.

6 MH(FP)(S)A 1981, s 22; CPA 2004, s 135: vehicles, caravans or houseboats are expressly excluded.

7 MH(FP)(S)A 1981, s 3(2) was, of course, enacted before the Family Law (Scotland) Act 1985, s 25, discussed above. Since the presumption of common ownership will usually apply, the scope of s 3(2) of the MH(FP)(S)A 1981 and s 103(2) of the CPA 2004 is greatly reduced. Ironically, it can be argued that the remedies under ss 3(2) and 103(2) are more sophisticated than that of a common owner at common

law. However, it is possible that the provisions may be capable of being interpreted as including household goods owned in common by the defender and the applicant: *sed quaere*.

8 The Court of Session or the sheriff court: MH(FP)(S)A 1981, s 22; CPA 2004, s 135.
9 MH(FP)(S)A 1981, s 3(1); CPA 2004, s 103(1); *Welsh v Welsh* 1987 SLT (Sh Ct) 30.
10 MH(FP)(S)A 1981, s 3(3); CPA 2004, s 103(3).
11 MH(FP)(S)A 1981, s 3(4); CPA 2004, s 103(4); *Welsh v Welsh* 1987 SLT (Sh Ct) 30.
12 MH(FP)(S)A 1981, s 3(2); CPA 2004, s 103(2).
13 MH(FP)(S)A 1981, ss 2(5)(a) and 3(2); CPA 2004, ss 102(5)(a) and 103(2).
14 MH(FP)(S)A 1981, ss 2(5)(a) and 3(2); CPA 2004, ss 102(5)(a) and 103(2).
15 MH(FP)(S)A 1981, s 2(5)(b); CPA 2004, s 102(5)(b).
16 Discussed at para **4.5** ff.
17 MH(FP)(S)A 1981, s 22; CPA 2004, s 135.
18 Since the bed is common property and A and B each own a one-half *pro indiviso* share of its value, an action for division and sale is competent to enable A to realise his or her share. This is discussed in the context of heritage in **Ch 5.** Theoretically, A could attempt to sell his or her one-half *pro indiviso* share of the bed, if anyone would like to buy half a bed!
19 Household goods inherited from third parties are expressly excluded by the Family Law (Scotland) Act 1985, s 25(1).
20 MH(FP)(S)A 1981, s 3(3)(c); CPA 2004, s 103(3)(c).

MONEY AND SECURITIES

4.7 As stated above money and securities are expressly excluded from the definition of household goods and, therefore, the presumption of equal shares in household goods.[1] The ownership of money or securities will therefore be determined by the ordinary property rules, ie in accordance with the separate property system. For example, if spouse or civil partner (A) deposits £5,000 in a bank account in her name, the money in the account *prima facie* belongs to her. It is open to spouse or civil partner (B) to claim that he transferred the money to A to invest on his behalf and consequently the investment belongs to B. B will have the benefit of the presumption against donation[2] and he is not restricted in the type of evidence he can bring to substantiate his claim.[3]

Problems have arisen in relation to joint bank accounts. When an account is opened in the joint names of spouses or civil partners, depending on the terms of the agreement with the bank, this may oblige the bank to honour cheques and withdrawals by either spouse or civil partner. In the case of a deposit or savings account in joint names, the bank may be obliged to pay money over to either of the spouses or civil partners when called upon to do so. But the fact that the account is in joint names does not determine the ownership of the money in it. It is no more than part of the agreement with the bank that both parties can draw from the account.

Where one spouse or civil partner has been the sole contributor of the funds into a joint account, in the absence of evidence of donation, it will be presumed that the account was opened for the administrative convenience only of the parties, and the money in the account belongs to the contributing spouse or civil partner. Where *both* spouses or civil partners contributed to the fund, it will be readily inferred that they intended the account to be used as a common purse and that the money in the account is owned in common.[4]

Where a spouse or civil partner draws on a joint account to buy property, *prima facie* the property belongs to the purchaser outright – even though the account was opened for administrative purposes only.[5] However, where a spouse or civil partner purchases household goods, the presumption of equal shares will apply by virtue of s 25 of the Family Law (Scotland) Act 1985.[6]

Similar principles will apply to money investments.

1 Family Law (Scotland) Act 1985, s 25(3)(a).
2 Discussed at para **4.3**.
3 *Smith v Smith* 1933 SC 701.
4 That is, the court will infer donation to the extent necessary to give each spouse a half share of the money in the account.
5 Unless there is evidence that the property was bought as a joint investment.
6 Discussed at para **4.5** ff.

SAVINGS FROM HOUSEKEEPING

4.8 It is interesting to note that one of the harshest consequences of the system of separate property was where a husband provided his wife with a housekeeping allowance and the wife, being thrifty, was able to save some of the money. Because the husband had intended the money to be used to run the home, donation could not be inferred. Consequently, the husband was the owner of the savings made by the wife.[1] The Married Women's Property Act 1964 attempted to alleviate the position. It provided that savings made by a wife from a housekeeping allowance made to her by her husband should be presumed to be owned jointly by the spouses in the absence of an agreement to the contrary. The 1964 Act was defective in that it was not applicable to savings made by a husband from a housekeeping allowance paid to him by his wife: in these circumstances, any savings would still be owned by the wife!

This discriminatory element has been removed and the provision amended to include civil partners. Section 26 of the Family Law (Scotland) Act 1985 provides:

> 'If any question arises (whether during or after a marriage or civil partnership) as to the right of either party to a marriage or as the case may be of a partner in a civil partnership to money derived from any allowance made by either party or partner for their joint household expenses or for similar purposes, or to any property acquired out of such money, the money or property shall, in the absence of any agreement between them to the contrary, be treated as belonging to each party or partner in equal shares.'

It will be clear that s 26 of the 1985 Act applies to allowances made by one spouse to the other spouse and civil partner to civil partner. The allowances must be for 'their joint household expenses or for similar purposes'. It is not thought that money given to a spouse or civil partner for payment of mortgage instalments would be included within the definition.[2]

Money or property 'derived from the allowance' has been given a wide meaning. In *Pyatt v Pyatt*,[3] Lord Fraser held that the prize money won by a wife on the Littlewoods Football Pools was 'derived from' the allowance when the wife had taken the stake money from her housekeeping. The winnings had resulted both from the allowance which had provided the stake money and the wife's luck. Since the source of the stake money had been essential, the prize money had been derived from the allowance and consequently the husband was entitled to half the winnings.

The application of s 26 of the Family Law (Scotland) Act 1985 can lead to some odd results. Consider the following example. Spouse or civil partner (A) gives B a housekeeping allowance. B uses some of the allowance to bet on a horse. B wins £10,000 and puts £5,000 in a building society account and buys a second-hand caravan with the remaining £5,000. Following *Pyatt v Pyatt*[4] A is entitled to half the £5,000 in the building society account, ie £2,500, and is an owner in common of the caravan.[5] A is not entitled to choose to have the full £5,000 in the account in lieu of the half share of the caravan.[6]

1 *Smith v Smith* 1933 SC 701; *Preston v Preston* 1950 SC 253. This did not apply to savings from aliment paid by a husband when the couple were separated.

2 *Tymoszczuk v Tymoszczuk* (1964) 108 Sol Jo 676 (interpreting the similar phrase in the Married Women's Property Act 1964), but cf *Re John's Assignment Trusts, Niven v Niven* [1970] 2 All ER 210 (Note), [1970] 1 WLR 955.

3 1966 SLT (Notes) 73.

4 1966 SLT (Notes) 73.

5 Family Law (Scotland) Act 1985, s 25 is inapplicable since caravans are expressly excluded from the definition of household goods: FL(S)A 1985, s 25(3)(b).

6 Moreover, if B used the £10,000 together with £10,000 of his own savings to buy a pony, A would own a quarter of the pony! Only domestic animals are excluded from the definition of household goods: FL(S)A 1985, s 25(3)(c).

POLICIES OF ASSURANCE

4.9 Where A takes out an insurance policy for the benefit of B, B has no rights in the policy until it is delivered to B or the rights under the policy have been intimated to B. However, there is an exception to this principle where a spouse or civil partner takes out a life policy on his or her own life for the benefit of the other spouse or civil partner (or children). In these circumstances, the policy is deemed to be held by the insured in trust for the beneficiaries who take an immediate right without the necessity of delivery or intimation of the policy to them.[1]

1 Married Women's Policies of Assurance (Scotland) Act 1880, s 2; Civil Partnership Act 2004, s 132.

Chapter 5

The legal consequences of marriage and civil partnership

PART III: THE MATRIMONIAL AND FAMILY HOME

INTRODUCTION

5.1 The most important heritable property[1] that spouses or civil partners are likely to have is their matrimonial or family home.[2] A married couple or civil partners are likely to live in accommodation which is owned by one or both of them. When property is purchased, the disposition in favour of the buyer must be registered in the Land Register of Scotland.[3] Until registration, the buyer does not have a real right in the property, ie he or she is not the owner with a title which is good against the world; as against the seller. However, the buyer will have a personal right to sue for breach of contract if the seller disposes of the property to a third party before registration.[4]

Many couples are unable to purchase a house outright and have to borrow the necessary sum from a bank or other institutional lender (the heritable creditor). Until the loan is repaid, the bank will usually have a heritable security (often referred to as a mortgage) over the house; this enables the heritable creditor to sell the house if the loan (and interest thereon) is not repaid.[5] The only form of heritable security is the standard security,[6] which is itself registered in the Land Register.

Some couples cannot afford to buy their home. Instead, they will simply rent accommodation. Legislation from 1974 provides that a lease of residential property cannot be granted for more than 20 years, but this is now the subject of numerous exceptions.[7] Importantly, these include private residential tenancies. Since 1 December 2017, this is the only form of private sector lease that can be entered into.[8] In practice, most residential leases are not for long periods. As a result of legislation,[9] tenants enjoy a considerable measure of security of tenure in both the public and private housing sectors. The person who has security of tenure is the tenant. Joint tenancies are possible, or the tenancy may be in the name of one of the spouses or one of the civil partners.

It will be obvious that where, one spouse or one civil partner owns the property or holds the tenancy, the other spouse or civil partner may experience difficulties in relation to the continued occupation of the matrimonial or family home if their relationship breaks down. As a result of the Matrimonial Homes (Family Protection) (Scotland) Act 1981, the rights of a spouse to occupy the *matrimonial* home have been greatly improved. Under the Civil Partnership Act 2004,[10] a civil partner has similar rights in respect of the *family* home. These rights will be discussed in this chapter. Before doing so, consideration must be given to the operation of the system of separate property on the question of the ownership of the matrimonial or family home.

1 This may also be referred to as 'immoveable' property.

2 For general discussion of the issues in this chapter from the standpoint of property law, see G L Gretton and A J M Steven, *Property, Trusts and Succession* (4th edn, 2021, Bloomsbury) ch 11.

3 See Land Registration etc. (Scotland) Act 2012, s 50(2) and (3).

4 If the third party is aware of the preceding contract, the transfer in their favour can be set aside under the so-called 'offside goals rule'. See G L Gretton and A J M Steven, *Property, Trusts and Succession* (4th edn, 2021, Bloomsbury) paras 4.48–4.51.

5 See *Zinda v Bank of Scotland Plc* [2011] EWCA Civ 706; [2012] 1 WLR 728 at para 17 per Munby LJ.

6 Standard securities are regulated by the Conveyancing and Feudal Reform (Scotland) Act 1970. This legislation is now the subject of a review by the Scottish Law Commission. See Scottish Law Commission, Discussion Paper on Heritable Securities: Pre-default (Scot Law Com DP No 168, 2019).

7 Land Tenure Reform (Scotland) Act 1974, s 8.

8 See Private Housing (Tenancies) (Scotland Act 2016.

9 See in particular: Housing (Scotland) Act 2001 and the PH(T)(S) Act 2016. Discussion of these statutes is outwith the scope of this book.

10 Sections 101–112.

THE OWNERSHIP OF THE MATRIMONIAL OR FAMILY HOME

Title in the name of one of the spouses or civil partners

5.2 When a person purchases heritable property, title to which is taken in that person's name, it is a cardinal principle of the law of property that

that person is the owner of the property. For example, if a person buys a house, title to which is taken in his or her name, he or she is the owner of the house. This is an inevitable consequence of a system of separate property. The fact that the house is to be used as the matrimonial or family home is irrelevant to the question of its ownership.

When a house is purchased solely from the funds of one of the spouses or civil partners then the application of the separate property principle is justified. But in practice it is more likely that a house will be purchased through the means of a loan and a standard security. A couple will often agree to pool their resources in order to acquire their house. For example, both may make a direct financial contribution to the deposit and/or the mortgage instalments. Alternatively, the spouses or civil partners may agree that while one spouse or civil partner's earnings are used to pay the instalments, the earnings of the other will be used for household expenses. In these circumstances, the other spouse or civil partner will have made an *indirect* contribution to the acquisition of the matrimonial or family home. Yet if the title has been taken in the name of the first spouse or civil partner, then he or she will be the sole owner of the house even though it could not have been purchased without the direct or indirect financial assistance from the other spouse or civil partner. The injustice of the application of the separate property principle in these circumstances is readily apparent.

In England, a spouse who has made a direct or indirect financial contribution towards the acquisition of the matrimonial or family home, owned by the other spouse may obtain an interest in the property because, in these circumstances, a court can infer that the couple intended that the other spouse was holding the property on a constructive trust for the benefit of the first spouse. The extent of the first spouse's interest in the house is proportional to the size of his or her contribution. Such a solution is highly unlikely in Scots law due to the general rejection of the constructive trust.[1]

If a spouse or civil partner (A) obtained the funds from spouse or civil partner (B) by saying that the title would be taken in joint names, then B could sue A in delict if this did not happen.[2] If B transferred the money in the erroneous belief that title would be taken in joint names, then even in the absence of fraud on the part of A, spouse or civil partner, B would have a claim for recompense under the principles of unjustified enrichment.[3]

Where a spouse or civil partner has made a direct or indirect contribution to the acquisition of a house, title to which has been taken in the name of the other spouse or civil partner, it is possible to regulate the ownership of the *value* of the property by agreement. While this agreement need not be in writing,[4] it is thought that such an agreement will not be readily inferred. Even if such an agreement existed it would only be binding between the spouses or civil partners and would not prevent the spouse or civil partner who has the title from selling the property to a third party who is entitled to rely on the title as it appears in the Land Register.[5]

1 Compare Norrie 1995 JR 209 and Gretton (1997) 3 Edin LR 281 at 312 to 316. See also *Johnston's Tr v Baird* [2012] CSOH 117; 2012 GWD 25-114 where an argument that there was an implied trust failed.

2 *Marshall v Lyall and Marshall* (1859) 21 D 514.

3 Similarly an action in unjustified enrichment would lie if spouse B or civil partner B made improvements to the property in the belief that the house was his or hers: *Newton v Newton* 1925 SC 715. It is important to note that it is the law of obligations which provides spouse B or civil partner B with a remedy, not the law of property. This was recognised by Lord Hope in the English case of *Stack v Dowden* [2007] UKHL 17. As these issues will in practice be of more importance for cohabitants, they are explored in greater depth at para **8.4**.

4 Requirements of Writing (Scotland) Act 1995, s 1(1) and (2); *Denvir v Denvir* 1969 SLT 301.

5 For further discussion of these property issues, see Joe Thomson *Scots Private Law* (2006, Bloomsbury) Chs 2–4.

Title in the name of both of the spouses or civil partners

5.3 Spouses and civil partners nowadays typically take title to their home in both names. While this will alleviate many of the problems discussed in the previous section, to take title in both names raises its own difficulties.

Where title to a house is taken in both names, the property is regarded as common property.[1] This means that while the property is possessed undivided, each of the spouses or civil partners has his or her own separate title to half of the property, ie each owns a one-half *pro indiviso* share of the value of the property.[2] During his or her lifetime, each co-owner is entitled to dispose of their share to a third party without the knowledge or consent of the other co-owning spouse or civil partner (although in practice, few would want to buy a half share of a house).[3] Similarly, co-owners are free to dispose of his or her one-half *pro indiviso* share by will.

Complications have arisen from the conveyancing practice of taking the title in the names of both spouses or civil partners *and the survivor*. This is known as a special destination. For example, if the property is taken in the names of both parties and the survivor, on the death of one of the parties, his or her share of the property will automatically pass to the survivor. The survivor will take the deceased's *pro indiviso* share burdened with the deceased's debts up to the value of the property.[4]

There are other difficulties. While the spouses remain free to dispose of their share during their lifetime,[5] a special destination may prevent a spouse disposing of his or her share by will. Where both spouses have contributed to the purchase of the property, the courts will readily infer from a special destination to the survivor that there is a contractual relationship between the parties and neither can revoke the arrangement by testamentary deed.[6] Where only one of the parties has purchased a house, this principle does not apply to the party who bought the property and he or she remains free to dispose of his or her *pro indiviso* share by will – but not, of course, the other party's share. Since the latter has in effect received his or her share as a gift, the court will readily imply that the donee took the gift under the condition that the donor should obtain that share if the donor is the survivor and consequently the donee cannot dispose of his or her share by will. But even in these circumstances, the donee is free to dispose of his or her share during his or her lifetime.[7] The same difficulties arise if title is taken in the name of both civil partners or cohabitants and the survivor.

At common law, a particular difficulty arose if the couple divorced or had their civil partnership dissolved. For example, title to a family home is taken in the names of A and B and the survivor. Suppose A and B are civil partners. When their civil partnership is dissolved, they agree that B should have the former family home. If A conveys his one-half *pro indiviso* share to B, B becomes the sole owner of the house. But the survivorship destination to A of B's original *pro indiviso* share has not been evacuated.

If B dies a one-half *pro indiviso* share of the property will automatically be transferred to A.[8] If both A and B contributed to the purchase of the house, there will be an implied agreement that B could not dispose of his original one-half *pro indiviso* share by will: so A will obtain a half share even if B had willed the house to his new civil partner, C. To avoid this result, at the time of the dissolution of their civil partnership *both* A and B must convey their one-half *pro indiviso* shares to B thus evacuating the special destination of B's share. Alternatively, A and B could expressly agree to renounce all rights of succession to each other's property thereby evacuating the special destinations.[9]

The law was complex and held pitfalls for the unwary or badly advised. However, the Succession (Scotland) Act 2016 provides that a special destination is rendered ineffective on death following divorce or on dissolution or annulment. This is done by having a statutory fiction that if the special destination has not been evacuated, the person who would succeed under it is deemed to have died before the deceased.[10] Accordingly, where title to heritable property is taken by A with a special destination to B or by A and B with a special destination to the survivor, then if A and B divorce or have their civil partnership dissolved, if B subsequently dies without having evacuated the destination, A is deemed to have died before B for the purpose of inheriting under the special destination. Therefore, A does not acquire the property or B's *pro indiviso* share from B's estate.[11]

---

1 Common property is one of the two types of co-ownership recognised by the law. The other, joint property, is restricted to trustees and unincorporated associations. See G L Gretton and A J M Steven, *Property, Trusts and Succession* (4th edn, 2021, Bloomsbury) ch 10.

2 If the title is in joint names, it is presumed that *prima facie* each owner has a one-half *pro indiviso* share. If the proportions are not to be so, then the parties should have an agreement stipulating what the actual proportions are.

3 But see *McLeod v Cedar Holdings Ltd* 1989 SLT 620 where H took out a further heritable security over property owned by H and W. H had forged W's signature. The Inner House granted W reduction in respect of her *pro indiviso* share.

4 *Fleming's Trustee v Fleming* 2000 SC 206.

5 *Steele v Caldwell* 1979 SLT 228.

6 *Perrett's Trustees v Perrett* 1909 SC 522; *Hill v Hill* [2016] CSOH 10.

7 *Hay's Trustee v Hay's Trustees* 1951 SC 329, cf *Povey v Povey's Exr* [2014] CSOH 68; 2014 SLT 643.

8 *Gardner's Executor v Raeburn* 1996 SLT 745.

9 *Redfern's Executors v Redfern* 1996 SLT 900.

10 Succession (Scotland) Act 2016, s 2, replacing Family Law (Scotland) Act 2006, s 19. But see: J Robbie *Death, Divorce and Defective Drafting* (2018) 22 Edin LR 307.

11 As a result of this rule, the title to property may become inaccurate. For example, A acquires property in A's own name with a destination over to A's civil partner, B. The civil partnership is dissolved. A dies. As a result of the new rule, B is deemed not to have survived A and the property remains in A's estate. But, as far as title is concerned, it remains subject to the special destination and it will not be evident from the Land Register that there has been a dissolution. B may therefore appear to be the owner of the property because of the special destination. In ignorance of the law or in bad faith, B may transfer the property to a third party who will attempt to acquire title through the special destination to B. Section 2(4) of the Succession (Scotland) Act 2016 provides that when the third party has acquired title in good faith and for value in such circumstances, the title acquired is not challengeable on the ground that the special destination was rendered ineffective by the dissolution and the property remains in A's estate. A's estate can recover the proceeds of B's sale to the third party under the law of unjustified enrichment.

THE OCCUPATION OF THE MATRIMONIAL OR FAMILY HOME

5.4 In the previous section, we discussed the question of the ownership of the matrimonial or family home. In this section we shall consider the different but related question of the occupation of the matrimonial or family home. There are two situations:

(1) where one spouse or civil partner has the title to the property or is the tenant, and the other spouse or civil partner has no real right in the property; and

(2) where both spouses or civil partners have a title to the property, ie they are common owners of the property.

Where one spouse or civil partner has title or is the tenant

5.5 At common law the owner or the tenant had the right of exclusive possession of the property. Thus, for example, if spouse A owned the matrimonial home, spouse A could tell spouse B to leave: if B refused, A could obtain an interdict preventing B access to the house. Where A was under a duty to aliment B, this duty did not extend to allowing B to continue to occupy the matrimonial home.[1] The common law rule that a spouse who owned or was the tenant of a matrimonial home was entitled to order the non-owning spouse to leave was radically altered by the Matrimonial

Homes (Family Protection) (Scotland) Act 1981.[2] A similar legal regime was introduced for civil partners by the Civil Partnership Act 2004.[3]

1 *MacLure v MacLure* 1911 SC 200; *Millar v Mill*ar 1940 SC 56.
2 See generally, E M Clive *The Law of Husband and Wife in Scotland* (4th edn, 1997, W Green/Sweet & Maxwell), Ch 15.
3 Sections 101–112.

The nature of the statutory rights

5.6 By s 1(1) of the 1981 Act and s 101(1) of the 2004 Act, where one spouse or civil partner, 'the entitled spouse' or 'entitled partner', is the owner or tenant of the matrimonial or family home[1] and the other spouse, 'the non-entitled spouse' or 'non-entitled partner' is not the owner or tenant,[2] then the non-entitled spouse or non-entitled civil partner has the following statutory rights:

(a) if in occupation, to continue to occupy the matrimonial or family home;

(b) if not in occupation, to enter into and occupy the matrimonial or family home.[3]

These statutory rights of a non-entitled spouse or civil partner to occupy the matrimonial or family home expressly include the right to do so 'together with any child of the family'.[4]

The effect of this provision is to give the non-entitled spouse or non-entitled civil partner a positive right to occupy the matrimonial or family home together with any child of the family. 'Matrimonial home' and 'family home' have wide meanings. They include any house, caravan, houseboat or other structure which has been provided as, or has become, a *family* residence.[5] Although the term 'family residence' is used, it is clear that it is not limited to a family where there are children. It is enough that a house has been acquired with the intention that it should be used as a family home; the couple do not need to have lived there.[6]

Conversely, if the house was acquired without the intention that it should be used as a family residence, nevertheless it can become a matrimonial or family home. For example, if spouse A bought a flat before meeting and marrying spouse B, it will become a matrimonial home if B lives there after their marriage.[7] If there are two or more family residences, for example a town house and a holiday cottage, the non-entitled spouse or civil partner will have a statutory right to occupy both (or more) houses. On the other hand, a matrimonial or family home does not include a residence provided for one spouse or civil partner to live in separately from the other spouse or civil partner even if children of the family also reside there.[8]

A child of the family includes any child or grandchild of either spouse or civil partner or any person brought up or treated by either spouse or civil partner as if he or she was a child of that spouse or civil partner. The age of the child or person is irrelevant.[9] For example, a disabled adult son or daughter of either spouse or civil partner will be a child of the family for the purposes of the 1981 and 2004 Acts.

The statutory rights arise as soon as the parties marry or register their civil partnership and the entitled spouse or civil partner acquires a family residence. The rights continue throughout the marriage or civil partnership even if the couple separate. But if they do not cohabit for a continuous period of two years during which the non-entitled spouse or civil partner does not occupy the matrimonial or family home, then the statutory rights come to an end.[10] Having lost the statutory rights in this way, the non-entitled spouse or civil partner cannot apply for a declarator that they exist even though the couple may have become reconciled and resumed cohabitation.[11] The statutory rights also cease when the marriage or civil partnership ends in death, divorce or dissolution.[12] Most importantly, the rights of the non-entitled spouse or civil partner are not defeated if, during the marriage or civil partnership, the matrimonial or family home is sold or otherwise disposed of to a third party.[13]

1 Or is permitted by a third party to occupy the home: Matrimonial Homes (Family Protection) (Scotland) Act 1981, s 1(1); Civil Partnership Act 2004, s 101(1). This only arises if the third party has waived the right to occupy the home in favour of the entitled spouse: MH(FP)(S)A 1981, s 1(2); CPA 2004, s 101(3); *Murphy v Murphy* 1992 SCLR 62.

2 Or is not permitted by a third party to occupy the home: MH(FP)(S)A 1981, s 1(1); CPA 2004, s 101(1).

3 MH(FP)(S)A 1981, s 1(1); CPA 2004, s 101(1).
4 MH(FP)(S)A 1981, s 1(1A); CPA 2004, s 101(2).
5 MH(FP)(S)A 1981, s 22; CPA 2004, s 135: any garden or outbuildings, for example a garage, are included.
6 *O'Neill v O'Neill* 1987 SLT (Sh Ct) 26.
7 But it will not be matrimonial or partnership property for the purpose of fair division under the Family Law (Scotland) Act 1985, s 9(1)(a): discussed in **Ch 7.**
8 MH(FP)(S)A 1981, s 22: CPA 2004. This includes a house provided by a spouse or civil partner for himself or herself; or a house provided by a spouse or civil partner for the other spouse or civil partner; or a house provided for one spouse or civil partner by a third party.
9 MH(FP)(S)A 1981, s 22; CPA 2004, s 101(7).
10 MH(FP)(S)A 1981, s 1(7); CPA 2004, s 101(6A).
11 MH(FP)(S)A 1981, s 1(8); CPA 2004, s 101(6B).
12 Where, on divorce or dissolution, the court makes an incidental order entitling the applicant spouse or civil partner to continue to occupy the matrimonial or family home after the divorce or dissolution, certain of the rights in s 2 of the MH(FP)(S) A 1981 and s 102 of the CPA 2004, which enable a non-entitled spouse or civil partner to take steps in relation to the upkeep of the home and its contents, will continue: FL(S)A 1985, s 14(5) and (5A). Nevertheless, it is common and accepted practice to incorporate craves for relief under the 1981 Act or 2004 Act in divorce or dissolution proceedings: *Nelson v Nelson* 1988 SLT (Sh Ct) 26.
13 Discussed in detail at para **5.10**.

Upkeep and maintenance of the matrimonial home

5.7 For the purpose of securing the statutory rights of occupation, a non-entitled spouse or civil partner has the right, without the consent of the entitled spouse or civil partner, *inter alia,* to pay any rent, mortgage instalments, etc, instead of the entitled spouse or civil partner; to carry out essential repairs; to carry out non-essential repairs approved by a court as appropriate for the reasonable enjoyment of the occupancy rights; and to take any other steps necessary to ensure the occupancy of the matrimonial or family home.[1] The court has the power to apportion such expenditure between the spouses or civil partners.[2]

1 Matrimonial Homes (Family Protection) (Scotland) Act 1981, s 2(1); Civil Partnership Act 2004, s 102(1). The court is the Court of Session or the sheriff court.
2 MH(FP)(S)A 1981, s 2(4); CPA 2004, s 102(4).

Regulatory orders

5.8 By s 3 of the Matrimonial Homes (Family Protection) (Scotland) Act 1981 and s 103 of the Civil Partnership Act 2004 the court has the power to regulate the spouse or civil partner's occupancy of the matrimonial or family home. An order may be sought by either the entitled or non-entitled spouse or civil partner. The court can make orders declaring or enforcing the applicant's rights of occupation, restricting the non-applicant's occupancy rights and regulating the occupancy rights of both parties. While the court is obliged to declare that the applicant has occupancy rights when it is satisfied that the property constitutes a matrimonial or family home,[1] the exercise of its other powers under s 3 and s 103 is discretionary. By s 3(3) and s 103(3) the court is obliged to make such orders as appears to the court to be just and reasonable having regard to all the circumstances of the case including:

(a) the conduct of the spouses and civil partners in relation to each other and otherwise;

(b) the respective needs and financial resources of the spouses or civil partners;

(c) the needs of any child of the family;

(d) the extent (if any) to which the matrimonial or family home is used in connection with a trade, business or profession of either spouse or civil partner; and

(e) whether the entitled spouse or civil partner offers or has offered to make available to the non-entitled spouse or civil partner any suitable alternative accommodation.

Interim orders are possible if considered necessary or expedient[2] and compensation is available for loss or impairment of occupancy rights.[3] However, a court cannot make an order under s 3(3) or s 103(3) if its effect would be to exclude the entitled spouse or civil partner from the matrimonial or family home. While the power to grant declarator of a non-entitled spouse or civil partner's statutory rights is important, in practice little use has been made of the court's powers to make regulatory orders under s 3(3) or s 103(3).[4]

1 Matrimonial Homes (Family Protection) (Scotland) Act 1981, s 3(3); Civil Partnership Act 2004, s 103(3). Indeed, it would appear that declarator is essential before other relief can be given under s 3 or s 103: *Welsh v Welsh* 1987 SLT (Sh Ct) 30.

2 MH(FP)(S)A 1981, s 3(4); CPA 2004, s 103(4): the non-applicant spouse or civil partner must have been afforded an opportunity of being heard or represented in court.
3 MH(FP)(S)A 1981, s 3(7); CPA 2004, s 103(8).
4 Where a s 103(3) order is in force when a qualifying civil partnership ends because the civil partnership has been converted into a same sex marriage, the order continues as if made under MH(FP)(S)A 1981, s 3(3): Marriage and Civil Partnership (Scotland) Act 2014, s 11(8). On qualifying civil partnerships, see para **1.19** above.

Exclusion orders

5.9 By s 4 of the 1981 Act and s 104 of the 2004 Act the court has the power to exclude either of the spouses or civil partners from the matrimonial or family home. The order may be sought by either the entitled or non-entitled spouse.[1] By s 4(2) of the 1981 Act the court:

> '*shall* make an exclusion order if it appears to the court that the making of an order is *necessary* for the protection of the applicant or any child of the family from any *conduct* or *threatened* or reasonably apprehended conduct of the non-applicant spouse which is or would be injurious to the physical or mental health of the applicant or child'.[2]

In spite of the mandatory wording of s 4(2), by s 4(3)(a) the court shall not make an exclusion order if it would be unjustified or unreasonable having regard to all the circumstances of the case, including the factors specified in s 3(3).[3] The wording of s 104(2) of the 2004 Act is a little different. It provides that:

> '... the court *is* to make an exclusion order if it appears to it that to do so is *necessary* for the protection of the applicant or any child of the family from any *conduct*, or any *threatened* or reasonably apprehended conduct, of the non-applicant partner which is or would be injurious to the physical or mental health of the applicant or child'.[4]

Once again, even if the necessity criterion is satisfied, the court is not to make an exclusion order if it appears to the court that it would be unjustified or unreasonable to do so having regard to all the circumstances, including the matters specified in s 103(3). Interim exclusion orders are available[5] but the necessity criterion must still be satisfied.[6]

The construction of s 4 of the 1981 Act initially caused the Scottish courts much difficulty. At first there was a reluctance to grant an interim exclusion order when the court was proceeding on affidavit evidence. In *Bell v Bell*[7] and *Smith v Smith*,[8] the Inner House of the Court of Session held that the necessity criterion in s 4(2) was a 'high and severe' test. The judges indicated that it would be unlikely to be satisfied unless the applicant was living in the matrimonial home at the time of the application. This caused considerable apprehension until the Lord Justice-Clerk (Wheatley) attempted to remove such fears in *Colagiacomo v Colagiacomo*:[9]

> 'If there is any misconception that following *Bell v Bell* an interim exclusion order will only be granted if the parties are both occupying the matrimonial home, the sooner that misconception is removed the better. The fact that only one of the parties is occupying the matrimonial home is a factor to be taken into account but is not per se to be regarded as a conclusive one.'[10]

Although exclusion orders were granted in later cases where the applicant had left the matrimonial home,[11] s 4(1) of the 1981 Act was amended expressly to provide that an application for an exclusion order can be made, 'whether or not that spouse [the applicant] is in occupation at the time of the application'.[12]

In *Bell v Bell*[13] and *Smith v Smith*[14] the judges also indicated that an exclusion order should not be made if a matrimonial interdict prohibiting the molestation of the applicant would be sufficient protection.[15] This could lead to a 'Catch 22' situation: a spouse could not be granted an interim exclusion order unless there had been an application for a non-molestation interdict, but if such an interdict were obtained, an exclusion order would not be granted without evidence that the other spouse had been in breach of the interdict.[16]

However, in *Brown v Brown*,[17] Lord Dunpark held that a matrimonial interdict was not a pre-requisite for an exclusion order, although in considering whether it would be unjustified or unreasonable to make the order, the sheriff or Lord Ordinary must consider, *inter alia*, whether a matrimonial interdict would suffice.[18] Moreover, when granting a s 4 order, the judge should state the reasons why an interdict did not afford sufficient protection.[19] On the facts of *Brown*, an interdict was not enough since the husband was violent only when he was drunk and this conduct would not be affected by the existence of an interdict.[20] In *Roberton v Roberton*[21] the Inner House held that a sheriff was entitled to grant an interim exclusion order because it was almost impossible to frame an effective interdict given the husband's unreasonably intrusive and jealous nature: the exclusion order was therefore necessary to protect the wife from injury to her health.

Lastly, there are dicta in *Bell v Bell*[22] to support the contention that an interim exclusion order should only be made if the court is satisfied that the applicant would be in danger of 'serious injury or irreparable damage' if the order is not granted. In *McCafferty v* McCafferty,[23] the Inner House of the Court of Session held that these dicta were an unnecessary gloss on the necessity test which stipulates that it is sufficient that the non-applicant's conduct or threatened or reasonably apprehended conduct 'is or would be injurious to the physical or mental health of the applicant or child'.

While these developments were concerned with exclusion orders under the 1981 Act, it is submitted that the same principles are applied to exclusion orders under the 2004 Act.

It has never been doubted that the criterion for an exclusion order is not easy to satisfy. The applicant must satisfy the court that the order is *necessary* for the protection of the applicant or any child of the family because the non-applicant's conduct (or threatened or reasonably apprehended conduct) is, or would be, injurious to the physical or mental health of the applicant or child.[24] The fact that, on a balance of convenience test, it is desirable that the applicant and the child of the family should have exclusive occupation of the matrimonial home will not suffice.[25] Although s 4(2) of the 1981 Act and s 104(2) of the 2004 Act expressly include harm to the applicant's or child's mental as well as physical health,[26] this must be occasioned by the non-applicant's *conduct* and not merely be the result of the breakdown of the marriage or civil partnership.[27]

It should also be remembered that, even if the necessity test is satisfied, the court can refuse an exclusion order if in all the circumstances of the case, including the factors listed in s 3(3) of the 1981 Act and s 103(3) of the 2004 Act, it would be unjustified or unreasonable to do so.[28] But, as Lord Dunpark observed in *Brown v Brown*,[29] the Inner House of the Court of Session:

> 'had difficulty in envisaging circumstances in which an order which is necessary for the protection of the spouse may be "unjustified or unreasonable" …'.

Nevertheless, the court has suspended the operation of an exclusion order for three months in order to enable the defender to find alternative accommodation. This is difficult to accept given that the exclusion order was *ex hypothesi* 'necessary'.[30] In *McCafferty v McCafferty*,[31] Lord Dunpark said that in an application for an exclusion order the court should ask four questions:

> '(1) What is the nature and quality of the alleged conduct?
>
> (2) Is the court satisfied that the conduct is likely to be repeated if cohabitation continues?
>
> (3) Has the conduct been or, if repeated, would it be injurious to the physical or mental health of the applicant or to any child of the family?
>
> (4) If so, is the order sought necessary for the future protection of the physical or mental health of the applicant or child?'[32]

The necessity for an exclusion order will only be established if the court is satisfied that a matrimonial interdict will not afford sufficient protection, but a matrimonial interdict is not a pre-requisite for an exclusion order.

It will be clear that the success of an application for an exclusion order will greatly depend on the readiness of the judge at first instance, the Lord Ordinary or the sheriff, to find the necessity test satisfied. This is important, for an appellate court will not interfere with a judge's discretion unless 'no reasonable Lord Ordinary [or sheriff] could have reached the decision, and that he was completely wrong'.[33]

Whatever the difficulties inherent in the legislation and experienced in practice, it cannot be doubted that the protections afforded by s 4 and s 104 are an important step in the protection of the victims of domestic abuse.[34]

The necessity criterion can be criticised as too narrow, but it will clearly cover at least the most blatant forms of domestic abuse. But there is much weight in the contention that where a relationship is breaking down, the needs of any children of the family should be paramount and that the courts should have the power to exclude a spouse or civil partner from the matrimonial or family home when giving paramount consideration to the welfare of the children of the failing relationship, on the balance of convenience it is desirable that the person looking after the children should have exclusive occupation of the home. To some extent, this has been remedied by s 76 of the Children (Scotland) Act 1995 whereby a local authority can apply to the sheriff for an exclusion order excluding the 'named person' from the child's family home.[35] The order will be granted where the sheriff is satisfied 'that the child has suffered, is suffering, or is likely to suffer, significant harm as a result of any conduct, or any threatened or reasonably apprehended conduct, of the named person'; that exclusion 'is necessary for the protection of the child'; and that it 'would better safeguard the child's welfare than the removal of the child from the family home'.[36]

The Domestic Abuse (Scotland) Act 2018 addresses domestic abuse by creating an offence of engaging in a course of abusive behaviour[37] towards a partner or ex-partner.[38] The offence of domestic abuse is aggravated where a child is involved.[39]

---

1 See, for example, *Brown v Brown* 1985 SLT 376; *Millar v Millar* 1991 SCLR 649 where the applicant was the entitled spouse. Note that a local authority can raise an action in the sheriff court for an exclusion order under s 76 of the Children (Scotland) Act 1995, discussed at para **14.6** ff.

2 Italics added.

3 See para **5.8**. Exclusion orders are also not available if the matrimonial or family home is part of an agricultural tenancy or has been let as an incident of employment: Matrimonial Homes (Family Protection) (Scotland) Act 1981, s 4(3)(b); Civil Partnership Act 2004, s 104(3)(b).

4 Italics added.

5 MH(FP)(S)A 1981, s 4(6); CPA 2004, s 104(6). The non-applicant spouse or civil partner must be afforded an opportunity of being heard or represented before the court. It has been held that affidavit evidence is of little value to the defender and a proof should take place at an early stage unless the circumstances are exceptional: *Armitage v Armitage* 1993 SCLR 173.

6 *Bell v Bell* 1983 SLT 224; *Smith v Smith* 1983 SLT 275; *Ward v Ward* 1983 SLT 472; *Roberton v Roberton* 1999 SLT 38.

7 1983 SLT 224.
8 1983 SLT 275.
9 1983 SLT 559.
10 1983 SLT 559 at 562.
11 See, for example *Ward v Ward* 1983 SLT 472; *Brown v Brown* 1985 SLT 376.
12 Law Reform (Miscellaneous Provisions) (Scotland) Act 1985, s 13(5). In *Millar v Millar* 1991 SCLR 649 a spouse obtained an exclusion order although she had left the home ten months before: the delay was not the fault of the pursuer.
13 *Bell v Bell* 1983 SLT 224.
14 *Smith v Smith* 1983 SLT 275.
15 Matrimonial interdicts are granted under the Matrimonial Homes (Family Protection) (Scotland) Act 1981, s 14. The equivalent for civil partners are relevant interdicts which are granted under the Civil Partnership Act 2004, s 113.
16 As happened in *Smith v Smith* 1983 SLT 275.
17 1985 SLT 376.
18 MH(FP)(S)A 1981, s 4(3); CPA 2004, s 104(3).
19 *McCafferty v McCafferty* 1986 SLT 650.
20 See also, for example, *Oliver v Oliver* 1988 GWD 26-1110.
21 1999 SLT 38.
22 1983 SLT 224 at 231, per Lord Robertson and at 232, per Lord Grieve.
23 *McCafferty v McCafferty* 1986 SLT 650 at 652 per Lord Justice-Clerk (Ross); at 654 per Lord Robertson and at 655 per Lord Dunpark.
24 In *Barbour v Barbour* 1990 GWD 3-135, for example, it did not appear that an exclusion order was necessary to protect anyone. Cf *Raeburn v Raeburn* 1990 GWD 8-424.
25 *Smith v Smith* 1983 SLT 275. In *Hampsey v Hampsey* 1988 GWD 24-1035, the Sheriff Principal (Caplan) held that a sheriff has 'no power to grant an exclusion order simply because the best interests of the child required it'. See also *Millar v Millar* 1991 SCLR 649.
26 *McCafferty v McCafferty* 1986 SLT 650. In *Roberton v Roberton* 1999 SLT 38, the court held that the wife's deteriorating health was caused by the husband's obsessive, jealous behaviour and was not merely the result of the tension which often arises when a marriage is breaking down.
27 *Matheson v Matheson* 1986 SLT (Sh Ct) 2.
28 It is ironic that the needs of the children is one of the factors listed in the MH(FP)(S)A 1981, s 3(3) and CPA 2004, s 103(3), and is, therefore, only relevant when considering whether it would be unjustified or unreasonable to make an exclusion order!
29 *Brown v Brown* 1985 SLT 376 at 378. See also *Millar v Millar* 1991 SCLR 649 at 651, per the Sheriff Principal (Maguire).
30 *Mather v Mather* 1987 SLT 565.
31 1986 SLT 650.
32 1986 SLT 650 at 656.
33 *McCafferty v McCafferty* 1986 SLT 650 at 655, per Lord Robertson. In *Brown v Brown* 1985 SLT 376, Lord Dunpark held that an appellate court could only interfere if the judge at first instance did not apply the proper test or the decision was wholly

unwarranted on the facts. In *Coster v Coster* 1992 SCLR 210, an appeal from a sheriff refusing an exclusion order was allowed on the basis that the sheriff had given too much weight to whether the pursuer had alternative accommodation available rather than the averments of serious assault by the defender. See also *Roberton v Roberton* 1999 SLT 38.

34 Where a s 104(4) order is in force when a qualifying civil partnership ends because the civil partnership has been converted into a same sex marriage, the order continues as if made under MH(FP)(S)A 1981, s 3(4): Marriage and Civil Partnership (Scotland) Act 2014, s 11(8). On qualifying civil partnerships, see para **1.19** above.

35 Children (Scotland) Act 1995, s 76(1).

36 Children (Scotland) Act 1995, s 76(2) and discussed at para **14.6** ff.

37 Domestic Abuse (Scotland) Act 2018, s 2.

38 DA(S)A 2018, s 11.

39 DA(S)A 2018, s 5.

Statutory rights and third parties

5.10 A non-entitled spouse or non-entitled civil partner's statutory right of occupancy is not prejudiced as the result of the entitled spouse or civil partner's dealings with the property.[1] Dealings include the sale or lease of the matrimonial or family home or the grant of a heritable security over it. For example, while an entitled spouse may still sell the matrimonial home, the purchaser will take the property subject to the non-entitled spouse's statutory rights of occupancy. Moreover, by s 6(1)(b) of the 1981 Act and s 106(1)(b) of the 2004 Act, the purchaser is not entitled to occupy the matrimonial or family home or any part of it while the non-entitled spouse or civil partner continues to enjoy statutory rights of occupation in relation to the property.

Although this provision is laudable in so far as it protects the non-entitled spouse or non-entitled partner's statutory rights *vis-à-vis* third parties, it clearly causes conveyancing difficulties as the statutory rights are not registered in the Land Register. Thus, a third party could buy a house in good faith and in reliance upon the Register only to find that it is not possible to occupy the property because it is a matrimonial or family home in which the seller's non-entitled spouse or non-entitled civil partner has statutory rights of occupancy.

The 1981 Act and the 2004 Act provide various solutions to this problem. A non-entitled spouse or civil partner can renounce in writing the statutory rights in relation to a particular matrimonial or family home provided that at the time it was made, the non-entitled spouse or civil partner swore or affirmed before a notary public that the renunciation was made freely and without coercion of any kind.[2] Where such a renunciation is made, the property is no longer subject to statutory rights of occupancy.[3]

Similarly, occupancy rights are not effective against a third party if the non-entitled spouse or non-entitled civil partner has consented to the dealing.[4] When a non-entitled spouse or civil partner refuses to consent to the dealing, the court has power to dispense with the consent on the ground that it is being unreasonably withheld.[5] A non-entitled spouse or civil partner will be taken to have withheld consent unreasonably if:

(a) the entitled spouse or civil partner had been led to believe that the consent would be forthcoming and there has been no change of circumstances which would prejudice the non-entitled spouse or civil partner; or

(b) having taken all reasonable steps, the entitled spouse or civil partner has been unable to obtain an answer to a request for consent.[6]

In all other cases, the onus rests on the entitled spouse or civil partner to show that the non-entitled spouse or civil partner has unreasonably withheld consent to the dealing. Before the court could consider the issue, the proposed dealing had to have reached a stage of negotiations where price and other conditions of the sale had been agreed.[7] This effectively prevented the entitled spouse or civil partner from selling the house on the open market without first obtaining the non-entitled spouse or civil partner's consent. It is possible for the court to dispense with consent even though negotiations have not reached that stage provided that the house is sold within the period specified in the order at no less than the price stipulated by the court in the order.[8] In determining whether the consent is being unreasonably withheld the court will consider all the circumstances of the case, including the factors listed in s 3(3) of the 1981 Act and s 103(3) of the 2004 Act.[9] In *O'Neill v O'Neill*[10] where the non-entitled spouse had no intention of living in the house but was merely withholding consent as a bargaining lever in relation to a financial settlement on divorce, the court indicated that her consent was being withheld unreasonably. If the court dispenses with the non-entitled spouse's consent to the dealing,[11] the third party is not affected by the statutory rights.

There are also exceptions when the entitled spouse or civil partner entered into a binding obligation in respect of the dealing before the marriage or registration of the civil partnership.[12] If the entitled spouse or civil partner has permanently ceased to be entitled to occupy the matrimonial or family home, for example by selling it to a third party, the non-entitled spouse or civil partner's statutory rights cease to be exercisable against the third party if the non-entitled spouse or civil partner has, at any time thereafter, not occupied the property for a continuous period of two years.[13] For example, spouse or civil partner, A, is the entitled party. A sells the matrimonial home to X in 2018. Spouse or civil partner, B, the non-entitled party, leaves the matrimonial home in January 2020. Provided B does not occupy the matrimonial or family home for any period during the next two years, B's statutory rights of occupation will not be enforceable against X after January 2022.

In practice the most important exceptions are to be found in s 6(3)(e) of the 1981 Act and s 106(3)(e) of the 2004 Act.[14] These provide respectively that the non-entitled spouse or civil partner's statutory rights are not enforceable against a third party where:

> 'the dealing comprises a transfer [for value] to a third party who has acted in good faith, if there is produced to the third party by the transferor—
>
> (i) a written declaration signed by the transferor ... declaring that the subjects of the transfer are not or were not at the time of the dealing, a matrimonial or family home in relation to which a spouse or civil partner of the transferor has or had occupancy rights; or
>
> (ii) a renunciation of occupancy rights or consent to the dealing which bears to have been properly made or given by the non-entitled spouse or civil partner ...'.[15]

Provided the third party is in good faith, then if there is such a written declaration, a transferee *for value*, for example a buyer, will take the property free from the occupancy rights of the transferor's non-entitled spouse or civil partner. If the written declaration is false, the non-entitled spouse or civil partner will have recourse against the entitled spouse or civil partner for compensation for loss of occupancy rights as a result of their fraud.[16] The provision is so worded that it enables a transferor who is not married or in a civil partnership to declare that the property is not a matrimonial or family home. But it also enables a transferor who is married or in a civil partnership and whose spouse or civil partner does have statutory rights to make a written declaration when the property which is subject to the dealing is not *in fact* a matrimonial or family home. A similar written declaration is used to prevent the rights of a heritable creditor[17] being prejudiced by a non-entitled spouse or civil partner's statutory rights of occupation.[18]

To summarise. A is an entitled spouse or civil partner, B is A's non-entitled spouse or civil partner with statutory rights of occupation in respect of the matrimonial or family home owned by A. A transfers the property to C who acts in good faith and gives value. If A has made a written declaration that the house is not subject to statutory rights of occupation, then C will take it free of B's statutory rights. If C is in bad faith, ie knows about B or does not give value, then B's statutory rights will prevail over C even if C obtained a written declaration from A. But if C later transfers the property to D who is in good faith and gives value, it has been enacted that D will take the property free of B's statutory rights.[19] If D then transfers the property to E, E takes free of B's statutory rights, even if E is not in good faith or has not given value.

Where a dealing has occurred and the third party has taken the property subject to the non-entitled spouse or civil partner's statutory rights, the third party can apply to a court for an order dispensing with the consent of the non-entitled spouse or civil partner to the dealing, if the consent was being unreasonably withheld.[20] If successful, the third party will then take the property free from the non-entitled spouse or civil partner's statutory rights.

Since the Matrimonial Homes (Family Protection) (Scotland) Act 1981 came into effect some 40 years ago, in spite of initial conveyancing difficulties, these provisions have been the cause of little, if any, litigation. In particular, where a third party has relied on a s 6(3)(e) declaration, there has been no reported case in which a non-entitled spouse has claimed that occupancy rights are nevertheless enforceable against the third party because of an absence of good faith. There is no reason to believe that the position will not be the same under s 106(3)(e) of the Civil Partnership Act 2004.

---

1 Matrimonial Homes (Family Protection) (Scotland) Act 1981, s 6(1)(a); Civil Partnership Act 2004, s 106(1)(a). This protection does not apply where the entitled spouse occupies the home by permission of a third party or shares the occupation of the home with a third party: MH(FP)(S)A 1981, s 6(2)(a) and (b); CPA 2004, s 106(2)(a) and (b).

2 MH(FP)(S)A Act 1981, s 1(5) and (6): CPA 2004, s 101(5) and (6). It is not necessary that the non-entitled spouse or civil partner comes to Scotland to swear or affirm provided it is done before a person authorised to administer oaths or receive affirmations under the law of the country where the non-entitled spouse swears or affirms.

3 MH(FP)(S)A 1981, s 6(3)(a)(ii); CPA 2004, s 106(3)(a)(ii).

4 MH(FP)(S)A 1981, s 6(3)(a)(i); CPA 2004, s 104(3)(a)(i).

5 MH(FP)(S)A 1981, s 7(1); CPA 2004, s 107(1). The other grounds for dispensation are that the non-entitled spouse or civil partner is unable to consent because of physical or mental disability; or cannot be found after reasonable steps have been taken to trace the spouse; or is under the age of 16. This last reason could only arise in the case of a marriage or registration of a civil partnership celebrated abroad MH(FP)(S)A, s 7(1)(d).

6 MH(FP)(S)A 1981, s 7(2); CPA 2004, s 107(2).

7 *Fyfe v Fyfe* 1987 SLT (Sh Ct) 38.

8 MH(FP)(S)A 1981, s 7(1A) and (1B); CPA 2004, s 107(1A) and (1B). There are similar provisions where the proposed dealing is the grant of a heritable security: 1981 Act, s 7(1C) and (1D); 2004 Act, s 107(1C) and (1D). If the application for dispensation is refused and the non-entitled spouse or civil partner continues to live in the house, he or she can be ordered to make payments to the entitled spouse or civil partner: MH(FP)(S)A 1981, s 7(3A); CPA 2004, s 107(3A).

9 MH(FP)(S)A 1981, s 7(3); CPA 2004, s 107(3).

10 *O'Neill v O'Neill* 1987 SLT (Sh Ct) 26. The house was only a matrimonial home because the husband had hoped that his wife would live there: see para **5.6**.

11 The court will proceed as expeditiously as possible, but there must be evidence to justify dispensing with consent: see *Longmuir v Longmuir* 1985 SLT (Sh Ct) 33.

12 MH(FP)(S)A 1981, s 6(3)(c); CPA 2004, s 106(3)(c).

13 MH(FP)(S)A1981, s 6(3)(f); CPA 2004, s 106(3)(f). Continuity is not broken even if during that period the non-entitled spouse or civil partner had taken court proceedings to assert his or her statutory rights. But the time during which the proceedings were taken does not count towards the two years; MH(FP)(S)A 1981, ss 9A, 15; CPA 2004, s 111A. These provisions in effect reverse *Stevenson v Roy* 2002 SLT 446.

14 MH(FP)(S)A 1981, s 6(3)(e); CPA 2004, s 106(6)(e).

15 The time of the dealing in the case of a sale of the property is the date of delivery of the deed transferring title to the property: CPA 2004, s 106(4).

16 MH(FP)(S)A 1981, s 3(7); CPA 2004, s 103(8).
17 For example, a bank.
18 MH(FP)(S)A 1981, s 8(1) and (2); CPA 2004, ss 108(1) and (2).
19 MH(FP)(S)A 1981, s 6(1A); CPA 2004, s 106(1A).
20 MH(FP)(S)A 1981, s 7; CPA 2004, s 107.

Where both spouses and civil partners have legal title or are joint tenants

5.11 The statutory rights of occupancy of the matrimonial or family home are only available to a non-entitled spouse or civil partner, ie a spouse or civil partner who has no real right of ownership in the property. Where a spouse or civil partner has ownership, at common law there is an entitlement to occupy it. Both the Matrimonial Homes (Family Protection) (Scotland) Act 1981 and the Civil Partnership Act 2004 contain important provisions which strengthen the position of spouses and civil partners who are co-owners of their matrimonial or family residence. These provisions will be discussed in this section.

Although it is contrary to principle that a co-owner or co-tenant can be ejected by the other from the common property, there was a suggestion in *Price v Watson*[1] that this was possible. Section 4(7) of the MH(FP)(S) A 1981 and s 104(8) of the CPA 2004 clarify the position: it provides that where both spouses or both civil partners are entitled, or permitted by a third party, to occupy a matrimonial home, it shall be incompetent for one spouse to bring an action of ejection from the matrimonial home against the other spouse.

While at common law either co-owner could carry out necessary repairs and pay essential outgoings, there was no power to carry out non-essential repairs. The 1981 Act and the 2004 Act give co-owners who are spouses or civil partners the power to do so and allows a court to apportion the expenditure between them.[2]

Where the spouses or civil partners are common owners of the matrimonial or family home, each spouse or civil partner is free to sell his or her own half *pro indiviso* share of the property without the agreement of the other.[3] This could lead to problems where the purchaser insisted on occupying the property. Section 9(1) of the 1981 Act and s 109(1) of the 2004 Act provide that the right to occupy the matrimonial or family home enjoyed by a co-owning spouse or civil partner is not to be prejudiced by reason only of any dealing of the other spouse or civil partner in respect of the property and that a third party shall not by reason only of such a dealing be entitled to occupy the matrimonial or family home or any part of it. The effect of these provisions is that, while a co-owning spouse or civil partner is still entitled to sell his or her one-half *pro indiviso* share, the purchaser of the *pro indiviso* share is unable to occupy the matrimonial or family home while the other co-owning spouse or civil partner continues to reside there.

Where property is held in common, either co-owner is, in principle, entitled to obtain a decree of division and sale to realise his or her share of the value of the property. The court has no discretion at common law to refuse the decree. In *Dickson v Dickson*,[4] for example, the Lord Ordinary (Kincraig) held that a husband was entitled to a decree of division and sale in respect of property he owned in common with his wife; it was irrelevant that she would not agree to the sale because she wished to use the house as a home for herself and the children of the family. Thus, by applying for a decree of division and sale, a spouse could frustrate the underlying purpose of owning a matrimonial home, ie to provide a home for the co-owning spouse and their family.

Section 19 of the 1981 Act and s 110 of the 2004 Act provide a partial solution to this problem. Where a matrimonial or family home is owned in common by a married couple or civil partners, if one of the spouses or civil partners brings an action for the division and sale of the property, the court has a discretion, after having regard to all the circumstances of the case, to refuse or postpone the granting of the decree, or only to grant the decree subject to conditions. The court is expressly directed to consider the factors listed in s 3(3) of the 1981 Act and s 103(3) in the 2004 Act and whether the spouse or civil partner bringing the action has offered to make suitable alternative accommodation available to the other spouse or civil partner.[5]

It is not clear where the burden of proof lies in respect to s 19 of the 1981 Act and s 110 of the 2004 Act applications: there are few reported cases on division and sale. In *Hall v Hall*,[6] the Sheriff Principal, arguing by analogy with dispensation of consent under s 7 of the 1981 Act,[7] held that the onus lay on the (pursuer) spouse seeking the sale to show that the sale is reasonable. On the other hand, in *Berry v Berry*,[8] Lord Sutherland held that as a co-owner has a *prima facie* right to an action of division and sale, the onus lay on the defender to show why it was unreasonable for the sale to go ahead. In practice, however, the court will not allow a sale to go ahead when the continued occupation of the matrimonial home is clearly in the interests of the defender and the family. There is a more general unresolved property law question as to whether in place of division and sale, one co-owner is entitled to buy out the other.[9]

The needs of children are important.[10] In *Crow v Crow*,[11] Lord Wylie held that s 19 of the 1981 Act had made very material inroads into the rights of *pro indiviso* proprietors who were married. In particular, he stressed that the needs of the family were crucial. Accordingly, he had no hesitation in postponing the grant of a decree of division and sale beyond a date when the marriage would be terminated by divorce.[12] So, for example, if a spouse or civil partner applies for an action of division and sale, the court could delay granting decree until any children of the marriage or civil partnership reach the age of 18, even though the couple may divorce before the youngest child has reached that age.

It is important to note that s 19 of the 1981 Act and s 110 of the 2004 Act are only applicable when the co-owners are spouses or civil partners. If after divorce or dissolution, an ex-spouse or civil partner applies for an action of division and sale, he or she must be granted a decree.[13] Moreover, if, during the marriage or civil partnership, a spouse or civil partner sells his or her one-half *pro indiviso* share to a third party, the third party is entitled to a decree of division and sale as s 19 and s 110 only apply when both co-owners of the matrimonial or family home are married to or in a civil partnership with each other.[14]

Where both spouses and civil partners are co-owners of the matrimonial or family home, ie entitled spouses, the court has the same powers under s 3 of the 1981 Act and s 103 of the 2004 Act to make regulatory orders in respect of its occupation as it has when there is an entitled and non-entitled spouse or civil partner.[15] Similarly, the court may make an exclusion order under s 4 of the 1981 Act and s 104 of the 2004 Act where both spouses or civil partners are entitled in exactly the same way as in the case of an entitled and non-entitled spouse or civil partner.[16] The availability of exclusion orders as an important step towards the protection of victims of domestic violence cannot be overestimated.

---

1 1951 SC 359.

2 Matrimonial Homes (Family Protection) (Scotland) Act 1981, s 2(4) and (6); Civil Partnership Act 2004, s 102(4) and (6).

3 See para **5.3.**

4 1982 SLT 128.

5 MH(FP)(S)A 1981, s 19(a) and (b); CPA 2004, s 110(a) and (b). The offer must be of specific alternative accommodation; a general offer to help a co-owning spouse find somewhere to live is not enough. See *Hall v Hall* 1987 SLT (Sh Ct) 15.

6 1987 SLT (Sh Ct) 15. See also *Milne v Milne* 1994 SLT (Sh Ct) 57, where the approach in *Hall* was followed.

7 Discussed at para **5.10**.

8 1988 SCLR 296. The sale was ordered in this case. The most appropriate method of sale is by private treaty in open market: *Berry v Berry* (*No 2*) 1989 SLT 292. Where a spouse refused to pay a capital sum payment as financial provision on divorce, he was forced to sell his *pro indiviso* share of the former matrimonial home to his co-owning former spouse: *Scrimgeour v Scrimgeour* 1988 SLT 590. This was an exceptional case. See: Grant Knight, *Is division and sale a useful remedy?* Fam LB 2015, 137, 4–6.

9 See, for example, *Gray v Kerner* 1996 SCLR 331 and *Collins v Sweeney* 2014 GWD 12-214. For discussion, see C Anderson, *Property: A Guide to Scots Law* (2016, W Green) paras 9-32–9-40.

10 See, for example, *Milne v Milne* 1994 SLT (Sh Ct) 57 (W and children lived in home for 18 years: not fair and reasonable that they should have to move). Significantly, in *Berry v Berry* 1998 SCLR 296, the couple had no children; but a home was not required for the children in *Hall v Hall* 1987 SLT (Sh Ct) 15, yet the sale was refused. In *Rae v Rae* 1991 SLT 454, *Berry* was distinguished on the ground that, in *Rae*, the home was required for the wife and child of the marriage.

11 1986 SLT 270.

12 A divorce action was pending in this case.

13 *Burrows v Burrows* 1996 SC 378. H agreed to refrain from bringing an action of division and sale for five years after the couple divorced; although H could not raise the action during that period, he had an absolute right to division and sale after the five years had expired.

14 However, this 'dodge' may be caught by the Matrimonial Homes (Family Protection) (Scotland) Act 1981, s 9(1)(a) which provides that the co-owning spouse's rights 'in that home' are not to be prejudiced by any dealing of the other spouse: Civil Partnership Act 2004, s 109(1)(a) is to the same effect. Curiously, s 9(2) appears to apply ss 6(3) and 7 of the 1981 Act to the situation where both spouses are entitled. But these provisions would appear to be concerned with the statutory rights of occupancy of non-entitled spouses: it could hardly have been Parliament's intention

that, for example, a spouse could be compelled to sell his or her *pro indiviso* share on the grounds of withholding consent unreasonably. *Sed quaere*. CPA 2004, s 109(2) raises a similar question.

15 See para **5.8** ff.

16 See para **5.9** ff.

Tenancies

5.12 By s 13(1) of the 1981 Act and s 112(1) of the 2004 Act, a non-entitled spouse or civil partner can apply to a court for an order transferring the tenancy of the matrimonial or family home from the entitled to the non-entitled spouse or civil partner subject to the non-entitled spouse or partner paying just and reasonable compensation to the entitled spouse or civil partner.

Notice must be given to the landlord who must be given an opportunity to be heard in the proceedings. In deciding whether the tenancy should be transferred, the court is directed to consider the factors in s 3(3) of the 1981 Act and s 103(3) of the 2004 Act[1] and whether the non-entitled spouse or civil partner is suitable to become a tenant and to perform the obligations in the lease. There are exceptions where the matrimonial home is, for example, part of an agricultural holding or a croft.[2] An order granting an application under s 13(1) of the 1981 Act or s 112(1) of the 2004 Act can be made on granting a decree of divorce or dissolution or declarator of nullity of marriage or civil partnership.[3]

Where both spouses or civil partners are co-tenants there is a similar right to apply to a court for an order vesting the tenancy in the applicant's name solely, provided that the applicant pays just and reasonable compensation to the other spouse or civil partner.[4] Where an entitled spouse or civil partner is the tenant of a matrimonial or family home, the non-entitled spouse or civil partner retains possession of the tenancy and therefore the protections in the residential tenancies legislation if the entitled spouse or civil partner leaves home.[5]

1 See para **5.8**. Thus in *McGowan v McGowan* 1986 SLT 112, Lord Kincraig ordered the transfer of a tenancy in H's name to his wife. H had been violent during the marriage and had had an adulterous affair. W was living with the son of the marriage in

overcrowded conditions with her married daughter. Lord Kincraig thought it would be a 'travesty of justice' if H was allowed to retain occupation of the matrimonial home.

2 For a full list, see the Matrimonial Homes (Family Protection) (Scotland) Act 1981, s 13(7) and (8); Civil Partnership Act 2004, s 112(8).

3 MH(FP)(S)A 1981, s 13(2); CPA 2004, s 112(2).

4 MH(FP)(S)A 1981, s 13(9); CPA 2004, s 112(10).

5 MH(FP)(S)A 1981, s 2(8), reversing the decision in *Temple v Mitchell* 1956 SC 267; CPA 2004, s 102(8).

MATRIMONIAL AND RELEVANT INTERDICTS

5.13 A spouse or civil partner's right to occupy the matrimonial or family home can, of course, be undermined as a result of the other spouse or civil partner's abusive behaviour. Since this is so, it is thought to be convenient to discuss the law relating to matrimonial and relevant interdicts in this section.

By way of historical background, in the leading case of *Tattersall v Tattersall*, the Lord President (Emslie) opined[1] that 'interdict in the law of Scotland is designed only to prevent the apprehended commission of a wrong'. Interdict is granted at common law to protect property rights. In *MacLure v MacLure*,[2] for example, a husband who owned a hotel which was also used as the matrimonial home obtained an interdict against his wife who had no real right in the property from entering the hotel. Interdict is also granted to protect the integrity of the person and therefore one spouse can obtain interdict against molestation by the other.[3]

An interdict must be granted in sufficiently precise terms to leave the defender in no doubt as to what he or she can or cannot do and that the conduct prohibited should be no wider than is necessary to curb the defender's illegal actions. Thus, in *Murdoch v Murdoch*[4] an interim interdict preventing a husband from telephoning his wife or calling at her house was incompetent by reason of being too wide.

The major drawback of an interdict at common law was the question of enforcement. Where there was an alleged breach of interdict, a petition and complaint had to be brought with the concurrence of the Lord Advocate or procurator fiscal, to establish to the courts that a breach of the interdict had taken place.[5] The action was civil and the police had no power to arrest a person merely because he or she was in breach of interdict, though they could, of course, intervene if a crime or offence, for example an assault, had occurred.

Under the Matrimonial Homes (Family Protection) (Scotland) Act 1981 and the Civil Partnership Act 2004, there is a system of matrimonial and relevant interdicts to which the court must, in certain circumstances, attach a power of arrest.[6] Where a power of arrest is attached to an interdict, a police constable may arrest the defender without warrant if the constable has reasonable cause to suspect that the defender is in breach of an interdict.[7]

Section 14(1) of the 1981 Act and s 113(1) of the 2004 Act provide that it shall not be incompetent for a court to entertain an application by a spouse or civil partner for a matrimonial or relevant interdict by reason only that the spouses or civil partners are living together. This clarifies the doubt which had existed at common law about the competency of such an application.[8]

By s 14(2) of the 1981 Act and s 113(2) of the 2004 Act a matrimonial or relevant interdict means an interdict, including an interim interdict, which:

(a) restrains or prohibits any conduct of one spouse or civil partner towards the other spouse or civil partner or a child of the family; or

(b) prohibits a spouse or civil partner from entering or remaining in –

    (i) a matrimonial or family home,

    (ii) any other residence occupied by the applicant spouse or civil partner,

    (iii) any place of work of the applicant spouse or civil partner,

    (iv) any school attended by a child in the permanent or temporary care of the applicant spouse or civil partner.

In relation to s 14(2)(b)(i) and s 113(2)(b)(i), it will be clear that the effect of such an interdict is to exclude the defender from the matrimonial or family home. Where the applicant is a non-entitled spouse or civil partner or both applicant and defender are entitled, the interdict cannot prohibit the defender from entering his or her home, and resort must be made to s 4 or s 104 for an exclusion order; the interdict can be granted as ancillary to that order. Even where the applicant is an entitled spouse or civil partner and the defender non-entitled, the interdict can only be granted as ancillary to a s 4 or s 104 exclusion order unless the defender has not been given leave to exercise his or her statutory rights.[9] As a result, before a s 14(2)(b)(i) or s 113(2)(b)(i) interdict is granted, in the vast majority of cases the applicant must have obtained an exclusion order which will only be granted if it is necessary to do so.[10]

Where a matrimonial or relevant interdict is made which is ancillary to an exclusion order the court *must* attach a power of arrest to such an interdict.[11] In relation to any other matrimonial or relevant interdict, for example, one that restrains or prohibits any conduct of one person towards the other, under MH(FP)(S)A, s 14(2)(a) or CPA 2004, s 113(2)(a), the court must attach a power of arrest if it is satisfied that it is necessary to do so to prevent the interdict being breached.[12] When a power of arrest is attached to a matrimonial or relevant interdict, a police constable may arrest the non-applicant spouse without a warrant if the constable has reasonable cause to suspect that the defender is in breach of the interdict.[13]

Where the court considers that an interdict may not be sufficient to stop the identified behaviour, it is competent to make a non-harassment order under the Protection from Harassment Act 1997, s 8(5).

It is worth adding to this section that the Domestic Abuse (Scotland) Act 2018 creates an offence consisting of abusive behaviour towards a partner or ex-partner.[14] The offence is aggravated if the behaviour is directed at a child or if one party uses a child to direct the behaviour to the other person. The offence is also aggravated if the child sees, hears or is present during an incident of behaviour from one party to the other.[15]

---

1 *Tattersall v Tattersall* 1983 SLT 506 at 509.

2 1911 SC 200.

3 Historically, this was certainly the case if the spouses were living apart. The Matrimonial Homes (Family Protection) (Scotland) Act 1981, s 14(1) and Civil Partnership Act 2004, s 113(1) allow for a spouse or a civil partner to apply for a matrimonial or relevant interdict even where the couple is still living together.

4 1973 SLT (Notes) 13.
5 *Gribben v Gribben* 1976 SLT 266.
6 MH(FP)(S)A 1981, s 14; CPA 2004, s 113. The Protection from Abuse (Scotland) Act 2001, s 1(1A) imposes a duty on a court to attach a power of arrest to a matrimonial or relevant interdict which is ancillary to an exclusion order under s 4(1) of MH(FP)(S) A 1981 or s 104(1) of CPA 2004.
7 PA(S)A 2001, s 4.
8 See note 3 above.
9 MH(FP)(S)A 1981, s 14(3), (4) and (5); CPA 2004, s 113(3), (4) and (5).
10 On exclusion orders, see para **5.9** above.
11 PA(S)A 2001, s 1(1A).
12 PA(S)A 2001, s 1(2)(c).
13 PA(S)A 2001, s 4.
14 The Domestic Abuse (Scotland) Act 2018, s 11 defines 'partner' as (a) spouses or civil partners of each other; (b) persons living together as if spouses or civil partners; and (c) persons in an intimate personal relationship with each other. Whether someone is a person's ex-partner is to be determined accordingly.'
15 DA(S)A 2018, s 5.

PROTECTION WHEN A STANDARD SECURITY IS BEING ENFORCED

5.14 A creditor in a standard security has a right to enforce the security on default by the debtor.[1] The usual cause of default is not keeping up with the loan repayments. Enforcement usually leads to the sale of the property to recover the debt. When the property is residential, the Conveyancing and Feudal Reform (Scotland) Act 1970, as amended by the Home Owner and Debtor Protection (Scotland) Act 2010, provides that the creditor must normally obtain the permission of the court to enforce.[2] Certain pre-action requirements have to be complied with.[3] The court must be satisfied also that it is reasonable, in the circumstances, to enforce.[4] Here it must have regard to a number of specified matters, including the nature of and the reasons for the default and the ability of the debtor and any other person residing at the property to secure reasonable alternative accommodation.[5] When the enforcement proceedings commence, it is competent for an 'entitled resident' to apply to the court to continue the proceedings or make any other order that the court thinks fit.[6] The definition of an 'entitled resident' includes the non-entitled spouse or non-entitled civil partner of the debtor or proprietor[7] of the property if it is in whole or in part a matrimonial or family home.[8] In determining the application, the court has to have regard to the same specified matters mentioned above, including the ability to find reasonable alternative accommodation.[9] The need for a court order to enforce is removed where the debtor voluntarily surrenders the property when the creditor begins the enforcement, but where there is a non-entitled spouse or civil partner they must also consent.[10]

---

1 See generally, Scottish Law Commission Discussion Paper on Heritable Securities, 2021, Discussion Paper No 173.
2 Conveyancing and Feudal Reform (Scotland) Act 1970, s 24.
3 CFR(S)A 1970, s 24(5)(a) and s 24A, and the Applications by Creditors (Pre-Action Requirements) (Scotland) Order 2010 (SSI 2010/317).
4 CFR(S)A 1970, s 24(5)(b).
5 CFR(S)A 1970, s 24(7).
6 CFR(S)A 1970, s 24B(1).
7 The proprietor of the property may not necessarily be the same person as the debtor. For example, where A and B grant a standard security over their house to secure their child, C's, debt. This is relatively unusual.
8 CFR(S)A 1970, s 24C(1)(b) and (c). A former spouse does not qualify: see *Hoblyn v Barclays Bank Plc* [2014] CSIH 52, 2015 SCLR 85.
9 CFR(S)A 1970, s 24B(2).
10 CFR(S)A 1970, s 23A. This provision superseded the Matrimonial (Family Protection) (Scotland) Act 1981, s 20 (repealed).

PROTECTION WHEN SPOUSE OR CIVIL PARTNER HAS BEEN SEQUESTRATED

5.15 Where an individual has become bankrupt, the estate of that person vests in a trustee in sequestration who will sell the assets in an attempt to meet, in part, the individual's debts. The Bankruptcy (Scotland) Act 2016, s 113 provides special protection for spouses or civil partners past and present of the debtor in relation to a home.[1] This can apply in the situation where either the sequestrated spouse or civil partner wholly owns the home or co-owns it with that spouse or civil partner. For the home to be sold, either that spouse or civil partner must consent, or the permission of the sheriff must be obtained.[2] The sheriff can refuse to give consent for a period not exceeding three years if this is reasonable in the circumstances having regard to specified factors.[3] Alternatively, the sheriff can give consent subject to conditions. There is a similar provision for where the trustee raises an action of division and sale.[4]

---

1 The provision also applies to a trustee acting under a trust deed for creditors.
2 Bankruptcy (Scotland) Act 2016, s 113(1).
3 B(S)A 2016, s 113(2).
4 B(S)A 2016, s 113(3). See *Accountant in Bankruptcy v Brooks* [2020] SAC (Civ) 15, 2020 GWD 38-488; [2020] SAC (Civ) 15.

Chapter 6

Divorce and dissolution

INTRODUCTION

6.1 Divorce is the legal end to a marriage. Dissolution is the legal end to a civil partnership. By way of historical background, divorce on the ground of adultery was recognised at common law since the time of the Reformation and divorce for desertion was introduced by statute in 1573.[1] Until the Divorce (Scotland) Act 1938, these remained the only two grounds of divorce. The 1938 Act introduced further grounds: cruelty, incurable insanity, sodomy and bestiality.[2] With the exception of incurable insanity, the grounds of divorce were fault-based and divorce was perceived as a punishment for the defender's matrimonial offence.

Divorce for incurable insanity was manifestly a no fault ground and to this can be traced the idea that divorce should be regarded as a remedy to enable a spouse to be released from such a marriage. This view of divorce gradually became more prevalent. For example, as the result of judicial and statutory developments,[3] any requirement of moral fault on the part of a defender was whittled away from the concept of cruelty so that the pursuer could obtain a divorce whenever the defender's conduct was detrimental to the pursuer's health.

By the 1960s the movement for the reform of divorce law on the basis of a 'no fault' ground of irretrievable breakdown of marriage had built up considerable momentum.[4] The Law Commission took the view that a system based on the matrimonial offence did not achieve the objectives of a good divorce law which were:

> '(1) to buttress, rather than to undermine, the stability of marriage; and
>
> (2) where, regrettably, a marriage has irretrievably broken down, to enable the empty legal shell to be destroyed with the maximum fairness, and the minimum bitterness, distress and humiliation'.[5]

However, the Law Commission considered that it was impracticable to make irretrievable breakdown of marriage the sole ground of divorce. How was breakdown to be established without some form of inquisitorial procedure alien to an adversarial system of adjudication? Who would have the task of assessing a marriage in order to establish the reason why it had irretrievably broken down? The Scottish Law Commission recommended merely the addition of new separation grounds to the existing grounds of divorce but considered that the legal effect of the grounds was that they established that a marriage had in fact broken down.[6]

In England, a compromise was reached between the concept of no fault divorce based on irretrievable breakdown and the existing matrimonial offences in the Divorce Reform Act 1969, later consolidated in the Matrimonial Causes Act 1973. Although irretrievable breakdown was to be the sole ground of divorce, it could only be established by proof of at least one of five guideline facts, which included modified versions of the previous matrimonial offences and two new facts based on separation.[7]

The Divorce (Scotland) Act 1976 follows a similar compromise. In its Report on the Reform of the Ground of Divorce[8] the Scottish Law Commission recommended important changes to the ground of divorce which were implemented in the Family Law (Scotland) Act 2006. An additional ground of divorce, that an interim gender recognition certificate has been issued to either party, was added by the Gender Recognition Act 2004.

The grounds for the dissolution of a civil partnership mirror those of divorce, with one important exception: adultery is not a ground for the dissolution of a civil partnership.[9]

---

1 Act of 1573 (c 55).

2 The Divorce (Scotland) Act 1938 also enabled a marriage to be dissolved on the ground of the presumed death of one of the spouses.

3 Most importantly, the Divorce (Scotland) Act 1964, s 5.

4 See, for example, *Putting Asunder: A Divorce Law for Contemporary Society* (1996) Society for Propagation of Christian Knowledge.

5 Reform of the Grounds of Divorce: The Field of Choice (Cmnd 3123), para 15.

6 Divorce: The Grounds Considered (Cmnd 3256) (1967).

7 Matrimonial Causes Act 1973, s 1.

8 Scot Law Com No 116.

9 See s 117(3) of the Civil Partnership Act 2004.

GROUNDS OF DIVORCE OR DISSOLUTION

6.2 Section 1 of the Divorce (Scotland) Act 1976 and s 117 of the Civil Partnership (Scotland) Act 2004 set out the two grounds for divorce or dissolution. They are: (a) that the marriage or civil partnership has broken down irretrievably; or (b) that an interim gender recognition certificate under the Gender Recognition Act 2004 has, after the date of the marriage or the date of the registration of the civil partnership, been issued to either of the spouses or civil partners.

Irretrievable breakdown

6.3 Where a pursuer raises an action for divorce or dissolution on the ground of irretrievable breakdown, two matters must be considered. First is that the relationship has, in fact, broken down irretrievably in the view of one of both of the parties. The conduct of either party as a contributing factor to the failure of the relationship is irrelevant and is often merely a symptom of the relationship breakdown. Secondly, the court may grant decree if, but only if, it is established to the satisfaction of the court that the marriage or civil partnership has broken down irretrievably. It is submitted that, under the present system of divorce in Scotland, provisions should be built into the system to establish whether reconciliation is possible and to encourage this where possible.

As a result of the fact that the current law is a compromise between the concept of irretrievable breakdown and conduct, the full implications of a no fault theory of divorce or dissolution have been largely ignored. Section 1(1)(a) of the Divorce (Scotland) Act 1976 and s 117(2)(a) of the Civil Partnership Act 2004 provide that irretrievable breakdown of marriage or civil partnership is a ground of divorce or dissolution. However, irretrievable breakdown is only relevant if, and only if, it is established in accordance with later provisions in the legislation. Section 1(2) of the D(S)A 1976 and s 117(3) of the CPA 2004 provide that irretrievable breakdown will be taken to be established on proof of:

(a) the defender's adultery (this does not apply to dissolution of a civil partnership);

(b) the defender's behaviour being such that the pursuer cannot reasonably be expected to cohabit with the defender;

(c) the non-cohabitation of the parties for one year with the defender's consent; or

(d) the non-cohabitation of the parties for two years.

Thus, a pursuer will be unable to obtain a divorce or dissolution on the ground of irretrievable breakdown unless he or she can establish one of the facts set out in s 1(2) of D(S)A 1976 or s 117(3) of CPA 2004. This is both a necessary and sufficient condition for establishing irretrievable breakdown. So, even if a marriage or civil partnership has irretrievably broken down, if the pursuer has been unable to establish one of the facts, divorce or dissolution will not be granted. Conversely, a pursuer will be entitled to a divorce or dissolution if one of the facts is established, even though the marriage or civil partnership has not, in fact, irretrievably broken down. The concept of fault has therefore not been eroded from the law.[1]

It is significant that the legislation contains no provisions for compulsory attempts at reconciliation nor is there any obligation on solicitors to discuss with clients the possibility of reconciliation.[2] If, however, it appears to the court that there is a reasonable prospect of reconciliation, the court can continue the action for an attempt to be made,[3] but in practice it is less likely that reconciliation is possible once the action has begun. It is interesting to note that Professor Joe Thomson's position was that it is hypocritical to regard irretrievable breakdown as the ground of divorce or dissolution: the provisions of s 1(2) of the D(S)A 1976 and s 117(3) of the CPA 2004 constitute grounds for divorce and dissolution in Scots law, not simply facts or guidelines to determine whether a marriage or civil partnership has, in fact, irretrievably broken down.

---

1 The phrase could as well be 'abracadabra': see W A Wilson 'Divorce for Abracadabra' 1976 SLT (News) 27. From April 2022, the law in England and Wales was changed to allow no fault divorce and dissolution. See Matrimonial Causes Act 1973, s 1 (as amended by the Divorce, Dissolution and Separation Act 2020) and Civil Partnership Act 2004, s 44 (as amended by the DDSA 2020).

2 Cf the Matrimonial Causes Act 1973, s 6. However, a Court of Session *Practice Note* of 11 March 1977 enjoins practitioners to encourage clients to seek marriage counselling if the clients might benefit. There are also provisions in the Court of Session and sheriff court rules under which parties can be advised to attempt mediation in respect of the residence of any children of the marriage. Note that s 24 of the Children (Scotland)

Act 2020 has introduced a pilot scheme whereby, before a court can make an order under s 11(1) of the Children (Scotland) Act 1995, the parties should attend a meeting to be given information about options available to resolve the dispute (unless cause is shown as to why the parties should not attend such a meeting).

3 Divorce (Scotland) Act 1976, s 2(1); Civil Partnership Act 2004, s 118.

Establishment of irretrievable breakdown

Adultery

6.4 By s 1(2)(a) of the Divorce (Scotland) Act 1976, irretrievable breakdown of marriage is established if 'since the date of the marriage the defender has committed adultery'.

Adultery has been defined as voluntary sexual intercourse between a married person and a person of the opposite sex, not being the married partner. The sexual intercourse must be voluntary; thus, a woman who is the victim of rape is not guilty of adultery.[1]

The physical requirements of adultery were discussed by Lord Wheatley in *MacLennan v MacLennan*.[2] The pursuer sought a divorce on the ground of his wife's adultery. She had gone to the United States and returned with a child which the pursuer could not have fathered. Her defence was that she had conceived the child as a result of artificial insemination from a donor (AID). Although Lord Wheatley regarded the wife's conception of a child by AID without her husband's consent as 'a grave and heinous breach of the contract of marriage', it did not amount to adultery. Adultery involved a mutual surrender of the sexual and reproductive organs and some degree of penile penetration of the woman's vagina was necessary: in Lord Wheatley's words, adultery necessitated 'physical contact with an alien and unlawful sexual organ, and without that element there cannot be what the law regards as adultery'.[3] He therefore dismissed the argument that adultery could be committed by a woman 'when alone in the privacy of her bedroom, she injects into her ovum by means of a syringe the seed of a man she does not know and has never seen'.[4]

A defender's adultery is only relevant if it has occurred 'since the date of the marriage'. Thus, if a man commits adultery while married to his wife

(A) and subsequently divorces A and marries wife (B), B cannot rely upon his pre-marital adultery to found an action of divorce. A single isolated act of adultery will suffice.

Where the defender has been found guilty of rape or incest by a United Kingdom court, evidence of the conviction can be used to establish adultery provided a third party identifies the defender as the person convicted.[5] Moreover, a finding of adultery in earlier matrimonial proceedings is admissible in divorce proceedings to establish adultery, but, once again, a third party must identify the defender as the party in the earlier proceedings.[6]

Section 1(3A) of the D(S)A 1976 provides: 'For the avoidance of doubt, in relation to marriage between persons of the same sex, adultery has the same meaning as it has in relation to marriage between persons of different sexes.' This means that a same sex spouse can be divorced on proof of adultery if that spouse has sexual intercourse with a person of the opposite sex during the marriage, but not if he or she engaged in homosexual sex during the marriage. Engagement in homosexual sex would constitute unreasonable behaviour.

This is in contrast with civil partnerships where adultery, as a means of establishing irretrievable breakdown, is not included in s 117(3) of the CPA 2004. Engagement in homosexual or heterosexual sex would constitute unreasonable behaviour.

In an action of divorce by proof of adultery, the pursuer may be met by certain defences. It should be noted that, as a result of s 14 of the Family Law (Scotland) Act 2006, collusion is no longer a bar to divorce on any of the grounds of divorce.

---

1 *Stewart v Stewart* 1914 2 SLT 310.
2 1958 SC 105.
3 *MacLennan v MacLennan* 1958 SC 105 at 114.
4 1958 SC 105 at 114. AID without the husband's consent could give rise to a divorce based on the Divorce (Scotland) Act 1976, s 1(2)(b).
5 Law Reform (Miscellaneous Provisions) (Scotland) Act 1968, s 10; *Andrews v Andrews* 1971 SLT (Notes) 44.
6 LR(MP)(S)A 1968, s 11.

Defences to Adultery

Lenocinium

6.5 Two defences are available in law to challenge a pursuer's action in divorce proceedings where adultery is used to establish irretrievable breakdown. They are: *lenocinium* and *condonation*.[1]

The common law defence of *lenocinium* was preserved by s 1(3) of the Divorce (Scotland) Act 1976. The defence of *lenocinium* is difficult to define.[2] The essence of the defence is that the pursuer actively promoted the defender's adultery or was art and part of the behaviour. This would cover, for example, a husband who encouraged his wife to take up prostitution or a wife who suggested to her husband that they should join a 'spouse swapping' party. The defence can be illustrated by the leading case of *Gallacher v Gallacher*,[3] where a husband sent a letter to his wife entreating her to do something to enable him to divorce her. A few months later, the wife fell in love with another man. In divorce proceedings based on adultery, the action failed on account of *lenocinium*. The court refused to accept the husband's contention that the adultery arose as a result of the wife's passion for her lover rather than his letter.

It is important to stress that before *lenocinium* can be established, the pursuer must actively encourage the defender's adultery. In *Thomson v Thomson*,[4] the pursuer thought that his wife was having an affair. When she asked him for money to visit friends, he suspected she was going to meet her lover. He gave her the money she requested but had her followed by an inquiry agent, who discovered her committing adultery. The wife's defence of *lenocinium* failed on the ground that since she believed she had succeeded in keeping the knowledge of her affair from her husband, he could not have been actively encouraging her to commit adultery when he gave her the money she requested – albeit that he suspected how she would use it. Similarly, it is not *lenocinium* to hire inquiry agents to watch a spouse suspected of adultery.[5]

1 Divorce (Scotland) Act 1976, s 1(3).

2 For a comprehensive background of these defences, see Thompson, *Family Law in Scotland*, 3rd edn, pp 130–134, paras 6.4 and 6.5. A lack of case law where these defences are pled suggests they are infrequently relied upon in modern-day divorce proceedings but they still appear to exist as bars to divorce under Scots law. The Court

in *Douglas v Douglas* [2018] 11 WLUK 644 gave a comprehensive outline of the history of *lenocinium* as a defence and considered whether it applied to the facts; it was ultimately held it did not.

3 See *Gallacher v Gallacher* 1928 SC 586.

4 1908 SC 179.

5 For proposals that *lenocinium* should be replaced by a defence of actively promoting or encouraging adultery, see Report on Family Law (Scot Law Com No 135) Recommendation 67. This recommendation was not implemented by the Family Law (Scotland) Act 2006.

Condonation

6.6 The defence of condonation is in s 1(3) of the Divorce (Scotland) Act 1976. The defender's adultery will not succeed in establishing the ground of irretrievable breakdown if it has been 'condoned by the pursuer's cohabitation with the defender in the knowledge or belief that the defender has committed the adultery'. Section 13(2) of the 1976 Act provides that for the purposes of the Act 'the parties to a marriage shall be held to cohabit with one another only when they are in fact living together as man and wife'.[1] Thus, the parties must, in fact, live together as 'man and wife' before the defence is operative; verbal forgiveness[2] or an isolated act of sexual intercourse will not suffice.

But s 1(3) must be read with s 2(2) of the 1976 Act. Section 2(2) provides that adultery will not be condoned unless the pursuer has continued or resumed cohabitation with the defender at any time after the end of a period of three months from the date on which cohabitation was continued or resumed.

It is thought that s 1(3) of the D(S)A 1976 only operates as a defence in relation to the adultery on which the action is founded. Thus, if the pursuer cohabited in the knowledge or belief that the defender committed adultery with A, it would not operate as a bar to an action based on the defender's adultery with B. Similarly, if the pursuer knew or believed that the defender had committed specific acts of adultery, s 1(3) would not operate in relation to other acts of adultery which subsequently came to the pursuer's knowledge.

As noted above, adultery is not a means of establishing irretrievable breakdown in an action for dissolution of a civil partnership.

1 'Man and wife' must be read as referring to same sex as well as opposite sex spouses: Marriage and Civil Partnership (Scotland) Act 2014, s 4.
2 This was the position at common law: *Annan v Annan* 1948 SC 532.

Behaviour

6.7 By s 1(2)(b) of the Divorce (Scotland) Act 1976, and s 117(3)(a) of the Civil Partnership Act 2004, irretrievable breakdown of marriage or civil partnership is established if:

> 'since the date of the marriage [or registration of the civil partnership] the defender has at any time behaved (whether or not as a result of mental abnormality and whether such behaviour has been active or passive) in such a way that the pursuer cannot reasonably be expected to cohabit with the defender'.

The defender's conduct must have occurred after the date of the marriage or registration of the civil partnership; a spouse or civil partner's behaviour before the marriage or registration of the civil partnership is irrelevant. Thus, for example, a husband cannot use s 1(2)(b) to obtain a divorce on the ground that he was induced to marry the defender as a result of her fraudulent misrepresentation that she was pregnant by him: as the wife's behaviour, ie the misrepresentation, took place *before* the date of the marriage.[1] Similarly, one civil partner who discovers that the other civil partner had committed a heinous offence before the registration of their civil partnership, cannot rely on this offence to obtain a dissolution.[2]

Before s 1(2)(b) of the D(S)A 1976 or s 117(3)(a) of the CPA 2004 is applicable, the defender must have behaved in such a way that the pursuer cannot reasonably be expected to cohabit with the defender. What does behaviour mean in this context? A mere physical condition does not *per se* constitute behaviour. For example, if a defender is incontinent, that in itself does not amount to behaviour. But if an incontinent spouse knowingly and deliberately refused to wear protective underwear, the refusal to do so could constitute behaviour. However, it is settled that symptoms of an illness can in certain circumstances amount to behaviour. If for example, a spouse or civil partner became violent as a result of an illness or acquired brain injury, the violence would clearly constitute behaviour. But it can be difficult to determine when the symptom of an illness is merely a physical condition and when it amounts to behaviour. Thus, a husband's sleepiness and general lack of interest in his family caused by schizophrenia has been held to amount to behaviour[3] and bad personal hygiene as a result of disseminated sclerosis has not.[4]

The inclusion of the wording, 'whether such behaviour has been active or passive' within D(S)A 1976 and CPA 2004 may be a solution to this problem. In *Thurlow v Thurlow*[5] it has been accepted in England that where, as a result of a debilitating illness, a spouse is unable to fulfil the obligations of marriage, this failure can constitute behaviour for the purposes of divorce. As the 1976 and 2004 Acts have expressly enacted that behaviour may be passive,[6] it is thought that the principle in *Thurlow* has been transplanted into Scots law. Thus, for example, if an illness prevents a spouse from fulfilling the obligations of married life, this passive behaviour – as opposed to the illness – can amount to the estabishment of grounds for divorce.[7]

The fact that a defender's behaviour is caused by mental illness is irrelevant: s 1(2)(b) of the D(S)A 1976 and s 117(3)(a) of the CPA 2004 expressly state that conduct will constitute behaviour 'whether or not as a result of mental illness'.[8] Whether or not the behaviour was intentional is also of no consequence.[9]

The pursuer must establish that the defender behaved 'in such a way that the pursuer cannot reasonably be expected to cohabit with the defender'. The test is a compromise between a subjective and objective test. The criterion is whether the particular pursuer can, at the time of the action,[10] reasonably be expected to cohabit with the defender. In *Stewart v Stewart*, a divorce was granted to a wife whose husband had told his wife that he had been 'associating with another woman'. Divorce was granted on the basis that the husband's behaviour was intolerable to the matrimonial relationship; the absence of evidence that the husband's relationship was adulterous was irrelevant.[11]

A highly sensitive spouse or civil partner may not reasonably be expected to put up with conduct which a spouse or civil partner of ordinary fortitude could withstand.[12] But because of the phrase 'reasonably be expected', seemingly trivial behaviour (for example, snoring)[13] or socially useful behaviour (membership of a lifeboat or mountain rescue team) will not establish irretrievable breakdown for divorce or dissolution, however sensitive the pursuer may be. In *Taylor v Taylor*,[14] the court held that the defender could not bring evidence to try to establish that, because of her Christian religious beliefs, the pursuer had to forgive his conduct and therefore it was not unreasonable for her to continue living with him!

The range of behaviour which could satisfy s 1(2)(b) of the D(S)A 1976 and s 117(3)(a) of the CPA 2004 is as wide as human conduct. It includes both physical[15] and verbal abuse. Moreover, as Lord Davidson explained in *Hastie v Hastie*,[16]

> 'conduct on the part of a defender, by word or act, may be of such a nature that even if there is no risk of a repetition it is so destructive of a marriage relationship as to make it unreasonable to expect the pursuer to cohabit with the defender'.

Lord Davidson makes clear that behaviour does not have to be a course of conduct and a single act may suffice if the test is met.

In relation to sexual behaviour, this would include, for example, excessive demands for sexual relations, wilful and unjustified refusal of sexual relations,[17] and sexual relations with a third party. Thus, while homosexual relations with a third party do not amount to adultery, they will constitute unreasonable behaviour.[18] Excessive drunkenness[19] or abuse of other drugs would also suffice.

The mere fact that the pursuer has continued to cohabit with the defender after the alleged behaviour took place does not *per se* prevent the pursuer relying upon it for the purposes of s 1(2)(b) of the D(S)A 1976 or s 117(3)(a) of the CPA 2004. Persons who are or have been the victims of domestic abuse may continue to live with their spouse or civil partner after the abuse for many reasons such as fear, protection of children, or because they simply have nowhere else to go.[20] But where the alleged behaviour is objectively trivial, the longer the pursuer remains with the defender, the more difficult it will be to establish that the pursuer cannot reasonably be expected to cohabit with the defender as a result of that conduct. The pursuer's conduct after separation, for example forming a new relationship, may be used as evidence to establish that the pursuer cannot reasonably be expected to live with the defender.[21]

By s 3(1) of the D(S)A 1976 and s 121 of the CPA 2004 if a decree of separation[22] has previously been granted in respect of the same, or substantially the same facts, an extract of the decree may be regarded as sufficient proof of these facts in an action for divorce or dissolution on the ground, inter alia, of behaviour, but the court must still receive further evidence from the pursuer of what has occurred between the parties since the date of the decree.[23] Finally, where the behaviour relied upon led to a criminal conviction of the defender by a United Kingdom court, s 10 of the Law Reform (Miscellaneous Provisions) (Scotland) Act 1968 is applicable.[24]

There are no specific defences in relation to s 1(2)(b) of the D(S)A 1976 or s 117(3)(a) of the CPA 2004.

---

1 On fraudulent misrepresentation, see para **2.17** ff.

2 Cf *Hastings v Hastings* 1941 SLT 323.

3 *Fullarton v Fullarton* 1976 SLT 8. However, the effect of the behaviour on the pursuer was not serious enough for the divorce to be granted.

4 *Grant v Grant* 1974 SLT (Notes) 54.

5 [1975] 2 All ER 979, [1976] Fam 32.

6 There is no express reference to passive behaviour in the Matrimonial Causes Act 1973, s 1(2)(b).

7 If this thesis is accepted doubt must be cast on such pre-1976 cases as *H v H* 1968 SLT 40, where a wife's inability to have sexual relations which was caused by neurotic depression was held not to constitute cruelty. However, this inability would now amount to passive behaviour and the fact that it was a symptom of an illness is irrelevant.

8 In so doing the Divorce (Scotland) Act 1976 follows the policy of the Divorce (Scotland) Act 1964, s 5; *Williams v Williams* [1963] 2 All ER 994, [1964] AC 698, HL.

9 See *Fullarton v Fullarton* 1978 SLT 8

10 In *Findlay v Findlay* 1991 SLT 457, H drank and stayed out late. W suspected H was seeing another woman. The couple separated. At the time of the proof, W was living with another man. Her association was not *per se* enough to conclude that she could no longer reasonably be expected to cohabit with H. Lord Prosser stressed that there had to be a causal link between H's behaviour and the conclusion that W could not reasonably be expected to live with H. On the facts, H's behaviour led to W's separation and new relationship: there was therefore a causal link. Accordingly, because she was now living with another man, she could not reasonably be expected to cohabit with H at the time of the divorce action. See also *Knox v Knox* 1993 SCLR 381.

11 1987 SLT (Sh Ct) 48.

12 See, for example, *Livingstone-Stallard v Livingstone-Stallard* [1974] 3 All ER 766, [1974] Fam 47; *O'Neill v O'Neill* [1975] 3 All ER 289, [1975] 1 WLR 1118, CA. In *Meikle v Meikle* 1987 GWD 26-1005, a wife who came from a town background and went to live on her husband's hill farm obtained a divorce on the grounds that her husband spent too much time at work and she was disillusioned with life in the country. However, the fact that a husband had to work long hours in order to support his family has been held not to be sufficient to amount to unreasonable behaviour: *Ross v Ross* 1997 SLT (Sh Ct) 51.

13 Assuming, of course, that snoring constitutes behaviour.

14 2001 SCLR 16.

15 The assault need not be directed at the pursuer: *AB v CB* 1959 SC 27.

16 1985 SLT 146 at 148: wife's false accusation that husband was engaging in an incestuous association. See also *MacLeod v MacLeod* 1990 GWD 14-767: husband's unfounded suspicions of wife's adultery.

17 In *Mason v Mason* (1980) *Times,* 5 December, CA, a wife's limitation of sexual intercourse to once a week was held in England not to be such that her husband could no longer reasonably be expected to cohabit.

18 *White v White* 1966 SC 187.

19 *Campbell v Campbell* 1973 SLT (Notes) 82.

20 See, for example, *Britton v Britton* 1973 SLT (Notes) 12; *Bradley v Bradley* [1973] 3 All ER 750, [1973] 1 WLR 1291, CA. See Jessica J Eckstein, (2011) 'Reasons for staying in intimately violent relationships: comparisons of men and women and messages communicated to self and others'. *Journal of Family Violence*, Vol 26, Issue 1.

21 *Findlay v Findlay* 1991 SLT 457; *Knox v Knox* 1993 SCLR 381.

22 See para **6.12**.

23 This will usually simply be that the parties have neither lived together nor had sexual relations since the date of the decree of separation.

24 Discussed in the context of adultery at para **6.3**.

Non-cohabitation for one year with the defender's consent

6.8 By s 1(2)(d) of the Divorce (Scotland) Act 1976 and s 117(3)(c) of the Civil Partnership Act 2004 irretrievable breakdown of marriage or civil partnership is established if:

> 'there has been no cohabitation between the parties [or civil partners] at any time during a continuous period of one year after the date of the marriage [or registration of the civil partnership] and immediately preceding the bringing of the action and the defender consents to the granting of the decree [or decree of dissolution of the civil partnership]'.

First, there must be no cohabitation between the parties for the requisite period. Section 13(2) of the 1976 Act provides that 'the parties to a marriage shall be held to cohabit with one another only when they are in fact living together as man and wife'.[1] Interpreted literally, a couple not *in fact* living together as 'man and wife' are not cohabiting for the purpose of s 1(2)(d). The reason *why* they are not in fact living together is irrelevant. Thus, for example, if a couple is not living together because the one party is in prison or in hospital or working abroad, they are not cohabiting within the meaning of the D(S)A 1976.

Conversely, a couple may not be cohabiting within the meaning of s 13(2) of the D(S)A 1976 even though they live in close physical proximity. They will only be treated as cohabiting if they are in fact living together '*as man and wife*'. The absence of sexual relations will be an important factor in determining whether they are living in that capacity – but absence of sexual relations alone will probably not be enough. But if sexual relations have ceased, or the spouses provide no services for each other, or if they have no joint social life, then it is possible to argue that they are not living together as husband and wife even though they occupy the same house.[2]

There is no equivalent of s 13(2) in the CPA 2004. It is submitted, however, that the concept of non-cohabitation for the purposes of s 117(3)(c) should be interpreted in a similar way.

The non-cohabitation must be for a continuous period of at least one year after the date of the marriage or registration of the civil partnership and immediately preceding the bringing of the action. By s 2(4) of the D(S)A 1976 and s 119(3) of the CPA 2004, resumption of cohabitation for a period or periods not exceeding six months in all does not break the continuity of the period of non-cohabitation but does not count towards it.

Example 1

A leaves B on 1 January 2021. The couple resume cohabitation on 1 July 2021. They separate on 1 October 2021. The action can be brought after 1 April 2022. The three-month period of cohabitation between 1 July and 1 October 2021 is less than six months and therefore does not break the continuity of the one year's non-cohabitation but does not count towards it.

Example 2

A leaves B on 1 January 2021. The couple resume cohabitation on 1 November 2021. They separate on 30 June 2022. The period of cohabitation between 1 November 2021 and 30 June 2022 is greater than six months. The continuity of the non-cohabitation after the separation on 1 January 2021 is broken and it is therefore impossible to establish that they have not cohabited for a continuous period of a year from that date. A divorce or dissolution based on continuous non-cohabitation for a year immediately preceding the bringing of the action can only be brought on 1 July 2023.

Finally, the defender must positively consent to the granting of the decree. Consent can be withdrawn at any time before decree. Moreover, in *Boyle v Boyle*,[3] Lord Maxwell held that 'it is perfectly open to a defender to withhold consent for any reason he thinks fit or for no reason'.[4] Thus, the defender may use his or her consent as a bargaining counter between the parties in reaching agreement over ancillary matters such as financial provision on divorce or dissolution.

The divorce or dissolution can proceed as a simplified application for divorce or dissolution.[5] The pursuer is able to use s 3 of the D(S)A 1976 or s 121 of the CPA 2004 if a decree of separation has previously been granted on the ground of non-cohabitation.[6]

---

1 'Man and wife' must be read as referring to same sex as well as opposite sex spouses: Marriage and Civil Partnership (Scotland) Act 2014, s 4.
2 See, for example, *Samurai v Al-Samurai* [2014] CSOH 95.
3 1977 SLT (Notes) 69. See also *Donnelly v Donnelly* 1991 SLT (Sh Ct) 9.
4 1977 SLT (Notes) 69 at 69.
5 Simplified divorce and dissolution procedure is discussed at para **6.11** ff.
6 Discussed in relation to behaviour at para **6.5**.

Non-cohabitation for two years

6.9 By s 1(2)(e) of the Divorce (Scotland) Act 1976 and s 117(3)(d) of the Civil Partnership Act 2004, irretrievable breakdown of marriage or civil partnership is established if 'there has been no cohabitation between the [spouses or civil partners] at any time during a continuous period of two years after the date of the [marriage or the date of registration of the civil partnership] and immediately preceding the bringing of the action'.

In relation to the meaning of non-cohabitation and continuity of non-cohabitation, establishment of irretrievable breakdown resulting from non-cohabitation for two years raises precisely the same legal issues as those in s 1(2)(d) and s 117(3)(c).[1] The difference is, of course, that the period of non-cohabitation is two years and the consent of the defender is *not* necessary. Accordingly, a defender can be divorced against his or her will. The rationale behind this is that since the parties have not cohabited for two years, the marriage or civil partnership has, in fact, broken down irretrievably and consequently should legally be brought to an end.

The divorce or dissolution can proceed as a simplified application for divorce or dissolution.[2] The pursuer is able to use s 3 of the D(S)A 1976 or s 121 of the CPA 2004 if a decree of separation has previously been granted on the ground of non-cohabitation.

1 The six-month resumption of cohabitation rule under the Divorce (Scotland) Act 1976, s 2(4) and Civil Partnership Act 2004, s 119(3) also applies to non-cohabitation for two years. Discussed at para **6.8**.
2 Simplified divorce procedure is discussed at para **6.13** ff.

Divorce or dissolution on the ground that either party has been issued with an interim gender recognition certificate

6.10 The second ground of divorce is set out in s 1(1)(b) of the D(S)A 1976, and of dissolution in s 117(2)(b) of the CPA 2004. As we have seen,[1] a post-operative transgender person can apply for a gender recognition certificate when the acquired gender will be recognised as the applicant's sex. Where the applicant is married or is a party to a civil partnership, only an interim gender recognition certificate will be issued. The grant of an interim gender recognition certificate to a spouse or civil partner is a ground of divorce[2] or dissolution.[3] *Either* party to the marriage or civil partnership can seek a divorce or dissolution on this ground. The divorce or dissolution can proceed as a simplified application for divorce or dissolution.[4]

With the introduction of same sex marriage and the availability of civil partnerships to different sex couples, the Gender Recognition Act 2004 has been amended.[5] The rules apply to protected Scottish marriages and protected Scottish civil partnerships. These are marriages solemnised in Scotland and civil partnerships registered in Scotland.[6] Where the applicant for a gender recognition certificate is a party to a protected Scottish marriage or a protected Scottish civil partnership *and* the application contains a declaration that the applicant wishes the marriage or civil partnership to continue after a full gender recognition certificate has been issued, accompanied by a statutory declaration by the applicant's spouse or civil partner that he or she wishes the marriage to continue after the issue of a full gender recognition certificate, then the Gender Recognition Panel will issue a full gender recognition certificate and the marriage or civil partnership will continue. If the applicant's spouse or civil partner does not consent to the marriage or civil partnership continuing after the issue of a full gender recognition certificate, the Panel will issue an interim gender recognition certificate. The interim gender recognition certificate can be submitted to the court to establish the ground for divorce under s 1(1)(b) of the D(S)A 1976 or s 117(2)(b) of the CPA 2004. The applicant can then apply to a sheriff for a full gender recognition certificate which, if the application was made within six months of the issue of the interim gender recognition certificate, the sheriff must grant.[7] While the marriage continues even though a full gender recognition certificate has been granted by the sheriff, the interests of the non-consenting spouse or civil partner are protected as s 1(3B) of D(S)A 1976 and s 117(3A) of CPA 2004 provide that the right to obtain a divorce which arose when the interim gender recognition certificate was issued does not lapse when the full gender certificate is granted.

---

1 See para **2.12**.
2 Divorce (Scotland) Act 1976, s 1(1)(b).
3 Civil Partnership Act 2004, s 117(2)(b).
4 Simplified divorce or dissolution procedure is discussed at para **6.13**.
5 By the Marriage and Civil Partnership Act 2014, Sch 2 and Civil Partnership (Scotland) Act 2020, Sch 2.
6 GRA 2004, s 25; see meaning of 'protected Scottish civil partnership' and 'protected Scottish marriage'.
7 GRA 2004, s 4E(2).

Postponement of decree where religious impediment to remarry exists

6.11 The grant of a decree of divorce, but not of dissolution of a civil partnership, may be postponed if s 3A of the Divorce (Scotland) Act 1976 is applicable. In certain religions, for example, Judaism, a woman who has been divorced under Scots law is not allowed to enter a religious marriage unless she has also been divorced under the law of her religion. This may involve her husband divorcing her by delivering to her a document of divorce. In Judaism this is known as a Get.[1] If the husband refuses to do so, the woman will be unable to re-marry in accordance with her religion. Section 3A gives the court power to postpone the grant of decree of divorce until a religious divorce has taken place. So, in our example, if a husband is seeking a divorce from his wife, the wife can apply under s 3A to have the grant of the decree of divorce postponed until he divorces her under the law of their religion so that she will have no religious impediment to having a religious marriage in the future.

The power to postpone grant of decree arises '[n]otwithstanding that irretrievable breakdown of a marriage has been established in an action of divorce'. The pursuer in our example is therefore being denied a remedy to which he would otherwise be legally entitled. This is done for religious reasons, namely because the applicant is prevented from entering into a religious marriage by virtue of a requirement of that religion and the other party can remove or contribute to the removal of the impediment which prevents the religious marriage. In addition, the court must be satisfied that it is just and reasonable to postpone the grant of the decree.[2] The court can recall the postponement when it has received a certificate from the relevant religious body that the other party has acted to remove the impediment.[3] Where the wife is seeking a divorce from her husband, postponement of the decree will not help the wife to obtain a religious divorce from her husband if he does not want to divorce her.

1 See: Deanna Levine, *Divorce Law, the Jewish client and the Get,* SLT 2009, 12, 61–68.

2 Divorce (Scotland) Act 1976, s 3A(1)(b)(ii).

3 It can also recall the postponement even though this has not occurred: D(S)A 1976, s 3A(4).

JUDICIAL SEPARATION

6.12 Judicial separation may be used where spouses wish to separate but not wish to divorce or dissolve their civil partnership. It is less relevant to the modern-day legal system where there is less stigma attached to divorce and dissolution. The grounds for judicial separation are exactly the same as the grounds for divorce or dissolution and the same defences apply.[1]

The marriage or civil partnership still subsists and the spouses and civil partners remain under their obligation to aliment each other[2] and their obligations of fidelity and tolerable behaviour continue. Thus, for example, a divorce can be sought on the establishment of adultery committed after the decree of separation has been granted. If a decree of separation is obtained, the same facts can be used as a ground for a subsequent divorce or dissolution.[3]

1 Divorce (Scotland) Act 1976, s 4; Civil Partnership Act 2004, s 120.
2 Discussed at para **3.8** ff. A pursuer can seek a decree of separation without craving for aliment: *Gray v Gray* 1991 SCLR 422.
3 Divorce (Scotland) Act 1976, s 3; Civil Partnership Act 2004, s 121.

Procedural matters

Proof and simplified procedure

6.13 As a general principle, a divorce or dissolution cannot be granted unless the ground of action has been proved, whether or not the action has been defended.[1] There is no need for corroboration but there must be evidence emanating from a source other than a party to the marriage or the civil partnership.[2] But where an action is undefended, unless the court otherwise directs, proof is by way of affidavits instead of parole evidence.

A simplified procedure[3] – in effect a do-it-yourself divorce or dissolution – is possible.[4] However, its scope is severely restricted. An application can proceed if and only if:

(1) the party relies on the facts set out in s 1(2)(d) of D(S)A 1976 (no cohabitation for one year with consent of defender to

decree or s 1(2)(e) of D(S)A 1976 (no cohabitation for two years); or s 117(3)(c) or (d) of the CPA 2004; or s 1(1)(b) of the D(S)A 1976 or s 117(2)(b) of the CPA 2004 (the divorce or dissolution is based on the issue of an interim gender recognition certificate);

(2) in relation to a divorce based on s 1(2)(d) of the D(S)A 1976, or a dissolution based on s 117(3)(c) of the CPA 2004, the other spouse or civil partner consents;

(3) there are no proceedings pending in any court which could have the effect of bringing the marriage or civil partnership to an end;

(4) there are no children of the marriage or of the family under the age of 16;

(5) neither party is seeking financial provision on divorce or dissolution;

(6) neither party is suffering from a mental disorder; and

(7) s 3A of the D(S)A 1976 does not apply.

The simplified procedure is an exception to the rule that in divorce actions the evidence from a source other than one or both of the spouses is required.

---

1 Proof is on the balance of probabilities: Divorce (Scotland) Act 1976, s 1(6) and the Civil Partnership Act 2004, s 117(8).

2 Civil Evidence (Scotland) Act 1988, ss 1(1), 8(1) and (3). See, for example, *Taylor v Taylor* 2001 SCLR 16.

3 See www.scotcourts.gov.uk for updated information on the procedure for simplified divorce.

4 Rules of Court of Session 1994, rr 49.72–49.80; Act of Sederunt (Ordinary Cause Rules) Amendment (Civil Partnership Act 2004) 2005, SSI 2005/638, rr 33A.66–33A.75.

The case for reform

6.14 In its Discussion Paper, *The Ground for Divorce: Should the law be changed?*[1], the Scottish Law Commission put forward a radical proposal that divorce should be obtained by the lapse of a period of time after the giving of notice of intention of divorce – delayed divorce on demand. However, this proposal was abandoned and, instead, the SLC recommended a reduction from two years to one year for no cohabitation with the defender's consent and five years to two years, otherwise.[2] These recommendations came into force through the Family Law (Scotland) Act 2006. Until recently, calls for more radical change seemed to have dissipated but the debate has been reignited following a movement for substantial reform to divorce laws in England and Wales, bolstered by the case of *Owens v Owens*.[3] The reforms to the law in relation to divorce and dissolution of civil partnerships in England and Wales came into force in April 2022.[4] Briefly, one or both members of the couple can apply to court for a 'divorce order' or a 'dissolution order' which dissolves the marriage or civil partnership on the (sole) ground that it has broken down irretrievably; there is a minimum of 20 weeks from the start of the proceedings before the party or parties can confirm that they wish the application for a divorce or dissolution order to go ahead; the court will then grant a 'conditional order'; the divorce or dissolution order cannot be granted before the end of the period of six weeks from the making of the conditional order.

It remains to be seen what steps the Scottish government will take to address the need for reform to Scots law on divorce and dissolution.

---

1 Scot Law Com, Discussion Paper No 76 (1988).

2 Report on Reform of the Ground of Divorce, Scot Law Com, Discussion Paper 116 (1989). See Divorce (Scotland) Act 1976, s 1(2)(d) and (e).

3 [2018] UKSC 41: Mrs Owens petitioned for divorce on the ground that her marriage had broken down irretrievably on the basis of her husband's unreasonable behaviour. Mr Owens defended the petition and refused to agree that the marriage had irretrievably broken down. In order to establish the ground that her husband had behaved in a way that meant she could not reasonably be expected to cohabit with him, Mrs Owens gave 27 detailed examples of the unreasonable behaviour she alleged. The court sympathised with Mrs Owens but was forced to dismiss the appeal on the basis that the ground had not been established. The only way Mrs Owens could, therefore, be granted a divorce was to rely on the non-cohabitation ground without consent which, at the time, was five years in England and Wales (as opposed to two years in Scotland). Baroness Hale stated that Owens was a 'troubling case' (para 46), and the Court used the opportunity to urge Parliament 'to consider whether to replace a law which denies to Mrs Owens any present entitlement to a divorce in the above circumstances' (para 45).

4 See Matrimonial Causes Act 1973, s 1 (as amended by the Divorce, Dissolution and Separation Act 2020) and Civil Partnership Act 2004, s 44 (as amended by the DDSA 2020).

CONCLUSION

6.15 This chapter has primarily been an attempt to outline the substantive Scots law of divorce and dissolution of a civil partnership. In theory, the right to a divorce or dissolution is restrictive but, in practice, generally, little difficulty is experienced in establishing the necessary grounds. The vast majority of divorces and dissolutions are undefended and there have been few reported decisions on the legal difficulties which the grounds in the Divorce (Scotland) Act 1976 and the Civil Partnership Act 2004 raise. In short, it would appear that in relation to establishing a ground of divorce or dissolution, as opposed to ancillary matters such as financial provision and the residence of children, the role of the court is largely administrative. But there must still be cases where a marriage or civil partnership has, in fact, irretrievably broken down, yet divorce or dissolution is not possible because a ground under s 1(2) of the D(S) A 1976 or s 117(3) of the CPA 2004 cannot be established.[1]

It should be accepted that in twenty-first-century society there is and will continue to be a high rate of matrimonial and civil partnership breakdown.[2] The primary concerns of a modern divorce or dissolution law should be to attempt to protect the children of the relationship as much as possible and to provide a fair system for the reallocation of the family's income and capital. Now that the law in England and Wales has been reformed to allow for no fault divorce and dissolution, it is submitted that it is a good time for Scots law to follow the same reform and move towards a no-fault system of divorce and dissolution of civil partnerships.

---

1 See the English case of *Owens v Owens* [2018] UKSC 41. See also fn 3 of para **6.13**.

2 At present, approximately one in three marriages ends in divorce. It is thought that this is similar for civil partnerships.

Chapter 7

Financial provision on divorce and dissolution

INTRODUCTION

7.1 A major function of contemporary family law is to provide a system of rules whereby a couple's capital and income can be redistributed in a just way when their marriage or civil partnership ends in divorce or dissolution. Before the enactment of the Family Law (Scotland) Act 1985, Scots law left this important matter largely to the discretion of the judges.[1] The Scottish Law Commission considered the options for reform in a very full and detailed report[2] which led to the system of financial provision on divorce in the Family Law (Scotland) Act 1985.[3] The 1985 Act has been amended by the Civil Partnership Act 2004[4] so that the same system of financial provision applies on the dissolution of a civil partnership as on divorce. Provision for the breakdown of cohabitation is discussed in Chapter 8. Before considering this system in detail, several important issues must be discussed.

For many couples whose relationship breaks down there is little property or income to be redistributed. Nevertheless, where couples do have considerable assets, they are entitled to a rational system of redistribution of their property and income when their marriage or civil partnership ends in divorce or dissolution. A major difficulty in determining the criteria for financial provision is that any system must endeavour to accommodate the different kinds of marriages and civil partnerships which end in divorce or dissolution. These include short childless marriages; civil partnerships where both parties work; medium-term marriages or civil partnerships where there are dependent children; long marriages or civil partnerships where a spouse or civil partner has given up paid employment to look after the children of the family and has no prospect of a job in the future; and a civil partnership or marriage where one partner or spouse has provided all the income while the other ran the home.

The Scottish Law Commission concluded that, given the variety of marriages, there was no one principle which, if followed, would produce a satisfactory financial settlement in every case. For example, in a short childless marriage or civil partnership it is simply not fair – even if it were practicable – that a spouse or civil partner should as a result of financial provision be placed in the same financial position he or she would have enjoyed if the marriage or civil partnership had not broken down. On the other hand, if a spouse or civil partner has given up a career in order to look after the children of the family and has, in effect, been an unpaid homemaker for many years, why should he or she lose the expectation that the other spouse or civil partner would maintain them in old age merely because the marriage or civil partnership has ended in divorce or dissolution? Again, even after a short marriage or civil partnership, the financial needs of a spouse or partner who is unable to earn because they are looking after dependent children may not be met merely by the equal division of the spouses' or civil partners' capital assets. Accordingly, the Scottish Law Commission took the view that it was necessary to provide a set of principles or objectives which were to be achieved by a system of financial provision on divorce but which at the same time would allow the courts to retain a considerable degree of discretion so that orders could be made which took account of the particular circumstances of the marriage or civil partnership in question.

Finally, it must be stressed at the outset that the provisions of the Family Law (Scotland) Act 1985 are concerned only with financial provision for *spouses and civil partners*. In Scots law children have an independent right to aliment from their parents or those who have accepted them as children of their family.[5] When, for example, a marriage breaks down, the children will often live with one of their parents and not with the other. In these circumstances the absent parent, ie the parent with whom the child does not live, is obliged to pay maintenance until the child is 16.[6] In addition, there is the possibility that the parents will have to pay aliment to the child. A child's claims for maintenance and/or aliment are determined *before* a court considers financial provision for the spouses or civil partners. In this way, Scots law gives primacy to the financial needs of the children of a family when a marriage or civil partnership ends in divorce or dissolution.

1 See the Divorce (Scotland) Act 1976, s 5(2). For a short discussion of the pre-1985 law, see the second edition of this book (1991, Butterworths), pp 120 ff.

2 Report on Aliment and Financial Provision (Scot Law Com No 67).
3 The Family Law (Scotland) Act 1985 came into force on 1 September 1986. On the effect of the 1985 Act on the practice of solicitors, see *The Impact of the Family Law (Scotland) Act 1985 on Solicitors' Divorce Practice* (November 1990) Scottish Office Central Research Unit Papers.
4 Part 2 of Sch 28 to the Act.
5 Family Law (Scotland) Act 1985, s 1(1)(c) and (d).
6 On maintenance calculation, see paras **10.11** ff.

THE NATURE OF THE ORDERS

7.2 In an action for divorce or dissolution[1] and, in accordance with s 8(1) of the Family Law (Scotland) Act 1985, a party may apply to the court[2] for one or more orders to be made by way of financial provision for the applicant.

1 The regime on financial provision also applies in an action of declarator of nullity of marriage or a civil partnership: Family Law (Scotland) Act 1985, s 17.
2 That is the Court of Session or the sheriff court, as the case may require: FL(S)A 1985, s 27.

(1) An order for the payment of a capital sum or the transfer of property

7.3 The court has the power to make orders for the payment of a capital sum and/or a transfer of property.[1] Such an order can be made either at the date of divorce or dissolution or within a period specified by the court.[2] The court can stipulate that the order is to come into effect at a specified future date.[3] For example, if a married couple's only substantial asset is the matrimonial home and this would have to be sold to raise the finance necessary for the payment of a capital sum, the court may delay the operation of such an order until a specified date, for instance when the youngest child of the family has reached the age of 18 and the property is no longer required as a home for the family.

The court can order that a capital sum be paid by instalments.[4] This is important where a couple's assets are not in an easily realisable form. For example, if a spouse or civil partner was granted a capital sum of £50,000 but the other spouse or civil partner's assets were tied up in a small business, the court could order that the £50,000 be paid in five annual instalments of £10,000. It will also be useful where a spouse or civil partner has few capital assets but a high income. The advantages of a capital sum payable by instalments over periodical allowances is that the total capital sum awarded cannot be varied,[5] which may make instalments an advantageous option as it will not be perceived by the payer as an indefinite financial burden.

A property transfer order obliges one of the parties to transfer the ownership of his or her property to the other. For example, if a husband and wife are common owners of the matrimonial home, the court could order the husband to transfer his one-half *pro indiviso* share of the house to the wife.[6] This is useful where the children of the parties are to reside with the wife after the divorce. A property transfer order and a capital sum payment can be made in the same action: but neither has a preference over the other.[7]

---

1 Family Law (Scotland) Act 1985, s 8(1)(a) and (aa). The court can also order a capital sum payment in respect of lump sums due under pension schemes: FL(S)A 1985, s 8(1)(ba). See para **7.8**.

2 FL(S)A 1985, s 12(1)(a) and (b).

3 FL(S)A 1985, s 12(2). See, for example, *Little v Little* 1990 SLT 230, approved by the Inner House 1990 SLT 785. In this case, the major asset – the defender's interest in a pension fund – was not in an easily realisable form thus justifying the court in delaying payment of one-half of the capital sum for six years.

4 FL(S)A 1985, s 12(3).

5 The date or method of payment of an order can be varied on a material change of circumstances: FL(S)A 1985, s 12(4).

6 H and W would both convey their one-half *pro indiviso* shares to W.

7 FL(S)A 1985, s 8(1)(a) and (aa). See *McKinnon v McKinnon* 2008 GWD 12-226. Whether there should be a property transfer order or a capital sum payment 'will depend on the facts of each case': ibid at para 10.

---

(2) Periodical allowances

7.4 The court has power to make an order for the payment of a periodical allowance.[1] It is an axiomatic principle of the Family Law (Scotland) Act 1985 that before ordering a periodical allowance the court must be satisfied that the payment of a capital sum or a transfer of property order is inappropriate or insufficient in the circumstances.[2] Moreover, a periodical allowance can only be made if it is justified by one of the principles in ss 9(1)(c), (d) or (e).[3] Thus, the whole thrust of the 1985 Act is that the 'normal' orders for financial provision should take the form of capital sum payments or transfer of property orders rather than periodical allowances. This is to encourage 'a clean break' with the consequence that the spouses or civil partners cease to be economically dependent on each other after the divorce or dissolution. It is for this reason that the court's power to order a capital sum to be paid by instalments is so important.

Only in exceptional circumstances should orders for periodical allowances be made. The order can be for a definite or indefinite period, or until a specified event happens.[4] If there has been a material change of circumstances, a periodical allowance can be varied or recalled and an order for a periodical allowance can be converted into the payment of a capital sum or property transfer order.[5] A periodical allowance ends with the death, marriage or registering a civil partnership of the payee;[6] it continues if the payer dies, although the executor can apply to the court to recall the order.[7]

---

1 Family Law (Scotland) Act 1985, s 8(1)(b). The court can also make a pension sharing order: s 8(1)(baa). Pension sharing orders are discussed at para **7.8** ff.

2 FL(S)A 1985, s 13(2). 'If a pursuer seeks an award of periodical allowance she must aver and prove that the conditions in section 13(2) are satisfied. If she does not do so, the principle of the '"clean break" embodied in the 1985 Act prevents the court from considering the question of periodical allowance at all': *Mackin v Mackin* 1991 SLT (Sh Ct) 22 at 24, per the Sheriff Principal (Ireland). Where the pursuer has obtained a substantial capital sum payment and/or property transfer order, it is most unlikely that the criteria in s 13(2) will be satisfied and no periodical allowance should be made: *McConnell v McConnell* 1995 GWD 3–145. See also: *W v W* 2012 SCLR 591.

3 FL(S)A 1985, s 13(2). The principles are discussed in detail at paras **7.18–7.20**. See *Thirde v Thirde* 1987 SCLR 335. The pursuer's pleadings must refer to the principle(s) in FL(S)A 1985, s 9(1)(c)–(e) being relied upon.

4 FL(S)A 1985, s 13(3). See, for example, *Mitchell v Mitchell* 1993 SLT 419.

5 FL(S)A 1985, s 13(4). The making of a maintenance calculation in respect of a child living with the payee is a material change of circumstances: FL(S)A 1985, s 13(4A). Any variation or recall can be backdated to the date of the application or, on cause shown, to an earlier date: FL(S)A 1985, s 13(4)(b). On variation, the periodical allowance can be made for a definite or indefinite period or until a specified event

happens: FL(S)A 1985, s 13(5), impliedly incorporating, *inter alia*, s 13(2). See, for example, *Kerray v Kerray* 1991 SLT 613.
6 FL(S)A 1985, s 13(7)(b).
7 FL(S)A 1985, s 13(7)(a) and (4).

(3) Incidental orders

7.5 In addition, the court has the power to make incidental orders. These are listed in s 14 of the Family Law (Scotland) Act 1985. They include an order for the sale of the couple's property,[1] the valuation of their property[2] and a declarator as to the ownership of any disputed property.[3] The court can also make an order regulating the occupation of the matrimonial or family home and the use of its furniture and plenishings,[4] including an order regulating liability as between the parties for outgoings in respect of the home and its contents.[5] Under these provisions the court can exclude one of the parties from the property. As long as an order subsists as to the occupation of the matrimonial or family home and its contents, the occupant retains[6] the powers of management conferred by the Matrimonial Homes (Family Protection) (Scotland) Act 1981 and the Civil Partnership Act 2004.[7] The provisions of the 1981 Act and the 2004 Act protecting a spouse or civil partner's occupancy rights against dealings with third parties do not apply.

Other incidental orders include an order that security should be given for any financial provision[8] and an order as to the date from which any interest on any amount awarded should run.[9] In *Geddes v Geddes*,[10] the Inner House of the Court of Session held that a court could order interest to run from a date *prior* to the date of decree provided it was justified by the principles in s 9 of the FL(S)A 1985 and reasonable to do so.[11] For example, where spouses or civil partners (A and B) separate and A lives in the matrimonial or family home until the divorce or dissolution five years later, B is *prima facie* entitled to a capital sum payment of half the net value of the house at the date of separation, the relevant date.[12] The court can order interest on the capital sum payment to run from the relevant date rather than the date of divorce, ie B will get the capital sum payment *plus* five years' interest on that sum. The interest represents consideration for A's exclusive use of the matrimonial home for five years.[13] The provision is also useful where payment of a capital sum is postponed until a future date because the payer's assets are not easily realisable at the date of divorce or dissolution. For example, a spouse or civil partner has pension interests and rights under a life insurance policy. These are not easily realisable. In these circumstances the court can make a capital sum order and defer payment for several years. But it can also order that interest on the capital sum is to be paid to the payee during this period thus compensating the payee for the deferment of the payment.[14]

Powers also exist for the payment or transfer of property to a trustee or curator *bonis* on behalf of a party to the marriage or civil partnership,[15] and for setting aside or varying any term in an antenuptial or postnuptial marriage settlement or any corresponding settlement in respect of a civil partnership.[16] The court can also dispense with the need for one of the parties to execute a deed and can order the sheriff clerk to do so instead: this power exists where the deed is concerned with moveable as well as heritable property.[17] Finally, the court can make any ancillary order which is expedient to give effect to the principles set out in s 9 of the FL(S) A 1985, or any order made under s 8(2) of the same Act.[18]

Armed with this plethora of powers, the court can make orders for financial provision which can be tailor-made for the particular couple concerned.

1 Family Law (Scotland) Act 1985, s 14(2)(a). See for example, *Porter v Porter* 1990 SCLR 752; *Reynolds v Reynolds* 1991 SCLR 175. Because of the exceptionally uncertain state of the current property market, the court may order the sale of the former matrimonial home giving the pursuer the free proceeds (or a proportion thereof) instead of making an order for a capital sum payment based on a valuation of the property: *Smith v Smith* [2009] CSOH 2. In *Thomson v Thomson* 2003 Fam LR 22 the sale of the former matrimonial home was delayed until a seven-year-old child had completed his primary education at a local school. It has been held that this order cannot be sought post decree to enforce a capital sum order which has not been paid: *Amin v Amin* 2000 SLT (Sh Ct) 115. *Sed quaere* if the incidental order is an ancillary order rather than an order for financial provision. Sale was ordered *post*-divorce in *Jacques v Jacques* 1995 SLT 963 at the Inner House stage.

2 FL(S)A 1985, s 14(2)(b).

3 FL(S)A 1985, s 14(2)(c).

4 FL(S)A 1985, s 14(2)(d); see *Little v Little* 1989 SCLR 613, approved by the Inner House 1990 SLT 785. By FL(S)A 1985, s 14(3), orders under s 14(2)(d) and (e) of the 1985 Act can be made only on or after divorce or dissolution; this is because before divorce or dissolution these matters are regulated by the Matrimonial Homes (Family Protection) (Scotland) Act 1981 and the Civil Partnership Act 2004.

5 FL(S)A 1985, s 14(2)(e).
6 FL(S)A 1985, s 14(5), (5A) and (5B).
7 That is MH(FP)(S)A 1981, s 2 and the CPA 2004, s 102.
8 FL(S)A 1985, s 14(2)(f). See, for example, *Macdonald v Macdonald* 1995 SLT 72. It would appear that the order must be made to secure an order for financial provision, eg the payment of a capital sum: *Trotter v Trotter* 2001 SLT (Sh Ct) 42.
9 FL(S)A 1985, s 14(2)(j).
10 *Geddes v Geddes* 1993 SLT 494; cf *Kennedy v Kennedy* 2004 Fam LR 70.
11 On the s 9 principles, see paras **7.6** ff.
12 Discussed at para **7.7** ff.
13 See, for example, *Welsh v Welsh* 1994 SLT 828.
14 *Bannon v Bannon* 1993 SLT 999.
15 FL(S)A 1985, s 14(2)(g).
16 FL(S)A 1985, s 14(2)(h). A contract of copartnery is not a marriage settlement for the purposes of this section.
17 Section 14(2)(ja) (moveable property); Courts Reform (Scotland) Act 2014, s 38(2)(f) (heritable property).
18 FL(S)A 1995, s 14(2)(k). See *McDonald v McDonald* 1993 SCLR 132; *Murley v Murley* 1995 SCLR 1138; *Lindsay v Lindsay* 2005 SLT (Sh Ct) 81. In *Murdoch v Murdoch* [2012] CSIH 2, 2012 Fam LR 2 the court held that it was competent for the pursuer to seek a principal order in her favour – in this case a property transfer order – and an incidental order – in this case a counter balancing payment – in favour of the defender, ie the pursuer can seek an order against herself. This approach was 'consistent with common sense': ibid at para 22. But before such an order is competent it must be necessary to do justice between the parties: *R v C* 2013 GWD 22-431.

THE PRINCIPLES

7.6 In an application for financial provision, s 8(2) of the Family Law (Scotland) Act 1985 provides that the court shall make such order, if any, as is justified by the principles set out in s 9 of the 1985 Act, and is reasonable having regard to the resources of the parties.[1] Resources include the couple's present and foreseeable resources.[2] Thus the court's discretion is limited in that the order must be justified by the s 9 principles but the discretion is still wide as even if justified by the principles, the order must still be reasonable in the light of the couple's resources.

This discretion can be used to reduce an award of financial provision which is otherwise due in the light of both the payer's[3] and payee's[4] resources at the date of the divorce or dissolution. For example, if one party is *prima facie* entitled to a capital sum payment of £100,000 but the other party's resources have substantially declined since the couple separated, the court can reduce the capital sum to be paid because it is not reasonable for the payer to pay such a large amount in the light of his or her resources at the date of divorce.[5] However, this discretion cannot be used *to increase* an award beyond that justified by the s 9 principles.[6] A discussion of the s 9(1) principles follows.

1 Family Law (Scotland) Act 1985, s 8(2)(a) and (b). The onus rests on the party seeking financial provision to establish both these considerations: *Fraser v Fraser* 2002 Fam LR 53.

2 So, for example, a spouse's interest in a pension fund is a resource for these purposes: *Gribb v Gribb* 1995 SCLR 1007, 1996 SLT 719. But in determining what is reasonable, the court is not entitled to allow the issue of expenses, for example, the effect of the legal aid clawback, to determine that choice of orders: see *McKinnon v McKinnon* 2008 GWD 12-226.

3 *Buczynska v Buczynski* 1989 SLT 558 (capital sum reduced because payee (wife) had resources which did not constitute matrimonial property). On the other hand, in *Cunniff v Cunniff* 1999 SC 537, W received an outright transfer of the matrimonial home even though this would lead to the bankruptcy of H!

4 *Welsh v Welsh* 1994 SLT 828.

5 In *Wallis v Wallis* 1993 SLT 1348, there are *dicta* in the speeches of Lord Keith at 1351 and Lord Jauncey at 1352 to the effect that amending legislation might be necessary to achieve this result: however, it is thought that the FL(S)A 1985, s 8(2)(a) and (b) do not inhibit a court reducing an award in the way described above. While (a) and (b) are cumulative in the sense that an award must be justified by s 9 principles and reasonable in the light of the parties' resources, it does not follow that the court can make no order at all if the order which is *prima facie* justified by the s 9 principles is unreasonable in the light of the payer's resources: instead the court can *reduce* the award to a reasonable level. In these circumstances, it is still justified by s 9 principles. *Sed quaere.*

6 *Latter v Latter* 1990 SLT 805. FL(S)A 1985, s 8(2)(a) and (b) are cumulative in this sense; see discussion in preceding note. If otherwise, the s 9 principles would be otiose and the financial provision would simply be whatever the court in its discretion regarded as reasonable.

Principle 9(1)(a): The net value of the matrimonial or partnership property should be shared fairly between the parties to the marriage or civil partnership.

7.7 The first principle is s 9(1)(a) of the Family Law (Scotland) Act 1985. This provides that the net value of the matrimonial or partnership property should be shared fairly between the parties. The *net* value of the matrimonial or partnership property is the value of the property at the relevant date[1] minus any outstanding debts incurred by the parties: (a) during the marriage or civil partnership; or (b) before the marriage or registration of the civil partnership in so far as the pre-marital or pre-registration debts relate to matrimonial or partnership property. For example, if the couple's only property is a house bought during the marriage or civil partnership by means of a loan secured by a standard security over the property, the net value of the property at the relevant date will be the value of the house after deducting the outstanding loan.[2] Potential liability for any capital gains tax which might be incurred by a payer if property has to be realised in order to pay financial provision is not taken into account in determining the net value of the property. Instead, it will be a relevant factor in deciding whether it is reasonable in the light of the payer's resources that he or she should pay the amount of financial provision to which the payee is otherwise entitled under the s 9 principles.[3]

The relevant date is the date on which the parties cease to cohabit as spouses or civil partners, or the date of service of the summons in the action of divorce or dissolution if they continue living together.[4] Thus, if a couple ceases to cohabit in June 2022, that will be the relevant date for this purpose even though the action for divorce or dissolution may not be brought until several years later.[5] In law, a couple is deemed not to cohabit unless 'they are in fact living together as man and wife'.[6] Therefore, the relevant date may occur before a couple finally separate if they were not in fact living together 'as man and wife', albeit residing in the same house.[7] However, the cohabitation status of the parties is one of a number of relevant factors to be taken into consideration. For example, in *McLeish v McLeish*,[8] the parties disputed the relevant date – the wife claiming that it was January 2019, the husband claiming it was October 2016. Between these dates, the parties did not live together, but the husband regularly stayed at the wife's property. The sheriff took this, and a number of other findings into consideration (eg, socialising, sexual relations, attending events together, etc) and found the relevant date to be January 2019. The Sheriff Appeal Court upheld the sheriff's decision and stated, 'no one factor is determinative and the decision depends upon a consideration of all the relevant factors in the particular circumstances of the case ... The nature of cohabitation was but one factor'. In arriving at its decision, the

Sheriff Appeal Court referred *Banks v Banks,*[9] the leading case on relevant date, and to Lord Carloway's dicta,

> 'The task of the Court is to determine when the parties ceased to cohabit, having regard to the statutory provision that cohabitation occurs only when parties are "in fact living together as husband and wife". That is, as the provision itself states, a matter of fact. The ultimate determination of the issue must depend upon the particular circumstances of a given case. As a generality, the Court must look at the issue objectively; no doubt taking into account the illustrative factors mentioned by Professor Clive. There may, of course, be many others which emerge as relevant. The intention of the parties cannot be determinative of the issue. In that sense, there is no absolute requirement for one of the parties to have decided that the marriage or relationship has run its course or that such a decision should have been communicated by one party to the other. However, the intention of the parties and any communication of them to each other may be relevant factors in the equation.'

Accurately determining the relevant date is important as it will follow that the net value of the matrimonial property may be significantly affected where the relevant date is later, or earlier, than that claimed by one or other party.

---

1 Family Law (Scotland) Act 1995, s 10(3).

2 FL(S)A 1985, s 10(2)(a) and (b). The value of a house should not be discounted if it is still subject to a clawback provision in favour of a local authority. But the fact that there may be a clawback if the house must be sold is a relevant factor in determining whether it is reasonable to order the amount of financial provision otherwise due under the s 9 principles: *Sweeney v Sweeney* 2004 SLT 125; *Stuart v Stuart* 2001 SLT (Sh Ct) 20. Where property was encumbered before the marriage or civil partnership, and subsequently becomes matrimonial or partnership property, then the encumbrances at the relevant date must be proportioned as between pre-marital or pre-partnership debts and debts incurred during the marriage or partnership: this can be very complex. Only the latter are used to determine the net value of the matrimonial or partnership property: *Willson v Willson* [2008] CSOH 161.

3 *Sweeney v Sweeney* 2004 SLT 125; *Sweeney v Sweeney (No 2)* 2005 SLT 1141; *Coyle v Coyle* 2004 Fam LR 2. Expenses are not a relevant factor in determining what is reasonable: *McKinnon v McKinnon* 2008 GWD 12-226.

4 FL(S)A 1985, s 10(3). See: *McLeish v McLeish* [2022] SAC (Civ) 12.

5 This is subject to the FL(S)A 1985, s 10(7) which determines the relevant date after unsuccessful attempts at reconciliation. For discussion of s 10(7), see E M Clive *The*

Law of Husband and Wife in Scotland (4th edn, 1997, W Green/Sweet & Maxwell), p 445.

6 FL(S)A 1985, s 27(2). The phrase 'man and wife' must be interpreted to include same-sex spouses: Marriage and Civil Partnership (Scotland) Act 2014, s 4. This provision does not appear to have been amended to include civil partners, but it is thought that similar principles apply.

7 *Buczynska v Buczynski* 1989 SLT 558, *Samurai v Al-Samurai* [2014] C50 H 95 (Spouses cease) to cohabit as man and wife, when wife sent a solicitor's letter informing him she wanted a divorce, albeit that they continued to live under the same roof but as separated persons. For full discussion of the meaning of cohabitation see para **6.7**. The statutory definition of cohabitation for the purpose of divorce is identical to that in FL(S)A 1985, s 27(2).

8 [2022] SAC (Civ) 12. See also *M v M* [2021] SC EDIN 31.

9 *Banks v Banks* 2005 Fam LR 116, at para [33]. See also Morven Douglas, *Relevant date disputes*, Fam LB 2022, 178, 5–8.

(i) Matrimonial and partnership property

7.8 Matrimonial and partnership property is defined[1] as *all* the property belonging to the spouses, civil partners or either of them at the relevant date that was acquired by the spouse(s) or civil partner(s):

(a) before the marriage or registration for use by them as a family home or as furniture or plenishings for such a home, ie the family home and its contents; or

(b) during the marriage or partnership *but before the relevant date.*

The following property is excluded:

(a) property acquired before marriage or registration, with the important exception of property acquired for use as a family home and its contents;

(b) property acquired by a spouse or civil partner *after* the relevant date; and

(c) property acquired during the marriage or civil partnership from a third party by way of gift or succession.

We shall now consider the definition of matrimonial or partnership property in some detail.

The only property acquired before the marriage or registration which can constitute matrimonial or partnership property is the family home if it was acquired for this purpose and its furniture and plenishings. Any other kind of property, such as a business which was acquired before marriage, is *not* matrimonial or partnership property;[2] moreover, any increase in value of such property does not constitute matrimonial property even if the increase in value is attributable to the efforts of the spouses during the marriage.[3]

In *F v R*,[4] the court held that a property purchased by a husband in his sole name prior to the parties' relationship was not matrimonial property as it was clear from the evidence that the parties were not a couple and, at the time of purchase of the property, the husband was not contemplating family life with his wife, and the wife understood this to be the case. Compare this to *Mitchell v Mitchell*,[5] where the Inner House of the Court of Session held that a house bought before the marriage would be treated as matrimonial property only if it was acquired by the purchaser *with the intention* that it was to be used as a family home for the purchaser and the other partner.

Consider the following examples:

(1) A buys a house. If A marries B, the house is not matrimonial property even if A and B live there because A did not acquire the house with the intention that it should be a family home for A and B.[6]

(2) A buys a house when she is cohabiting with B with the intention that it should be a family home for A and B. If A and B marry, the house is matrimonial property as it was bought before the marriage with the intention that it should be a family home for A and B. It does not matter that at the time it was acquired A did not intend to marry B; it is enough that it was intended as a family home for A and B.[7]

(3) A buys a house when she is cohabiting with B with the intention that it should be a family home for A and B. A and B separate. A registers a civil partnership with C. The house is not partnership property as it was not acquired by A with the intention that it should be a family home for A and C.

(4) A buys a house during his marriage to B. The house is matrimonial property. A and B divorce. A remains in the house. A marries C. The house is not matrimonial property *vis-à-vis* the second marriage because it was not acquired with the intention of being a family home for A and C.[8]

(5) A buys a house during her marriage to B. The house is matrimonial property. A and B divorce. A remains in the house. A and B remarry. The house is matrimonial property because, although acquired before the second marriage, it was bought with the intention of being used as a family home for A and B, albeit when they were parties to the first marriage.[9]

(6) A buys a house during his marriage to B. The house is matrimonial property. A and B divorce. A sells the house and buys a new property. A and B remarry. The house is not matrimonial property because it was bought before the second marriage when A did not intend it to be used as a family home for A and B.

In *Corbett v Corbett*[10] before she married, the wife was the tenant of a local authority house. She decided to buy the property as an investment. Her cohabitant did not wish to contribute to the purchase of the house. After the house was purchased, the couple married. It was held that the house was not matrimonial property. At the time of purchase the house was already a family home: consequently, it had not been *bought* with the intention that it should be the couple's family home but simply as an investment. However, the court accepted that a house could be bought both as an investment and with the intention that the purchaser would live in it with the person who subsequently becomes a spouse or civil partner, ie that it should be a family home: in these circumstances, the house would be matrimonial or partnership property.

This area of the law remains very significant as more and more couples cohabit before they marry. It is particularly relevant in cases of dissolution of civil partnerships where the couple were cohabiting in a house belonging to one of the partners before the civil partnership was registered.

Where a spouse or civil partner owned a house before the marriage or registration, if he or she conveys a one-half *pro indiviso* share of the property to the other spouse or civil partner during the marriage or civil partnership, only the transferee's one-half *pro indiviso* share constitutes matrimonial or partnership property: the transferor's one-half *pro indiviso* share is not matrimonial or partnership property and therefore is not subject to fair sharing under s 9(1)(a).[11]

The current law may leave the less financially secure party to a divorce or dissolution at risk of being awarded little or no financial provision on divorce because the family home, which is often the main or only asset of a marriage or civil partnership, does not meet the definition of matrimonial or partnership property. For example, in *Maclellan v Maclellan*,[12] the wife sought a capital sum of half of the value of a croft where she had lived with her husband for their 26 years of marriage. However, the croft had been purchased by the husband before the parties had married and therefore, was not matrimonial property. As there was no other matrimonial property, no award was made.

All property acquired by spouses or civil partners during the marriage or civil partnership but before the relevant date is *prima facie* matrimonial or partnership property. This includes the house, furniture, motor cars, jewellery, savings and investments. It is irrelevant whether, as a matter of property law, the property is owned individually or in common. For example, although money, vehicles and pets are not household goods[13] and therefore are not presumed to be owned in common, they nevertheless constitute matrimonial or partnership property if acquired during the marriage or civil partnership. Where a spouse or civil partner owns a business prior to or during the marriage or civil partnership, then the question of it being matrimonial or partnership property can be a very complex matter.[14]

Any property acquired by way of gift *from a third party* or inheritance is excluded from the calculation of net matrimonial or partnership property.[15] Several points should be noted. First, gifts from one spouse or civil partner to the other constitute matrimonial or partnership property. For example, if A gives her civil partner, B, a ring, or B gives A a watch, both the ring and watch are matrimonial or partnership property: the exception only applies if A or B receives a gift from a third party, for example their parents.

Secondly, where a gift from a third party or an inheritance increases in value during the marriage or civil partnership, the increase in value does *not* constitute matrimonial or partnership property and is excluded.[16]

However, where a gift of money from a third party or an inheritance is used by a spouse or civil partner to buy property during the marriage or the partnership, the property acquired is matrimonial or partnership property. For example, A inherits £200,000 in shares. A sells shares worth £100,000 to purchase a house. The house is matrimonial or partnership property but the £100,000 in unsold shares is not because they remain part of her inheritance. As Lord McLean observed:[17]

> '... any property acquired by the parties during the marriage but before separation is matrimonial property even if it is purchased with funds which one of the parties has acquired by way of gift or succession. The funds themselves before their application in acquiring the property, would not, according to s 10(4), be matrimonial property'.

Property acquired after the relevant date but before the divorce or dissolution is not matrimonial or partnership property for the purpose of s 9(1)(a) – although it would be a part of a spouse or civil partner's resources for the application of other provisions in the Family Law (Scotland) Act 1985. A redundancy payment paid before the relevant date is matrimonial or partnership property but *not* if paid after the relevant date.[18] A tax refund paid after the relevant date in respect of income earned before the relevant date is matrimonial or partnership property.[19]

Most importantly, matrimonial and partnership property includes the portion of any rights or interests of either spouse or civil partner:

(a) under a life policy or similar arrangement; and

(b) in any benefits under a pension which either party has or may have (including such benefits payable in respect of the death of either party), which is referable to the period of marriage or civil partnership before the relevant date.[20]

It is necessary to determine the cash equivalent transfer value (CETV) of the pension at the relevant date.[21] After this is received, the parties must apportion it to determine the part which is referable to the period of marriage before the relevant date.[22] Where a lump sum is payable under the pension scheme on the death of one of the parties, the court on ordering a capital sum payment under s 8(1) of the FL(S)A 1985 can direct the trustees or managers to pay the whole or part of the lump sum when it becomes due to the other party to the marriage or civil partnership. This is known as a 'pension lump sum order'.[23]

It is possible for the spouses or civil partners to share a pension when it matures. This is done by the parties reaching agreement (a qualifying agreement)[24] or by obtaining a pension sharing order under s 8(1)(baa) of the FL(S)A 1985.[25] The basic state pension cannot be shared. Where there is to be pension sharing the court cannot make a pension lump sum order under s 12A of the 1985 Act.[26] The idea is that on divorce or dissolution the transferor spouse or civil partner's shareable rights in his or her pension arrangement are subject to a debit of the appropriate amount, and the transferee spouse or civil partner becomes entitled to a credit of that amount which is enforceable against the person responsible for running the pension scheme.[27] The pension credit can then be used to purchase rights in the pension arrangement in the transferee's own name. The pension will become payable when the transferee retires.

Most pension sharing is achieved by qualifying agreements. Before any agreement is signed, the transferor must have intimated to the managers of the pension scheme his or her intention to have his or her pension rights shared with the transferee.[28] The agreement must then be registered in the Books of Council and Session.[29] Qualifying agreements cannot be made after the parties have divorced or the partnership has been dissolved. Alternatively, the court can make a pension sharing order which will specify the percentage value or the amount to be deducted from the transferor's pension rights.[30] On divorce or dissolution, the parties send the decree, the qualifying agreement or pension order to the pension scheme managers; this should be done within two months of the extract decree.[31]The pension sharing can then be effected.[32] Pension sharing is an attractive option for younger persons who have their own career and sufficient funds to withstand the financial difficulties which usually accompany the breakdown of a relationship. Older payees might prefer to have the family home or an immediate capital sum payment since they will have less time to build up an alternative source of income for their retirement.[33]

---

1 Family Law (Scotland) Act 1985, s 10(4) and (4A). In *AB v CD* [2006] CSOH 200, where H set up a trust to manage his property in favour of a company which he controlled, the court nevertheless held that some of the property technically owned by

the trust still constituted matrimonial property belonging to H; H had simply treated the trust as a 'piggy bank'.

2 See *LWT or T v GPT* [2021] CSOH 6 in which business franchises formed prior to the parties' marriage did not constitute matrimonial property.

3 *Wilson v Wilson* 1999 SLT 249

4 *F v R* [2018] SC EDIN 51; 2018 Fam LR 146.

5 1995 SLT 426.

6 The house *would* be a matrimonial home for the purpose of the Matrimonial Homes (Family Protection) (Scotland) Act 1981: see para **5.6** ff.

7 *Mitchell v Mitchell* 1995 SLT 426 at 427, per the Lord Justice-Clerk (Ross).

8 *Ranaldi v Ranaldi* 1994 SLT (Sh Ct) 25.

9 These were the facts in *Mitchell v Mitchell* 1995 SLT 426.

10 2009 WL 2392276.

11 *Willson v Willson* [2008] CSOH 161. See also: *B v B* [2012] CSOH 21.

12 1988 SCLR 399

13 That is for the purposes of the FL(S)A 1985, s 25: discussed at para **4.5** ff.

14 See *SCA v MMA* [2020] CSIH 66 which demonstrates the complexities of determining ownership and valuation of businesses held by the husband's family. Note also that acute difficulties can arise in the valuation of such a business. Where the business is a partnership, the increase in the value of a spouse's capital account during the marriage is matrimonial property but land in the spouse's name may be owned on behalf of the partnership and not constitute matrimonial property: *Marshall v Marshall* [2007] CSOH 16. In *K v K* 2013 GWD 26-530 H deliberately ran down a business after the relevant date which W subsequently rescued. The value of the business at the relevant date was not treated as matrimonial property on the basis that it was not fair that W should compensate H in respect of property which he had squandered and abandoned: *sed quare*? Surely special circumstances existed under FL(S)A 1985, s 10(6)(c) to deviate from equal sharing in W's favour. On s 10(6), see paras **7.11** ff below.

15 Family Law (Scotland) Act 1985, ss 10(4) and 10(4A).

16 *Whittome v Whittome (No 1)* 1994 SLT 114 at 125, per Lord Osborne, disapproving the dictum of Lord Marnoch in *Latter v Latter* 1990 SLT 805. Lord Marnoch appeared to accept these strictures in *Wilson v Wilson* 1999 SLT 249. See, more recently, *F v R* 2018 Fam LR 146 in which there was a dispute over the status of an investment portfolio and property owned by the husband and acquired before the marriage.

17 *Davidson v Davidson* 1994 SLT 506 at 508. These provisions must not be construed too technically. If, for example, A's parents wish to give A and B a house as a wedding present, the fact that they give A the money to pay for the house and the missives of sale are signed by A would not prevent the house being regarded as a gift from A's parents and therefore *not* matrimonial property: see, for example, *Latter v Latter* 1990 SLT 805. In *Willson v Willson* [2008] CSOH 161, Lord Drummond Young held that funds owned by W before marriage or funds which were the realisation of property owned before marriage or acquired by gift or succession from a third party do not become matrimonial property merely because they are deposited in a joint bank account during the marriage. See also *JA v WA* [2017] CSOH 93.

18 *JA v WA* [2017] CSOH 93, in which the portion of a redundancy payment attributable to the marriage was considered to be matrimonial property. See also *Tyrrell v Tyrrell* 1990 SLT 406 where the court refused to treat a redundancy payment as analogous to an interest under a life policy or pension.

19 *Macritchie v Macritchie* 1994 SLT (Sh Ct) 72 and *Simpson v Simpson* 2007 Fam LR 134 in which the husband was the tenant of a farm throughout the marriage; a farm payment to which the husband was not yet entitled at the time of separation of the parties was not matrimonial property.

20 FL(S)A 1985, ss 10(5), 10(5A)

21 This information must be given by the pension scheme managers to the member on request within specified time limits. On valuation, see generally the Pensions on Divorce etc (Provision of Information) Regulations 2000, SI 2000/1048.

22 The formula is A × B/C where A is the CETV, B is the period of membership within the marriage and before the relevant date and C is the total period of membership before the relevant date.

23 FL(S)A 1985, s 12A.

24 Welfare Reform and Pensions Act 1999, s 28(1)(f); Pensions on Divorce etc (Pension Sharing) (Scotland) Regulations 2000, SI 2000/1051, regs 3 and 5.

25 The order is defined in FL(S)A 1985, s 27. See: *Douglas v Douglas* 2019 Fam LR 12

26 FL(S)A 1985, s 8(4), (5) and (6).

27 WRPA 1999, s 29.

28 Pensions on Divorce etc (Pension Sharing) (Scotland) Regulations 2000, SI 2000/1051, reg 2(e).

29 WRPA 1999, s 28(3)(b).

30 FL(S)A 1985, s 27. The court can include in the order provisions about the apportionment between the parties of any charges in respect of the costs of pension sharing: s 8A.

31 WRPA 1991, ss 28(7) and (8).

32 Where a spouse or civil partner is entitled to compensation payable under the Pensions Act 2004, the court is disempowered from making a pension sharing order or a pension lump sum order out of such compensation: FL(S)A 1985 ss 10(4A) and (5A). But once the compensation is paid, the proportion referable to the period of the marriage or civil partnership is matrimonial or partnership property and is subject to fair division and subject to all the orders under s 8 except those relating to pensions. If a pension lump sum order has already been made, references to the pension are to be taken as references to any compensation that has been paid out: ss 12A(7ZA), (7ZB) and (7ZC). Any agreements which contain provisions in relation to pensions remain liable to be set aside or varied by the court even if the Board of the Pension Protection Fund assumes responsibility for the pension scheme: ss 16 (2A), (2B) and (2C).

33 The detailed issue of pensions and pension sharing is complex and problematic and beyond the scope of this book. For further reading, see: *McDonald v McDonald* [2017] UKSC 52; John Speir, *Pensions after McDonald v McDonald – When B changed from being a zero to a potential special circumstance*, Fam LB 2017, 149, 1–5; and the Case Comment on *R v R* 2018 Fam LR 63 and *LV v IV* 2018 Fam LR 128 Fam LB 2019, 157, 7–8. See also *Douglas v Douglas* [2019] SC PER 4.

(ii) Identifying matrimonial and partnership property

7.9 In applying the principle in s 9(1)(a) of the Family Law (Scotland) Act 1985, the first task is to identify the matrimonial or partnership property which should be shared fairly between the parties. This can often be a source of contention between the parties. The principle in *Little v Little*[1] remains relevant, where the Inner House of the Court of Session held that there was no need for the court to calculate a single value of the total matrimonial property at the relevant date; moreover, the court could leave out certain items, for example a couple's motor cars or personal possessions, if this would have no practical result on the claim for financial provision. In addition, it was accepted that the matrimonial home could be excluded if a property transfer order was desirable in the circumstances of the case.[2] It is submitted that the approach of the Inner House runs counter to the express language of ss 10(4) and (4A) of the FL(S)A 1985 which refers to *all* the couple's property at the relevant date and therefore a court should still proceed to calculate the total net value of their property at that date.[3]

Let us consider a typical example:

A bought a house for £100,000 shortly before he married B. A bought the house intending that it should be used as their family home. A paid a down-payment of £10,000 and raised the rest of the price by a loan secured by a standard security over the house. Title to the house was taken in A's name. When A and B separated after 16 years of marriage, the house was worth £140,000 with an outstanding loan of £2,000. During the marriage A bought a car, a horse and golf clubs: these were worth £16,000, £9,000 and £1,000 respectively at the time of separation. During the marriage B bought furniture and a van: these were worth £4,000 and £6,000 respectively at the time of separation. B also inherited a ring worth £10,000 at the time of separation. A had contributed to an occupational pension scheme which he joined four years before A and B married. The CETV of A's interest in the scheme when A and B separated was £120,000. A's shares that he bought before the marriage were worth £60,000 at the time of separation. B's savings made from her earnings during the marriage were worth £10,000. After separation, B won £5,000 on the lottery. The relevant date is the date when the parties ceased to cohabit, ie the date on which A and B separated. At that date, the net value of the matrimonial property consists of the following:

(1) The matrimonial home. While the property was acquired by A *before* marriage, it was acquired with the intention to use it as a family home for A and B and therefore qualifies as matrimonial property. Its net value at the relevant date was: £140,000 – £2,000 (outstanding mortgage) = £138,000.

(2) A's car, horse and golf clubs, ie property acquired by him during the marriage and before the relevant date was worth: £16,000 + £9,000 + £1,000 = £26,000.

(3) B's furniture and van, ie property acquired by her during the marriage and before the relevant date, but excluding the diamond ring which was acquired by way of succession from a third party, was worth: £4,000 + £6,000 = £10,000.

(4) B's savings made during the marriage and before the relevant date are worth £10,000. A's shares are excluded as he acquired them *before* marriage. B's lottery winnings are excluded because she acquired them *after* the relevant date.

(5) The proportion of A's interest in the occupational pension scheme which is referable to the period of marriage before the relevant date has to be calculated. A has been in the scheme for 20 years, 16 of which were during the marriage and before the relevant date. At the relevant date CETV is £120,000. Therefore, the portion referable to the period of marriage is:

$$\pounds 120{,}000 \times \frac{16}{20} = \pounds 96{,}000$$

Thus, the total value of the net matrimonial property at the relevant date is £280,000.

By s 10(1) of the FL(S)A 1985, fair sharing of matrimonial and partnership property is *prima facie* equal sharing. In the example, A and B are each *prima facie* entitled to £140,000. As B already owns property valued at £20,000, ie £10,000 furniture and a van and £10,000 savings, A must transfer £120,000 to B. In deciding whether this should be done, the court must consider whether it is reasonable to do so in the light of the couple's resources.[4] These will include the non-matrimonial property belonging to the spouses, ie A's shares worth £60,000 and B's ring and lottery win which are worth £10,000 and £5,000 respectively, ie £15,000. In these circumstances, it is thought that it would be reasonable to order A to make a payment to B of £120,000 – to be paid in instalments if his capital is not easily realisable.

It should be emphasised that it is the net value of matrimonial or partnership property which is subject to fair division. If, for example, C has assets worth £100,000 and D has no assets but has incurred credit card debts of £20,000, the outstanding debt must be deducted from the value of C's assets. Thus, the net value of the matrimonial property is £80,000. It might be thought that to obtain an equal division of the property, C should transfer £40,000 to D. But D still has a debt of £20,000 and once it is paid D is left with only £20,000 while C has £40,000. In these circumstances, in order to achieve an equal division, C must make a capital sum payment of £50,000 to D. so that after the debt is paid both C and D are left with £30,000 from the property.[5] While this result is fair if D's debt was incurred for the benefit of the family, it is less so if D had done so for selfish or self-indulgent reasons. However, if that were the case, the court could deviate from a 50:50 division in C's favour on the ground that D dissipated the matrimonial property.[6]

---

1 1990 SLT 785.

2 The court maintained that the court's discretion to depart from equal sharing in special circumstances under the Family Law (Scotland) Act 1985, s 10(1) and (6) was wide enough to exclude certain items from being treated as matrimonial property at all. However, it is thought that the discretion only operates *after* all the couple's matrimonial property at the relevant date has been valued: see para **7.11** ff. See *Jacques v Jacques* 1995 SLT 963; *R v R* 2000 Fam LR 43.

3 Nevertheless the Inner House continues to allow judges at first instance considerable latitude: 'The sheriff decided to take a broad and practical approach, without finding it necessary to do what is required by a strict reading of s 10(4) of the Act, which is to take into account all the property belonging to the parties or either of them at the relevant date which is comprised within the definition of matrimonial property … The question whether it was necessary to value every item of property comprised in the matrimonial property and to calculate a single lump sum representing the net value of the entirety of it was a matter for the discretion of the sheriff': *Jacques v Jacques* 1995 SLT 963 at 965, per the Lord President (Hope).

4 FL(S)A 1985, s 8(2)(b).

5 See, for example, *Russell v Russell* 2005 Fam LR 96 and *Lindsay v Lindsay* [2007] Fam LR 18.

6 FL(S)A 1985, s 10(6)(c). See also: *Peberdy v Peberdy* 2020 Fam LR 59 (wife's conduct in delaying proceedings) and *McCallion v McCallion* [2020] CSIH 43 (husband's conduct adversely affected the value of the matrimonial property). See para **7.14**.

(iii) Valuation Date: The Wallis v Wallis problem

7.10 It must always be remembered that the fund that is to be shared fairly is the net value of the matrimonial or partnership property *at the relevant* date.[1] However, there may be several months or years between the relevant date on which parties ceased to cohabit and the conclusion of the financial provision award. For example, consider the following situation: A and her civil partner, B, own the family home in common. At the relevant date the house is worth £100,000, ie A and B have a one-half *pro indiviso* share worth £50,000. After separation, B remains in the family home. At the time of the dissolution, the house is worth £120,000. B wishes to live in the house. In these circumstances, it might be thought sensible that A transfers her one-half *pro indiviso* share to B in return for a counter-balancing capital sum payment of £60,000, ie the value of A's *pro indiviso* share of the property *at the date of dissolution.*

However, in *Wallis v* Wallis,[2] it was held that the maximum capital sum payment which could be awarded in this situation was half the value of the house *at the relevant date*, ie £50,000 in our example. Accordingly, if a property transfer order was made, B would receive an asset worth £60,000 in return for a capital sum payment of £50,000, ie B would obtain a windfall of £10,000. This result is clearly unfortunate.[3] To deal with the *Wallis* problem, s 10(3A) was added to the Family Law (Scotland) Act 1985. This provides that *when a property transfer order is made*, the date when the property being transferred is to be valued is no longer to be the relevant date but the 'appropriate valuation date'. The appropriate valuation date is to be the date agreed by the parties or in the absence of such an agreement, the date on which the property transfer order is made: this will usually be the date of divorce or dissolution. So, in the example, in the absence of an agreement between A and B, the house will be valued at the date of dissolution rather than the relevant date so that B must make a capital payment of £60,000 to A and no longer receives the *Wallis* windfall. Given that s 10(3A) is only triggered when the court intends to make a transfer of property order under s 8(1)(aa), it is designed to make the smallest possible inroad into the fundamental principle that for the purpose of fair sharing under s 9(1)(a) the property is valued at the relevant date.

In the absence of a date agreed between the parties, the appropriate valuation date is to be the date when the property transfer order is made, ie the date of divorce or dissolution. But s 10(3A) also provides that in exceptional circumstances the appropriate valuation date can be determined by the court being a date as near as may be to the date when the transfer of property order is made. In *Willson v Willson*,[4] the wife obtained a transfer of property order of the husband's one-half *pro indiviso* share of the former matrimonial home. Due to delays on the part of the husband, if the value of the property had increased at the date of the order, Lord Drummond Young was prepared to treat the delay as exceptional circumstances and revert to an earlier date as the appropriate valuation date when the house had a lower value. It was unfair that the husband should benefit from the higher value as the wife had paid the mortgage and running costs of the house since the relevant date. However, if, because of even further delays on the husband's part, the value of the house had fallen substantially at the date of the order, this would be the appropriate valuation date.

Nevertheless, difficulties can be anticipated in determining the appropriate valuation date. Consider the following example:

> At the relevant date, A and B are owners in common of a family home valued at £300,000; A has investments valued at £250,000 and B has investments valued at £50,000. The net matrimonial property is therefore £600,000 and both are entitled to an equal share ie £300,000. As B already has property worth £200,000, ie B's one-half *pro indiviso* share of the house (£150,000) and B's investments (£50,000), A has to make a capital sum payment to B of £100,000. At the time of divorce, the value of the house is £500,000. A's investments are worth £750,000 but B's have collapsed and are worthless. B seeks a property transfer order of A's one-half *pro indiviso* share of the property. Under *Wallis*, A's share is valued at the relevant date, ie £150,000. Given that B is entitled to £100,000 from A, B need only transfer £50,000 to A in return

for A's share of the house. Under s 10(3A), A's share will be valued at the appropriate date, the date of the transfer order, ie £250,000. B is still only entitled to £100,000 from A and now B must transfer £150,000 in respect of the transfer of A's one-half *pro indiviso* share to B. Given that A's investments have prospered and that B's have failed, would these constitute exceptional circumstances when the court could depart from the rule that *prima facie* the appropriate valuation date is the date of divorce? For in our example, although B's *pro indiviso* share of the house has also risen since the relevant date, B has no other assets and cannot afford to purchase A's share if it is valued at the date of divorce as opposed to the relevant date.

It should also be noted that, where one spouse or civil partner wishes to take over the matrimonial or family home after divorce or dissolution, then, if the property requires to be mortgaged, he or she must meet the criteria to be a mortgage holder as laid down by the mortgage lender.[5]

---

1 Family Law (Scotland) Act 1985, s 10(2).

2 1992 SLT 672 (IH); 1993 SLT 1348 (HL).

3 The inequality that might derive from using the property valuation on the relevant date can be seen in some pre-section 10(3A) cases. In *Dible v Dible* 1997 SLT 787, for example, at the relevant date the matrimonial property was valued at £164,000: this included a house valued at £59,000. W obtained a property transfer order of the house which at the time of divorce was worth £83,000. The sheriff ordered H to make a capital sum payment of £12,000 so that she received approximately 60 per cent of the value of the matrimonial property at the relevant date. (The sheriff thought a 40:60 split was fair sharing in the circumstances.) On appeal, following *Wallis v Wallis* 1993 SLT 1348, it was held that the sheriff should have ignored the increase in value of the house when considering the appropriate balancing capital sum payment, ie the property transfer accounted for only £59,000 of what was due as opposed to £83,000. Consequently, the capital sum payment was increased by £21,000 to £33,000. Again, the injustice inherent in *Wallis* is readily apparent. Although criticised, the decision was binding on the courts: *Kennedy v Kennedy* 2004 Fam LR 70: *Christie v Christie* 2004 SLT (Sh Ct) 95. Courts became reluctant to make property transfer orders unless there was other matrimonial property and the transferee's 'windfall' could be treated as her share of that property. The injustice could also be alleviated by an award of interest on the transferor's capital sum being backdated to the relevant date. Where the house was owned in common, instead of a property transfer order, the court could make an order for the sale of the property, enabling both parties to benefit from any increase in its value since the relevant date: Family Law (Scotland) Act 1985, s 14(2)(a): *Lewis v Lewis* 1993 SCLR 33; *Jacques v Jacques* 1995 SLT 963; *McCaskill v McCaskill* 2004 Fam LR 123 (incidental orders for sale of property owned in common).

4 [2008] CSOH 161.
5 *N v N* 2021 SLT (Sh Ct) 250.

(iv) Special circumstances

7.11 By s 10(1) of the Family Law (Scotland) Act 1985, fair sharing is *prima facie* equal sharing of the net value of all the matrimonial and partnership property. However, s10(1) also provides that the court can depart from equal sharing if justified by special circumstances. It is important to appreciate that the provision is general. It is always open to argue that the facts of a particular case constitute special circumstances which justify the court deviating from the principle that fair sharing means equal sharing. Nevertheless, it is expressly enacted that special circumstances include those listed in s 10(6) of the 1985 Act. Whether or not to deviate from the fair sharing is equal sharing principle, is a matter entirely at the discretion of the court and a judge is not obliged to deviate when there are facts which amount to special circumstances in s 10(6).[1]

The special circumstances listed in s 10(6) of the 1985 Act are discussed below.

1 *Douglas v Douglas* [2019] SC PER 4, *Jacques v Jacques* 1997 SC (HL) 20.

(a) The terms of any agreement between the parties on the ownership or division of any of the matrimonial or partnership property.[1]

7.12 The most common example of such an agreement is a joint minute tendered to the court hearing the divorce or dissolution in which the parties have agreed how certain items of matrimonial or partnership property are to be divided. The parties may also have entered an agreement made before the marriage or registration on how the matrimonial or partnership property should be divided on divorce or dissolution.[2] Such agreements are increasing in popularity and often deal with all the couple's property.[3] On the other hand, the agreement might relate to a particular piece of property. For example, while a gift made by one spouse or civil partner to another is matrimonial or partnership property, the couple might agree expressly or impliedly that gifts *inter se* should be excluded from fair sharing under s 9(1)(a) of the Family Law (Scotland) Act 1985.

1 Family Law (Scotland) Act 1985, s 10(6)(a).
2 *Fox v Fox* [2019] SC STI 3, where the husband founded on a verbal agreement made before the marriage that his pre-marriage savings which contributed to the deposit, fees and purchase of the matrimonial home, should be returned to him if the couple divorce. The sheriff stated that, if such an agreement was a prerequisite to marriage, the husband 'could and should have obtained it in writing'.
3 For a more detailed discussion on ante nuptial or registration agreements, see para **7.22**.

(b) The source of the funds or assets used to acquire any of the matrimonial or partnership property where those funds or assets were not derived from the income or efforts of the parties during the marriage.[1]

7.13 Where a spouse or civil partner buys property during the marriage or civil partnership from funds which were not matrimonial or partnership property, for example the proceeds of the sale of a house prior to the marriage or registration or pre-marital or pre-civil partnership savings, the court can use this provision to give the spouse or civil partner an increased share of the matrimonial or partnership property purchased from these funds.[2] Although property acquired from a third party as a result of gift or inheritance is excluded from the definition of matrimonial or partnership property, where a spouse or civil partner uses funds acquired by gift or inheritance during the marriage or civil partnership to reduce a mortgage on a matrimonial or family home or to buy an item to be used in the marriage or civil partnership, this will *prima facie* be matrimonial or partnership property which is subject to fair sharing.[3] In these circumstances, the court has been prepared to deviate from the principle that equality is fairness in order to compensate the party who purchased the property as it was not bought from funds deriving from the income or efforts of the parties during the marriage. But, in *Fox v Fox*,[4] a husband unsuccessfully claimed that monies derived from work bonuses and a life insurance payment should not be included in the calculation of matrimonial property.

Conversely, if the property did derive from the income and efforts of the parties during the marriage or civil partnership, there is no ground for deviation under s 10(6)(b) of the Family Law (Scotland) Act 1985. This can lead to some harsh decisions. For example, if A worked to support B, a spouse or civil partner who, by choice rather than circumstance, has no paid employment and does not contribute financially to the household, then any property A acquired during the marriage, for example if she purchased the rented accommodation in which the couple lived, would be subject to equal division between them. There is no room for deviation under s 10(6)(b) as the property was acquired as a result of A's income and efforts during the marriage: s 10(6)(b) only applies when the funds did *not derive from the income and efforts of the parties during the marriage or civil partnership.*

1 Family Law (Scotland) Act 1985, s 10(6)(b).

2 See, for example, *Douglas v Douglas* [2019] SC PER 4 in which both parties relied on a s 10(6)(b) source of funds argument claiming that elements of their pension funds had been used to acquire the matrimonial property.

3 *Fox v Fox* [2019] SC STI 3 in which the husband claimed that a gift given to him by his mother and which he used to reduce the mortgage of the matrimonial home, should be considered a loan and, as such, should be considered special circumstances to justify unequal sharing in his favour.

4 See fn 3, above.

(c) Any destruction, dissipation or alienation of property by either party.[1]

7.14 This provision enables the court to deviate from the principle that fair sharing is equal sharing when a spouse or civil partner has destroyed, dissipated or alienated matrimonial property before or after the relevant date.[2] This provision is additional to the general protection in s 18 of the Family Law (Scotland) Act 1985 against transactions likely to defeat claims for, *inter alia*, financial provision on divorce or dissolution.[3]

1 Family Law (Scotland) Act 1985, s 10(6)(c).

2 *R v R* 2018 SCLR 695.

3 FL(S)A 1985, s 18, is discussed at para **7.23** ff. This provision should perhaps have been applied in *K v K* 2013 GWD 26-530.

(d) The nature of the family or partnership property, the use made of it (including use for business purposes or as a matrimonial home) and the extent to which it is reasonable to expect it to be realised or divided or used as security.[1]

7.15 This is probably the most important of the special circumstances which may justify deviation from the principle that fair sharing is equal sharing. If spouse A uses the family home for business purposes, it might be unreasonable to order A to sell the property in order to realise its value to make a capital payment to spouse B. In those circumstances, the court could allow A to retain the property and order A to pay to B whatever capital sum A could afford to compensate B for the loss of B's *prima facie* entitlement to half the value of the house. This capital sum need not be equivalent to half the net value of the house, ie the court could decrease B's share, but it would normally still be substantial. A could be required to raise the capital by a second mortgage or the capital sum could be paid by instalments out of A's income. Alternatively, if A is to retain the property in which the business exists, then it is still possible to arrive at equal sharing without unfairness by transferring other substantial assets to B.[2] Similarly, while a spouse's business assets acquired during the marriage constitute matrimonial property, the court may award less than half their net value to the other spouse as clearly they may not be easily realisable.[3]

Where there are children of the family who need a home, the court could order that the family home be transferred outright to the spouse or civil partner who is looking after the children. If the children reside with A, her share of the rest of the matrimonial property would be reduced proportionately even if the reduction does not fully compensate B for the loss of half the value of all the matrimonial property.[4] In *Cuniff v Cuniff*,[5] the court ordered that the husband transfer his one-half *pro indiviso* share of the family home to the wife, even though he would then face bankruptcy. The fact that the party who continues to live in the family home may, in the view of the other party, not be able to afford to continue living in the family home, is not a matter for the court to determine.[6]

It should be noted that this provision is concerned with the use made of the property as a matrimonial home. In *Hales v Hales*,[7] after the couple separated the wife continued to live in the former matrimonial home. Subsequently she began a new relationship and her partner moved into the house. He suffered a brain aneurism and the house was modified by Glasgow City Council at significant cost so as to be suitable for the partner's ongoing needs. In the action for divorce, the wife resisted the proposed sale of the house on the basis of special circumstances under s 10(6)(d) due to the substantial modifications that had been carried out and her inability to finance similar modifications on an alternative property. The court held that the defence was irrelevant as s 10(6)(d) referred to the matrimonial home and was therefore confined to the circumstances of the parties to the marriage and their children.

---

1 Family Law (Scotland) Act 1985, s 10(6)(d).

2 *McConnell v McConnell (No 2)* 1997 Fam LR 108.

3 *Morrison v Morrison* 1989 SCLR 574; *Crockett v Crockett* 1992 SCLR 591. Alternatively, the capital sum could be ordered to be paid by instalments or payment delayed until a later date, with interest to run on the capital sum from the date of divorce (or earlier). In *Sweeney v Sweeney (No 2)* 2005 SLT 1141, the Inner House of the Court of Session accepted that there could be a deviation under s 10(6)(d) even though the assets, which were difficult to realise, had been invested by H in his business between the relevant date and the date of divorce. But in the event the court preferred to take account of this, not by awarding W less than 50 per cent, but by making the capital sum payable by instalments.

4 In *Cooper v Cooper* 1989 SCLR 347, the wife obtained a property transfer of the matrimonial home even though it was the couple's major capital asset (however, the husband did not require accommodation as he was seriously ill). In *JR v AR* 2012 GWD 39-765, W received a larger share of the proceeds of the sale of the former matrimonial home so that she could purchase a suitable home for herself and their children. The sheriff accepted that an unequal share of the proceeds would be appropriate referring to 'a legitimate objective under the principles of the Act: namely that account should be taken of the parties' housing needs'. A pension sharing order was made in respect of W's pension to offset the imbalance and achieve equal division.

5 1999 SC 537. See also *Peacock v Peacock* 1994 SLT 40 the couple had few assets except their house, title to which was in joint names. W looked after the children and H was unemployed and unable to contribute to the children's aliment. W had paid the mortgage instalments after H left. The Inner House of the Court of Session ordered H to transfer his one-half *pro indiviso* share of the house to W in return for W's assignation to him of her interest in a small life policy. The fact that there was little matrimonial property apart from the house which was required as a home for the children constituted special circumstances reducing H's share of the net value of the house to nil.

6 *Scott v Scott* [2021] 5 WLUK 503 and *Adams v Adams (No 1)* 1997 SLT 144 in which the Lord Ordinary (Gill) refused to transfer the matrimonial home to W because she could not afford to run that house which was too big for her and the children.

7 2012 GWD 7-123.

(e) Actual or prospective liability for any expenses of valuation or transfer of property in connection with the divorce or dissolution of the civil partnership[1]

7.16 In applying the principles in s 9 of the Family Law (Scotland) Act 1985, generally, *prima facie* the conduct of either party is not taken into account.[2] For example, if a marriage or civil partnership has irretrievably broken down on the establishment of A's adultery or a B's behaviour, this is irrelevant and does not affect the principle that fair sharing of matrimonial property *prima facie* means equal sharing. Where a spouse or civil partner's conduct has adversely affected the financial resources of the couple, for example by dissipation of assets or unreasonably refusing to find employment, the conduct will be relevant.[3] Often, of course, such conduct may well have already been taken into account by virtue of s 10(6)(c) of the FL(S)A 1985, ie deviation from equality of sharing as a result of destruction, dissipation or alienation of property.[4] The reason why, as a general rule, misconduct is not relevant is that the principle in s 9(1)(a) is intended to recognise that a spouse or civil partner deserves a fair share of the matrimonial or partnership property as a result of his or her contribution to the marriage or civil partnership; responsibility for its breakdown should not undermine that entitlement unless the spouse or civil partner's conduct has adversely affected the assets which are to be divided.

1 Family Law (Scotland) Act 1985, s 10(6)(e).
2 FL(S)A 1985, s 11(7). See, for example, *Gracie v Gracie* 1997 SLT (Sh Ct) 15.
3 FL(S)A 1985, s 11(7)(a), (b). See: *McCallion v McCallion* [2020] CSIH 43.
4 See para **7.14**.

Principle 9(1)(b)	Fair account should be taken of any economic advantage derived by either person from contributions by the other, and of any economic disadvantage suffered by either person in the interests of the other person or of the family.

7.17 This principle is intended to compensate a spouse or civil partner who, whether before or during the marriage or partnership, has either:

(1) made a contribution to the economic advantage of the other, for example, by putting money into the other person's business or working in the business as an unpaid employee, or by one person making contributions from inheritances or pre-relationship savings[1] or

(2) has suffered an economic disadvantage in the interests of the other party or the family, for example, by one person giving up a well-paid job to look after children.[2]

Where a spouse or civil partner has suffered an economic disadvantage, there need not be a corresponding economic advantage to the other; it is sufficient if the economic disadvantage was sustained in the interests of the other party or the family.[3] 'Economic advantage' is defined in s 9(2) and includes gains in capital, income and earning capacity; 'economic disadvantage' is to be construed accordingly.[4] Contributions include indirect and non-financial contributions, for example the upkeep of the family home or contributing to a family business. A 'contribution' made by a spouse or civil partner in keeping the home and caring for the family is expressly recognised.[5] In *Bradbury v Bradbury*,[6] the wife pursuer sought and was awarded a capital sum and periodical allowance on the basis of the contribution that she had made to the husband's farm (which did not constitute matrimonial property) and to the upbringing of their children over the course of their 22-year marriage. Where items of matrimonial or partnership property have increased in value between the relevant date and the date of divorce or dissolution, the courts have consistently refused to allow s 9(1)(b) to be used to give the applicant a share in the increase in value of the asset because the increase is not a result of any economic contribution of the applicant during that period. Nor is the increase in value a special circumstance for deviation under s 10(1) of the 1985 Act.[7]

It is important to note that principle 9(1)(b) also applies to economic advantages made, economic disadvantages suffered and contributions made by a party *before* the marriage or registration took place.[8] Thus, for example, if A had worked before a couple married or registered a civil partnership in order to support B when B was undergoing training for a profession, that contribution could be taken into account under s 9(1)(b) of the Family Law (Scotland) Act 1985 even though it was made before the parties married or registered their civil partnership.

By s 11(2) of the FL(S)A 1985, the court must consider whether the economic advantages or disadvantages sustained by either spouse have been balanced by the economic advantages or disadvantages sustained by the other. It is only when there is an economic imbalance in the applicant's favour that an award can be made. As the Lord Ordinary (Lady Smith) observed in *Coyle v Coyle*:[9]

> 'It is important to recognise that Parliament did not, in the 1985 Act, provide that whenever a couple divorce after a marriage in which one has been the breadwinner and one has been the homemaker, the latter must receive extra compensatory financial provision on divorce.'

In *Douglas v Douglas*[10] Sheriff Collin stated that,

> 'While each case will to some extent turn on its own facts, it seems to me that the case law supports the general position … that [t]here is a recognition that the relative economic advantages and disadvantages enjoyed and suffered by parties to a marriage, where (typically) the wife gives up employment to care for children and provide domestic services, will often cancel each other out, at least to the extent that unequal division is not justified in the wife's favour by section 9(1)(b).'

Claims under this principle are particularly difficult to quantify.[11] In *Douglas v Douglas* (above) by the end of the marriage, the parties had little to show economically for their years together and the sheriff relied on the strength of the parties' evidence to arrive at any resulting imbalance under s 11(2)(a).

The court will also have to determine whether or not any resulting imbalance has been or will be corrected by a fair sharing of the value of the matrimonial or partnership property under principle 9(1)(a) or otherwise.[12] Since any awards under principle 9(1)(b) must take the form of capital sum payments or property transfer orders, in practice principles 9(1)(a) and (b) are considered together. Thus, a claim under s 9(1)(b) has been met by making a property transfer order which gave the transferee not only a fair share of the matrimonial property but also the increase in value of the house between the relevant date and the date of divorce: this increase in value satisfied the s 9(1)(b) claim.[13] Again a claim by a wife under s 9(1)(b) was used to justify refusing to give the husband a share of the matrimonial property which had all been purchased by the wife.[14] In particular, having determined that a spouse or civil partner should receive compensation under principle 9(1)(b) for contributions to the family during the marriage or the civil partnership, the court may decide that the most appropriate form it should take is an outright transfer of the family home to the spouse or civil partner even though they would thereby receive more than half the value of the matrimonial or civil partnership property to which she was *prima facie* entitled under principle 9(1)(a).[15]

Section 9(1)(b) has been used where there is no matrimonial or partnership property which is subject to fair sharing under s 9(1)(a). In *Ranaldi v Ranaldi*,[16] the couple's home was not matrimonial property therefore the wife was not entitled to a share of its value under principle 9(1)(a). However, during the marriage, the wife had taken in boarders, paid off the loan over the property and enhanced its value. As a result of principle 9(1)(b), she was awarded a capital sum payment of half the increase in the value of the property during the marriage. A similar approach was taken in *Bradbury v Bradbury*[17] when a farmer's wife obtained a capital sum in respect of her contribution to running a farm which was not matrimonial property and therefore not subject to fair division under s 9(1)(a) of the FL(S)A 1985.

As in principle 9(1)(a), in applying principle 9(1)(b) a spouse or civil partner's conduct is irrelevant unless it has adversely affected the financial resources of the couple.[18]

In *McCallion v McCallion*[19] the husband's conduct was found to have had an adverse effect on the net value of the matrimonial property.

Principle 9(1)(b) of FL(S)A 1985 was originally intended to recognise the economic contributions made by women who had followed the traditional role of caring for children and maintaining the family household within the marriage.[20] The economic contribution so made and the economic disadvantages sustained in doing so were to be compensated by an award under s 9(1)(b) of the FL(S)A 1985. This has been problematic for two main reasons. First, it is unrealistic to assess the economic value of caring for a child and maintaining a family home and to balance this with the financial contributions made by the working parent to the caring parent to allow him or her to carry out the role. Secondly, since only capital sum payments and/or transfer of property orders are available under s 9(1)(b) of the 1985 Act, the courts may be reluctant to make an award if there are no capital assets. However, it is submitted that a capital sum payment is nevertheless appropriate in these circumstances – to be paid by instalments out of the working parent's future income.[19] The solution to the limitations of s 9(1)(b) has been to award periodical allowances under principle 9(1)(e). Professor Joe Thomson was of the view that this is often a distortion of the function of principle s 9(1)(e). Instead, recourse should be made to principle 9(1)(b), which has been designed to compensate the party in this situation. Professor Thomson also held the view that the under-utilisation of s 9(1)(b) is perhaps the most disappointing feature of the way in which the FL(S)A 1985 has been applied in practice.[21]

---

1 See *JA v WA* 2018 SCLR 157: The court held that the three items of heritable property should be sold and the proceeds divided in proportions of two-thirds to the pursuer and one-third to the defender to reflect the contributions that the pursuer had made from gifts, inheritances and pre-marital property.

2 In *Dougan v Dougan* 1998 SLT (Sh Ct) 27 Sheriff Morrison awarded the wife pursuer a capital sum, stating that '… it is quite clear that the pursuer suffered an economic disadvantage in giving up a well-paid position in the interests of the family and, even though the marriage was a short one, the disadvantage to the pursuer was substantial'. In *P v P* [2012] CSIH 15, while the court was satisfied that W had undoubtedly suffered economic disadvantage as a result of giving up her employment in London, she had not averred that she had done so in order to care for their child: accordingly, the s 9(1)(b) test was not satisfied.

3 In *Galloway v Galloway* 2003 Fam LR 10, H transferred 25 per cent of the shares in a private company to W. H administered the fund and took the dividends. W paid tax on the dividends at the higher rate. This was held to be an economic disadvantage.

4 Family Law (Scotland) Act 1985, s 9(2). It is suggested that 'construed accordingly' means: economic disadvantage means disadvantage suffered whether before or during the marriage or civil partnership and includes losses in capital, in income and earning power. It therefore does not include losses which arise *after* the divorce or dissolution, including loss of earning power. Yet we cannot calculate loss of earning power unless we consider how the claimant is likely to fare in the employment market after divorce or dissolution. The view that future losses should not be compensated was upheld by the sheriff in *Dougan v Dougan* 1998 SLT (Sh Ct) 27.

5 FL(S)A 1985, s 9(2).

6 [2021] CSOH 113; 2021 Fam LR 157.

7 See para **7.11**.

8 Contributions made after a couple have separated but before the divorce or dissolution are also included.

9 2004 Fam LR 2 at 9. Lady Smith also suggested that before there could be a claim under s 9(1)(b) there has to be an identifiable economic advantage to one spouse which

derives from an identifiable contribution by the other: *sed quaere*. In the context of economic disadvantage at least, it is thought that it is enough if the economic disadvantage was sustained in the interests of the other party or the family.

10 [2019] SC PER 4.

11 See *F v R* 2018 Fam LR 146 in which the sheriff stated that 'an element of broad brush is inevitably required'.

12 *JA v WA* 2018 SCLR 157 (Unequal sharing of matrimonial property resulted because the value of the property derived from the husband's contribution by way of gift, inheritance and pre-marital assets.) See also *Harris v Harris* 2013 Fam LR 122 (Pursuer's economic disadvantage in using her inheritance to reduce the mortgage over the former matrimonial home was compensated by deviation from equal sharing of the matrimonial property in her favour as a result of s 10(6)(b) special circumstances.) An award under FL(S)A 1985, s 9(1)(b) is intended to be *additional* to fair sharing of matrimonial property under s 9(1)(a); therefore it is thought that an imbalance will not have been corrected unless as in *Harris* the payee has obtained more than half the net value of the matrimonial or partnership property under s 9(1)(a). In *Louden v Louden* 1994 SLT 381, the wife's share of the matrimonial property was increased to 55 per cent.

13 *Coyle v Coyle* 2004 Fam LR 2.

14 *Symanski v Symanski (No 2)* 2005 Fam LR 2.

15 *Cunniff v Cunniff* 1999 SC 537.

16 1994 SLT (Sh Ct) 25. See also *De Winton v De Winton* 1998 Fam LR 110.

17 *Bradbury v Bradbury* [2021] CSOH 113.

18 FL(S)A 1985, s 11(7)(a).

19 [2020] CSIH 43. The court stated that, '… the reclaimer's conduct did have an adverse effect on the matrimonial property. It is not necessary for there to be a finding of culpability; all that is required is that there has been conduct which adversely affects the matrimonial property. The quality of the conduct, and whether it is culpable in any way, may be a factor which the court might wish to address in deciding whether and to what extent, an adjustment should be made, but it is not a precondition for allowing conduct to be taken into account'. In *Skarpaas v Skarpaas* 1991 SLT (Sh Ct) 15, the husband's alcoholism was held to amount to such conduct and increased the wife's claim.

20 See, for example, *Dougan v Dougan* 1998 SLT (Sh Ct) 27 where the wife was awarded a capital sum to reflect that she had given up paid work to look after the couple's child.

21 It would appear that this solution was overlooked by Lord Hope in *Miller v Miller; McFarlane v McFarlane* [2006] UKHL 24. This was an appeal to the House of Lords in an English case. Nevertheless, Lord Hope took the opportunity to call for reform of the Family Law (Scotland) Act 1985 because a Scottish court could not award a periodical allowance under s 9(1)(b) to compensate a wife who had sustained economic disadvantage in looking after a family. But even if the husband has no capital assets at the date of divorce, a Scottish court can make an order for a capital sum to be paid by instalments over a long period out of the husband's future income. See Clive 'Financial Provision in Divorce' 2006 10 Edin LR 413.

Principle 9(1)(c)	Any economic burden of caring (i) after divorce, for a child of the marriage under the age of 16 years or (ii) after dissolution of a civil partnership, for a child who has been accepted by both partners as a child of the family or in respect of whom they are by virtue of sections 33 and 42 of the Human Fertilisation and Embryology Act 2008, the parents,[1] should be shared fairly between the persons.

1 On ss 33 and 42 of the 2008 Act see para **9.2**.

7.18 Where there are dependent children of a marriage or civil partnership[1] which ends in divorce or dissolution, there cannot usually be a clean break as in most cases it will be in the children's best interests to retain contact with both parties.[2] Maintenance calculation[3] and/or aliment for children of the family must be determined before the court will consider claims by the parties for financial provision on divorce or dissolution. But the party who looks after the children may suffer economic disadvantages in doing so, for example, he or she may not be able to take up full-time employment or may have to pay for childcare.

Principle 9(1)(c) was intended to ensure that the economic burden of childcare is shared fairly between the parties after divorce or dissolution. In practice this meant that the party who looked after the children received additional financial provision in recognition of the economic burden of childcare. But where maintenance calculation is paid, an element of the maintenance is to provide support for the parent who cares for the child. Accordingly, there has been a reduction of claims for financial provision based on principle 9(1)(c). In *Fox v Fox*,[4] the wife (and child's mother) argued for an unequal division to reflect that she had the greater burden on her in looking after the parties' child after divorce. The husband (and child's father) had already been assessed by the Child Maintenance Service (CMS) and had not missed a payment. The sheriff did not consider that an unequal division was justified in terms of s 9(1)(c).

In determining financial provision under principle 9(1)(c) the court must consider:

(a) any decree or arrangement for the aliment of the child of the marriage or civil partnership;

(b) any expenditure or loss of earning capacity caused by the need to care for the child;

(c) the need to provide suitable accommodation for the child;

(d) the age and health of the child;

(e) the education, financial or other circumstances of the child;

(f) the availability and cost of suitable child care facilities or service;

(g) the needs and resources of the persons; and

(h) all the other circumstances of the case.[5]

The court may also take into account the fact that the party from whom financial provision is sought is supporting a person who is maintained as a dependant in his or her household, whether or not he or she owes an obligation of aliment to that dependant;[6] For example, where, after divorce or dissolution, one spouse or civil partner is living with a new partner and his or her children, and is supporting members of that household financially, then the court may, if it thinks fit, take this into account in making a s 9(1)(c) decision. A party's misconduct is again irrelevant unless it has adversely affected the financial resources of the couple. This is because principle 9(1)(c) recognises that by contributing to the family by caring for the children, the claimant deserves financial provision.[7]

Unlike orders under principles 9(1)(a) and (b), the court has the power when applying principle 9(1)(c) to make an order for a periodical allowance provided it is satisfied that a capital sum or property transfer is inappropriate or insufficient to satisfy the requirements of s 8(2) of the Family Law (Scotland) Act 1985.[8] Thus, where a couple has little or no capital assets so that it is not reasonable in the light of their resources to make a capital sum payment or a property transfer order, a periodical allowance may well be justified under principle 9(1)(c).[9] If a periodical allowance is made, it could – subject to recall or variation – last until the youngest child of the marriage or civil partnership reaches the age of 16.[10] If the couple has extensive capital assets, financial provision under principle 9(1)(c) could take the form of the payment of a capital sum or property transfer order *in addition* to any financial provision under principles 9(1)(a) or (b). Alternatively, if the capital assets were not so extensive, principle 9(1)(c) could be used to justify the transfer of the family home to the party who is looking after the children even though that party would thereby receive more than half the value of the matrimonial or partnership property to which he or she was *prima facie* entitled under principle 9(1)(a).[11]

---

1 Children of a marriage or civil partnership include children who have been accepted by the spouses or civil partners as a child of the family: Family Law (Scotland) Act 1985, s 27.

2 See **Ch 12**.

3 See para **10.11**.

4 [2019] SC STI 3; [2018] 8 WLUK 325 Sheriff Collins stated that '... the enactment of the 1991 Act has greatly reduced the scope for reliance on section 9(1)(c), because of the elements taken into account in making a child maintenance assessment. Assessment is now based principally on the income of the non-resident parent, not the needs or resources of the resident parent or the child . Although section 9(1)(c) has not been wholly superseded by the 1991 Act, it has been observed that the courts should in particular now be slow to make a capital payment for revenue expenses in respect of a child the jurisdiction in respect of which lies with the CMS ... Put another way, the making (or adjustment) of a capital payment is not, in the normal case, to be used as a device to supplement the periodical child maintenance payments which the other party has been assessed as liable to make, effectively in lieu of aliment for the child.'

5 FL(S)A 1985, s 11(3)(a)–(h).

6 FL(S)A 1985, s 11(6).

7 FL(S)A 1985, s 11(7).

8 FL(S)A 1985, s 13(2). See *B v B* [2012] CSOH 21 where six instalments of capital were payable instead of an order for periodical allowance.

9 See *Wilson v Wilson* 2013 Fam LR 113 (periodical allowance of £500 until the child reached the age of 16 to begin after expiry of a periodical allowance of £1,000 per month for 18 months to be paid to W under s 9(1)(d)): see para **7.19** below.

10 A periodical allowance could be competent beyond the child's sixteenth birthday if the pursuer had incurred a substantial economic burden until the child reached 16 but the defender's means were not sufficient to pay the appropriate periodical allowance which would compensate the pursuer by the time the child reached 16: see the older case of *Monkman v Monkman* 1988 SLT (Sh Ct) 37.

11 See, for example, *Cunniff v Cunniff* 1999 SC 537; *Connolly v Connolly* 2005 Fam LR 106. Here a child had a significant disability and the child's mother could only work part-time to allow for her to care for the child. Her s 9(1)(c) claim was to be satisfied by the increase in value of her share of the family homes when they were finally to be sold. See also, *JR v AR* [2012] 11 WLUK 581.

Principle 9(1)(d)	A person who has been dependent to a substantial degree on the financial support of the other person should be awarded such financial provision as is reasonable to enable the person to adjust over a period of not more than three years from the date of the decree of divorce or dissolution to the loss of that support.

7.19 The purpose of this principle is to provide financial support for a spouse or civil partner who has been financially dependent on the other spouse or civil partner to enable him or her to adjust to life after the divorce or dissolution for up to three years.[1] The financial provision can take the form of a periodical allowance provided the court is satisfied that a capital sum or property transfer is inappropriate or insufficient to satisfy the requirements of s 8(2) of the Family Law (Scotland) Act 1985.[2] This matter is comprehensively discussed in *Neill v Neill*,[3] in which the Sheriff Appeal Court states:

> 'The meaning could not be clearer: the court shall not make an order for periodical allowance unless such an order is both justified by one of the principles referred to and the court is satisfied that an order for payment of capital or for transfer of property (etc) would be inappropriate or insufficient to satisfy the requirements of s.8(2) – which, reading short, are that the order is justified by the s.9 principles and is reasonable having regard to the parties' resources. Putting that another way, if possible the court is to achieve the s.9 principles by making an order for payment of capital (in the broadest sense); only if that cannot be achieved, either because such an order would not be sufficient to achieve the principles, or would be inappropriate, is the court to make an order for periodical allowance.'[4]

The payment of any periodical allowance is restricted to a maximum period of three years. It might be thought that a three-year maximum period is too short to enable a spouse or civil partner to adjust to life after divorce or dissolution but the view was taken that it was not the function of the law on financial provision to act as a panacea for the general problem of unemployment. Moreover, it should also be noted that any financial provision awarded under principle 9(1)(d) is *additional* to any capital sum or property transfer order awarded by virtue of principles 9(1)(a) or (b) and any financial provision awarded under principle 9(1)(c), which can last until the youngest child reaches the age of 16.[5]

Before the s 9(1)(d) principle applies, the applicant must have been financially dependent to a substantial degree on the other spouse or civil partner. For example, where a spouse or civil partner has been able to find a job during the period between separation and divorce or dissolution, the principle may not be triggered at all or any support awarded will not be for the maximum period of three years.[6] However, provided one person has continued to receive aliment from the other person, the first person can expect some financial provision under this principle even if he or she has obtained part-time employment.[7]

In making any order the court must have regard to:

(a) the age, health and earning capacity of the applicant;

(b) the duration and extent of the dependence prior to divorce or dissolution (thus for example, a person who has been a party to a short marriage and has given up a job only shortly before the divorce, is unlikely to receive a periodical allowance for the maximum three years, as opposed to a person who has been dependent for many years before the divorce);[8]

(c) the applicant's intention to undertake a course of education or training;

(d) the needs and resources of the parties; and

(e) all the other circumstances of the case.[9]

The court may also take into account the fact that the party from whom financial provision is sought is supporting a person who is maintained as a dependant in his or her household whether or not he or she owes an obligation of aliment to that dependant.[10] Unlike s 9(1)(a), (b) and (c) principles, the applicant's misconduct will be taken into account not only when it has affected the couple's financial resources but also if it would be manifestly inequitable to leave the conduct out of account.[11] This is because principle 9(1)(d) is based on equitable considerations and is not a recognition of what a spouse or civil partner has earned or will earn as a result of his or her contributions to the marriage or civil partnership.

Given that financial provision under principle 9(1)(d) is *additional* to any financial provision awarded under principles 9(1)(a), (b) or (c), it is submitted that it will be useful in helping a spouse or civil partner to adjust to life after divorce or dissolution. It will be particularly valuable when the applicant intends to embark on a course of further education or retraining. But by restricting the payment of any periodical allowances under this principle to a maximum of three years, any order will not be perceived by the payer as an indefinite financial burden.

---

1 See *Wilson v Wilson* 2013 Fam LR 113 where the court ordered the husband to pay periodical allowance of £1,000 to the wife in line with the s 9(1)(d) principle. The Sheriff Principal stated, 'periodical allowance is part of the matrix of fair sharing and equitable distribution of assets and liabilities on divorce ... factors to be taken into account by the court do not refer to the needs of the person claiming but rather "the needs and resources of the persons" ie the parties to the marriage'. *Morrison v Morrison* 1989 SCLR 574; *Maitland v Maitland* (9 December 1991, unreported) Sh Ct.

2 Family Law (Scotland) Act 1985, s 13(2).

3 2021 Fam LR 2.

4 2021 Fam LR 2, [para] 31.

5 Nevertheless, in *Miller v Miller; McFarlane v McFarlane* [2006] UKHL 24 Lord Hope argued that the courts should have discretion in exceptional circumstances to award periodical allowances under s 9(1)(d) which could extend beyond three years. Otherwise, it could be unfair to women who have given up their careers to look after their families but were facing difficulties in finding employment. But with respect this overlooks the power of the court to make a substantial capital sum payment under s 9(1)(b) to be payable in instalments out of the husband's future income: these instalments could be payable for far longer than three years: see also discussion at para **7.17** note 21.

6 *Dever v Dever* 1988 SCLR 352 (six months' support); *Muir v Muir* 1989 SCLR 445 (one year's support); *Miller v Miller* 1990 SCLR 666 (none at all!).

7 In *L v L* 2003 Fam LR 101 W received a periodical allowance under s 9(1)(d) where a delay was anticipated in the payment by H of a substantial capital sum.

8 *Sheret v Sheret* 1990 SCLR 799 (the marriage lasted around 12 months; the wife craved for a periodical allowance of £135 until either she remarried or died. She was awarded £40 a week for 13 weeks!

9 FL(S)A 1985, s 11(4).

10 FL(S)A 1985, s 11(6).

11 FL(S)A 1985, s 11(7)(b).

Principle 9(1)(e)	A person who at the time of divorce or dissolution seems likely to suffer serious financial hardship as a result of the divorce or dissolution should be awarded such financial provision as is reasonable to relieve him of hardship over a reasonable period.

7.20 Principle 9(1)(e) is intended to be a 'long stop' measure where adequate financial provision for a spouse or civil partner cannot be achieved by applying the previous four principles. It deals with the situation where, *at the time of the divorce or dissolution*, the applicant is not able to work, for example, due to age or ill health, and will suffer serious financial hardship as a result.[1] The principle does not apply if the applicant is overtaken by illness or other misfortune *after* the date of divorce or dissolution: that is not the concern of a previous spouse or civil partner.

Again, financial provision can take the form of a periodical allowance provided the court is satisfied that a capital sum payment or property transfer is inappropriate or insufficient to satisfy the requirements of s 8(2) of the Family Law (Scotland) Act 1985.[2] In making any order, the court must have regard to:

(a) the age, health and earning capacity of the applicant;

(b) the duration of the marriage or civil partnership;

(c) the standard of living of the parties during the marriage or civil partnership;

(d) the needs and resources of the parties; and

(e) all the other circumstances of the case.[3]

The court may also take into account the fact that the party from whom financial provision is sought is supporting a person who is maintained as a dependant in his or her household whether or not he or she owes an obligation of aliment to that dependant.[4] Moreover, the applicant's misconduct will be taken into account not only when it has affected the couple's financial resources, but also when it would be manifestly inequitable to leave the conduct out of account.[5] This is because principle 9(1)(e) is clearly based on equitable considerations and accordingly an applicant's responsibility for the breakdown of the marriage or civil partnership should be a relevant consideration. Nevertheless, it should be stressed that conduct will only be relevant when it would be *manifestly* inequitable to ignore it.

Recourse to the s 9(1)(e) principle is, in today's society, relatively rare. For example, if there has been a long (traditional) marriage during which the wife has given up employment to look after the family, then even if at the date of the divorce, due to her age, she is unable to enter the labour market, the s 9(1)(e) principle will not necessarily be applicable. For in the circumstances of this type of marriage, the wife may have obtained substantial financial provision under principles 9(1)(a) and (b), which may include an entitlement to a share of the husband's interests under any life policies or occupational pension schemes. Nevertheless, in such cases, the courts have made awards of periodical allowance to persons who may still suffer serious financial hardship as a result of the divorce or dissolution.[6]

Moreover, the serious financial hardship must arise *from the divorce or dissolution.* In *G v G*,[7] financial provision was not awarded in respect of s 9(1)(e) because the wife wished to continue maintaining her horses. Lady Wolffe found that, '... there must be a causal connection between the hardship and the divorce ... any hardship that might arise here was caused principally by the pursuer's maintenance of the horses and not, "as a result" of the divorce'. Where a couple has very limited resources principle 9(1)(e) should be inapplicable because any periodical allowance awarded simply reduces the amount of income support, universal credit and other benefits to which the payee would otherwise be entitled as a single person. But the fact that the applicant was not being financially supported by the defender immediately before the divorce or dissolution is not in itself enough to prevent a claim under principle 9(1)(e). In *Haugan v Haugan*,[8] the defender had failed to aliment his wife during the marriage. The Inner House of the Court of Session held that she was not precluded from using s 9(1)(e) merely because, if she was divorced without any financial provision, she would be no worse off financially than she was while married. The absence of support during the marriage was, however, a relevant factor in determining the amount she should be awarded.

In *Smith v Smith*,[9] the husband opposed the wife's claim under s 9(1)(e) on the basis that she would find herself in no worse a financial position than many other families. The court stated that '"serious financial hardship" should be assessed by reference to the circumstances of the parties … and not according to some undefined objective minimum subsistence provision'.[9] This principle was re-stated in *Neill v Neill,*[10] where it was stated that 'serious hardship must be assessed having regard to the parties' particular circumstances and not according to some objective or uniform standard of poverty'.

It was the considered view of Professor Joe Thomson that it should only be in very exceptional circumstances that s 9(1)(e) should be relevant, and that courts can use s 9(1)(b) to achieve a fairer outcome.[11] In *Smith v Smith*,[12] the court awarded a periodical allowance under both s 9(1)(d) and (e).

If a periodical allowance is ordered under this principle, while subject to recall or variation, it is not limited to any maximum period and can continue until the payee remarries or dies.[13] The fact that it gives rise to a potentially life-long financial burden for the payer is another reason why principle 9(1)(e) should be applicable only in the most exceptional circumstances.

---

1 *Johnstone v Johnstone* 1990 SCLR 358. In this case the wife had epilepsy. The husband appealed unsuccessfully against the sheriff's decision to award periodical allowance under s 9(1)(e) for an unlimited period.

2 Family Law (Scotland) Act 1985, s 13(2). See *Neill v Neill* 2021 Fam LR 2 above at para **7.19**.

3 FL(S)A 1985, s 11(5).

4 FL(S)A 1985, s 11(6).

5 FL(S)A 1985, s 11(7).

6 See *Johnstone v Johnstone* above at fn 1.

7 2016 Fam LT 30.

8 2002 SC 631.

9 2010 SLT 372.

10 2021 Fam LR 2, [para 42].

11 *Stott v Stott* 1987 GWD 17-645. The husband had a very low income and no capital assets. If there had been no divorce, any award of aliment for the wife would have been no greater than the income support and other benefits she would receive if she did divorce. Yet the court awarded her a periodical allowance. In Professor Joe Thomson's view, the s 9(1)(e) claim should have been rejected because the wife's financial situation was the same whether or not she remained married, therefore no financial hardship arose from *the divorce*.

12 [2009] CSOH 2; 2010 SLT 372.

13 FL(S)A 1985, s 13(7)(b); *Johnstone v Johnstone* 1990 SCLR 358.

Conclusion

7.21 The Family Law (Scotland) Act 1985, s 9 principles provide sophisticated guidelines which judges must use when exercising their discretion in making orders for financial provision on divorce or dissolution. Principles 9(1)(a) and (b) give recognition through the payment of capital sums and property transfer orders of the economic and other contributions made by the parties to the marriage or civil partnership and provide compensation for any economic disadvantages suffered by them in the interests of the family. As such, they constitute a major step towards a system of deferred community of property and, in effect, perceive marriage and civil partnership as basically an equal relationship between the parties. It may be that more use could be made of s 9(1)(b). At the same time, principle 9(1)(c) recognises the need to provide financial provision for the party who sustains an economic burden as a result of continued involvement in caring for any child of the family after the divorce or dissolution;[1] and principle 9(1)(d) is designed to help a spouse or civil partner to adjust to life after divorce or dissolution – though in this case a periodical allowance is restricted to a maximum period of three years. The final principle is a 'long stop' for very exceptional cases where at the time of the divorce or dissolution serious economic hardship is likely to arise as a result of the divorce or dissolution. The effect of an award under s 9(1)(e) can go against the 'clean break' principle between the parties, which was one of the major aims of the legislation. Finally, unless it has adversely affected the couple's financial resources, misconduct is irrelevant except in relation to principles 9(1)(d) and (e) where it should only be taken into account in so far as it would be manifestly inequitable *not* to do so.[2] This, of course, is consistent with a no-fault system of divorce and dissolution.[3]

Where appropriate, it is important to use all the principles in order to achieve a financial settlement which can best satisfy the claimant's needs: often this will be an attempt to ensure that the party looking after the children can continue to live in the family home.

---

1 Maintenance calculation has overtaken the issue by providing an element of financial support for the parent who cares for the child: see paras **7.18** and **10.11**.

2 It is also significant that periodical allowances are most likely to be awarded under these principles.

3 On the operation of the Family Law (Scotland) Act 1985 in practice, see *The Impact of the Family Law (Scotland) Act 1985 on Solicitors' Divorce Practice* (November 1990) Scottish Office Central Research Unit Papers.

AGREEMENTS FOR FINANCIAL PROVISION

7.22 It was a cardinal principle of the pre-1985 law that a spouse could validly discharge his or her right to apply for financial provision on divorce.[1] Spouses could agree for themselves the appropriate redistribution of their property and thus achieve an economic 'clean break' on divorce. The problem was that because of the uncertainty on what, if any, financial provision a court was likely to order if the case was litigated, lawyers had difficulty in advising their clients on what, in the circumstances of the marriage, constituted a fair settlement. The introduction of the s 9 principles has now given greater certainty as to the outcome of litigation and lawyers are now in a much better position to negotiate financial settlements on behalf of their clients. Written agreements, both pre- and post-marriage or civil partnership, are now a common and effective way for parties to regulate financial matters in the event of divorce and dissolution. Parties are able to have the authority and autonomy to regulate their own affairs in a manner of their choosing, with the appropriate legal direction and advice.

Prior to the Family Law (Scotland) Act 1985, an agreement on financial provision to be made on divorce could not be set aside unless there was evidence of a vitiating factor such as error, fraud, undue influence or misrepresentation. Such principles are drawn from the common law principles within contract law, a written agreement being a binding contract between the parties who enter into it. Therefore it was, and still is, important for the parties to receive separate legal advice on the terms of any agreement to ensure each party's individual interests are protected. The introduction of s 16 of the Family Law (Scotland) Act 1985, gives the courts limited additional powers to set aside or vary agreements on financial provision to be made on divorce or dissolution.[2]

First, any term in an agreement relating to the payment of a periodical allowance may be varied or set aside provided there is an express term in the agreement to this effect.[3] This can be done at any time after the divorce or dissolution has been granted.[4]

Secondly, any term relating to a periodical allowance can be varied or set aside if the payer has become bankrupt or a child maintenance calculation has been made.[5] This can be done on, or at any time after, granting decree of divorce or dissolution.

Thirdly, and most broadly, on granting decree of divorce or dissolution,[6] the court may set aside or vary any agreement or any term of such an agreement that was not 'fair and reasonable' at the time it was entered into.[7]

The leading case in which a variation of a minute of agreement was sought in terms of s 16 is *Gillon v Gillon (No 3)*,[8] which sets out the principles to be applied when dealing with such issues. The five principles identified in *Gillon* can be summarised as follows: (1) It is necessary to examine the agreement from the point of view of both fairness and reasonableness. (2) Such examination must relate to all the relevant circumstances leading up to and prevailing at the time of the execution of the agreement, including amongst other things the nature and quality of any legal advice given to either party. (3) Evidence that some unfair advantage was taken by one party of the other by reason of circumstances prevailing at the time of negotiation may have a cogent bearing on the determination of the issue. (4) The court should not be unduly ready to overturn agreements validly entered into. (5) The fact that it transpires that an agreement has led to an unequal and possibly a very unequal division of assets does not by itself necessarily give rise to any inference of unfairness and unreasonableness.

Since the introduction of s 16 of the FL(S)A 1985, it has been clear that the court is generally unwilling readily to reduce, vary or set aside an agreement that appears, on the face of it, to have been validly entered into between parties.[9] Crucially, it is the time of the agreement, rather than any later date, which is the relevant period in considering whether the agreement should be varied or set aside. If unfairness later transpires, that is irrelevant for the purposes of s 16.

In cases where reduction or variation is sought, it is essential that the key elements of the case are presented to the court to allow the court to understand the nature and circumstances pertaining to the making of the agreement. Relevant evidential factors which the court will seek to consider have included: (a) The practical financial or other consequences of the existing arrangement. (b) Why that consequence is unfair or unreasonable at the time the agreement was entered into. (c) Whether there is any offsetting to take into account. (d) What, specifically, would be the minimum intervention required to alleviate any unfairness or unreasonableness as at the date of separation having regard to the effect on both parties?[10] While the onus lies on the pursuer to establish that the agreement is not fair and reasonable, it is not necessary to prove that it was *both* unfair and unreasonable.[11] It is an objective test and the agreement is considered from the point of view of both parties.

The nature and quality of legal advice received in relation to the agreement is an important factor,[12] but the fact that the same solicitor advised both parties is not *per se* sufficient to render an agreement unfair.[13] The fact that a spouse has been overgenerous in agreeing financial provision and then changes his or her mind is also not sufficient, on its own, to allow the agreement to be set aside.[14] However, if the agreement was of no benefit to one of the parties when it was entered into, then it may be considered an extreme case where setting aside is deemed appropriate.[15] The court is able to look to relevant circumstances present at the time the agreement was entered into in order to inform its assessment of unfair or unreasonableness. In particular, in *M(C) v M(M)*,[16] the sheriff made various findings in relation to the nature of the parties' relationship, including that the defender was in a subservient position, was at risk of manipulation and was subject to control and abuse by the pursuer. Psychological evidence assisted the defender in successfully seeking that the agreement be set aside.

---

1 *Dunbar v Dunbar* 1977 SLT 169; *Thomson v Thomson* 1982 SLT 521; *Elder v Elder* 1985 SLT 471.

2 These include agreements made before as well as during a marriage (or civil partnership): *Kibble v Kibble* 2010 SLT (Sh Ct) 5.

3 Family Law (Scotland) Act 1985, s 16(1)(a); *Mills v Mills* 1989 SCLR 213. It does not matter if the agreement refers – wrongly – to alimentary payments rather than periodical allowances: *Drummond v Drummond* 1995 SCLR 428, 1996 SLT 386.

4 FL(S)A 1985, s 16(2)(a); *Mills v Mills* 1989 SCLR 213; *Drummond v Drummond* 1995 SCLR 428, 1996 SLT 386.

5 FL(S)A 1985, s 16(3).

6 FL(S)A 1985, s 16(2)(b). The court may also exercise its power within such period as the court may specify on granting decree. Although the court cannot set aside

the agreement until in a position to grant decree of divorce or dissolution, this does not prevent the court having a preliminary hearing to determine whether or not the agreement is fair: *Gillon v Gillon (No 2)* 1994 SLT 984.

7 FL(S)A 1985, s 16(1)(b).

8 1995 SLT 678.

9 *Inglis v Inglis* 1999 SLT (Sh Ct) 59.

10 *Bradley v Bradley*, 2018 SC (SAC) 7.

11 *Clarkson v Clarkson* 2008 SLT (Sh Ct) 2.

12 *Gillon v Gillon (No 1)* 1994 SLT 978; *M(C) v M(M)*, 2021 SLT (Sh Ct) 319.

13 *Worth v Worth* 1994 SLT (Sh Ct) 54.

14 *Anderson v Anderson* 1991 SLT (Sh Ct) 11. Where the defender acted without legal advice but did so voluntarily and in full knowledge of what he was doing.

15 *M(C) v M(M)* 2021 SLT (Sh Ct) 319.

16 Ibid.

Procedural matters

7.23 By the Family Law (Scotland) Act 1985, s 18, a spouse or civil partner who has made a claim for an order for financial provision[1] may, no later than a year from the date of disposal of the claim, apply to the court for an order setting aside or varying any transfer of, or transaction involving, property which was effected by the other party no more than five years before the date of making the claim.[2] The court will make such an order if satisfied by the challenger that the transaction had, or was likely to have, the effect of defeating, in whole or in part, the applicant's claim for financial provision. This is an objective criterion: there is no need to establish that the transfer was intended by the transferor to defeat the applicant's claim. In *J v J*,[3] the parties were married for three years. Early in the marriage, the husband won around £11 million on the lottery. This money was considered matrimonial property. The purchase of the winning lottery ticket had been funded by money that the husband had taken from the till of his parents' shop, where he worked. His parents claimed that the ticket money belonged to them, therefore, the lottery winnings belonged to them. However, they were unable to prove to the satisfaction of the court that the husband (their son) was acting as agent for them. Shortly before the couple separated, the husband transferred around £8 million into his parents' bank accounts. Nevertheless, the money was still considered matrimonial property and, in line with the principle of fair sharing under s 10(1) of the 1985 Act, the wife was entitled to a capital sum of around £4.8 million. The husband claimed that he no longer had the funds available to pay the capital sum to his wife. The wife pursuer asked the court for an order under s 18 to set aside the transaction by which the husband transferred the money to his parents, on the basis that it had the effect of defeating the wife's claim for financial provision. An order under s 18 was granted.

An order under s 18 of the 1985 Act does not prejudice the rights of a third party in or to the property where the third party has acquired the property or any rights therein in good faith and for value or has derived title to such property or rights from any person who has done so. Thus, for example, if three years before A's claim for financial provision A's civil partner, B, transferred £20,000 to a third party, C, the court could set aside the transfer unless C was in good faith and had given value in respect of the money, for example if C had sold to B a painting worth £20,000.[4]

Finally, in an action for financial provision,[5] the court can order either party to provide details of his or her resources.[6]

It should also be remembered that before the determination of an action for divorce, dissolution or declarator of nullity, the court has the power to make an award of interim aliment to a party to the action.[7] Only periodical payments can be awarded which are payable until the date of the disposal of the action[8] when the court will make orders for financial provision.

---

1 The section also applies to an action for aliment, or variation or recall of a decree of aliment or order for financial provision.

2 The court has also the power to interdict the party from entering into such a transfer or transaction.

3 2021 SLT 1152; 2021 Fam LR 88. See also: *M v M* [2011] CSOH 33.

4 In *M v M and Wards Estate Trustees Ltd* 2009 SLT 608 prior to the divorce H had transferred assets into a trust for the benefit of children from previous relationships. Because the trustees had not given value, the court granted an interim interdict preventing the trustees from distributing the trust funds to the beneficiaries.

5 Or actions for aliment or interim aliment.

6 FL(S)A 1985, s 20. See, for example, *AF v AF* 2019 Fam LR 74.

7 FL(S)A 1985, s 6. Interim aliment can also be awarded in actions for aliment: *Mc Geoch v Mc Geoch* 1998 Fam LR 8.

8 FL(S)A 1985, s 6(3).

Chapter 8

Cohabitants

INTRODUCTION

8.1 One of the features of today's society is the increase in couples who choose to live together without marrying or registering a civil partnership. The most recent figures on cohabiting couples in Scotland date from the 2011 Census. Scotland's Census, which should have taken place in 2021, was postponed until 2022 due to the impact of the COVID-19 pandemic. The results of the 2022 census will not be available in time for the publication of this book. In 2011, of the 2.4 million families living in households in Scotland, 9% (217,000) were cohabiting couple families.[1] It is estimated that there has been a gradual increase in the number of cohabiting couples over the last decade or so. This was artificially boosted between 2020 and 2022 due to the prohibition of gatherings during the pandemic which led to a decrease in marriage ceremonies and a corresponding increase in cohabitations. The general annual increase in couples choosing to cohabit (pre- and post-pandemic) has seen 51.6% of all babies being born to unmarried parents.[2] In some cases, the cohabiting couple may eventually marry, for example, if they decide to have children. But for others their relationship continues simply as cohabitation. How should the law respond to such relationships? At one extreme the law could pay no regard to the fact that the couple live together and instead treat them as single persons in law. At the other end of the spectrum, the law could treat them as though they were married or in a civil partnership, thereby thrusting the legal obligations of marriage or civil partnership on persons who had chosen not to enter a legal institution.[3] Prior to 2006, cohabitants in Scots law had no statutory rights to any financial claim against their former cohabitant on breakdown of the relationship. If one party sought financial compensation, his or her only option (in the absence of an agreement between them), was to raise an action based on unjustified enrichment.[4] The purpose of this chapter is to give an account of the major rights and obligations which arise from cohabitation.

1 National Records of Scotland, Census 2011. There are no annual NRS statistics available on the number of cohabitation households in Scotland. This is because there is no legal requirement to register a cohabitation.

2 See: National Records of Scotland website at: https://www.nrscotland.gov.uk/statistics-and-data.

3 The Scottish Law Commission, in its Annual Report 2021, states that its Report on Cohabitation and accompanying draft Cohabitation Bill will be published in summer 2022.

4 *Shilliday v Smith* 1998 SC 725.

COHABITATION

8.2 There is limited legislation applicable to the breakdown or end of a cohabitation. What law there is can be found in s 25 to s 29 of the Family Law (Scotland) Act 2006. The fact that a couple is living together does not in itself generate rights and duties. It is only when a couple live together as if they were married or in a civil partnership that they will be regarded as cohabitants for the purposes of s 25 to s 29 of FL(S)A 2006.[1] In determining whether a couple is living together as if they were married or in a civil partnership, the court will consider, *inter alia*, the following factors:[2]

(a) the length of the period during which A and B have been living together (or lived together);[3]

(b) the nature of their relationship during that period; and

(c) the nature and extent of any financial arrangements subsisting or which subsisted during that period.

The court may also consider such matters as:[4]

(a) social acceptance as a couple;[5]

(b) the stability of the parties' relationship;

(c) emotional commitment; and

(d) whether one party has told the other that the relationship is over.[6]

It will be clear that before a couple will be treated as living together as though they were married or in a civil partnership, their relationship must exhibit enough of the above characteristics. This is ultimately a question of fact to be determined by the court. Because cohabitation has to be inferred from the facts of a particular relationship, unlike marriage or registration of a civil partnership, there will always be an inevitable degree of uncertainty as to when cohabitation as spouses began or, indeed, ended.

One of the most important and welcome features of Scots law is that there is no set minimum period of cohabitation, that must have elapsed before the couple acquire rights and obligations. In *Harley v Robertson*,[7] the sheriff observed that, had the defender not conceded that there was a cohabitation (after seven months), in terms of s 25 he 'would not have found on the evidence before [him] that the pursuer had established cohabitation in terms of that provision'. However, in *Harley v Thompson*,[8] 12 months' cohabitation, coupled with other characteristics, was regarded as a relationship of cohabitation for the purposes of s 25. The length of a relationship will be a relevant factor in determining whether a relationship has the element of stability necessary for the inference to be drawn that the parties were, in fact, living together as though they were married.

For many years, only opposite sex couples were recognised as cohabitants for legal purposes. However, in *Ghaidan v Godin-Mendoza*,[9] the House of Lords accepted that statutes which gave rights to different sex couples would have to be construed as including same sex couples to avoid unlawful discrimination under Article 13 of the European Convention on Human Rights read in conjunction with Article 8 (right to respect for private and family life, home and correspondence). In *Telfer v Kellock*,[10] the Lord Ordinary (Lady Smith) accepted that the Damages (Scotland) Act 1976 would have to be interpreted in this way. However, with the introduction of same sex marriage the relevant law applies to same sex as well as different sex cohabitants.[11]

---

1 Family Law (Scotland) Act 2006, s 25(1)(a) and (b). Since the introduction of same sex marriage any reference in an enactment to persons living together as if they were in a civil partnership ceases to have effect: Marriage and Civil Partnership (Scotland) Act 2014, s 4(4).

2 FL(S)A 2006, s 25(2).

3 *Harley v Robertson* [2011] 12 WLUK 328 (a claim under s 28(2) of the 1985 Act was allowed to proceed after just seven months of cohabitation).

4 See: *Crake v Supplementary Benefits Commission* [1982] 1 All ER 498 (the court held that the fact that a man and woman lived together would not, of itself, equate to them living as husband and wife. Other aspects of the relationship must be considered.

5 In *M v T* [2011] 11 WLUK 503 the sheriff stressed the importance of how the couple presented themselves to their family and the public 'given the public nature of the institution of marriage which underpins the issue' (at para 30). See also para 24 where the sheriff lists the factors referred to by Professor Clive in *Husband and Wife,* (1997), 4th edn.

6 *Garrad v Inglis* 2013 WL 6980541; 2014 GWD 1-17. The sheriff found that the relationship ended when the defender informed the pursuer that their relationship was over and she consulted her accountant about related financial matters.
7 [2011] 12 WLUK 328 (and fn 3 above).
8 2015 Fam LR 45.
9 [2004] 3 WLR 113.
10 2004 SLT 1290.
11 Marriage and Civil Partnership (Scotland) Act 2014, s 4.

SOME LEGAL CONSEQUENCES OF COHABITATION[1]

Personal effects

8.3 Unlike spouses, cohabitants are *not* under an obligation to aliment each other in terms of s 1 of the Family Law (Scotland) Act 1985. On the other hand, for the purpose of obtaining income support, the needs and resources of a couple living together in the same household as if they were married or civil partners are aggregated.[2] Similarly they are liable relatives.[3] When a person is injured, his or her cohabitant is a relative for the purposes of the Administration of Justice Act 1982.[4] If a person dies as a result of personal injuries, his or her cohabitant is a member of the deceased's immediate family for the purposes of the Damages (Scotland) Act 2011.[5] It is thought that cohabitants would be treated in the same way as a couple who are married or in a civil partnership for the purpose of the doctrine of good faith laid down in *Smith v Bank of Scotland*.[6]

1 There are important rights enjoyed by cohabitants under housing legislation: these are beyond the scope of the current text.
2 Social Security Contributions and Benefits Act 1992, s 137(1) (definition of 'couple').
3 Social Security Administration Act 1992, s 78(5) and (6).
4 Sections 8, 9 and 13 (definition of 'relative'). The 1982 Act is discussed above at para **3.6**.
5 Section 14. The 2011 Act is discussed above at para **3.6**.
6 1997 SC (HL) 111, discussed above at para **3.5**.

Property issues

8.4 The Family Law (Scotland) Act 2006 contains important property rights for cohabitants. For the purposes of the 2006 Act, s 25(1)(a) states that cohabitant means a member of a couple consisting of a man and a woman who are or were living together as if they were husband and wife.[1] or as civil partners. But in determining whether a couple are cohabitants, the court is expressly directed by s 25(2) to have regard to how long the couple have been living together, the nature of their relationship during that period and the nature and extent of any financial arrangements which subsisted between them. Section 25(2) is problematic. To give the definition of cohabitant in s 25(1) and then redefine it in s 25(2) is intellectually incoherent. The provision would have made more sense if it had stated that the factors in s 25(2) were to be considered in determining under s 25(1) whether or not a couple was living together as husband and wife or civil partners. Alternatively, having determined that a couple was living together as husband and wife or civil partners, the provision could have stated that in exercising its discretion to make awards of financial provision on separation or death,[2] the court should have regard to the factors in s 25(2).

Section 26 provides that, in any question as to the respective rights of ownership of cohabitants in household goods, there shall be a rebuttable presumption that each cohabitant has an equal share in any household goods acquired during the period of cohabitation. The presumption does not apply to household goods acquired by gift or succession from a third party. Household goods are defined[3] as any goods, including decorative or ornamental goods, kept or used at any time during the cohabitation for their joint domestic purposes in any residence in which the couple was cohabiting. These would include all kinds of domestic furniture and appliances. But because the goods must be used for *joint* domestic purposes, it would not include a wristwatch as opposed to a grandfather clock. The provision only applies to goods, ie moveable property. There is therefore no presumption of common ownership in heritable property, for example the house or flat where the couple lives. Section 26(4) expressly excludes money and securities, road vehicles and pets from the definition of 'household goods'. Unlike the analogous provision for spouses and civil partners in s 25 of the Family Law (Scotland) Act 1985,[4] there is no equivalent of s 25(2) under which the presumption cannot be rebutted 'by reason only that … the goods in question were purchased from a third party by either party alone or by both in unequal shares'. It would therefore appear that in relation to cohabitants such evidence could of itself rebut the presumption. It is difficult to see how the factors listed in s 25(2) of the 2006 Act could be used to prevent a couple being treated as cohabitants for the purpose of this section although, of course, the nature and extent of their financial arrangements could be evidence which could be used to rebut the presumption.

Section 27 provides that any savings made from housekeeping allowances by cohabitants or any property bought with such money, should be owned in common between the cohabitants. The rule is subject to any agreement to the contrary between the parties. Unlike the analogous provision for spouses and civil partners under s 26 of the Family Law (Scotland) Act 1985,[5] s 27(3) expressly provides that property does not include the house or flat which the cohabitants used as their sole or main residence. Again, it is difficult to see how the factors in s 25(2) of the 2006 Act could be used to prevent a couple being treated as cohabitants for the purpose of this section, although their financial arrangements could contain an agreement that any savings from an allowance or any property bought from such savings should not be owned in equal shares.

It is important to emphasise that these provisions are irrelevant in determining the ownership of heritable property which remains governed by the ordinary rules of property law. This is particularly important in relationship to the ownership of the property in which the couple lives. Accordingly, where title is registered in the names of both cohabitants, they are common owners. But if title is registered in the name of only one of the cohabitants, only that cohabitant is the owner of the property. This can give rise to unfairness if the non-owner has directly contributed to the purchase of the property, or has relieved the owner of expenditure by paying household bills, or providing services thus indirectly contributing to the acquisition of the property.

As stated by Lord Hope in *Stack v Dowden*,[6] it may be possible for a remedy to be found in the law of unjustified enrichment. This important matter has become the subject of robust legal argument in recent case law, which will be discussed in more detail below at para 8.6, in relation to s 28 of the 2006 Act. However, it is helpful to look at previous similar case law on this matter. For example, in *Satchwell v McIntosh*,[7] title was taken in the name of one of the cohabitants, but the other had directly contributed to the purchase price and had paid for some refurbishments. Although the defender was the owner of the property, under principles of unjustified enrichment, the pursuer recovered the monies that she had paid. In *McKenzie v Rutter*,[8] the parties agreed to sell their existing properties to purchase a house. Only one of the parties sold their property in order to buy the house, title to which was nevertheless taken in joint names. Both were therefore common owners. When the cohabitant who had not sold her property insisted on an action of division and sale of the house, her share of the proceeds was paid to the other cohabitant for otherwise she would have been unjustifiably enriched.

1 The phrase 'husband and wife' must be construed as including same sex spouses and accordingly same sex cohabitants are included: Marriage and Civil Partnership (Scotland) Act 2014, s 4.
2 On these see below at paras **8.6** and **8.7**.
3 Family Law (Scotland) Act 2006, s 26(4).
4 Discussed above at para **4.5**.
5 Discussed above at para **4.8**.
6 [2007] UKHL 17.
7 2006 SLT (ShCt) 117. See also *Shilliday v Smith* 1998 SC 725 where the pursuer successfully sued the defender for recovery of monies paid by her for materials and work on a property owned by the defender and in which the couple had intended to live after their marriage.
8 2007 SLT (Sh Ct) 117.

The occupation of the family home

8.5 Cohabitants may experience difficulties in relation to the occupation of their family accommodation when their relationship begins to break down. The Matrimonial Homes (Family Protection) (Scotland) Act 1981 provides some relief. There are generally two situations which occur.

(a) A couple is cohabiting and one partner is entitled to occupy the house and the other partner is not entitled.

The non-entitled partner may apply to a court for the grant of occupancy rights in relation to the house in which they are cohabiting.[1] Occupancy rights can be granted for a period not exceeding six months,[2] although the initial period can be extended for further periods of up to six months with no overall limit. A non-entitled partner's rights of occupation are the same as those of a non-entitled spouse.[3]

A cohabiting couple is defined as a man and a woman who are living with each other as if they were man and wife.[4] In determining whether a couple is cohabiting for the purpose of an application for occupancy rights under s 18(1) of the Matrimonial Homes (Family Protection) (Scotland) Act 1981, the court is directed to consider all the circumstances of the case, including the length of their relationship and whether they have any children.[5] The couple must be cohabiting as man and wife at the time of the conduct giving rise to the application for occupancy rights,[6] but the applicant need not be residing in the house at the time of the application. The longer they have been apart, of course, the less likely the court will exercise its discretion under s 18(1) and grant occupancy rights.[7]

When an order granting occupancy rights is in force, certain provisions of the 1981 Act, similar to those of a married couple, apply to the partners.[8] In particular, regulatory and exclusion orders are available under s 3 and s 4 of the 1981 Act.[9] By s 18A of the 1981 Act the court can grant a domestic interdict: (a) restraining or prohibiting the defender's conduct towards the pursuer or any child in the pursuer's permanent or temporary care; and (b) prohibiting the defender from entering or remaining in: (i) a family home occupied by the pursuer and the defender; (ii) any other residence occupied by the pursuer; (iii) the pursuer's place of work; and (iv) any school attended by a child in the pursuer's care. Where the defender is an entitled partner or has statutory rights of occupation under s 18(1) of the 1981 Act, a domestic interdict cannot be granted prohibiting the defender from entering or remaining in the family home occupied by the pursuer unless it is ancillary to an exclusion order under s 4 of the 1981 Act. Tenancy transfer orders under s 13 of the 1981 Act are also available.[10] However, the non-entitled partner's occupancy rights are not protected from dealings by the entitled partner with third parties.[11]

(b) Both partners are entitled to occupy the house.

Here there is no need for an application under s 18(1) of the 1981 Act. But the same provisions of the 1981 Act apply to the couple as though a s 18(1) order was in force.[12] The entitled partners do not have to be residing together at the time of the proceedings; it is enough that they were living together at the time of the conduct which gave rise to the action. Thus, for example, in *Armour v Anderson*,[13] where entitled joint tenants were living together as man and wife at the time of the man's misconduct, his partner obtained a tenancy transfer order in an action brought ten months after she had left the house.

It must be stressed that when one partner is non-entitled, the protection afforded by these provisions of the 1981 Act do not apply unless and until there has been a successful application by the non-entitled partner for occupancy rights. Thus, in the older case of *Clarke v Hatten*,[14] an entitled partner was unable to use the 1981 Act to obtain a domestic interdict as the non-entitled partner whose violence she had fled, had not applied for occupancy rights.[15] It is now the case that the entitled partner could seek an interdict at common law and a power of arrest under the Protection of Abuse (Scotland) Act 2001, s 1. In contrast, a non-entitled spouse or civil partner has statutory rights of occupation of the matrimonial or family home as a result of simply being married or registering a civil partnership.

---

1 Matrimonial Homes (Family Protection) (Scotland) Act 1981, s 18(1).
2 MH(FP)(S)A 1981, s 18(1).
3 MH(FP)(S)A 1981, s 18(6).
4 The phrase 'man and wife' must be construed as including same sex spouses and accordingly same sex cohabitants are included: Marriage and Civil Partnership (Scotland) Act 2014, s 4.
5 MH(FP)(S)A 1981, s 18(2). In *Armour v Anderson* 1994 SLT 1127, it was emphasised that s 18(2) applies only to determine whether a couple are cohabiting for the purpose of a s 18(1) application.
6 *Armour v Anderson* 1994 SLT 1127.
7 Ibid The applicant moved out of the jointly tenanted home 10 months before raising an action to suspend her former partner's occupancy rights, to seek summary ejection and an interdict against him entering the property without permission. See also: *Verity v Fenner* 1993 SCLR 223 (couple lived apart for 11 months; applicant had a home in Northern Ireland; occupancy rights not granted).
8 MH(FP)(S)A 1981, s 18(3).
9 For discussion of ss 3 and 4 see above at paras **5.8–5.9**.
10 MH(FP)S)A 1981, s18(3). See, for example, *Souter v McAuley* 2010 SLT (St Ct) 121.
11 For discussion see above at para **5.10**.
12 MH(FP)(S)A 1981, s 19. Unlike the position of entitled spouses or civil partners, there is no restriction on the grant of a decree in an action of division and sale where the house is owned in common by the entitled partners: for discussion see above at

para **5.11**.

13 1994 SLT 1127. The same principle would apply if an entitled partner sought an exclusion order under s 4 of the 1981 Act against the other entitled partner.

14 1987 SCLR 527.

15 It would have been different if both partners had been entitled because MH(FP)(S) A 1981, s 18(3) would operate.

Financial provision where cohabitation ends otherwise than by death

8.6 Under s 28 of the Family Law (Scotland) Act 2006, a cohabitant can apply for financial provision when the cohabitation has ended otherwise than by death. The right to apply arises when the couple ceases to cohabit.[1] This is ultimately a question of fact. While clear cases can be envisaged, for example where one cohabitant is in jail or hospital, in practice the same rules with regard to when a married or civilly partnered couple ceases to cohabit are applied to cohabitation.[2] An application under s 28 must be made within a year of the parties ceasing living together. (This means that the application should be lodged in court and served on the other party.) Failure to do so will result in the application being time barred.[3] Where a couple has cohabited, separated and then resumed cohabitation, the first period of cohabitation can be taken into account provided the action is brought within one year from the date when the second period of cohabitation came to an end.[4] The strict adherence to s 28(8) can place some parties at a disadvantage, for example, a victim of domestic abuse may be reluctant to make an application soon after separation. In the case of *Courtney's Executors v Campbell*,[5] the parties cohabited in a house purchased by the defender from 2010 to May 2013. Title was held by the defender alone. Two sums of money were paid by the pursuer to the defender amounting to £100,000. After the couple separated in 2013, the pursuer sought legal advice in August 2014 for recompense for the monies paid. It was suggested that the delay in making the application was, in part, because the defender's son was ill and subsequently died and because the pursuer was unaware of the procedure open to him. Thereafter, the pursuer died and his executors sued the defender for the payments made by the deceased. The Outer House held that the 'subsidiary principle' applied; namely that where a claim can be made under s 28, but is not made timeously, a party cannot simply fall back on the common law of unjustified enrichment. Further, Lord Beckett stated that he was not satisfied that the pursuer had pled 'special and strong' circumstances that would entitle them to the remedy sought. This decision, however, was regarded as highly controversial.[6] It is of note that in March 2019 (post-*Courtney's Executors v Campbell*), the Law Society of Scotland published a report suggesting that 'legislation be introduced to provide the court with discretion to accept an application under section 28 in particular circumstances after 12 months from the date on which the parties ceased to cohabit … "on cause shown" or on "special cause shown"'.[7]

In *Pert v McCaffrey*,[8] the pursuer did not raise an action under s 28 within the required 12 months. She then raised an action for unjustified enrichment seeking re-payment of monies paid to her former cohabitant defender by the trustee in bankruptcy. The five-Judge Inner House of the Court of Session stated,

> 's 28 is not a remedy which is alternative to an action for recompense but one which is additional to any common law remedy otherwise available. The failure to exercise the right to make an application under s 28 timeously does not bar the use of such remedies. In this respect the court must disagree with *Courtney's Exrs v Campbell*'.[9]

Assuming the party has made the claim timeously, by s 28(2) of the 2006 Act the court can make the following orders:

(a) an order for the payment to the applicant of a capital sum of an amount specified in the order;

(b) an order to pay the applicant such amount as may be specified in the order 'in respect of any economic burden of caring, after the end of the cohabitation, for a child of whom the cohabitants are parents';[10] and

(c) such interim order as the court thinks fit.

The court can specify the date on which payments must be paid and that a capital sum should be payable in instalments.[11]

In relation to s 28(2)(b), the court can order periodical payments as well as a capital sum. For the purpose of this provision, a child is a person under the age of 16 of whom the cohabitants are the parents.[12] It does not include a child who has been accepted or treated by the applicant and the defender (or both) as a child of the family. This is surprising as such cohabitants may sustain economic loss after the breakdown from having to care for a child who has been living with them in the same way as cohabitants who are the child's parents.

In considering whether to make any of these orders the court must consider the matters listed in s 28(3) of the 2006 Act. These are:

(a) whether, and if so to what extent, the defender has derived economic advantage from contributions made by the applicant; and

(b) whether, and if so to what extent, the applicant has suffered economic disadvantage in the interests of the defender and any relevant child.

While it may be readily apparent how fair account of the economic advantages received by the defender and the economic disadvantages suffered by the applicant can form the basis of an order under s 28(2)(a) it is difficult to see why it is applicable to an order under s 28(2)(b) which expressly stipulates that its purpose is to compensate the applicant for the economic burden of caring for a child of the cohabitation after it has come to an end.[13]

The factors in s 28(3) are, of course, important in respect of a claim for a capital sum under s 28(2)(a). These are the economic advantages received by the defender from contributions made by the applicant and economic disadvantages sustained by the applicant in the interests of the defender and a relevant child. For the purposes of s 28(2)(b), a relevant child is a person under the age of 16 who is either a child of whom the cohabitants are the parents or who is or was accepted by the cohabitants as a child of their family.[14] The acceptance criterion seems to be the same as creates liability to aliment a child under s 1(1)(d) of the Family Law (Scotland) Act 1985.[15]

Contributions include indirect and non-financial contributions made by looking after any relevant child or any house in which the couple lived.[16] Economic advantage includes gains in capital, income and earning capacity; economic disadvantage includes losses in capital, income and earning capacity.[17] In the case of *M v* S,[18] the approach by Lord Ericht was to award to the pursuer two distinct awards. The first reflected the various economic benefits derived by the defender by the contributions made by the purser to the monthly mortgage of the farm in which they lived and which was owned by the defender. The second to reflect the economic disadvantage suffered by the purser in the interests of the parties' two children, the pursuer having reduced her working hours to spend time with, and care for the children. Lord Ericht followed Lord Hope in *Gow v Grant*[19] in stating: '... the purpose of the exercise of making an award under section 28 is to achieve fairness between the parties. In my opinion, the award of the sum of £912,000 sought by the pursuer would achieve that fairness. The sum is targeted at redressing two specific disadvantages, being the paying of half the mortgage payments and the loss of income due to caring for the children'.

Unlike s 9(1)(b) of the Family (Scotland) Act 1985 (the analogous principle which applies in relation to financial provision on divorce or dissolution,[20]) s 28(3) does not take account of any economic disadvantage sustained or economic advantages obtained before the couple began to cohabit.

In deciding whether to make an order for a capital sum payment under s 28(2)(a), s 28(4) provides that the court has to consider the matters in ss 28(5) and (6). First, the court must consider the extent to which any economic advantage derived by the defender from the applicant's contributions is offset by any economic disadvantage sustained by the defender in the interests of the applicant and any relevant child. Second, the court must consider the extent to which any economic disadvantage sustained by the applicant in the interests of the defender or any relevant child is offset by any economic advantage the applicant has derived from the defender's contributions. It is only if, after this balancing exercise, there is an economic imbalance in favour of the applicant that an award of financial provision can be made under s 28(2)(a). This balancing process is familiar from s 9(1)(b) of the 1985 Act.[21] But unlike spouses and civil partners, cohabitants are not under any obligation to aliment one another. Even so, it is thought that in most relationships it would be unusual if there were not some economic advantages and disadvantages to offset under this provision.

In *Gow v Grant*,[22] the Second Division of the Court of Session took an extremely narrow view of the function of s 28. The court stated[23] that the objective of the section was 'limited in scope: it was intended to enable the court to correct any clear and quantifiable economic imbalance that might have resulted from cohabitation. The section was not designed to confer a general power to deal with any wider financial issues that might have arisen between the parties'. It was 'in the nature of compensation for an imbalance of economic advantage or disadvantage'.[24]

Given this approach to the purpose of the provision, it is not surprising that the court went on to hold that the only relevant economic disadvantage was that sustained 'in the interests' of the defender, ie that the applicant suffered economic disadvantage in a manner intended to benefit the defender. Although the defender had encouraged the applicant to sell her house – her only capital asset – she had not done so in his interest as she had used the proceeds of the sale to pay her debts and make a loan to her son as well as contributing to the couple's extravagant lifestyle.

The decision of the Court of Session in *Gow v Grant* was overturned by the Supreme Court.[25] The underlying principle of s 28 was one of fairness. The purpose of s 28 was to achieve fairness in the assessment of compensation for contributions made or economic disadvantages suffered in the interests of the relationship.[26] While the economic disadvantage which the applicant sustained had to be in the defender's interests, Lord Hope argued that the provision,

> 'does not say that this must have been his interests only, or that the fact that it was in the applicant's interests also means that it must be left out of account. Still less does it say that "interests" have to be equated with economic advantage or benefit. … Provided that disadvantage has been suffered in the interests of the defender to some extent, the door is open to an award of a capital sum even although it may also have been suffered in the interests of the applicant'.[27]

The overriding principle was one of fairness rather than precise economic calculation having regard to where the parties were at the beginning of the cohabitation and where they were at the end. The disadvantage that Mrs Gow suffered when she sold her house was her loss of the benefit of the increase in value of her property. She was therefore entitled to compensation for that loss as some of the proceeds of the sale had been used to finance their lifestyle when she cohabited with Mr Grant.

Given that Lord Hope took the view that s 28 was designed to correct imbalances arising out of a non-commercial relationship where parties are quite likely to make contributions or sacrifices without counting the cost or bargaining for a return, it is not surprising that Lord Hope accepted Lady Hale's contention that in an application under s 28 'it is quite impracticable to work out who has paid for what and who has enjoyed what benefits in kind during the cohabitation as people do not keep such running accounts and the cost of working out in detail is quite disproportionate to the task of doing justice between the parties'.[28] In short, a broad brush approach is required. As the principle in s 9(1)(b) of the Family Law (Scotland) Act 1985 provides similar compensation for spouses and civil partners,[29] Lord Hope considered that,

> '... it may be helpful to refer to cases decided under section 9(1)(b) when the court is considering what might be taken to be an economic advantage, disadvantage or contribution for this purpose or how the economic burden of caring for a child is to be dealt with under section 28(2)(b). An assessment of what is in the interests of any relevant child cannot sensibly be reduced to purely financial factors'.[30]

The decision of the Supreme Court in *Gow v Grant* has transformed this area of the law.[31] Section 28 is seen as a way of achieving economic fairness between the parties when their relationship breaks down. While the court must still engage in a balancing exercise, this is to be done in a non-technical and practicable way: common sense rules rather than detailed accounts. In *Whigham v Owen*,[32] the couple had lived together for 27 years before they separated. During that time the defender had accumulated substantial assets of approximately £750,000 through the success of his business interests. The pursuer had given up her career and acted as the primary carer of their three children. As a result, she had assets of less than £10,000 when they ceased to cohabit. Following the Supreme Court's decision in *Gow v Grant*, the Lord Ordinary (Lord Drummond Young)[33] accepted that what was required in a s 28 claim was 'a rough and ready' calculation. In deciding on economic advantages and disadvantages and contributions, the calculation should take into account the factors that are relevant for that purpose in divorce cases.[34] Nor was there a need to calculate the award on a 'precise mathematical basis'. In the circumstances, Lord Drummond Young awarded the pursuer a capital sum of £250,000.[35]

As a result of the decision of the Supreme Court in *Gow v Grant* the judges at first instance have a wide discretion in s 28 applications. The view has rightly been expressed that parties must bring evidence of their financial position at the end of their relationship.[36] Evidence of their financial position at the beginning of their cohabitation would also be valuable.[37] Similarly, the parties must be able to produce some of the evidence of the facts that they wish the court to consider in any balancing exercise.[38] This is important since, as in all discretionary decisions, there is little scope for interference by appellate courts in s 28 claims.[39]

It will be noticed that in a cohabitant's claim for financial provision there is no equivalent of s 9(1)(a) of the FL(S)A 1985, ie fair sharing of the matrimonial or partnership property where fair sharing is *prima facie* equal sharing.[40] Although there is a presumption of common ownership of household goods,[41] this presumption does not apply in relation to valuable property such as savings and other investments, interests in a pension scheme or the family home.[42] It may be because many spouses and civil partners are content with the division of the matrimonial or partnership property under s 9(1)(a), that comparatively little use is made of s 9(1)(b). If there is no matrimonial or partnership property, the courts have taken a rather cavalier approach to the balancing process so that an award of some financial provision can be made under s 9(1)(b).[43] *Gow v Grant* remains the leading case on s 28 applications by cohabitants seeking financial provision on the breakdown of a cohabiting relationship.

---

1 Family Law (Scotland) Act 2006, s 28(1).

2 In *Banks v Banks* [2005] CSOH 144, the Lord Ordinary (Carloway) considered how the couple had socialised and managed their finances to determine when they had ceased to live together as husband and wife. In *M v T* 2011 GWD 40-828 the sheriff applied the same test (Couple had not stopped presenting themselves as cohabitants: cohabitation did not cease until they stopped doing so); *Garrad v Inglis* 2014 GWD 1-17 (Couple ceased to cohabit when, after physically separating for two months while the pursuer worked abroad, the defender told him that their relationship was over and began take steps to secure her position by for example changing her will.)

3 FL(S)A 2006, s 28(8). In *Simpson v Downie* [2012] CSIH 74; 2013 SLT 178 an action was raised within the one-year time limit. The defender sought to introduce a crave for financial provision on her own account in her defences, which were lodged outwith the one-year time period. The court held that the defender's claim was time barred.

4 *Douglas v Bell* 2014 Fam LR 2. To limit the claim to only the most recent period of cohabitation, the sheriff observed 'would fly in the face of normal human experience': ibid at para 42.

5 [2016] CSOH 136; 2017 SCLR 387.

6 Hector MacQueen 'Cohabitants, unjustified enrichment, contract and subsidiarity: Pert v McCaffrey' Fam LB 2020 (165) 4–6. See also: Hector MacQueen, 'Cohabitants in the Scottish Law of Unjustified Enrichment' [2019] *Acta Juridica* 419.

7 See: Law Society of Scotland, 'Rights of Cohabitants: Family Law (Scotland) Act 2006, sections 28 and 29' (March 2019).

8 2020 SC 259. While this decision disagreed with *Courtney's Exrs v Campbell*, Ms Pert was unsuccessful in her action on the basis that her claim for recompense should have been made by an action for specific implement and, in any case, her claim had prescribed in terms of s 6(1) of the Prescription and Limitation (Scotland) Act 1973.

9 Ibid at [para 24].

10 FL(S)A 2006, s 28(2). In *F v D* 2009 Fam LR 111, the sheriff awarded the applicant £3,000 under s 28(2)(b) in respect of the care of the child and £6,000 under s 28(2)(a) in respect of economic advantages given to the defender: as there was no evidence that the defender had suffered any economic disadvantages, the sheriff avoided having to engage in a balancing exercise demanded by s 28(5): s 28(5) is discussed below.

11 FL(S)A 2006, s 28(7). Payment of a capital sum by instalments was made in *M v S* 2008 SLT 871.

12 FL(S)A 2006, s 28(9). It will include a child of whom the cohabitants are the child's parent and second female parent under the Human Fertilisation and Embryology Act 2008 ss 33 and 43, discussed at para **9.2**.

13 In *M v S* 2008 SLT 871 the Lord Ordinary (Matthews) awarded the applicant only half of her prospective economic burden in caring for the child on the assumption that the cost of the upbringing of the child had to be shared fairly between the applicant and the defender. There is no statutory basis for this assumption.

14 FL(S)A 2006, s 28(9) and (10).

15 For discussion, see para **10.9**.

16 FL(S)A 2006, s 28(9).

17 Losses sustained by one cohabitant as a result of a wrong committed by the other are to be pursued in delict not a claim under s 28(2)(a) because the defender does not receive economic advantages from the wrong: *Cameron v Leal* 2010 GWD 19-379.

18 [2017] CSOH 151; 2018 Fam LR 26. See also: *T v W* [2020] 2 WLUK 702.

19 [2012] UKSC 29.

20 Discussed at para **7.17** above.

21 Ibid.

22 [2011] CSIH 25,2011 SC 618.

23 Ibid at para [4].

24 Ibid at para [3].

25 *Gow v Grant* [2012] UKSC 29,2013 SC(UKSC)1.
26 Ibid per Lord Hope at para [33]. In so doing, Lord Hope approved of the approach of Sheriff Miller in *Lindsay v Murphy* 2010 Fam LR 156.
27 Ibid at para [38], approving the approach of Sheriff Dunlop in *Mitchell v Gibson* 2011 Fam LR 53 .
28 Ibid at para [33].
29 Discussed at para **7.17** above.
30 *Gow v Grant* [2012] UKSC 29 at para [36].
31 For some of the difficulties before *Gow,* see *M v S* 2008 SLT 871 and the discussion in the 6th edition of this book at para **8.6**.
32 [2013] CSOH 29.
33 Who, ironically, gave the judgment of the Second Division in *Gow v Grant.*
34 [2013] CSOH 29 at para 10.
35 Lord Drummond Young stated that, if they had been married, he would have awarded the pursuer £368,000. This is because she would have been *prima facie* entitled to half the value of the matrimonial property under s 9(1)(a) of FL(S)A 1985, discussed at para **7.7** above.
36 *M v S* [2017] CSOH 152. See also: *Smith-Milne v Langler* 2013 GWD 13-284; 2013 Fam LR 58.
37 In *Whigham v Owen* 2013 SLT 483, Lord Drummond Young reiterated what Lord Hope stated in *Gow v Grant*, namely that, 'regard must be had to where the parties were at the beginning of the cohabitation and where they were at the end', para [9].
38 *M v* S [2017] CSOH 152. See also: Cameron *v Lukes* 2014 GWD 7-144; [2013 12 WLUK 32.
39 It should also be remembered that, theoretically at least, a court might not treat an applicant as a cohabitant for the purpose of a claim for financial provision because of the length and nature of the relationship and the financial arrangements between the parties during that period FL(S)A 2006, s 25(2).
40 Discussed above at paras **7.7–7.16**.
41 FL(S)A 2006, s 26. Also discussed at para **8.4**.
42 FL(S)A 2006, s 27(3).
43 See, for example, *Wilson v Wilson* 1999 SLT 249, discussed at para **7.17**.

Financial provision on intestacy[1]

8.7 Unlike a surviving spouse or civil partner,[2] a surviving cohabitant does not have legal rights in the deceased cohabitant's free moveable estate. Nor does a surviving cohabitant have prior rights in respect of the deceased cohabitant's intestate estate, ie when the deceased died without a will.[3] As around 75 per cent of Scots die intestate, a surviving cohabitant can find him or herself without any capital when the other cohabitant dies. Moreover, and perhaps, more importantly, where the deceased owned the family home in which they lived together, the surviving cohabitant can be evicted by the deceased's heirs on intestacy who will usually be the deceased's children or grandchildren.

However, by s 29(2) of the Family Law (Scotland) Act 2006, the surviving cohabitant has the right to apply for a share of the deceased cohabitant's property when he or she has died intestate. At the outset it is important to stress that the right only arises on an intestacy.[4] This means that the cohabitant's right can be defeated if the deceased makes a will before he or she dies. For example, A makes a will leaving all her property to a charity. A dies. As A died testate her surviving cohabitant, B, has no right to apply under s 29(2) and as B has no legal rights, B will have no redress against the deceased's estate.

Before an application can be brought the deceased must have been domiciled in Scotland immediately before death.[5]

Even if the deceased was domiciled in Scotland, the Act does not apply to any heritable property situated outwith Scotland. This is because under the rules of private international law, succession to land is governed by the law of the country where the land is situated. This matter was addressed in *Kerr v Mangan*,[6] in which the pursuer sought payment of a capital sum from the defender's net intestate estate which included heritable property in Ireland. Lady Smith stated, 'The conclusion that s 29 reformed the law of succession and is, accordingly, a part of the Scots law of succession is inescapable.'[7] Lady Smith further stated:

> 'If s 29 is not to be regarded as part of the law of succession then the normal rules of private international law applicable in succession matters would not apply. That would mean that a Scottish court had been given the power to order that foreign land be transferred to a cohabitant even if the relevant foreign law provides that it must devolve in a manner which excludes the cohabitant.'[8]

The deceased must also have been cohabiting with the applicant immediately before his death.[9] It is evident that it is not intended that a former cohabitant should have the right to make a claim under s 29(2). But the use of the word 'immediately' is unfortunate. Surely a surviving cohabitant should still have a claim under s 29(2) even if the deceased had been in hospital or a nursing home for several months before his or her death? To achieve this result the provision will have to be construed purposively and with sensitivity.

On an application by the surviving cohabitant, the court can make an order: (i) for payment of a capital sum to the applicant out of the deceased's net intestate estate; and (ii) for heritable or moveable property to be transferred from the deceased's net intestate estate to the applicant.[10] The court can specify the date on which the capital sum should be paid, that the capital sum can be paid in instalments and the date when the property should be transferred.[11] The claim must be brought within six months beginning with the day on which the deceased died.[12]

The definition of net intestate estate is significant. It is so much of the intestate estate as remains after provision has been made for the satisfaction of (a) inheritance tax; (b) other liabilities of the estate having priority over the prior rights and legal rights of a surviving spouse or civil partner; and (c) the prior rights and legal rights of a surviving spouse or civil partner. The last point is important. Where the deceased has died with a surviving spouse or civil partner as well as a surviving cohabitant, then the surviving cohabitant's claim under s 29(2) only applies to what remains of the estate *after* the prior rights and legal rights of the surviving spouse or civil partner have been satisfied. In many cases the prior rights and legal rights of the surviving spouse or civil partner will exhaust the estate[13] and the surviving cohabitant's right under s 29(2) will be valueless.[14]

However, in the majority of cases, the deceased will not be survived by both a spouse or civil partner as well as a cohabitant. A *former* spouse or civil partner does not have legal rights or prior rights in the intestate estates of their ex-spouse or civil partner, having obtained financial provision on divorce or dissolution.

It should also be noticed that in calculating the net intestate estate, no provision has to be made for the satisfaction of the legal rights – *legitim* – of the deceased's children (and their issue).[15] In other words, a surviving cohabitant's claim under s 29(2) is to be considered before the succession rights of the deceased's children are addressed. In short, it is the deceased's children, as opposed to a surviving spouse or civil partner, who will almost certainly 'lose out' when a claim is successfully brought under s 29(2).

In considering a claim under s 29(2), the court has to consider the following factors in section 29(3):

(i) the size and nature of the net intestate estate;

(ii) any benefit received, or to be received, by the surviving cohabitant as a result of the death, for example a pension or life insurance;[16]

(iii) the nature and extent of any other rights against or claims on the deceased's intestate estate. It is only at this stage that the court can take into account that the deceased's children (and their issue) have legal rights and are the heirs on intestacy; and

(iv) any other matter the court thinks appropriate.[17]

It should also be remembered that by virtue of s 25(2) the court could consider that, in the light of the length and nature of the relationship and the degree and extent of any financial arrangements which subsisted during the relationship, the applicant should not be treated as a cohabitant for the purpose of a claim under s 29(2). But these factors are surely very important considerations in determining what would be an appropriate award. In order to do so, the sheriff in *Savage v Purches*[18] had to treat them as other matters he considered appropriate under s 29(3). It is thought that he was correct to do so. However, the case illustrates the fundamental flaws in the structure of the Act.

There is only one subsection in the 2006 Act that gives a court specific guidance on how to exercise its discretion in a s 29(2) claim: s 29(4). This provides that an order under s 29(2) must not have the effect of awarding a surviving cohabitant an amount which is more than that to which he or she would have been entitled to as a surviving spouse or civil partner of the deceased. Put another way, the maximum order a surviving cohabitant can receive is the equivalent of the prior rights and the legal rights that he or she would have received out of the deceased's intestate estate if the survivor had been the deceased's spouse or civil partner.[19] Otherwise little guidance is given on how the court should exercise its discretion.

The difficulty is that the purpose of giving a surviving cohabitant a claim under s 29(2) is not clear. Is it to recognise the surviving cohabitant's economic contributions or to compensate for economic disadvantages sustained in the interests of the deceased. Is it to help a surviving cohabitant who has been financially dependent on the deceased by providing him or her with reasonable financial provision? Or should a surviving cohabitant be treated as a surviving spouse or civil partner unless there are compelling reasons not to do so?[20] What seems clear from case law is that judges are unhappy with the unfettered discretion they have been given under the Act[21] and that it is difficult for solicitors to advise clients on the success of a s 29(2) claim. In these circumstances, a cohabitant may well be advised to settle. This may account for the paucity of reported decisions.

---

1 It should be noted at the start of this section that, as part of its Tenth Programme of Law Reform, which includes Aspects of Family Law and, more specifically, the Rights of Cohabitants; and in light of the Consultation on the Law of Succession, which includes the rights of bereaved cohabitants in intestacy, the Scottish Law Commission did not include a review of s 29 of the Family Law (Scotland) Act 2006 in Discussion Paper No 170 – *Aspects of Family Law: Discussion Paper on Cohabitation.*

2 For discussion see para **3.17**.

3 For discussion see para **3.18**.

4 Family Law (Scotland) Act 2006, s 29(1)(a).

5 FL(S)A 2006, s 29(1)(b)(i). This may be difficult to establish: see *Chebotareva v Khandro* 2008 Fam LR 66.

6 [2014] CSIH 69; 2014 SLT 866.

7 Ibid at para [36].

8 Ibid at para [40].

9 FL(S)A 2006, s 29(1)(b)(ii).

10 FL(S)A 2006, s 29(2). See also s 29(4).

11 FL(S)A 2006, s 29(7) and (8).

12 FL(S)A 2006, s 29(6). There has been much discussion and criticism of the limitations of s 29(6). The Scottish Government is considering changes to the time limits to deliver fairer outcomes. See: The Scottish Government's *Consultation on the Law of Intestacy* (February 2019), Chapter 3: Cohabitants and Intestacy.

13 For discussion, see paras **3.17–3.18**.

14 In *Kerr v Mangan* [2014] CSIH 69, Lady Smith stated at para [33] that: 'There is no principle of general fairness underlying s 29 … [Sections 28 and 29] are structured differently and, in the case of s 29, a power is conferred without identifying any goal to be achieved.'

15 For discussion of legitim see para **3.17**.

16 In *Savage v Purches* 2009 SLT (Sh Ct) 36 one of the reasons that the cohabitant's claim was unsuccessful was that he had received a substantial lump sum and was in receipt of an annual income from the deceased's pension trustees.

17 In *Savage v Purches* (ibid), the sheriff, at para [16], utilised his discretion under s 29(3)(d) to consider the short term of the cohabitants' relationship 'in a way that does justice to the parties'.

18 Ibid.

19 This must include the amount that a surviving spouse or civil partner would receive in the unusual circumstances when a surviving spouse or civil partner is the deceased's heir on intestacy.

20 An approach with which Sheriff Principal Dunlop appears to have supported, albeit obiter, in *Kerr v Mangan* 2013 SLT (Sh Ct) 102, para [23].

21 See the stringent criticism of s 29 made by Lady Smith in *Kerr v Mangan* [2014] CSIH 96.

Chapter 9

Parents and children

INTRODUCTION

9.1 In Scotland, all children are born rights holders. Of course, very young children do not have active capacity[1] to exercise their legal rights and, consequently, in the early ages of childhood, it is usually the parents who ensure the child's rights are respected. The primary purpose of this chapter is to discuss how parentage is established. Before doing so, it is proposed by way of introduction to consider the starting place for a child's legal rights.[2]

Once a child is conceived, the foetus is protected by prohibiting an abortion other than those permissible by s 1(1) of the Abortion Act 1967, which states that a person shall not be guilty of an offence if a pregnancy is terminated by a registered medical practitioner provided two doctors in good faith are of the opinion:

- (a) that the pregnancy has not exceeded its twenty-fourth week and that its continuance would involve risk, greater than if it were terminated, of injury to the physical or mental health of the pregnant woman or any existing children of her family; or
- (b) that the termination is necessary to prevent grave permanent injury to her physical or mental health; or
- (c) that the continuance of the pregnancy would involve risk to her life, greater than if the pregnancy were terminated; or
- (d) that there is a substantial risk that if the child were born it would suffer from such physical or mental abnormalities as to be seriously disabled.[3]

As in all cases of medical treatment the patient, ie the woman, must consent. Where one of the grounds for a lawful termination under s 1(1)(a)–(d) is established, the consent of the genetic father is not required nor can he obtain an interdict to prevent the pregnancy being terminated.[4] Although s 1(1)(a) cannot be used after the twenty-fourth week of the pregnancy, there is no time limit in relation to the other grounds. A later abortion may be necessary, for example, if there has been a delay in establishing that the foetus is developing abnormally for the purposes of s 1(1)(d). Although not illegal *per se*, late termination, ie beyond twenty-four weeks, is not common in Scotland.[5]

Article 2 of the European Convention on Human Rights[6] provides: 'Everyone's right to life shall be protected by law.' It has been held that 'everyone' usually applies to persons who have been born; consequently, lawful termination of a foetus is not a breach of Article 2.[7]

An action in delict will lie when a child is born physically or mentally disabled as a result of injuries sustained in the womb. No action in delict will lie unless the child is born alive. It is only when the child is born alive that the child sustains harm and the delict is completed,[8] albeit that the injuries occurred while the child was a foetus. While there is no authority directly in point it is submitted that, in theory at least, an action may lie even where the injuries were caused as a result of the mother's negligence.[9] A child's right to the physical integrity of the person therefore extends to injuries suffered before the child was born. This conclusion is consistent with the *nasciturus* principle,[10] namely, that in matters of private law a child who is *in utero* should be deemed to be already born whenever this would operate for the benefit of the child.[11]

Where a baby is conceived because of a failed sterilisation procedure, the parents cannot recover damages for the economic cost of raising a healthy – if unplanned – child.[12] Where a child is born with a congenital disability, the increased costs incurred by the parents as a consequence of the child's special needs are recoverable, at least where the medical authorities failed to diagnose that the foetus had a genetic abnormality.[13] In both situations, the parents may be entitled to solatium.[14]

---

1 See **Ch 10**.

2 On the law of Parent and Child see generally A B Wilkinson and K Norrie *The Law Relating to Parent and Child in Scotland* (3rd edn, 2013) afterwards referred to as *Wilkinson and Norrie.*

3 Abortion Act 1967, s 1(1)(a)–(d).

4 *Kelly v Kelly* 1997 SC 285.

5 See *R (on the application of Crowter) v Secretary of State for Health and Social Care*

[2021] EWHC 2536 in which the matter of compatibility of late abortions (after 24-week time limit) with ECHR arts 2, 3, 8 and 14 is raised.

6 Convention for the Protection of Human Rights and Fundamental Freedoms (Rome, 4 November 1950; 213 UNTS 221; TS 71 (1953); Cmd 8969). Most, but not all, of the 1950 Convention has been incorporated into United Kingdom law as Sch 1 to the Human Rights Act 1998.

7 *Paton v United Kingdom* (1981) 3 EHRR 408, '"everyone" does not include the unborn', para [9].

8 *Hamilton v Fife Health Board* 1993 SC 369. For discussion see *Thomson's Delictual Liability* (6th edn, 2021, Bloomsbury Professional), Ch 13.

9 It has long been accepted that actions in delict are competent between parent and child for injuries sustained after the child's birth: *Young v Rankin* 1934 SC 499; *Wood v Wood* 1935 SLT 431.

10 *Nasciturus pro iam nato habetur quotiens de eius commodo agitur* – if it is to the child's benefit, he or she will be treated as having been born in relation to the legal issues arising from events that occurred while the child was *in utero*.

11 See *Stuart v Reid* 2014 Rep LR 107 – Lord Woolman awarded damages to family members after the grandfather was killed in a road accident. The third grandchild, who was born after the deceased's death, was awarded £14,000 to reflect that he had been deprived of his grandfather's society and guidance. See also: *Cohen v Shaw* 1992 SLT 1022.

12 *McFarlane v Tayside Health Board* 2000 SC (HL) 1. The husband and wife sought damages of £100,000 to cover the costs of maintaining the child and Mrs M also sought £10,000 for the pain, distress and discomfort of the pregnancy. Damages were payable to Mrs M only and included loss of earnings. It does not matter if the parent of the healthy child is disabled, for example, if the mother was blind: *Rees v Darlington Memorial NHS Trust* [2004] AC 309.

13 *McLelland v Greater Glasgow Health Board* 2001 SLT 446.

14 *McLelland v Greater Glasgow Health Board* 2001 SLT 446.

ESTABLISHING PARENTAGE

9.2 In the context of family law, the question of who is a parent would seem to be relatively straightforward. However, establishing parentage can raise difficulties that, in turn, can lead to conflict. For this reason, it is important to have rules that establish parentage.

With the technological and other developments in assisted reproductive technology and surrogacy arrangements (see below), there is a need to distinguish between a child's genetic parent[1] and legal parent.[2] This distinction is important as it sets out who has the legal authority to make decisions about the child's health, development and welfare; with whom the child should live; the regulation of contact for a non-resident parent; and who has the legal authority to act as the child's legal representative.[3]

1 Children (Scotland) Act 1995, s 15.
2 A legal parent is a person who has parental responsibilities and parental rights, or in whom parental responsibilities and parental rights have been vested by a court.
3 Children (Scotland) Act 1995, ss 1 and 2 set out parental responsibilities and parental rights.

Mother

9.3 In the not-so-distant past, there was little difficulty in determining who was a child's mother. Where a woman becomes pregnant through sexual intercourse with a male, carries the child in her womb throughout pregnancy and gives birth to the child, then this woman is the biological mother of the child. In this straightforward case, the biological mother is also the legal mother who, by virtue of carrying the child throughout pregnancy, has full parental responsibilities and parental rights regardless of her age or marital status.[1]

Advances in reproductive techniques raise complexities. If an ovum is donated by a donor (A) and then fertilised and the resulting embryo transferred into the donee's womb (B), the question arises as to who is the child's mother – A or B? There is a clear biological connection between A and the child meaning that A is the biological mother; there is no biological connection between B and the child. However, the law is clear that it is B who is the legal mother of the child. Section 33(1) of the Human Fertilisation and Embryology Act 2008 sets out the meaning of 'mother':

> 'The woman who is carrying or has carried a child as a result of the placing in her of an embryo or of sperm and eggs, and no other woman, is to be treated as the mother of the child.'

Sections 54 and 54A of HFEA 2008 deal with 'parental orders' in relation to surrogacy. Following from s 33(1), it is the surrogate who is, in law, the mother of the child. This means that the intended parent or parents are required to apply for a parental order. Several conditions common to both s 54 and s 54A must apply before a parental order may be granted. They include that the surrogate is not the applicant; the gametes of at least one of the applicants (or in a s 54A application, the applicant) were used to bring about the creation of the embryo; and the application must be made during the period of six months beginning with the day on which the child is born.[2]

For a s 54 application, the applicants must be: husband and wife; civil partners; or two persons living as partners in an enduring family relationship and outwith the prohibited degrees of relationship in relation to each other. However, in *Re X (Parental death of intended parent prior to birth)*,[3] the court granted a parental order to Mrs Y. Mr Y, whose gametes had been used along with those of Mrs X (the surrogate) had died when Mrs X was five months pregnant. Under a strict interpretation of s 54, a parental order would be granted only where a joint application was made by a couple and where the child has the gametes of at least one of the applicants.

1 C(S)A 1995, s 3(1)(a). See para **6.2**, fn 3 above.
2 Human Fertilisation and Embryology Act 2008, s 54(1)–(8A) and s 54A(1)–(8).
3 [2020] EWFC 39. The court was satisfied that Arts 8 and 14 of the European Convention on Human Rights were relevant to the decision and allowed the court to interpret the 2008 Act sufficiently widely to allow it to be 'read down' in a way that was compliant with ECHR.

Father

9.4 The legal status of a father is rather more complex than that of a mother. A child's biological father is determined solely by biological criteria. He is the man whose semen fertilised the ovum leading to the birth of the child. In other words, he must be genetically related to the child. There may be instances where there is a dispute over who is the biological father of a child and, for this reason, the law therefore proceeds on the basis of a series of presumptions which can be rebutted by evidence to the contrary.

By s 5(1)(a) of the Law Reform (Parent and Child) (Scotland) Act 1986 a man is presumed to be the father of a child if he was married to, or in a civil partnership with, the mother ('the parties') of the child at any time during the period beginning with the conception and ending with the birth of the child. This presumption applies when:

(a) the parties were married or in a civil partnership both at the date of conception and birth;

(b) the parties were married or in a civil partnership at the date of conception but not at the date of the birth: for example, if the father had died before the child's birth – a posthumous child – or the couple had divorced or had their civil partnership dissolved before the child's birth;

(c) the parties were not married at the date of conception but were married or in a civil partnership at the date of the birth;[1]

(d) the parties married or registered a civil partnership during the pregnancy but were not married or in a civil partnership at the date of birth.[2]

The s 5(1)(a) presumption does not apply where a child was conceived and born before the parties married or registered a civil partnership.[3] The presumption applies in the case of a void or voidable marriage or civil partnership; or irregular marriage in the same way as it applies in the case of a valid and regular marriage.[4]

By s 5(1)(b) of the Law Reform (Parent and Child) (Scotland) Act 1986, a man will be presumed to be the father of a child, if *both* he and the mother of the child have acknowledged that he is the father and the child has been registered as such.[5]

The presumptions in s 5(1)(a) and (b) of the 1986 Act may be rebutted by proof on a balance of probabilities[6] that the man was not the father of the child.

Where the presumptions apply, the presumptive father – or the mother if she alleges her husband or civil partner is not the father – can seek a declarator of non-parentage in the Court of Session or the sheriff court. Where the presumptions do not apply, a declarator of parentage may be sought in the Court of Session or the sheriff court.[7] Thus if a woman has a child, she can seek declarator that a particular man is the father of her child. Conversely, a man can seek declarator that he is the father of a woman's child, but this may raise the problem of consent to have the child DNA tested.[8] If declarator of non-parentage is granted, the presumptions in s 5 of the Law Reform (Parent and Child) (Scotland) Act 1986 are displaced; if declarator of parentage is granted, it will give rise to a presumption to the same effect as the decree.[9] The court shall not grant a decree of declarator unless it is satisfied that the grounds of action have been established by sufficient evidence.[10] Thus in an action of declarator of parentage, the pursuer – if it is the mother of the child – must establish, by evidence, that on the balance of probabilities the alleged man is the father of the child. Corroborated evidence is not required.[11] Similarly, if a man seeks a declarator of parentage, he must establish, by evidence, that on the balance of probabilities he is the father of the child.[12] Finally, in an action of declarator of non-parentage it must be established, by evidence, that on the balance of probabilities the Law Reform (Parent and Child) (Scotland) Act 1986 s 5 presumptions of paternity have been rebutted by, for example, evidence of non-access by the husband to his wife at the probable date of conception. In this context it should be noted that courts have recognised the possibility of abnormal gestation periods.[13]

Whether it is consequent on the s 5 presumptions or by the granting of a declarator of parentage that a man is declared to be the father of a child, he does not automatically obtain parental responsibilities and parental rights in relation to the child. Compare this to the status of the mother (see above). Parental responsibilities and parental rights are vested in parents by law. There are several ways in which a father may acquire parental responsibilities and parental rights over the child.

Section 3(1)(b) of the Children (Scotland) Act 1995 states that the father has parental responsibilities and parental rights if (i) he was married or in a civil partnership with the mother[14] of the child at the time of the child's conception or subsequently, ie this may be after the child is born, or (ii) if not married or in a civil partnership with the mother, the father is registered as the father on the child's birth certificate.[15] Interestingly, it need not be the biological father of the child who is registered on the child's birth certificate. Registration as the father on the birth certificate gives legal parental responsibilities and parental rights to the named father. It cannot change the biological relationship between the child and his or her biological father.

Section 4 of C(S)A 1995 allows the natural father to acquire parental responsibilities and parental rights over his child by signing a 'Parental Responsibilities and Parental Rights Agreement Form' (also known, colloquially, as a 'section 4 agreement') with the child's mother. This form must be signed by both the child's parents to acknowledge their agreement to share the parental responsibilities and parental rights over their child.[16] The father must not already have parental responsibilities and rights in relation to the child. Where the parents have two or more children together, a separate s 4 agreement form must be signed for each child. The signed agreement must be registered in the Books of Council and Session before it has legal effect.[17]

Where the father of the child has not acquired parental responsibilities and parental rights through the legal channels set out above, and where the father wishes to acquire parental responsibilities and parental rights in relation to his child, but the mother of the child is, for whatever reason, unwilling to agree to share parental responsibilities and parental rights with the father, then, as a last resort, the father can raise an action in court under s 11 of the C(S)A 1995.[18]

---

1 Cf the position at common law in *Gardner v Gardner* (1876) 3 R 695, (1877) 4 R (HL) 56.

2 For example, if the husband or male civil partner dies before the child is born.

3 This was also the position at common law: *Imre v Mitchell* 1958 SC 439; *James v McLennan* 1971 SLT 162.

4 Law Reform (Parent and Child) (Scotland) Act 1986, s 5(2). A difficulty might arise if a woman marries husband A or enters a civil partnership with partner A, and later goes through a ceremony of marriage or registers a civil partnership with B. If the woman has a child, both A and B have the benefit of the s 5(1)(a) presumption as the presumption applies both to the woman's valid marriage or CP with A and her void 'marriage' or 'CP' with B (by virtue of s 5(2)). In these circumstances it is submitted that A and B must attempt to establish paternity by evidence. It is irrelevant that the parties to the void marriage were not acting in good faith, ie knew it was void. Cf the Children (Scotland) Act 1995, s 3(2)(a) and (b), discussed at para **11.3**.

5 LR(PC)(S)A 1986, s 5(1)(b) and Sch 1, para 8. Cf the position at common law where no presumption arises from cohabitation: *A v G* 1984 SLT (Sh Ct) 65.

6 LR(PC)(S)A 1986, s 5(4). At common law, the presumption *pater est quem nuptiae demonstrant*, ie the father is the man to whom the marriage points, applied when the husband and wife were married at the date of conception. It was a presumption which could only be rebutted by evidence which established beyond reasonable doubt that the husband did not have access to the wife at the probable date of conception: see *S v S* 1977 SLT (Notes) 65. See also *Docherty v McGlynn* 1983 SLT 654.

7 LR(PC)(S)A 1986, s 7(2) and (3).
8 *Docherty v McGlynn* 1983 SLT 654.
9 LR(PC)(S)A 1986, s 5(3).
10 Civil Evidence (Scotland) Act 1988, s 8(1).
11 CE(S)A 1988, s 1(1). The doctrine of corroboration by false denial has been abolished: CE(S)A 1988, s 1(2).
12 See, for example, *Docherty v McGlynn* 1985 SLT 237, OH; *Campbell v Grossart* 1988 GWD 24-1004.
13 See, for example, *Currie v Currie* 1950 SC 10 (W gave birth 336 days after the couple last cohabited: held not to be an impossible period of pregnancy).
14 Section 1 of the Civil Partnership (Scotland) Act 2020 repeals the words 'same sex', thus extending civil partnership to persons of different sex.
15 Family Law (Scotland) Act 2006, s 23 and Registration of Births, Deaths and Marriages (Scotland) Act 1965, s 18.
16 It should be noted that, where both parents of a child are under the age of 16 years, the mother will have full parental responsibilities and parental rights by virtue of s 3(1)(a) of C(S)A 1995. If the parents then sign a 'section 4 agreement', the child's father will acquire parental responsibilities and parental rights 'whatever age they may be': C(S)A 1995, s 4(1). Also, under s 11(2)(b)(i) a court is empowered to grant an order imposing parental responsibilities and parental rights on a father who is under the age of 16 years (or if the person is not the parent of the child, the person must be at least 16 years of age).
17 C(S)A 1995, s 4(3).
18 C(S)A 1995, s 11(2)(b). See **Ch 11**.

Assisted reproduction

9.5 In cases involving assisted reproduction important statutory rules apply to determine the child's parentage. As we have seen, the woman who is carrying or has carried a child as a result of the placing in her of an embryo or of sperm and eggs, and no other woman, is to be treated as the mother of the child for all legal purposes.[1]

Where a woman is married at the time when she is artificially impregnated and the sperm used is not her husband's, her husband is to be treated as the father of the child for all legal purposes unless it is shown that he did not consent to the treatment.[2] This provision must be construed as applying to same sex marriages.[3] This means that, if A and B are same sex female spouses and B has a child by artificial insemination, A shall be treated as the parent of the child unless she did not consent to the treatment.

Similarly, where a woman is a party to a civil partnership at the time when she is artificially impregnated, the other civil partner is to be treated as the child's parent for all legal purposes unless it is shown that she did not consent to the treatment.[4] For these purposes, a marriage and civil partnership includes a void marriage or civil partnership if either or both spouses or civil partners believed that their marriage or civil partnership was valid.[5]

Where the treatment is provided by a person to whom a licence applies, when a woman and a man are not married at the time of the artificial impregnation,[6] the man will be the father of the child for all legal purposes if the agreed fatherhood conditions apply. These are that: (a) he gives notice to the person responsible that he consents to being the child's father; (b) the woman gives notice to the person responsible that she consents to him being so treated; (c) that she does not give a further notice that another man or woman should be the parent of the child; and (d) the mother and the man are not within the prohibited degrees of relationship.[7] There are similar provisions where the mother and another woman are not parties to a same sex marriage or a civil partnership. If the agreed female parenthood conditions apply,[8] the other woman will be the parent of the child for all purposes (except in relation to succession to a title etc).[9] She is called the second female parent.

Where a person is to be treated as a father or parent by virtue of s 35 and s 36 of the HFEA 2008 or as a parent by virtue of s 42 and s 43, no other person is to be treated as the father or parent of the child.[10] It is also provided that the donor of sperm used for treatment under the 2008 Act is not to be treated as the father of the child[11] and that a woman is not to be treated as the parent of the child merely because she has donated eggs to be used in treatment.

These provisions are of particular relevance to lesbian couples who are not married or in a civil partnership. They enable the mother's partner to be treated as her child's second female parent and, as we shall see, give her the opportunity to have parental responsibilities and parental rights in relation to the child. By s 4A of the Children (Scotland) Act 1995, the mother of the child may, by agreement with a second female parent, provide that the other parent shall have parental responsibilities and parental rights as if the other parent were treated as a parent by virtue of s 42 of HFEA 2008.

It is important to stress that these provisions only apply where the child has been conceived as a result of assisted reproduction. If a woman has conceived a child as the result of sexual intercourse, her female spouse or civil partner, or female cohabitant will not be the child's parent though the child may be accepted by them as a child of the family.[12]

1 HFEA 2008, ss 33 and 48(1). In relation to all these rules, legal purposes do not include the right to succeed to any title, coat of arms, honour or dignity: HFEA 2008, s 48(8).

2 HFEA 2008, ss 35(1) and 48(1).

3 Marriage and Civil Partnership (Scotland) Act 2014, s 4.

4 HFEA 2008, ss 42 and 48(1).

5 HFEA 2008, ss 49(1) and 50(1). The provisions do not apply if at the time a judicial separation was in force: ibid.

6 The sperm used must not be that of the man: in addition, there must be no other man who is the father of the child by virtue of s 35 and no other woman who is the parent of the child by virtue of ss 35 or 42.

7 HFEA 2008, ss 36, 37 and 48(1).

8 In substance they are the same as the agreed fatherhood conditions.

9 HFEA 2008, ss 43, 44 and 48(1).

10 HFEA 2008, ss 38(1) and 45(1). Note, however, ss 38(3) and 45(3) which appear to ensure that the presumption of paternity in s 5(1)(a) of the LR(PC)A 1986 is not automatically displaced by the provisions in the HFEA 2008: but since the 2008 Act only applies when the father is not genetically related to the child, the presumption will be easily rebutted and fatherhood will then be determined by the provisions of the 2008 Act.

11 HFEA 2008, s 41.

12 There are also provisions in the Act dealing with the situation where (a) the sperm is used or the embryo is transferred after the death of the donor who had consented to be the child's father (s 39); (b) the embryo is transferred after the death of a spouse or intended father (s 40); and (c) the embryo is transferred after the death of a civil partner or intended second female parent (s 46). Where these apply the particulars of the deceased as the child's father or parent can be entered into a relevant register of births; HFEA 2008, ss 39, 40 and 46. See also: *R v Human Fertilisation and Embryology Authority, Ex p Blood* [1997] 2 All ER 687, in which the Court of Appeal held that Diane Blood had the right under EU law to take her deceased husband's sperm to a clinic in Belgium for treatment. Mr and Mrs Blood had intended to start a family and Mr Blood died before Mrs Blood became pregnant. Mr Blood had not given his written consent for his sperm to be used. The storage and preservation of sperm from an unconscious man without his written consent was unlawful under HFEA 2008.

DNA PROFILING

9.6 In the past, in actions of declarator of parentage or non-parentage, blood test evidence was of immense importance. By taking blood samples from a child, the mother and the alleged or presumptive father, it was possible to establish that, because of his blood group, the man could not be the father of the child, ie blood tests could lead to an exclusionary result. If a non-exclusionary result was obtained, the blood tests merely established that any man within that blood group *could* be the child's father. In other words, blood tests could not establish that a man was genetically the child's father.

In the mid-1980s, DNA profiling overtook the utility of blood test evidence in terms of reliability of results and is used where a question arises over who is the father of a child. By taking samples of bodily fluid or tissue from the child, the mother and the alleged or presumptive father, it is possible by DNA profiling to establish positively whether the man is the child's father, ie an inclusionary result can be obtained. The value of DNA profiling evidence in determining issues of paternity is obvious. Nevertheless the law has been uncertain in its application[1] and several problems remain.

The first is to consider who has the power to consent to samples of blood, bodily fluid or tissue being taken from a child. In civil proceedings relating to the determination of parentage, where such a sample is sought from a child below the age of 16 by a party to the proceedings or a curator *ad litem*,[2] any person having parental responsibilities and parental rights may consent.[3] However, if a qualified medical practitioner takes the view that a child under 16 understands the nature and possible consequences of the tests, then the child has capacity to consent or withhold consent.[4] Where such a sample is sought from a person, for example, a baby, who is incapable of giving consent, by s 6 of the Law Reform (Parent and Child) (Scotland) Act 1986 the court has power to consent to the taking of a sample where:

(a) there is no person who is entitled to give such consent, for example if the child is an orphan; or

(b) there is such a person but it is not reasonably practicable to obtain his or her consent, for example if the child's parents are abroad, or a parent is unwilling to accept the responsibility of giving or withholding consent.[5]

A particular difficulty arises if the person with parental responsibilities and parental rights is the child's presumptive father. Consider the following example. A husband and wife are married at the date of the child's conception and birth. Section 5(1) of the 1986 Act will operate so that the husband will be presumed to be the child's father and consequently will have parental responsibilities and parental rights.[6] If the husband subsequently brings an action of declarator of non-parentage, can he consent to samples being taken from the child when the purpose of so doing is to rebut the s 5 presumption by establishing on the balance of probabilities that he is not the father? *Docherty v McGlynn*[7] is authority that a presumptive father may consent to samples being taken from a child but it is important to note that in this case he (the presumptive father) wished to do so to establish that he was in fact the child's genetic father. Could, therefore, a presumptive father rely on this presumption if his purpose was to deny that he was, in fact, the child's genetic father? In spite of *dicta* in *Docherty v McGlynn*[8] that he cannot do so, it is submitted that he can. Until the s 5 presumption is rebutted, the husband is the child's presumptive father and can act as the child's legal representative.[9] *It is in that capacity* that he has the power to consent to the blood or DNA test on the child. Even if his purpose is to establish that he is not the child's genetic father, this does not undermine the legality of his consent to samples being taken from the child which was given in his capacity as the child's legal representative. As we shall see,[10] the court may refuse to admit the evidence so obtained if it would be against the child's interests to do so.

The second problem is that it is a cardinal principle of Scots law that in civil proceedings the courts will not make an order to compel a person to submit to a DNA test against his or her will.[11] Similarly, the court will not make an order to compel a person with parental responsibilities and parental rights to consent to samples of blood, bodily fluid or tissue being taken from the child.[12] Moreover, it would appear that at common law the court could not make a direction that a sample should be given and then draw adverse inferences if a sample was refused.[13]

Section 70(1) of the Law Reform (Miscellaneous Provisions) (Scotland) Act 1990 provides that in civil proceedings the court[14] may request a party to the proceedings[15] to provide a sample of blood, bodily fluid or tissue or consent to such a sample being taken from a child in relation to whom the party has power to give consent. This provision still does not give the court the power to *compel* a person to give such a sample or consent to such a sample being taken from a child.

However, if the person refuses or fails to provide such a sample being taken from a child, 'the court may draw … such adverse inference, if any, … as seems to it to be appropriate'.[16] In *Smith v Greenhill*,[17] it was held that the court has discretion: (1) whether or not to draw an adverse inference at all; and (2) if it decides to do so, as to the nature of the inference. In this case, the pursuer, S, sought a declarator of parentage claiming to be the father of Mrs G's child. Mr G had also had sexual intercourse with Mrs G around the probable date of conception. Mr G refused to consent to samples being taken from the child. It was held that any adverse inference to be drawn from Mr G's refusal was not *per se* enough to rebut the presumption that Mr G was the father of the child.

Where a person had died, the Scottish courts were prepared to admit hospital records containing the blood group of the deceased where the deceased's blood group was necessary to determine a child's paternity by the use of blood tests.[18]

Finally, in *Docherty v McGlynn*,[19] the Inner House of the Court of Session held that, in the exercise of its inherent protective jurisdiction in relation to children, the court could intervene and refuse to admit such evidence if it was not in the child's interests to do so. Moreover, while it is expressly enacted that a court cannot exercise its powers under s 6(3) of the 1986 Act to consent to a blood sample being taken from a child unless satisfied that it would not be detrimental to the child's health to do so,[20] it is submitted that a court would not consent if the results of the blood tests would be contrary to the child's interests. In reaching its decision in *Docherty v McGlynn*,[21] the Inner House relied upon the English case of *S v S*,[22] where Lord Reid concluded that 'the court ought to permit a blood test of a young child to be taken unless satisfied that it would be against the child's interest'.[23]

In what circumstances will the courts either refuse to make a request under s 70(1) of the 1990 Act that a party to the proceedings should consent to a sample of blood, bodily fluid or tissue being taken from a child, or refuse to admit the results of blood or DNA tests which have been carried out on a child with the appropriate consents? While it is an ageing case, *Docherty v McGlynn*[24] reinforces the principle that a court, in making its decision, must consider the best interests of the child as its foremost consideration.

It is submitted that knowing the truth must always be in the interests of the parties and, only in exceptional circumstances will it be against the best interests of the child to withhold the truth about his or her biological parent(s).

---

1 See, for example, *Torrie v Turner* 1990 SLT 718, where the Inner House held that a court has no power to make a direction that a person should give a sample for the purposes of DNA screening though this could lead to a positive result of paternity.

2 A *curator ad litem* is a person appointed by the court to protect the interests of the child in the proceedings.

3 Law Reform (Parent and Child) (Scotland) Act 1986, s 6(1) and (2). On parental responsibilities and parental rights, see **Ch 11**.

4 Age of Legal Capacity (Scotland) Act 1991, s 2(4), discussed at para **10.2**.

5 LR(PC)(S)A 1986, s 6(3). It should be noted that s 6(3) of the 1986 Act applies to any person – not necessarily a child – who is incapable of consent, for example, a person suffering from mental illness that limits capacity.

6 Children (Scotland) Act 1995, s 3(1)(b)(i). See para **11.3**.

7 1983 SLT 645.

8 1983 SLT 645 at 746, per the Lord President (Emslie) approving *Whitehall v Whitehall* 1958 SC 252 and dicta in *Imre v Mitchell* 1958 SC 439.

9 C(S)A 1995, ss 3(1)(b)(i) and 2(1)(d). See **Ch 11**.

10 See below.

11 *Whitehall v Whitehall* 1958 SC 252; *Torrie v Turner* 1990 SLT 718.

12 *Docherty v McGlynn* 1983 SLT 645; Torrie v *Turner* 1990 SLT 718.

13 *Torrie v Turner* 1990 SLT 718. Cf the approach of Lord Cameron in *Docherty v McGlynn* 1983 SLT 645 at 650.

14 That is, the Court of Session or the sheriff court: Law Reform (Miscellaneous Provisions) (Scotland) Act 1990, s 70(4). The court may make the request *ex proprio motu*: LR(MP)(S)A 1990, s 70(1). Cf the position in the LR(PC)(S)A 1986, s 6(1).

15 A child's grandmother who defended an action of declarator of parentage in the capacity of executrix to her deceased son, the alleged father, has been held to be a party to the proceedings for this purpose: *MacKay v MacKay* 1995 SLT (Sh Ct) 30.

16 LR(MP)(S)A 1990, s 70(2).

17 1994 SLT (Sh Ct) 22.

18 *Docherty v McGlynn (No 2)* 1985 SLT 237, OH.

19 1983 SLT 645.

20 LR(PC)(S)A 1986, s 6(4).

21 *Docherty v McGlynn (No 1)* 1983 SLT 645.
22 *S v S* [1972] AC 24, HL.
23 [1972] AC 24 at 45.
24 *Docherty v McGlynn (No 1)* 1983 SLT 645.

LEGITIMACY AND ILLEGITIMACY

Historical background

9.7 It is worth looking briefly at the historical background to the status of illegitimacy as it sheds light on the current position in today's society. As stated above, the status of illegitimacy was abolished by s 1 of the Law Reform (Parent and Child) (Scotland) Act 1986. For centuries a child's rights in Scots law were dependent upon whether the child was legitimate. A child was legitimate if the parents were validly married at the date of the child's conception or birth or any time in between.[1] When the child was conceived during a valid marriage, the husband was presumed to be the child's father: *pater est quem nuptiae demonstrant.* Thus, for example, where a couple was validly married at the date of the child's conception the child was presumed to be the legitimate child of the husband even if the husband died before the child's birth. If a child was conceived and born out of wedlock, the child was considered illegitimate.[2]

Where the parents' marriage was void, a child conceived or born during the void marriage could be regarded as legitimate as a result of the doctrine of putative marriage. Before this doctrine was applicable, at least one of the parties must have entered into the 'marriage' in the *bona fide* belief that the marriage was valid, ie in ignorance of any impediment to the marriage. The error had to be one of fact not of law, for example, if a man and a woman married without realising they were uncle and niece, the doctrine was applicable (error of fact) but it did not apply if they had married in the belief that uncle and niece had capacity to marry each other under the law of Scotland (error of law).[3] A child who was conceived or born during a voidable marriage retained the status of legitimacy even if a declarator of nullity of marriage was subsequently obtained.[4] (Since the only ground of a voidable marriage is incurable impotency, the number of children involved was very small.)

When a child was born illegitimate, at common law the child could be legitimated by the subsequent valid marriage of the parents: legitimation *per subsequens matrimonium*. Although the effect of the doctrine was retrospectively to treat the child as legitimate from the date of birth, it did not apply if the child's parents lacked the capacity to marry each other at the date of the child's conception.[5] The law was changed by the Legitimation (Scotland) Act 1968.[6] This provided that a child would become legitimated as a result of the parents' subsequent marriage provided that the child was living at the date of the marriage and the father was domiciled in Scotland at that date.[7] It was irrelevant that the parents lacked capacity to marry at the date of the child's conception[8] but, unlike the common law position, the child was only treated as legitimate from the date of the marriage.[9] A marriage for the purposes of the Legitimation (Scotland) Act 1968 included a putative and voidable marriage.[10]

The law took pains to preserve a child's status of legitimacy. For example, the presumption *pater est quem nuptiae demonstrant* was only rebuttable by proof beyond reasonable doubt that the husband was not the father of the child.[11] Moreover, because of the scope of the doctrine of putative marriage and the possibility of legitimation by the subsequent marriage of a child's parents, the range of persons treated as legitimate was wide.

Nevertheless, it came to be considered reprehensible that the rights of children should continue to depend on the marital status of their parents. Legal discrimination against illegitimate children was held to a be a breach of Article 8 (right to respect for private and family life) of the European Convention on Human Rights.[12] The matter was considered by the Scottish Law Commission[13] and its recommendations were enacted in the Law Reform (Parent and Child) (Scotland) Act 1986. That Act has been amended by the Family Law (Scotland) Act 2006[14] so that the status of illegitimacy can finally be erased from Scots law.

---

1 Bell *Principles of the Law of Scotland* (10th edn, 1899) s 1624. If the child was conceived before marriage and the husband knew at the time of the ceremony that his wife was pregnant and he had had intercourse with her at the probable date of conception, there was a strong presumption that the child was the legitimate child of the husband: *Gardner v Gardner* (1876) 3 R 695, (1877) 4 R (HL) 56.

2 *James v McLennan* 1971 SLT 162.

3 *Purves' Trustees v Purves* (1896) 22 R 513.

4 Law Reform (Miscellaneous Provisions) Act 1949, s 4. See **Ch 2.**

5 Erskine *An Institute of the Law of Scotland* (8th edn, 1870) I, 67, 52; Bell's *Principles* 1627; *Kerr v Martin* (1840) 2 D 752.

6 This Act is no longer in force.

7 Legitimation (Scotland) Act 1968, s 1.

8 By L(S)A 1968, s 4, certain children who failed to be legitimated *per subsequens matrimonium* because their parents lacked capacity to marry at the date of their conception were to be treated as legitimate from the date of the commencement of the 1968 Act. Cf *Wright's Trustees v Callander* 1992 SLT 498.

9 L(S)A 1968, s 1(1).

10 L(S)A 1968, s 8(1).

11 See, for example, *Ballantyne v Douglas* 1953 SLT (Notes) 10 at 11, per Lord Patrick. Today, the presumption of paternity under the Law Reform (Parent and Child) (Scotland) Act 1986, s 5, can be rebutted by proof on a balance of probabilities: LR(PC)(S)A 1986, s 5(4).

12 Convention for the Protection of Human Rights and Fundamental Freedoms (Rome, 4 November 1950; 213 UNTS 221; TS 71 (1953); Cmd 8969). Most, but not all, of the 1950 Convention has been incorporated into United Kingdom Law as Sch 1 to the Human Rights Act 1998. See *Marckx v Belgium* (1979) 2 EHRR 330.

13 See Illegitimacy (Scot Law Com No 82).

14 FL(S)A 2006, ss 21 and 45(2) and Sch 3.

Chapter 10

Children's legal capacity and rights

INTRODUCTION

10.1 As stated at the beginning of Chapter 9, all children are born rights holders. The purpose of this chapter is to examine some of the most important legal rights that children have and how these rights are enforced. As a child grows and matures, there may be a conflict between the child's 'right' to self-determination and the parents' responsibilities and rights in relation to the child's upbringing. A full discussion of this important issue will take place in Chapter 11 which discusses parental responsibilities and parental rights in some detail. In this chapter, we are concerned with a child's capacity to enter into juristic acts and to seek redress when the child's rights have been infringed. We shall also consider when children may incur liability in respect of their actions. In this context, Scots law makes an important distinction between a child below 16 and a young person over that age. Section 1(1)(b) of the Age of Legal Capacity (Scotland) Act 1991 states that 'a person of or over the age of 16 years shall have legal capacity to enter into any transaction'. Note that this does not affect the age at which a child reaches the age of majority, which is age 18.[1] At the outset it must be emphasised that the treatment of the substantive law on many of these issues is not intended to be exhaustive.

1 Age of Majority (Scotland) Act 1969. See also s 97(1) of the Children and Young People (Scotland) Act 2014 which defines a child as 'a person who has not attained the age of 18'. Art 1 of the UNCRC also states, 'a child means every human being below the age of 18 years unless, under the law applicable to the child, majority is attained earlier'.

LEGAL TRANSACTIONS

Children under 16

10.2 In Scots law a child of any age has passive capacity, ie all children are rights holders and the child enjoys the full complement of legal rights, for example the right to own heritable and moveable property.[1] As a general rule, a child under 16 has no active capacity.[2] This means that the child cannot enter into juristic acts, for example make a contract. The child cannot pursue or defend actions when the child's rights have been infringed. Instead, a person entitled to act as the child's legal representative must enter into juristic acts for the child's benefit and pursue or defend actions on the child's behalf. The right to act as a child's legal representative is one of the parental responsibilities and parental rights[3] which, *prima facie*, parents have in respect of their children. Accordingly, it is the parent who will usually enter into a transaction[4] on behalf of the child. If a child purports to enter into a transaction without the capacity to do so, the transaction is void.[5] So, for example, if a child of ten purported to buy a mobile phone costing £1,000, the contract of sale is null. Where a parent enters into a contract on behalf of a child, the contract is valid even if it is to the child's disadvantage. Any remedy[6] the child may have is against the parent, not the other party to the contract.[7] If, for example, P enters into a contract with A on behalf of P's child, C, C has no remedy against A if the contract is disadvantageous to C but may have a remedy against P for failing to act as a reasonable and prudent person.[8]

However, there are important exceptions to the general rule of absence of legal capacity until the child reaches 16:

(i) A child under the age of 16 has legal capacity to enter into a transaction of a kind commonly entered into by persons of the child's age and circumstances *and* provided the terms of the contract are not unreasonable.[9] If 'commonly' is interpreted as 'not unusually or surprisingly' as opposed to 'often', the scope of this section is potentially very wide. Not only would it cover such transactions as the purchase of sweets or bus and rail tickets but also 'one-off' but not unusual contracts, such as the purchase of a bicycle or computer. It should also be noted that before the child is bound by the transaction, its terms must not be unreasonable.

(ii) A child aged 12 or over has the legal capacity to make a will;[10] the child can test on both heritable and moveable property.[11]

(iii) An adoption order or a permanence order (whether or not it contains a provision granting authority for the child to be adopted)[12] cannot be made in respect of a child aged 12 or over unless the child consents.[13]

(iv) A transaction includes giving any consent having legal effect.[14] Thus, giving consent to any surgical, medical or dental procedure or treatment on the child is a legal transaction. Where the child is under 16, the parent, as the child's legal representative, can give consent to such procedures or treatments on the child's behalf.[15] However, a child under 16 has capacity to consent if, in the opinion of a qualified medical practitioner attending the child, the child is capable of understanding the nature and possible consequences of the procedure or treatment.[16]

Several points should be noted. First, the child's capacity to consent is determined by the qualified medical practitioner, ie it is the qualified medical practitioner who decides whether the child is capable of understanding the nature and possible consequences of the procedure or treatment and consequently whether the child has legal capacity to consent. There is no lower age limit in s 2(4) of the Age of Legal Capacity (Scotland) Act 1991. What is important is the opinion of the medical practitioner.

Secondly, the language of s 2(4) of the ALC(S)A Act 1991 is enabling. It empowers a child under 16 to consent. It is silent on whether a child, whom the medical practitioner has decided does understand the nature and possible consequences of the proposed procedure or treatment, has capacity to refuse consent.[17] Since an invasion of bodily integrity is an assault in the absence of positive consent, it can be argued that inherent in the capacity to consent is the capacity to refuse consent, *viz* if a person does not positively consent, an invasion of bodily integrity cannot lawfully take place.[18] Further support for this view is to be found in s 186 of the Children's Hearings (Scotland) Act 2011. This section provides that even if a court or children's hearing specifically directs that a child should undergo medical examination or treatment, this does not override the right of a child who has s 2(4) capacity to refuse consent. Again, s 131A of the Education (Scotland) Act 1980 presupposes that a child with s 2(4) capacity can refuse to consent to medical procedures carried out by school doctors.

It should be noted that there is no 'best interests' provision in s 2(4). However, the English courts have been prepared to override a child's refusal to consent where the proposed procedure or treatment is in the best interests of the child.[19] It remains to be seen whether the Scottish courts will find a way to reach a similar conclusion. In practice, if a child is refusing to consent to a proposed procedure or treatment, the qualified medical practitioner may come to the conclusion that the refusal results from the child's lack of capacity to understand the nature and possible consequences of the procedure or treatment and, therefore, does not hold the child to possess the required s 2(4) capacity. In these circumstances, the medical practitioner would then ask the parent as the child's legal representative to consent on behalf of the child.[20]

(v) A child under 16 has legal capacity to instruct a solicitor in connection with any civil matter provided the child has a general understanding of what it means to do so. A child aged 12 or more is presumed[21] to be of sufficient age and maturity to have such understanding but a child below that age may instruct a solicitor if the child, in fact, has such understanding.[22]

(vi) If a girl under 16 has a baby, she will automatically have parental responsibilities and rights in respect of her child.[23] Although under 16, the mother may exercise her parental responsibilities and parental rights.[24] Where a boy under 16 is the father of a child and has parental responsibilities and rights in respect of the child, he is also able to exercise them.[25]

---

1 Age of Legal Capacity (Scotland) Act 1991, s 1(3)(e).

2 ALC(S)A 1991, s 1(1)(a).

3 Children (Scotland) Act 1995 (C(S)A), ss 1(1)(d) and 2(1)(d).

4 'Transaction' is defined as a transaction having legal effect: it includes unilateral transactions, the exercise of testamentary capacity, the exercise of a power of appointment, bringing or defending actions, acting as arbiter or trustee, acting as an instrumentary witness and giving consent having legal effect: ALC(S)A 1991, s 9.

5 ALC(S)A 1991, s 2(5).

6 See para **11.2**.

7 This is because the old remedy of reducing the contract as against the other party on the grounds of minority and lesion has been abolished: ALC(S)A 1991, s 1(5). On reduction on the grounds of minority and lesion, see *Wilkinson and Norrie* paras 1.18ff.

8 C(S)A 1995, s 10(1), discussed at para **11.2**.

9 ALC(S)A 1991, s 2(1)(a) and (b).
10 ALC(S)A 1991, s 2(2). A parent as the child's legal representative cannot make the child's will.
11 On children's rights to legitim out of their parents' moveable estate, see para **3.17**.
12 On adoption and permanence orders see Ch 13.
13 Adoption and Children (Scotland) Act 2007, ss 32 and 84(1) and (2).
14 ALC(S)A 1991, s 9.
15 For full discussion, see para **11.9**.
16 ALC(S)A 1991, s 2(4). For the purposes of s 2(4), the storage of gametes in accordance with the Human Fertilisation and Embryology Act 1990 is to be treated as a medical procedure and a person under the age of 16 can consent to the use of his cells for the purpose of research where the child is capable of understanding the nature of the research: ALC(S)A 1991, s 2(4ZA) and (4ZB).
17 In *Houston, Applicant* 1996 SCLR 943 there was a concession that a 15-year-old boy with s 2(4) capacity had the right to refuse to consent to medical treatment. This case concerned the detention of the boy under the Mental Health (Scotland) Act 1984, so the issue of s 2(4) capacity was not explored in depth in this case.
18 The patient does not have to say 'I refuse to consent': if the patient is silent, the proposed procedure or treatment cannot lawfully go ahead without the patient's positive consent. This is subject to the necessity principle where, for example, treatment can be carried out without consent if the patient is unconscious after an accident.
19 See: *F v F* [2013] EWHC 2683 (Fam); *Re M (child: refusal of medical treatment)* [1999] 2 FLR 1097; *Re W (a minor)* [1992] 4 All ER 627.
20 For full discussion, see para **11.9**.
21 A legal presumption is one where a court assumes a fact to be true until there is sufficient evidence to show otherwise.
22 ALC(S)A 1991, s 2(4A). If the child has s 2(4A) capacity he or she will also have capacity to sue or defend in civil proceedings: ALC(S)A 1991, s 2(4B).
23 Children (Scotland) Act 1995, s 3(1)(a).
24 ALC(S)A 1991, s 1(3)(g).
25 Ibid. He will have parental responsibilities and rights if he was registered as the child's father on or after 4 May 2006 or if the mother agreed he should have them. For discussion see para **11.3**.

YOUNG PERSONS AGED 16 BUT UNDER 18 YEARS OLD

10.3 A young person aged 16 years and over has active legal capacity to enter into any transaction.[1] However, when a young person has entered into a transaction between the ages of 16 and 18, the court has power to set the transaction aside if it is a prejudicial transaction.[2] The court can set aside such a transaction until the young person reaches 21.[3] A prejudicial transaction is defined as a transaction which an adult, exercising reasonable prudence, would not have entered into in the circumstances of the young person at the time of entering into the transaction and has caused or is likely to cause substantial prejudice to the young person.[4]

Certain transactions cannot be set aside. These include consent to adoption orders, consent to surgical, medical or dental procedures or treatment, transactions in the course of the young person's trade, business or profession, transactions induced by the young person's fraudulent misrepresentation as to age or transactions ratified by the young person after the age of 18 when he or she knew that it could be set aside.[5]

When a young person is between 16 and 18, all the parties to a proposed transaction may make an application to the court to have the transaction ratified.[6] The court cannot ratify the transaction if it is satisfied that an adult exercising reasonable prudence in the circumstances of the young person would not have entered into the transaction.[7] If the transaction is ratified, it cannot be set aside as a prejudicial transaction.[8] Thus for example, if A intends to purchase a house owned by B who is aged 17, A and B should apply to the court to have the proposed sale ratified. The court will ratify the proposed sale if satisfied that an adult exercising reasonable prudence would have sold the house if in B's position. Once ratified, B cannot set the sale aside on the ground that it is a prejudicial transaction.

1 Age of Legal Capacity (Scotland) Act 1991, s 1(1)(b).
2 ALC(S)A 1991, s 3(1).
3 ALC(S)A 1991, s 3(1).
4 ALC(S)A 1991, s 3(2). A typical example of a prejudicial transaction would be if the young person undertook a cautionary obligation.
5 ALC(S)A 1991, s 3(3).
6 ALC(S)A 1991, s 4.
7 ALC(S)A 1991, s 4(2)
8 ALC(S)A 1991, s 3(3)(j).

DELICTUAL LIABILITY

10.4 The Age of Legal Capacity (Scotland) Act 1991 does not affect delictual liability.[1] Where a child under 16 is injured by the wrongous or negligent act of another, the child's legal representative can sue for damages in delict on the child's behalf.[2] Where the young person is aged 16 or over, he or she has capacity to bring the action. If a child is injured by his or her parent an action for damages in delict is competent:[3] in these circumstances, a curator *ad litem* will be appointed for the child.

Conversely, children can be liable in delict for their wrongful acts if the requisite intention or negligence can be established. Since children are rarely wealthy or insured, there are few, if any, cases where they have been sued for damages in delict. This will not apply if a young person aged 17 causes injury through negligent driving because there is compulsory third-party insurance. More importantly, it has been held that a child can be guilty of contributory negligence leading to a reduction of the child's damages when he or she has been injured. In *McKinnell v White*[4] for example, Lord Fraser reduced the damages of a five-year-old child by 50 % on the basis that the child had been contributorily negligent when he ran in front of a speeding motorist. Lord Fraser justified his decision on the basis that any child living in an urban area would be bound to be aware by the age of five of the danger of traffic.[5] It should be noted that parents are not automatically vicariously liable for the delicts of their children,[6] but a parent will incur personal liability if, as a result of the parent's negligence, this caused or contributed to the child's delict, for example failure to supervise a child properly.[7]

Where a child's parent has died as a consequence of personal injury arising from a wrongful or negligent act of another, a child may claim damages in respect of the parent's death under the Damages (Scotland) Act 2011.[8] Damages are available for loss of support suffered or likely to be suffered as a result of the parent's death.[9] As a general rule, if the child is a dependent child,[10] 75% of the deceased's net income is assumed to have been spent in support of the family.[11] There is also compensation for the loss of non-patrimonial benefits, such as the parent's affection and guidance.[12]

---

1 Age of Legal Capacity (Scotland) Act 1991, s 1(3)(c).

2 A child under the age of 16 may have capacity to sue if the child has a general understanding of what it means to do so: ALC(S)A 1991, s 2(4A) and (4B), discussed at para **10.2**.

3 *Young v Rankin* 1934 SC 499; *Wood v Wood* 1935 SLT 431.

4 1971 SLT (Notes) 61.

5 1971 SLT (Notes) 61 at 62. See also *McCluskey v Wallace* 1998 SC 711 (four-year-old child held to be contributorily negligent); In *Jackson v Murray* [2015] UKSC 5 a

13-year-old was injured when she crossed a road after alighting from a school minibus. The Lord Ordinary assessed contributory negligence at 90%; an Extra Division of the Inner House reduced this to 70%; the UKSC reduced it to 50%.

6 But the parents would be liable if they had authorised the child's action or the child was acting as an employee of the parents.

7 *Hastie v Magistrates of Edinburgh* 1907 SC 1102; *Hardie v Sneddon* 1917 SC 1.

8 A child has title to sue even if he or she was born after the parent has died: *Cohen v Shaw* 1992 SLT 1022; *Stuart v Reid* [2014] 7 WLUK 1193.

9 D(S)A 2011, s 4(3)(a).

10 A child who is under 18 and to whom the deceased owed an obligation of aliment, D(S)A 2011, s 7(3).

11 D(S) Act 2011, s 7(1)

12 D(S)A 2011, s 4(3)(b). For full discussion, see *Thomson's Delictual Liability* (6th edn, 2021 Bloomsbury Professional), Ch 13.

MARRIAGE AND DOMICILE

10.5 A person has capacity to marry or register a civil partnership when aged 16 or over.[1] A young person has the capacity to acquire a domicile of choice on reaching 16.[2]

1 Marriage (Scotland) Act 1977, s 1; Civil Partnership Act 2004, s 86(1)(c).

2 Family Law (Scotland) Act 2006, s 22. Before then, the child will either have a domicile of dependence which follows that of the parents or else will be domiciled in the country with which the child has for the time being the closest connection.

CRIMINAL RESPONSIBILITY

10.6 In December 2021, the age of criminal responsibility in Scotland was raised from age eight to age 12.[1] This brings the age of criminal responsibility in line with the age of criminal prosecution, which is also age 12.[2] The age of criminal responsibility is not affected by any enactments of the Age of Legal Capacity (Scotland) Act 1991.[3]

Where a child aged 12 but not yet 16 has allegedly committed an offence, he or she cannot be prosecuted except on the instructions of, or at the instance of, the Lord Advocate.[4] More commonly, a child who has allegedly committed an offence will be referred to the Children's Reporter to determine if that child is in need of 'protection, guidance, treatment or control' and a compulsory supervision order.[5] Note that s 3 of the Age of Criminal Responsibility (Scotland) Act 2019 states that the Principal Reporter may not determine that the ground in s 67(2)(j) (the offence ground) applies where the child 'was under 12 years of age when the offence was committed'.

If a person aged 16 to 18 commits a criminal offence that will usually be dealt with by the courts. However, they may be called to a children's hearing if they are already subject to a compulsory supervision order from a children's hearing.[6] Offenders aged 16 to 21 can be sentenced to detention in a young offenders' institution; however, they may be temporality detained in an adult prison if a place is not available in a young offenders' institution.

---

1 Age of Criminal Responsibility (Scotland) Act 2019, s 1 amends s 41 of the Criminal Procedure (Scotland) Act 1995.
2 Criminal Procedure (Scotland) Act 1995, s 42(1).
3 Age of Legal Capacity (Scotland) Act 1991, s 1(3)(c).
4 Criminal Procedure (Scotland) Act 1995, s 42(1).
5 Children's Hearings (Scotland) Act 2011, s 66(1)(b) and s 66(2)(b). See generally **Ch 15**.
6 Children's Hearings (Scotland) Act 2011, s 199(7).

SPECIFIC AGE LIMITS

10.7 The Age of Legal Capacity (Scotland) Act 1991 does not affect any age limits laid down for specific purposes by other statutes. In a work of this compass, it is not possible to explore these limits in detail. Sometimes a statute gives a child capacity before the child reaches 16; for example, in Scotland a child aged 12 or more can apply for a maintenance calculation under s 7 of the Child Support Act 1991.[1]

Statutory age limits usually prevent a young person from engaging in a course of conduct until he or she reaches the age of 16 or beyond. Thus, for example, a young person has to be 17 or over before he or she can hold a licence to drive a motor car or motor cycle.[2] Parliament makes it a criminal offence to sell or supply particular goods or services to a child or young person below a particular age, for example, it is an offence to sell tobacco or nicotine vapour products to a child under 18.[3] It is also an offence for a person under 18 to buy or attempt to buy tobacco products.[4] Under s 102 of the Licensing (Scotland) Act 2005, it is an offence to sell alcohol[5] to a child or young person.[6] It is also a criminal offence for a person under 18 to buy or attempt to buy alcohol.[7] Similarly, there are offences relating to betting transactions involving children and young persons.[8]

In relation to sexual activity, the law is found in the Sexual Offences (Scotland) Act 2009. The 2009 Act distinguishes between a 'young child'[9] and an 'older child'.[10] A key distinction between these categories is in relation to consent. The 2009 Act defines consent as 'free agreement'.[11] Under the law, there is no reference to the ability of a young child to give consent. This means that any sexual activity with a young child will be a criminal offence irrespective of whether the young child apparently consented to the sexual activity. Further, it is no defence that the accused believed the child was 13 or over.[12]

It is also a criminal offence to have sexual intercourse, or engage in sexual activity, with an older child who is aged 13 but under 16.[13] The offence is committed even though the older child can give consent. It is a defence if the accused reasonably believed that the older child was 16 unless the accused has previously been charged with a sexual offence or there is a sexual harm order against the accused.[14] If both parties are between the ages of 13 and 16, both commit an offence where the sexual acts were consensual.[15] Again there is the defence of reasonable belief that the other party was 16. However, in both situations, there is a further defence that at the time when the sexual conduct took place, the difference in age between the parties did not exceed two years.[16] The 2009 Act makes no distinction under the law between heterosexual and homosexual sexual activity. So, for example, if a boy aged 15 has sex with another boy aged 14, both have a defence as the age difference between them is only one year. Where both parties are aged 16 or over they are free to engage in consensual sexual activity with each other.

---

1 On the Child Support Act 1991, see para **10.11**.

2 Road Traffic Act 1988, s 101.

3 Tobacco and Primary Medical Services (Scotland) Act 2010, ss 4 and 4A.

4 Tobacco and Primary Medical Services (Scotland) Act 2010, s 5. Note that it is also an offence under s 6 of this Act for a person aged 18 or over knowingly to buy tobacco products for a person under the age of 18.
5 Licensing (Scotland) Act 2005, s 102 prohibits the sale of alcohol to a child or young person. Note that it is also an offence for a child or young person to buy or attempt to buy alcohol.
6 'Child' and 'young person' are defined in s 147 of the Licensing (Scotland) Act 2005.
7 Licensing (Scotland) Act 2005, s 105.
8 See the Gambling Act (Scotland) 2005, ss 45–50.
9 Sexual Offences (Scotland) Act 2009, s 18.
10 SO(S) Act 2009, s 28.
11 SO(S) Act 2009, s 12.
12 SO)S) Act 2009, s 27.
13 SO(S) Act 2009, ss 28 to 36.
14 SO(S) Act 2009, s 39(1) and (2).
15 SO(S) Act 2009, s 37.
16 SO(S) Act 2009, s 39(3).

LITIGATION

10.8 *Prima facie* the general rule of legal capacity applies. Generally, where the child is under 16, any civil action must be pursued or defended on behalf of the child by the child's legal representative.[1] If the child has no legal representative or the legal representative refuses to act, the action can proceed in the child's name despite the fact that the child is under 16.[2] In any civil proceedings, the court can appoint a curator *ad litem* to protect the child's interests.[3]

If a child under 16 has legal capacity to instruct a solicitor, the child also has capacity to pursue or defend in civil proceedings.[4] While a young person aged 16 to 18 has legal capacity, the young person cannot assent to the variation of a trust until age 18;[5] in these circumstances, a curator *ad litem* will be appointed for a young person between the ages of 16 and 18.[6]

It should be noted that prescriptive or limitation periods do not begin to run against a child until he or she reaches 16.[7]

There are special rules which apply to witnesses who are under the age of 18. These are contained in the Vulnerable Witnesses (Scotland) Act 2004 and the Vulnerable Witnesses (Criminal Evidence) (Scotland) Act 2019. Discussion of these is beyond the compass of the present work.

---

1 See Children (Scotland) Act 1995, s 1(1)(d) and s 2(1)(d).
2 Age of Legal Capacity (Scotland) Act 1991, s 1(3)(f)(i).
3 ALC(S)A 1991, s 1(3)(f)(ii). This would arise if, for example, there was a potential conflict of interest between the child and the parents and the child's parents were acting as the child's legal representatives.
4 ALC(S)A 1991, s 2(4A) and (4B). On s 2(4A), see para **10.2**.
5 Trusts (Scotland) Act 1961, s 1(2).
6 ALC(S)A 1991, s 1(3)(f)(iii).
7 Prescription and Limitation (Scotland) Act 1973, ss 17(3), 18(3), 18A(2), 22B(4), 22C(3) (limitation); 6(4)(b) (five years' prescription); *McCabe v McLellan* 1994 SLT 346. There is no need for the young person's nonage (ie, below 16) to be causally related to the failure to pursue the action. In other words, there is a blanket protection due to nonage.

ALIMENT

10.9 A child has the right to be alimented by his or her parents. The law of aliment of children is to be found in the Family Law (Scotland) Act 1985. By s 1(1)(c) of the 1985 Act, an obligation of aliment is owed by a father or mother to his or her child. Both parents are under an obligation to aliment their children. Thus, liability must be divided between the father and the mother: aliment is not the primary responsibility of one parent of a child. The fact that the parents have never married each other is irrelevant. Although the statute speaks of 'father' and 'mother', it is thought that these words must be interpreted as including a parent's same sex spouse or civil partner or a child's second female parent who are parents of the child by virtue of s 35, s 42 and s 43 of the Human Fertilisation and Embryology Act 2008.[1]

Section 1(1)(d) of the 1985 Act places an obligation on a person to aliment a child who has been accepted by that person as a child of the family.[2] The absence of a blood tie is irrelevant. The obligation to aliment is therefore extended beyond parents and natural children to include, for example a step-parent or the cohabitant of the child's parent.[3] But s 1(1)(d) would equally apply where a grandparent brings up a grandchild or an uncle or aunt brings up a niece.[4] It is doubtful whether the acceptor must have a family before the child can be accepted since it is expressly provided by s 27 of the 1985 Act that family includes a one-parent family.[5]

Before the obligation arises under s 1(1)(d) the child must have been 'accepted' as a child of the family. This could give rise to difficulties. Consider the following example.

Example 1

The mother and father of a child are married and have a child together. The presumption of paternity in s 5 of the Law Reform (Parent and Child) (Scotland) Act 1986 will apply. If the father later rebuts the presumption and establishes that he is not the child's father, does he owe the child an obligation of aliment? Section 1(1)(c) does not apply as the husband is not the child's father. Section 1(1)(d) does not apply if the view is taken that the husband did not accept the child as a child of his family because he did not know that the child was not his and had therefore not agreed with his wife to accept another man's child as a child of the family.[6]

The difficulty can be avoided if the criterion was whether a person had 'treated' as opposed to 'accepted' the child as a child of the family.[7]

A child for the purposes of aliment means a person under 18 or a person between 18 and 25 who is reasonably and appropriately undergoing instruction at an educational establishment, or training for employment or for a trade, profession or vocation.[8] Thus, a parent's obligation to aliment a child continues while the child attends college or university or undertakes an apprenticeship.[9] The obligation to aliment a child with a disability and/or learning difficulties *prima facie* ceases when the child reaches 18[10] but will continue until age 25 if the child attends any course of instruction designed to maximise the child's potential for life.

The obligation of aliment is to provide such support as is reasonable in the circumstances[11] having regard to the factors which the courts use to determine the amount of aliment, ie the needs[12] and resources of the parties, their earning capacities and generally all the circumstances of the case.[13] Where two or more parties owe an obligation of aliment to a child, while there is no order of liability, the court in deciding how much, if any, aliment to award against any of those persons must have regard to the obligation of aliment owed to the child by the other person(s).[14] The following examples illustrate how this provision operates in practice.

Example 2

The mother and father of a child are married. They have a child, C. Both the mother and the father therefore have an obligation to aliment C: s 1(1)(c). In quantifying the amount of aliment that each parent should pay, the court must have regard to the criteria set out in s 4(1)(a) to (c). Thus, if one parent (P1) is unemployed and the other parent (P2) is in well-paid employment, the court could take the view that P1 should only be ordered to pay a fraction of the required aliment or, indeed, no aliment at all, leaving C to pursue a claim against P2.

Example 3

P1 and P2 are the parents of child, C. Both P1 and P2 therefore have an obligation to aliment C: s 1(1)(c). P1 later marries P3 who accepts C as a child of the family. P3 therefore has an obligation to aliment C: s 1(1)(d). In quantifying the amount of aliment P3 should pay, the court must have regard to the fact that both P1 and P2 owe an obligation of aliment to C. Thus, even if P3 is in employment, the court could take the view that P3 should only be ordered to pay a fraction of the required aliment, leaving C to pursue claims against P1 and P2.

Where a court makes an award of aliment in respect of a child under 16, it may include an amount for the reasonable expenses of the person having care of the child where these are incurred in looking after the child.[15]

An action for aliment can be brought by the child.[16] Thus, for example, an 18-year-old child who is attending university can bring a claim for aliment against his or her parents if they have refused to make an appropriate contribution towards his or her maintenance.[17] Where a child is below 18, an action can be brought on his or her behalf by the parent or guardian of the child or any person with whom the child lives or is seeking a residence order in respect of the child.[18] So if, for example, a grandmother is caring for her daughter's child, she can bring an action of aliment on the child's behalf against the child's mother and father. A woman, whether married or not, may bring an action for aliment on behalf of her unborn child as if the child had been born but no such action will be heard or disposed of prior to the birth of the child;[19] on granting decree after the birth, the court has power to backdate the aliment to the date of the child's birth.[20]

An action for aliment of a child can be brought even if the child is living with the defender; so, for example, a child can seek aliment from his or her parents while still living at home with them.[21] In these circumstances, the parents will have a defence if they can show that they are fulfilling their obligation of aliment and are continuing to do so.[22]

Where a couple has separated and a parent (P1), for example, has taken a child under 16 with him or her, then if P1 brings an action for aliment on behalf of the child against the other parent (P2), it is no defence to the action that P2 has offered to receive the child into P2's household and thereby fulfil the obligation of aliment.[23] This is because the question of where a child should live is *prima facie* an issue in proceedings for a residence order where the child's welfare will be the paramount consideration.[24] But where the child is aged 16 or over, P2 will have a defence to a claim for aliment if he or she had offered a home to the child which it was reasonable to expect the child to accept.[25] In determining whether it was reasonable for the child to accept such an offer, the defender's conduct will be taken into account.[26] For example, it might not be reasonable for a child aged 16 or over to accept a parent's offer of accommodation if that parent's unreasonable behaviour towards the other parent had led to the breakdown of the marriage and had been a cause of distress and the reason for the parent and child to leave the family home.[27]

While an action for aliment simpliciter is competent in both the Court of Session and the sheriff court,[28] in practice a claim is more likely to be made in the course of other proceedings, such as declarator of parentage, actions in relation to parental responsibilities and parental rights, separation, dissolution of a civil partnership, divorce and claims for financial provision on divorce or dissolution.[29] For example when a woman has a child, if she seeks declarator of parentage,[30] she can bring a claim for aliment on behalf of her child against the alleged father in the same proceedings: if parentage is established, aliment can be ordered from the father of the child. Similarly, in an action for divorce or dissolution, the pursuer can bring claims for aliment on behalf of the children of the marriage or family. These will include not just the spouses' or a civil partner's children, but any child who has been treated by both of them as a child of their family, not being a child who is placed with them as foster parents by a local authority or voluntary association.[31] Any claims for aliment for the child must be satisfied before the court will order financial provision for the spouses or civil partners. Where, at any stage in the proceedings, an action for divorce, dissolution or separation is dismissed, the court is not prevented from making, *inter alia*, an order for aliment for any child of the family.[32]

Aliment takes the form of periodical payments, whether for a definite or indefinite period or until the happening of a specified event.[33] The court cannot substitute a lump sum for a periodical payment.[34] But the court can order alimentary payments of an occasional or special nature to meet special needs which it would be unreasonable to expect the claimant to meet out of a periodical allowance.[35] This could, for example, be an order to pay school fees.[36] An award of aliment can be backdated to the date of the bringing of the action and, on special cause shown, to a date prior to the bringing of the action.[37]

On a material change of circumstances since the date of the original decree, an award of aliment can be varied or recalled.[38] An application to vary an award has to be made while the obligation to aliment subsists: it cannot be varied retrospectively when the child has become an adult.[39] The variation can be backdated but not beyond the date of the decree which is being varied.[40] When a variation is backdated, any sums paid under the order before variation can be ordered to be repaid.[41] While an interim award of aliment can be varied or recalled, there is no power to backdate the variation.[42] Where there has been an agreement relating to aliment it can also be varied on a material change of circumstances.[43]

There is no obligation on a child to aliment his or her parent, however wealthy the child or indigent the parent. Where a child is wealthy in his or her own right, a parent can use the child's income for the child's maintenance or education; resort will rarely be made to the child's capital for these purposes unless the parent's circumstances are so reduced that he or she cannot aliment the child.[44]

Where the person owning aliment fails to pay the sum of aliment ordained by the court, then the court has found that failure to make an alimentary payment cannot amount to a contempt of court,[45] the correct procedure being that the party seeking to enforce payment can apply for a warrant in the sheriff court in terms of s 4 of the Civil Imprisonment (Scotland) Act 1882.[46] Although this remains a competent disposal, it is rarely invoked as there are other forms of diligence available, for example, current maintenance arrestment and arrestment of assets other than earnings.

Finally, the discretionary nature of awards of aliment must be emphasised. What a child will actually receive as an award of aliment depends not only on the child's needs but also on the resources of his or her parents.[47] For children of low income families, awards of aliment will be small. Increasingly resort will have to be made to income support or universal credit for the basic maintenance of children whose parents are unemployed for whatever reason. Where the parents have separated, in the vast majority of cases their child's right to aliment cannot be enforced in the courts. Instead, an application must be made to the Child Maintenance Service for a maintenance calculation. It is to this statutory system of child support that we now turn.

---

1 Discussed at para **9.2**. Otherwise, a child of a lesbian couple would be disadvantaged with a resulting breach of the child's human rights.

2 This does not include foster carers where the child has 'been boarded out by a local or other public authority or a voluntary organisation'. See: Family Law (Scotland) Act 1985, s 1(1)(d).

3 See for example, *Telfer v Kellock* 2004 SLT 1290 (mother's deceased female partner died and the mother and her child sought damages). The court held that the deceased had accepted the child as 'a child of the family' – 'a child did not require to have two parents nor two heterosexual parents'.

4 See, for example, *Inglis v Inglis and Mathew* 1987 SCLR 608 (aunt and uncle had accepted the child as a child of the family).

5 Where a child has been accepted as a child of the family, the acceptor's obligation to aliment continues even if the acceptor no longer wishes a relationship with the child.

6 *Watson v Watson* 1994 SCLR 1097 (after blood and DNA tests showed that the husband was not the father of the child, he successfully raised an action to recall the grant of aliment).

7 'Treated' is now the criterion for the definition of a child of the family in other areas of Scots law, for example ancillary orders for parental responsibilities and parental rights on divorce or dissolution: Children (Scotland) Act 1995, s 12(4)(b).

8 FL(S)A 1985, s 1(5)(a) and (b). See, for example, *Jowett v Jowett* 1990 SCLR 348; *Park v Park* 2000 SLT (Sh Ct) 65.

9 Provided he or she is under 25.

10 *McBride v McBride* 1995 SCLR 1138. See also Helen McGinty, *Aliment for adults* Fam LB 2018, 151(Jan) 1–4.

11 FL(S)A 1985, s 1(2). The test for what is reasonable is objective and does not turn on the view of the parent: *Winter v Thornton* 1993 SCLR 389 (whether aliment should be paid for the child's *private* education).

12 In *McGeachie v McGeachie* 1989 SCLR 99 the child was an infant and the mother was in receipt of child benefit; the court reduced an award of aliment on the ground that it was too generous in the light of the baby's existing needs! To be fair, this was an application for interim aliment.

13 FL(S)A 1985, s 4(1). The court may take into account any support given by the defender to any person whom he or she maintains as a dependent in his or her household, whether or not the defender owes the dependent an obligation of aliment, for example, a cohabitant's children: FL(S)A 1985, s 4(3)(a). *Pryde v Pryde* 1991 SLT (Sh Ct) 26 suggests that a cohabitant's income could be relevant; and that it is the net, not gross, income to which the court should have regard. Conduct is irrelevant unless it would be manifestly inequitable to leave it out of account: s 4(3)(b). In *Walker v Walker* 1991 SLT 649, the court took the father's conduct in lying about his income into account. Section 4(3) of the FL(S)A 1985 is discussed in detail in the context of aliment between husband and wife: see para **3.9–3.10**.

14 FL(S)A 1985, s 4(2). See, for example, *Inglis v Inglis and Mathew* 1987 SCLR 608 (action of aliment by uncle and aunt, who had accepted the child, against the child's parents; court took into account the fact that the aunt and uncle also owed an obligation to aliment the child). In *Ahmed v Ahmed* 2004 Fam LR 14, the obligation to aliment the child was proportioned 20:80 between mother and father respectively.

15 FL(S)A 1985, s 4(4); *H v H* 2004 Fam LR 30.

16 FL(S)A 1985, s 2(4)(a). If the child is between 16 and 18, the child has legal capacity to pursue the action; if below 16, the child will have legal capacity to pursue the action if the he or she has capacity to instruct a solicitor by virtue of s 2(4A) of the Age of Legal Capacity (Scotland) Act 1991: see para **10.2**. If the 'child' is 18 or over, he or she must pursue the action; it is no longer competent for the parent to bring the action on behalf of the child: *Hay v Hay* 2000 SLT (Sh Ct) 95.

17 See *Jowett v Jowett* 1990 SCLR 348. In assessing the amount of aliment to award a student, the court takes into account the availability of student loans and part-time jobs: *Park v Park* 2000 SLT (Sh Ct) 65. There must be evidence of the student's outlays.

18 FL(S)A 1985, s 2(4)(c)(i) and (iii). On residence orders, see **Ch 12**.

19 FL(S)A 1985, s 2(5). This provision might be useful if the father was about to remove himself from the jurisdiction.

20 FL(S)A 1985, s 3(1)(c).

21 FL(S)A 1985, s 2(6).

22 FL(S)A 1985, s 2(7).

23 FL(S)A 1985, s 2(8).

24 The welfare principle is discussed in **Ch 12**.
25 FL(S)A 1985, s 2(8).
26 FL(S)A 1985, s 2(9).
27 See, for example, *McKay v McKay* 1980 SLT (Sh Ct) 111. In *Bell v Bell* (unreported) the father's offer was held to be unreasonable as his daughter had lived with her mother after the divorce and was currently engaged in higher education in a different town.
28 FL(S)A 1985, s 2(1).
29 FL(S)A 1985, s 2(2).
30 Law Reform (Parent and Child) (Scotland) Act 1986, s 7.
31 FL(S)A 1985, s 1(1)(c) and (d).
32 FL(S)A 1985, s 21.
33 FL(S)A 1985, s 3(1)(a): for example, aliment could be ordered until the child reaches 18.
34 FL(S)A 1985, s 3(2).
35 FL(S)A 1985, s 3(1)(b).
36 *McDonald v McDonald* 1995 SLT 72; *G v G* 2002 Fam LR 120; *H v H* 2004 Fam LR 30.
37 FL(S)A 1985, s 3(1)(c). The judge should give reasons why the award should be backdated; *Ahmed v Ahmed* 2004 SCLR 247.
38 FL(S)A 1985, s 5(1). The fact that the cost of maintaining a child increases as the child grows older has been held to be a material change of circumstances: *Skinner v Skinner* 1996 SCLR 334. The making of a maintenance calculation in respect of the child for whom the decree of aliment was granted is a material change of circumstances: FL(S)A 1985, s 5(1A).
39 *Paterson v Paterson* 2002 SLT (Sh Ct) 65.
40 FL(S)A 1985, s 5(2) incorporating s 3(1)(c); *Walker v Walker* 1991 SLT 649; cf *Hannah v Hannah* 1988 SLT 82. This is because the material change of circumstances must have arisen after the original decree was awarded. However, the variation will not be backdated unless it is established that the defender can afford to pay the backdated aliment: *Adamson v Adamson* 1996 SLT 427.
41 FL(S)A 1985, s 5(4).
42 *McColl v McColl* 1993 SLT 617; *Adamson v Adamson* 1996 SLT 427; *Ahmed v Ahmed* 2004 SCLR 247
43 FL(S)A 1985, s 7. See, for example, *H v H* 2004 Fam LR 30. The court has the power to backdate any variation: Family Law (Scotland) Act 1985, s 7(2ZA).
44 The parent on ceasing to act as the child's legal representative is liable to account for intromissions with the child's property but there is no liability if the child's money was used in the proper discharge by the parent of the parent's responsibility to safeguard and promote the child's welfare: C(S)A 1995, s 10, discussed at para **11.2**.
45 *ADM, Petitioner* [2014] SC 165.
46 *Jaworowska-Dziewirz v Wojciechowski* 2020 SLT (Sh Ct) 37.
47 It appears that a child of a wealthy parent should be awarded aliment that is to some extent commensurate to the parent's and his or her family's lifestyle: *H v H* 2004 Fam LR 30; *Ahmed v Ahmed* 2004 Fam LR 14.

THE CHILD SUPPORT ACT 1991

Who is covered by the Child Support Act 1991?

10.10 The central legal concept of the Child Support Act 1991[1] is that of the 'qualifying child'.[2] This concept is described in more detail below, but in general, a child is only a qualifying child when one or both of the child's parents are not living with the child. Each parent of a qualifying child is responsible for maintaining the child but is taken to have met that responsibility by making periodical payments of child support maintenance in accordance with the Act.[3]

Where a maintenance calculation requiring payments is made under the Act, it is the duty of the non-resident parent to whom the calculation is addressed to make those payments.[4] The person with day-to-day care of the child in effect meets his or her responsibility to maintain by looking after the child and need make no payments to, or for the benefit of, the child. In most cases covered by the Act, the child is being cared for by one of his or her natural parents ('the person with care'), who is separated from the other ('the non-resident parent'). However, the person with care need not be a parent and it is therefore possible for two persons to be non-resident parents for the purposes of the Act. The payments must be made either to the Child Maintenance Service (CMS) or to the resident parent. It is unwise to make payments in cash without a receipt. Payments made to any other party, such as to the child, will not be regarded by the CMS as having been made at all and the relevant CMS debt will remain and will be enforced.

A child is a qualifying child if one or both of the child's parents are 'non-resident parents'.[5] A parent is a non-resident parent if he or she is not living in the same household with the child and the child has his or her home with another person who is 'a person with care'.[6] A person with care is the person with whom the child has his or her home and who usually provides day-to-day care for the child. The person need not be an individual but may be, for example, a children's home. The prescribed categories for those who may not be persons with care are local authorities and foster carers looking after a child or children who have been boarded out with them by local authorities.[7]

A person only counts as a 'child'[8] for the purposes of the Act if he or she is:

(a) under 16; or

(b) under 20 and satisfies such conditions as may be prescribed.

Category (b) could cover, for example, children attending school or a further education college. A person between the ages of 16 and 20 is not a qualifying child if the child is engaged in advanced education or entitled to income support or income-based jobseeker's allowance or engaged in work-based training. In addition, a person who is or has been married or a party to a civil partnership is not a child and this includes cases where the person has celebrated a marriage or civil partnership which is void or a decree of nullity has been granted.

Where a person does not fall within the definition of 'child', that person is not a qualifying child for the purposes of the 1991 Act and therefore no maintenance calculation relating to him or her may be made.[9]

The definition of 'parent' is also important as a person cannot be either a parent with care or a non-resident parent unless he or she falls within the definition of parent. The Act defines 'parent' as 'any person who is in law the mother or father of the child'.[10] This means that the expression covers both natural and adoptive parents but not step-parents. Therefore, a person is not liable to maintain a step-child under the Act.[11] The Act makes special provision for determining disputes about parentage for its purposes.[12]

Thus, the Act is concerned with defining and enforcing the obligations of parents to maintain their natural and adopted children in those cases where at least one of the parents is neither living with nor looking after the child and the child is living with and being looked after by the other parent or a third party. In most cases to which the Act applies, the courts have no power to award aliment.

Before there can be any liability for child support, it is necessary, in terms of s 44 of the Child Support Act 1991, that both of the parents and the child should be either habitually resident (not necessarily domiciled) in the United Kingdom or, in respect of the non-resident parent, should fall with the terms of s 44(2A) of the CSA 1991 and Regulation 7A of the Child Support (Maintenance Arrangements and Jurisdiction) Regulations 1992.

1 References are to the Child Support Act 1991 as amended. For discussion of child support, see *Wilkinson and Norrie* Ch 14.
2 CSA 1991, s 3.
3 CSA 1991, s 1.
4 CSA 1991, s 1.
5 Child Support Act 1991, s 3. The term 'non-resident' parent replaces the original 'absent' parent.
6 CSA 1991, s 3.
7 Child Support (Maintenance Assessment Procedure) Regulations 1992, SI 1992/1813, reg 51.
8 CSA 1991, s 55.
9 However, since the person is not a qualifying child, he or she may be able to pursue an action for aliment in the courts: see para **10.9**.
10 CSA 1991, s 54. On the legal concept of parent see **Ch 9**.
11 This means that the child can pursue an action for aliment in the courts against a step-parent who has accepted the child as a child of the family. See: Family Law (Scotland) Act 1985, s 1(1)(d). Also discussed at para **10.9**.
12 CSA 1991, ss 26–28.

Maintenance calculations[1]

10.11 Under s 4 of the 1991 Act either the person with care, or the non-resident parent of a qualifying child may apply to the Child Maintenance Service (CMS) for a maintenance calculation to be made. By virtue of s 7 of the Act, a qualifying child who is habitually resident in Scotland and is aged 12 or over may apply for a maintenance calculation in his or her own right, provided no application has already been made by either a person with care or a non-resident parent under s 4.

Once a maintenance calculation has been made under s 4 or s 7 of the 1991 Act, the non-resident parent comes under a duty to make payments of the amounts specified in the calculation. CMS has powers to arrange for the collection and enforcement of child support maintenance.

Where payments are required under a maintenance calculation they may be made in a variety of ways. The CMS has several important powers with regard to payments. The first is to make a deduction from earnings order, which is, in effect, an instruction to an employer to deduct maintenance from earnings at source. Such orders may be used both to collect arrears and to collect current maintenance even where there are no arrears. There is no requirement for the CMS to show that there has been any default in payment before imposing an order, although an order should not be used 'in any case where there is good reason not to use it'.[2] The second is the regular deduction order which can be used where: (i) the non-resident parent has failed to pay an amount of child support maintenance; and (ii) that person has capital in some form of account. Payments can be ordered from that account to secure payments of arrears and current maintenance on a regular basis. Third is the lump-sum deduction order which can be used if the non-resident parent has failed to pay an amount of child support maintenance and has a deposit or other savings account from which the arrears can be paid. Finally, there is a liability order which can be made when the non-resident parent has failed to pay an amount of child support maintenance and can be enforced by the usual forms of diligence. A liability order can be appealed to the First Tier Tribunal on the grounds that the non-resident parent has paid the amount or that the amount said to be due is wrong. It must be emphasised that all these are administrative orders, ie they are imposed by the CMS without any intervention of a court. In addition, once a liability order has been granted, or if other forms of enforcement have failed, the CMS can apply to the sheriff court for one or more of the following orders: committal to prison, disqualification from driving, removal of a passport.[3]

This is an appropriate point at which to mention the obligation imposed on the CMS by s 2 of the Child Support Act 1991: ie when considering the exercise of any discretionary power conferred by the 1991 Act, the CMS is to 'have regard to the welfare of any child likely to be affected by its decision'.[4] This may be contrasted with the obligation of the court in s 11(7) of the Children (Scotland) Act 1995 to regard the welfare of the child as the paramount consideration in any proceedings relating to parental responsibilities and parental rights.

---

1 The term maintenance 'calculation' replaces the original maintenance 'assessment'.

2 Child Support Act 1991, s 29(4).

3 CSA 1991, ss 39, 39A, 40A and 40B.
Before these sanctions apply the court must be satisfied of the liable relative's wilful refusal or culpable neglect to pay: *Secretary of State for Work and Pensions v McNamara* 2005 SLT (Sh Ct) 125. In relation to the potential removal of a driving

licence or passport, the court must determine in the presence of the non-resident parent what his means are and whether he requires a passport or licence to earn his living.

4 CSA 1991, s 2.

The maintenance calculation

10.12 The basic rate of child support maintenance[1] is calculated as a percentage of the non-resident parent's gross weekly income:

- 12%, where there is one qualifying child;
- 16%, where there are two qualifying children; and
- 19%, where there are three or more qualifying children.

The basic rate applies provided the non-resident parent's gross income is less than £800 a week. If it is more than £800 the non-resident parent will pay 9%, 12% and 15% of that part of his or her income which exceeds £800 for one, two or more children respectively. The maximum gross weekly income is £3,000. The income of the person with care of the qualifying child is ignored as is the income of any new partner of the non-resident parent.[2] On the other hand, if the non-resident parent has one child[3] in his or her new family, the gross income is reduced by 12% before the formula is applied. If he or she has two children, the reduction is 16%. If there are three or more children, the reduction is 19%.

For example, a non-resident parent has two children and gross earnings of £600 a week. The maintenance calculation is £96, ie 16% of £600. If he or she has two children in his or her new family, the gross earnings are reduced by 16%, ie £504. The maintenance calculation is therefore reduced to £80.64, ie 16% of £504.

There can be a further reduction in the maintenance calculation if the non-residential parent has residential contact with a child from an earlier family. The reduction is as follows:

- 52–103 nights' residential contact: 1/7th reduction;
- 103–156 nights' residential contact: 2/7th reduction;
- 156–174 nights' residential contact: 3/7th reduction; or

- 174 + nights' residential contact: maintenance calculation is halved.

Here it is the maintenance calculation, not the gross income used for the calculation, that is reduced. Thus if, in our example, the non-resident parent has residential contact of 60 days with the children of his or her first family, the maintenance calculation is reduced by 1/7th, ie 1/7th of £96 = £13.70 a week. Only residential contact with the non-residential parent counts. Staying with the non-resident parent's mother or father, ie the child's grandparents, for example, will not lead to any reduction.

The non-resident parent may apply to have the normal maintenance calculation *reduced* because he or she is incurring special expenses.[4] These are:[5]

(a) high costs of exercising contact with his or her children;

(b) long-term illness or disability of a child living with him;

(c) debts incurred for the benefit of his or her earlier family while they were living together;

(d) boarding school fees paid for qualifying children: this is limited to the boarding part of the cost; and

(e) mortgage payments which he or she pays in respect of a home shared with the person with care and in which the person with care continues to live. The non-resident parent must have no real right of property in the house.

CMS used to ask the paying parent for vouching of his or her income. Since the 2012 regulations, CMS now asks HMRC for the gross income of the paying parent as disclosed in the most recent tax return. This often works straightforwardly, but those advising a parent in a child support case should take note of what the regulations say. If the paying parent has no gross income which is taxable in the UK only because his or her income is subject to a double taxation agreement, then the true gross income for child support purposes is the income on which the paying parent would have paid UK tax if the double taxation agreement had not operated.[6]

Furthermore, it is the habit of the officials of CMS to make assumptions even in the face of evidence. Where a young person has reached the age of 16 and is in full-time non-advanced education then that young person is a child for child support purposes. If the child has left school, then he or she may still be a child for these purposes if, in terms of the Child Support (Maintenance Calculation Procedure) Regulations 2000 (as amended), child benefit is payable in respect of him or her. HMRC will confirm to CMS whether child benefit is in payment, and CMS will often accept that information as confirming that the child still qualifies for child support maintenance. The criterion is, however whether child benefit is properly and lawfully payable[7] so that if the child benefit is being claimed fraudulently, or even in error, the child will no longer be a qualifying child for child support maintenance and the paying parent will no longer be liable. The paying parent may have to challenge the decision at a Tribunal.

One very common challenge to a maintenance calculation is, as might be expected, a challenge to the payer's income which is to be used as its basis. The challenge can be made by either parent, or even by both of them. The paying parent will say that the amount on which the calculation is based is erroneously large, and the receiving parent will say that it is too small. Difficulties most often arise when unearned income such as dividends fall to be taken into account. It is a common practice for a paying parent who is the effective owner of a small business to incorporate it so that the business is actually owned by the shareholders. A portion of the shares may then be put into the name of a new partner so that the dividends which are legally his or hers are accordingly reduced in value. Under child support law, if that parent is in a position to effect such a change, CMS or the Tribunal may recalculate the maintenance based upon his or her true earnings, treating all the dividends as belonging to the parent. If, of course, the new partner actually works in the business, and particularly if the new partner has contributed capital to it, the change of shareholding may be proper and the Tribunal will not recalculate the liability. The Child Support Maintenance Calculation Regulations 2012, regs 69–71 can be a busy field of work for the receiving parent's solicitor. The paying parent's solicitor will no doubt focus on regs 63–69.

Another frequent issue in variation cases is the diversion of income within a limited company. For example, it is possible that the director of a small company, particularly one in which there is only one fee-earner, may decide that despite having taken a certain level of dividends in previous years, he or she will nevertheless (in the year when he or she is asked to pay child support maintenance) leave a much greater share of profits in the business. This has the effect of reducing the amount on which he or she pays tax, and therefore the sum on which the child maintenance liability is calculated. If this is appealed by the resident parent, the Tribunal will consider whether the paying parent's action is commercially reasonable. It could be reasonable if, for example, he or she has to make provision for a bad debt or has to allow for the purchase of new equipment. If, however, the Tribunal decides that the retention of profits was unreasonable, CMS will be directed to recalculate the maintenance liability on the basis of a notionally commercially reasonable drawing of dividend.

There is an anomaly which has affected child support since the law was amended to make the receiving parent's income irrelevant. The anomaly is perhaps best illustrated by an example. A couple separates and their child remains with the mother (M). Both she and the father (F) earn modest salaries. CMS calculates F's liability in the usual way and M finds that she can get by reasonably well with that maintenance on top of her own earnings. Then M meets and begins to cohabit with a wealthy partner. She now has no need for her salary so she gives up work. Her financial needs are more than being met by her new partner but the amount that F pays has not altered. Then M's new relationship breaks down and she is once again on her own with her child. Her financial needs (and by extension those of the child) are now much greater, but the maintenance which F pays remains exactly the same.

---

1 See Child Support Act 1991, Sch 1 (as amended).

2 For many years the rules in respect of cohabitants discriminated against a non-resident parent who cohabited with a same sex partner. In *M v Secretary of State for Work and Persons* [2006] UKHL 11 the House of Lords held that this did not amount to a breach of the non-resident parent's human rights under Article 8 (right to respect for private and family life) or Article 1 of the First Protocol (right to possessions). The discrimination has been removed by amendments made by the Civil Partnership Act 2004.

3 The child can be his or her biological child or step-child.

4 CSA 1991, ss 28A–28F.

5 CSA 1991, Sch 4B.

6 *CH v SSWP & DN* [2015] UKUT 381 (AAC).

7 *NG v SSWP & JG (CSM)* [2015] UKUT 0020 (AAC).

Respective roles of the courts and the CMS

10.13 The jurisdiction of the courts to award aliment for qualifying children has been largely, but not entirely, replaced by the powers of the CMS to make maintenance calculations.[1] Section 8 of the Child Support Act 1991 provides that no court shall exercise any power which it would otherwise have to make, vary, or revive an award of aliment in any case where the CMS would have jurisdiction to make a maintenance calculation. In other words, it is not competent for the court to make any order which has the effect of awarding aliment in cases where a child support calculation may be made under s 4 or s 7 of the CSA 1991.[2] This has the effect of excluding the court's jurisdiction to award aliment under the Family Law (Scotland) Act 1985 in cases where at least one of the parents of the relevant child or children is a non-resident parent for the purposes of the 1991 Act. However, s 8 of the 1991 Act does not prevent an order for aliment being made against a person with care of the child. Accordingly, a child can sue the person caring for him or her for aliment even where a maintenance calculation could be made against the non-resident parent.

There are three exceptions to the general principle that no award of aliment may be made where a maintenance calculation could be made. First, under s 8(6) of the CSA 1991, an order for aliment may be made where the non-resident parent has more than enough assessable income to meet fully the maximum child maintenance allowable under the formula and there is such a maintenance calculation in place and the court is satisfied that the circumstances of the case make it appropriate for an award to be made. This is colloquially referred to as a 'top-up' award.[3] The great majority of non-resident parents will not be sufficiently well off to reach the threshold for top-up awards.

Secondly, under s 8(7) of the 1991 Act, an award for aliment may be made solely for the purpose of meeting some or all of the expenses incurred by a child in receiving instruction at an educational establishment or undergoing teaching for a trade, profession or vocation.[4]

Thirdly, under s 8(8) of the 1991 Act, an award of aliment may still be made where the child is disabled and the order is made solely for the purpose of meeting some or all of the expenses due to the disability. This exception applies where disability living allowance or personal independence payment is being paid in respect of the child, the child is 'blind, deaf or dumb' or is substantially and permanently disabled.[5]

These three exceptions apply where a person is a qualifying child for the purposes of the 1991 Act. Their effect is to allow the court to make an award of aliment – or vary an award or an alimentary agreement – even though a child maintenance calculation has been or could be made. But since the court's jurisdiction is only excluded in the first place where there is jurisdiction to make a maintenance calculation, it follows that the general law of aliment is still relevant in all cases where a child who is not a qualifying child is owed an obligation of aliment. Thus, for example, a university student may sue a parent for aliment and a step-child may sue a step-parent who has accepted the child as a child of his family.

In terms of s 9 of the 1991 Act, there is nothing to prevent persons entering into a maintenance agreement even though a child maintenance calculation has been or might be made.[6] The existence of such an agreement does not prevent any party to it from applying for a maintenance calculation provided the agreement has been in force for a year or more:[7] Such agreements prevent an application for a maintenance calculation until the expiry of that year.[8] Any provision of the agreement which purports to restrict the right to apply for a maintenance calculation is void. Thus, a paying parent should not agree, for example, to pay a lump sum to the resident parent in exchange for an agreement not to apply for child support maintenance. The resident parent in such a case could take and keep the lump sum, then wait for 12 months and then apply for child support maintenance, being no longer bound by the agreement not to do so. In any case, where the jurisdiction of the court to make an award of aliment would be excluded by s 8 of the 1991 Act, the court has no power to vary any maintenance agreement by inserting a provision requiring a non-resident parent to pay aliment or by increasing the amount payable under such an existing provision.

1 Child Support Act 1991, s 11.

2 It should be emphasised that the court's jurisdiction is excluded if a maintenance calculation *could* be made: there is no need for the calculation to have taken place before the court's jurisdiction is excluded.

3 See for example, *H v H* 2004 Fam LR 30.
4 Ibid.
5 CSA 1991, s 8(9).
6 The court also retains the power to make a maintenance order to enforce the terms of the agreement; s 8(5) of the 1991 Act. See *Otto v Otto* 2002 Fam LR 95.
7 CSA 1991, ss 4(10)(ab), 7(10) and 9(3).
8 CSA 1991, ss 4(10)(a), 7(10) and 9(3).

Chapter 11

Parental responsibilities and parental rights

INTRODUCTION

11.1 It is a hallmark of a democratic society that while parents have the primary responsibility to look after their children, they are free to bring them up in the manner which they deem best for the children's welfare. In order to enable them to fulfil their responsibilities, parents enjoy important rights in respect of the upbringing of their children. However, parental autonomy is not absolute. The criminal law protects children from serious physical, emotional or sexual or other abuse by their parents. Moreover, if a parent neglects or physically ill-treats a child, the child can be made subject to a compulsory supervision order under the Children's Hearings (Scotland) Act 2011 and can, if necessary, be removed from the parents.[1] With the intention of strengthening child protection measures across Scotland, the Scottish Government introduced a Named Person Service.[2] However, the Named Person Service was challenged in the UK Supreme Court and the information sharing provisions (which were central to the robust working of the service) were held to be incompatible with Article 8 of the European Convention on Human Rights.[3] In September 2019, the Scottish Government stated its intention to withdraw the Children and Young People (Information Sharing) (Scotland) Bill and to repeal Parts 4 and 5 of the Children and Young People (Scotland) Act 2014.

Scots law gives parents the rights, *inter alia*, to have the child living with them or determine generally where the child should live, to choose a child's religion, to decide how a child should be educated, to discipline the child, and to consent to medical or other treatment on the child's behalf. As maturity and understanding increases and the child's capacity to take decisions evolves, he or she will wish to make important decisions in relation to such matters as medical treatment for themselves. Accordingly, it is submitted that the nature of parental rights alter as the child matures. Throughout the child's childhood, the decision-making control that parents have diminishes as the child's capacity increases. When a child reaches the age of 16 years, the parental responsibilities and parental rights enjoyed by the parents cease to exist – except for the parental responsibility to provide guidance which continues until age 18 years.[4]

The purpose of this chapter is to examine the nature and extent of parental responsibilities and parental rights. We shall consider:

(1) what, in general, these parental responsibilities and parental rights are;

(2) who has parental responsibilities and parental rights; and

(3) some specific parental responsibilities and parental rights.

---

1 On the Children's Hearings (Scotland) Act 2011, see **Chs 14** and **15** below.

2 Children and Young People (Scotland) Act 2014, Part 4 whereby every child in Scotland would have a Named Person (other than the parent) to promote, support and safeguard the child's wellbeing. This is discussed in **Ch 14** below.

3 See *Christian Institute and others (Appellants) v The Lord Advocate (Respondent) (Scotland)* [2016] UKSC 51.

4 See ss 1 and 2 of the Children (Scotland) Act 1995.

WHAT ARE PARENTAL RESPONSIBILITIES AND PARENTAL RIGHTS?

11.2 A parent[1] has the following responsibilities to a child:[2]

(a) to safeguard and promote the child's health, development and welfare;

(b) to provide direction and guidance to the child in a manner appropriate to the stage of the child's development;

(c) if the child is not living with the parent, to maintain personal relations and direct contact with the child on a regular basis; and

(d) to act as the child's legal representative.[3]

These responsibilities supersede any analogous duties imposed on a parent at common law;[4] but they do not replace specific statutory duties, for example to aliment a child[5] or to ensure the child's education.[6] The parental responsibilities have to be carried out to the extent that it is practicable and in the interests of the child to do so.[7] A court may intervene where the parent's exercise of parental responsibilities may not serve the child's welfare. In *A v A*,[8] the court stated that, although it 'was conducive to a child's welfare if their absent parents maintained personal relations and direct contact with them on a regular basis … that principle was not to be applied without qualification or discrimination'.

In order to fulfil these responsibilities, a parent has the following rights:

(a) to have the child living with the parent or otherwise to regulate the child's residence;

(b) to control, direct or guide the child's upbringing in a manner appropriate to the child's stage of development;

(c) if the child does not live with the parent, to maintain personal relations and direct contact with the child on a regular basis; and

(d) to act as the child's legal representative.[9]

These parental rights supersede any analogous right enjoyed by a parent at common law[10] but they do not replace specific statutory rights.[11] Because these rights are given in order that parents can fulfil their parental responsibilities, they can only be exercised in so far as it is practicable and in the interests of the child to do so.[12]

Parental rights end when the child reaches 16.[13] Parental responsibilities also end when the child reaches 16, except the responsibility to provide guidance to a child which lasts until a young person reaches 18.[14]

When reaching any major decision in fulfilling parental responsibilities or exercising parental rights, the parent must have regard, so far as practicable, to the views of the child if the child wishes to express them.[15] Account should be taken of the child's age and maturity. At the time of writing (July 2022) there is a presumption in s 6(1) of the C(S)A 1995 that a child of 12 years of age or more is of sufficient age and maturity to form a view. The views of younger children are relevant if they have *in fact* sufficient maturity. Note that s 1(2) of the Children (Scotland) Act 2020 will repeal this presumption and insert new ss 6(1A) to (1D) to the Children (Scotland) Act 1995 Act.[16] This obligation to consult the child may be difficult to enforce, but it is indicative of the child-centred decision-making process which the Children (Scotland) Act 1995 is intended to promote. The obligation arises only in respect of *major* decisions: it is thought that the importance of a decision will be determined objectively rather than from the child or parent's perspective.

If two or more persons have parental rights, each can exercise a right without the consent of the other.[17] But a child cannot be removed from the United Kingdom without the consent of any other person (whether a parent or not) who has the parental rights relating to the child's residence or contact with the child.[18]

The parental responsibility in s 1(1)(a) of the C(S)A 1995 is sufficiently amorphous to cover a wide range of matters: the child's health, education, religion, discipline, etc. Similarly, the s 1(1)(b) responsibility is of wide import, ie the provision of direction and guidance for the child in every aspect of the child's life. The s 1(1)(c) responsibility is of the utmost significance. The 1995 Act proceeds on the basis that it is in a child's best interests to have the benefit of two parents; thus the responsibility – and corresponding right in s 2(1)(c) – of a parent to maintain personal relations and direct contact with the child when that parent no longer lives with the child. The parental rights in s 2(1)(a) and (b) are to help a parent fulfil the parental responsibilities in s 1(1)(a) and (b). We shall consider these responsibilities and rights in greater detail later in this chapter.

The parental responsibility[19] and parental right[20] to act as a child's legal representative enables a parent to enter into transactions on behalf of a child when the child lacks active legal capacity. When the child has capacity to enter into a legal transaction the parent cannot act as the child's legal representative.[21] The parent should consult the child before entering any major transaction[22] on the child's behalf; but if the other party to the transaction entered into it in good faith the transaction cannot be challenged on the ground of the legal representative's failure to consult the child.[23]

Where a parent, acting as the child's legal representative, administers the child's property[24] the parent must act as a reasonable and prudent person would act on his or her own behalf.[25] While enabled to do anything in relation to the property which the child could do if of full age and capacity,[26] the parent is liable to account to the child for the intromissions with the child's property.[27] This will usually occur when the child reaches 16. No liability is incurred by the parent in respect of funds which have been used in proper discharge of the parent's responsibility under s 1(1)(a), ie to safeguard and promote the child's health, development and welfare.[28]

If a parent enters into a transaction on behalf of a child under 16, the transaction cannot be set aside on the ground that it is prejudicial to the interests of the child. If the transaction involved the use of the child's own funds, redress may be sought by the child against the parent under s 10.[29]

'Transaction' is widely defined.[30] Consequently, the parent acting as the child's legal representative can enter into a wide range of juristic acts on behalf of the child as well as administer the child's own property.[31] Moreover, as legal representative, a parent can give consent on behalf of the child.[32] Thus, for example, while the responsibility to obtain medical care for a child falls within s 1(1)(a) of the C(S)A 1995, the duty and right to consent to medical treatment on the child's behalf derives from the parent being the child's legal representative.[33] It is also for this reason that a parent cannot consent to surgical, medical or dental treatment on the child if the child has gained the capacity to consent on his or her own behalf under s 2(4) of the Age of Legal Capacity (Scotland) Act 1991.[34]

Parents cannot abdicate parental responsibilities and rights but can arrange for them to be carried out by other people, for example a grandparent or other family member.[35] Liability for failure to fulfil the responsibilities remains with the parents.[36]

---

1 A parent is the child's genetic mother or father: Children (Scotland) Act 1995, s 15(1). In spite of the absence of a genetic relationship, a person is a parent if that person has adopted the child or if parentage is established by the Human Fertilisation and Embryology Act 1990, ss 27–30 or Part 2 of the Human Fertilisation and Embryology Act 2008: C(S)A 1995, s 15(1).

2 A child is a person below 18 years old: C(S)A 1995, s 15(1).

3 C(S)A 1995, s 1(1)(a), (b), (c) and (d).

4 C(S)A 1995, s 1(4).

5 Family Law (Scotland) Act 1985, s 1(1)(c) and (d), discussed at para **10.9**.

6 For example under the Education (Scotland) Act 1980, s 35.

7 C(S)A 1995, s 1(1); It is for the court to decide if it is practicable and in the interests of the child for a parent to carry out a parental responsibility. if it is not practicable and in the interests of the child for a parent to carry out a parental responsibility, it would appear that the responsibility no longer exists: *White v White* 1999 Fam LR 28; *sed quaere*?

8 [2020] 10 WLUK 613. See also *R v R* [2021] CSOH 69.

9 C(S)A 1995, s 2(1)(a)–(d).

10 C(S)A 1995, s 2(5).

11 For example under the Education (Scotland) Act 1980, s 37 (the right of a parent to home school a child).
12 C(S)A 1995, s 1(1).
13 C(S)A 1995, s 2(7).
14 C(S)A 1995, s 1(2)(a) and (b).
15 C(S)A 1995, s 6(1). The views of other persons having parental responsibilities and rights should also be considered.
16 When s 1(2) of the Children (Scotland) Act 2020 comes into force, the presumption of age 12 and over (in s 6(1) of the Children (Scotland) Act 1995) will be replaced by the principle that 'In considering whether the child is capable of forming a view, the person is to start with the presumption that the child is': s 6(1C).
17 C(S)A 1995, s 2(2).
18 C(S)A 1995, s 2(3) and (6). If the child's parents have such rights the consent of both is required.
19 C(S)A 1995, s 1(1)(d).
20 C(S)A 1995, s 2(1)(d).
21 C(S)A 1995, s 15(5).
22 On the duty to consult, see s 6(1) of the C(S)A 1995.
23 C(S)A 1995, s 6(2).
24 Where the child is the beneficiary under a trust or executory, the property may be administered by a judicial factor or the Accountant of Court: C(S)A 1995, s 9. Where a child is awarded damages, the court can order that the fund is to be administered by persons other than the parents, for example the Accountant of Court: C(S)A 1995, s 13. In the absence of any criticism or suspicion of the parents' ability to look after the child's funds, a defender is not obliged to raise s 13 proceedings. The court's discretion under s 13 is unfettered by the need to be satisfied that the administration of the damages could not be reasonably secured except by the appointment of a factor: *I v Argyll and Clyde Health Board* 2003 SLT 231. See also *S v Argyll and Clyde Acute Hospitals NHS Trust* 2009 SLT 1016.
25 C(S)A 1995, s 10(1)(a).
26 C(S)A 1995, s 10(1)(b); for example, *sell* the child's property, including heritage.
27 C(S)A 1995, s 10(1).
28 C(S)A 1995, s 10(2).
29 A parent is no longer a trustee for the purposes of the Trusts (Scotland) Act 1921: C(S) A 1995, Sch 4, para 6.
30 It has the same meaning as in s 9 of the Age of Legal Capacity (Scotland) Act 1991, discussed at para **10.2**: C(S)A 1995, s 15(1).
31 C(S)A 1995, s 15(5)(a).
32 C(S)A 1995, s 15(5)(b). However, a parent has no right to consent on behalf of the child to the storage of gametes under the Human Fertilisation and Embryology Act 1990: C(S)A 1995, s 15(7).
33 Discussed in detail at para **11.9**.
34 C(S)A 1995, ss 1(1)(d) and 2(1)(d).
35 C(S)A 1995, s 3(5), but note s 5(2) of C(S)A 1995.
36 C(S)A 1995, s 3(6).

WHO HAS PARENTAL RESPONSIBILITIES AND PARENTAL RIGHTS?

11.3 A child's mother automatically has parental responsibilities and rights in relation to her child.[1] It does not matter that she has never been married to the child's father; her age is also irrelevant.[2] A child's father automatically obtains parental responsibilities and rights in two situations.

First, if he is or was married to the child's mother at the date of the child's conception or at any time thereafter.[3]

Examples

(1) A husband and wife are married at the date of conception and birth. The husband is presumed to be the father of the child[4] and will automatically have parental responsibilities and parental rights.

(2) A husband and wife are married after the date of conception but before the birth. The husband is presumed to be the father of the child and will automatically have parental responsibilities and parental rights.

(3) A husband and wife marry after the date of conception and birth. The husband will *not* be presumed to be the father of the child unless the husband and wife acknowledge that the husband is the father of the child, and he has been registered as such.[5] If the husband's paternity is established, he will automatically acquire parental responsibilities and rights when he marries the child's mother.

For this purpose, marriage includes a voidable marriage and a 'marriage' which is void provided *both* parties believed in good faith that the marriage was valid (whether or not the error was one of fact or law).[6]

Where a father has not married the child's mother he will automatically obtain parental responsibilities and rights if he is presumed to be the father of the child because he was registered as the child's father.[7] This rule applied when the man was registered as the child's father on or after 4 May 2006, the date on which the Family Law (Scotland) 2006 came into force. Registration before 4 May 2006, did not, of itself, give the father parental responsibilities and parental rights; it raised the presumption that the man was the father of the child. Given that it is now more than 16 years since 4 May 2006, all men who are registered as the child's father will obtain parental responsibilities and parental rights over the child as well as being presumed to be the child's father.[8]

Where a woman is a parent by virtue of s 35 or s 42 of the Human Fertilisation and Embryology Act 2008, ie when she is married to, or in a civil partnership with, a man or a woman,[9] she will automatically have parental responsibilities and rights in respect of the child she is carrying[10] If another woman is to be treated as the child's second female parent by virtue of s 43 of HFEA 2008, ie when no man is to be treated as the father of the child under s 35 of the 2008 Act, and no woman is to be treated as a parent to the child under s 42 of the 2008 Act, and the mother has agreed that the other woman should be the child's second female parent,[11] she will automatically have parental responsibilities and parental rights if she was registered as the child's parent.[12]

Where none of these principles applies, there are two ways that a father[13] or the child's second female parent[14] can obtain parental responsibilities and parental rights. First, if the mother has not previously been deprived of some or all of her parental responsibilities and parental rights,[15] she may enter an agreement: (i) with the father under which he is to obtain the responsibilities and rights which he would have got if he had married the mother;[16;] or (ii) with the child's second female parent under which she is to obtain the responsibilities and rights she would have obtained if she had been a spouse of, or party to a civil partnership with, the mother.[17] Thus a father and second female parent can obtain *all*[18] the parental responsibilities and parental rights by agreement with the mother. The agreement will stipulate the appropriate date upon which the father or second female parent is to acquire the responsibilities and rights. It is expressly enacted that the mother and father have capacity to make such an agreement 'whatever age they may be'.[19] This means that if either or both are below 16, the age of legal capacity,[20] they can still enter into such an agreement and both will be able to exercise their parental responsibilities and rights in respect of their child.[21] However there is no such provision in respect of an agreement between the mother and the second female parent. Such an agreement does not have effect unless it is in the prescribed form and registered in the Books of Council and Session at a time when the mother still has the parental responsibilities and parental rights that she had when she made the agreement.[22] It is important to note that the father or second female parent acquires their responsibilities and rights solely by the mother's agreement. No court is involved and it is irrelevant that a court would take the view that it was not in the child's interests that the father or second female parent should have parental responsibilities and parental rights. Once registered, the agreement is irrevocable[23] except by court order.[24] Section 4 and s 4A agreements only enable a mother to give parental responsibilities and parental rights to the man who is the biological father of her child or the woman who is the second female parent: they cannot be used to give parental responsibilities and parental rights to other relatives of the child, for example the child's grandmother.

Secondly, the father or the second female parent could apply to the sheriff court or Court of Session under s 11 of the Children (Scotland) Act 1995 for an order giving him or her parental responsibilities and parental rights.[25] He or she has title to raise an action as a person who 'not having, and never having had, parental responsibilities and parental rights in relation to the child, *claims an interest*'.[26] The genetic and/or emotional ties towards the child are *per se* sufficient to constitute an interest.[27] The welfare of the child is the paramount consideration, and the court will give the father or second female parent parental responsibilities and parental rights only if it is in the child's best interests to do so. Further, there is no legal onus on the person bringing the action to prove that it is in the child's best interests. It is for the court to determine what is in the child's best interests.[28] In *Treasure v McGrath*,[29] the court held that the following factors should be considered: the degree of commitment that the applicant has towards the child; the degree of attachment between the applicant and the child; the importance of that commitment and attachment to the child's welfare; the reasons or motives behind the application; whether the applicant will take account of the child's views; any need to protect the child from the applicant's conduct; whether the applicant and any other person having parental responsibilities and parental rights will have to cooperate with each other in matters affecting the child and whether they will be able to do so; and whether it is better for the child that the order be made than no order being made at all. However, in *SM v AN*,[30] Lady Wise stated that the 'court must assess the evidence led and particular issues raised without reference to any checklist other than factors included as part of the statutory test'.

Any person, for example the child's grandparents or a step-parent, can apply under s 11(3)(a)(i) of the C(S)A 1995 to obtain parental responsibilities and parental rights. Again their genetic and/or emotional ties would constitute sufficient interest. Moreover, it is open to any person with an interest in the welfare of a child to apply under s 11(3)(a)(i) for a specific parental responsibility or parental right; for example a doctor seeking the right to regulate a child's medical treatment where an argument has arisen and parents are refusing to consent, and where the child does not have capacity.[31] It has been held that these provisions should not be interpreted restrictively and that Parliament should be presumed to have legislated in accordance with the UN Convention on the Rights of the Child and the European Convention on Human Rights. Thus a 14-year-old girl had title to sue for a contact order in respect of her half-brother and half-sister: the welfare of the children is the paramount consideration.[32]

Where a person aged 16 or over has *de facto* care or control of a child below that age then, if the person does not have parental responsibilities or parental rights in relation to the child, the person has a statutory responsibility to do what is reasonable in all the circumstances to safeguard the child's health, development and welfare.[33] Even though the person does not have the right to act as the child's legal representative,[34] in fulfilling the responsibility to safeguard the child's health the person can consent to any surgical, medical or dental treatment or procedure on behalf of the child. However, this right to consent applies only where:

(a) the child is not able to give such consent on his or her own behalf;[35] *and*

(b) it is not within the knowledge of the person that a parent of the child would refuse to give the consent in question.[36]

Thus, for example, a person who has care or control of a child cannot consent to a blood transfusion on behalf of the child where he or she knows that the child's parents, for religious reasons, will not allow the child to have a blood transfusion. If in fulfilling this responsibility the person must make a major decision, the child has to be consulted.[37] The responsibility does not arise when a person has care or control of a child at school.[38]

A child's parent can appoint a person to be the child's guardian in the event of the parent's death.[39] To be effective the appointment must be in writing and signed by the parent.[40] In addition, the parent must have been entitled to act as the child's legal representative at the date of the parent's *death*.[41] When a parent appoints a guardian, this is regarded as a major decision and there is a duty to consult the child.[42] An appointment as guardian does not take effect unless the person named in the deed accepts the appointment, either expressly or by acts which are not consistent with any other intention.[43] Once the appointment is accepted, the guardian automatically acquires the full complement of parental responsibilities and parental rights.[44] Where the child has a surviving parent, the parent's responsibilities and rights continue and are fulfilled and exercised along with the parental responsibilities and parental rights of the guardian.[45] Guardianship ends when the child reaches 18, the child or guardian dies, or it is terminated by an order under s 11 of the C(S)A 1995.[46]

---

1 Children (Scotland) Act 1995, s 3(1)(a).
2 Age of Legal Capacity (Scotland) Act 1991, s 1(3)(g).
3 C(S)A 1995, s 3(1)(b)(i). This would also be the case where the husband was the child's father by virtue of the Human Fertilisation and Embryology Act, s 35: on s 35 see para **9.2**.
4 Law Reform (Parent and Child) (Scotland) Act 1986, s 5(1)(a), discussed at para **9.2**.
5 LR(PC)(S)A 1986, s 5(1)(b), discussed at para **9.2**. If the registration took place on or after 4 May 2006, the father would automatically obtain parental responsibilities and parental rights.
6 C(S)A 1995, s 3(2)(a) and (b). Accordingly, if the wife is acting in bad faith, the husband does not obtain parental responsibilities and rights under this provision. The wife will, of course, have parental responsibilities and rights by virtue of being the child's mother. Cf s 5(1) and (2) of the LR(PC)(S)A 1986, discussed at para **9.2**.
7 C(S)A 1995, s 3(1)(b)(ii). This presumption of paternity arises under the LR(PC)(S)A 1986, s 5(1)(b) and Sch 1, para 8, discussed above at para **9.2**. This would also be the case when the man was the child's father by virtue of the HFEA 2008, s 35, ie the mother agreed that the man should be the child's father: on s 35, see para **9.2**.
8 FL(S)A 2006, s 23(4).
9 On HFEA 2008, s 42, see para **9.2**.
10 C(S)A1995, s 3(1)(c).
11 On HFEA 2008, s 43, see para **9.2**.
12 C(S)A 1995, s 3(1)(d).
13 Ie, who has not been registered as such.
14 Ie, who has not been registered as such.
15 For example, as a result of the child having been adopted or a s 11(2)(a) order or a permanence order. On adoption see **Ch 12**; on s 11 orders see para **12.4**; and on

permanence orders, see paras **13.13** and **14.7.** If the mother has been deprived of any parental responsibilities and rights, she cannot make such an agreement.

16 C(S)A 1995, s 4(1).

17 C(S)A 1995, s 4A(1).

18 Unless there is a s 11 order in force affecting some of the mother's responsibilities and rights, for example, if there was a residence order in favour of a third party. Such an order does not normally deprive the parent of his or her responsibilities and rights: C(S)A 1995, s 11(11), discussed at para **12.4.** Accordingly, for example, the mother could still enter into a s 4 agreement with the father, even if a residence order had been made in favour of the child's grandparents.

19 C(S)A 1995, s 4(1), but note that this is not the case for a s 4A agreement.

20 Discussed in **Ch 9.**

21 ALC(S)A 1991, s 1(3)(g): for discussion, see para **10.2**.

22 C(S)A 1995, s 4(2)(a) and (b). The date of registration is the appropriate date, ie it is the date when the father or second female parent obtains parental responsibilities and rights.

23 C(S)A 1995, s 4(4).

24 C(S)A 1995, s 11(11).

25 C(S)A 1995, s 11(1), (2)(b)(i) and (ii). Note that s 1(3)(g) of the Age of Legal Capacity (Scotland) Act 1991 recognises that a person under the age of 16 years can exercise parental responsibilities and parental rights. Therefore, there seems to be no reason why an applicant cannot be under the age of 16.

26 C(S)A 1995, s 11(3)(a)(i). Italics added.

27 In *X v Y* 2002 Fam LR 58 the homosexual man, X, who agreed to be a sperm donor for Y and her lesbian partner, obtained parental responsibilities and rights over the child although the case was defended by the mother and her same sex cohabitant.

28 C(S)A 1995, s 11(7)(a). See *White v White* 2001 SLT 485 (IH) in which the court stated, 'where a party seeks an order ... [T]he court must consider all the relevant material and decide what would be conducive to the child's welfare. That is the paramount consideration'.

29 2007 SCLR 447 (Sh Ct).

30 [2021] CSOH 60 at para 56.

31 C(S)A 1995, s 11(5) expressly excludes local authorities from the definition of 'person'. There is nothing to prevent a health board from claiming an interest.

32 *E v E* 2004 Fam LR 115.

33 C(S)A 1995, s 5(1).

34 C(S)A 1995, s 2(1)(d).

35 On the capacity of a child below 16 to consent to medical treatment etc, see the ALC(S)A 1991, s 2(4), discussed at para **10.2**.

36 C(S)A 1995, s 5(1)(a) and (b).

37 C(S)A 1995, s 6(1)(a). On the duty to consult the child see para **11.2**.

38 C(S)A 1995, s 5(2).

39 C(S)A 1995, s 7(1). A guardian of a child may appoint a person to be the child's guardian in the event of the guardian's death: s 7(2). The same rules apply as in the appointment of a guardian by the child's parent.

40 C(S)A 1995, s 7(1)(a)(i). The appointment will usually be in the parent's will or a codicil to the will. If the will or codicil is revoked, the appointment is also revoked: C(S) A 1995, s 8(4). Where the appointment is made in a deed other than a will or codicil, it is revoked if the deed is destroyed by the granter or the granter has another person destroy the deed in the granter's presence: s 8(3). If A appoints B to be the guardian, then B's appointment is revoked if A later appoints C to be the guardian unless it is clear that the appointment of C is an additional appointment: s 8(1). However, the appointment of B is not revoked unless the appointment of C is in writing and signed by A: s 8(2). It does not matter if the appointment of B is in an unrevoked will or codicil.

41 C(S)A 1995, s 7(1)(a)(ii).

42 C(S)A 1995, s 7(6).

43 C(S)A 1995, s 7(3). If two or more persons are appointed, any one can accept the appointment even if the other(s) refuse to do so unless the appointment otherwise provides.

44 Children (Scotland) Act 1995, s 7(5). This is subject to any s 11 orders and any parental responsibilities order in force at the time the appointment was accepted. Note that parental responsibility orders were repealed by the Adoption and Children (Scotland) Act 2007.

45 C(S)A 1995, s 7(1)(b). Each can exercise a parental right without the consent of the other: s 2(3), discussed at para 11.1.

46 C(S)A 1995, s 11(2)(h).

SPECIFIC PARENTAL RESPONSIBILITIES AND PARENTAL RIGHTS

11.4 In this section, we shall consider some of the most important parental responsibilities and parental rights.[1] Statutory parental responsibilities and parental rights are expressed in very general terms and it is valuable to consider specific aspects. The responsibility to safeguard and promote the child's health, development and welfare and to give the child direction and guidance will be considered along with the right to have the child living with the parent and the parent's right to control, direct or guide the child. The responsibility and right to act as the child's legal representative have already been discussed.[2] It must always be remembered that a parent is expected to fulfil the statutory responsibilities only in so far as it is practicable for the parent to do so.[3] However, in exercising parental rights there is a duty to consult the child when making a major decision and the parent must always act in the child's interests.[4] Accordingly, parental rights can be regarded as *prima facie* rights in the sense that any purported exercise of the right must further the child's welfare or, at least, must not be against the interests of the child. This is known as 'the welfare principle'.

If a purported exercise of a parental right is against the child's interests, there is no obligation on the child or a third party to act in accordance with the parent's decision. The ultimate arbiter of whether or not a purported exercise of parental rights is *in fact* contrary to a child's welfare is the Court of Session or the sheriff court which have the power to make any order in relation to parental responsibilities and parental rights.[5] Thus for example, a child or a third party can petition the court for a declarator that a purported exercise of a parental right by a parent is not in the interests of the child or that a parent's acts or omissions are in breach of the parent's statutory responsibilities.

---

1 For full discussion see Ch 7 of Wilkinson and Norrie, *The Law Relating to Parent and Child in Scotland* (SULI) 3rd edn; and Ch 4 and 5 of Griffiths, Fotheringham and McCarthy, *Family Law* (W Green) 4th edn.

2 At para **11.2**. They will arise incidentally in the present discussion.

3 Children (Scotland) Act 1995, s 1(1). There would, for example, be no failure to comply with s 1(1)(a) if a parent had to refuse a child's request for an expensive computer because the parent could not afford the cost.

4 C(S)A 1995, ss 1(1), 2(1) and 6. On the duty to consult, see para **11.2**.

5 C(S)A 1995, s 11(1) and (2). The orders listed in s 11(2) are 'without prejudice to the generality' of s 11(1).

Residence

11.5 Parents have the right to have their child live with them or otherwise to regulate their child's residence,[1] for example to allow the child to holiday with friends. It is generally accepted that children thrive in a stable home environment and consequently this right can be seen as enabling parents to fulfil their responsibility to promote the child's development.[2] It is only a *prima facie* right and must be exercised in the child's interests. Accordingly, parents may lose the right to have their child live at home if it would be against the child's interests to remain with or be returned to the parent.

The principles arising from the case of *J v C*,[3] a decision of the House of Lords in an English appeal,[4] are generally accepted as the basis for s 1(1) of the C(S)A 1995. The parents of a boy who had spent eight years in foster care due to his mother's illness, wanted the boy returned to their care and to live with them in Spain. Their position was that the welfare of a child was best served by allowing the child to live with his or her parents unless it was shown that it was not for the child's welfare to do so. The House of Lords decided that in spite of the fact that the parents' conduct was unimpeachable, the child should nevertheless remain with his foster carers in England. After eight-and-a-half years, the boy had become integrated into his foster family and to remove him to Spain would be likely to cause him distress and possible long-term psychological harm; the parents could not exercise their *prima facie* right to have their child live with them because it would be contrary to the child's interests to do so. This case is authority for the proposition that the parental right of residence is governed by the welfare principle.[5] In *W v G*,[6] the parents of a child both had parental responsibilities and parental rights. After separation, the child was resident with the mother; the father having regular residential contact. The father raised an action for a residence order to be granted in his favour based on the mother's drug use and unstable behaviour. The sheriff stated: 'Neither party has any greater right to a residence order than the other. The matter must be determined on the basis that [the child's] welfare is the paramount consideration.' A residence order was granted in favour of the father with the mother being granted residential contact. A parent cannot validly exercise his or her right if it is not in the best interests of the child to do so.

---

1 Children (Scotland) Act 1995, s 2(1)(a).
2 C(S)A 1995, s 1(1)(a).
3 [1970] AC 668, HL, [1969] 1 All ER 788.
4 But accepted as authoritative in Scotland.
5 See, in particular, the speech of Lord McDermott, [1970] AC 668 at 701. This is now enacted in s 1(1) of the C(S)A 1995.
6 *SW v SG* [2012] 10 WLUK 8; 2012 WL 4866914. See also *AY v MM* 2021 GWD 33-674.

Discipline

11.6 A parent has the right to control a child.[1] For some parents this can include an approach to discipline that involves the physical chastisement of the child. While there has been a growing societal movement away from the physical punishment of children, the movement has been slow moving, until now. In November 2020, the Children (Equal Protection from Assault) (Scotland) Act 2019 came into force. It is worthwhile briefly to chart the legal position prior to the 2019 Act.

Pre-2019 Act, the defence of 'reasonable chastisement' was available to a parent who would, otherwise, risk a charge of assault against his or her child. Article 3 of the European Convention on Human Rights states that: 'No one shall be subjected to torture or to inhuman or degrading treatment or punishment.'[2] Excessive physical ill-treatment of a child led to criminal proceedings for cruelty[3] and constituted grounds for referral to a children's hearing under the Children's Hearings (Scotland) Act 2011.[4] Section 51 of the Criminal Justice (Scotland) Act 2003[5] made clear that physical ill-treatment constituted an assault for which the parent was criminally responsible unless the parent could show that the assault was a 'justifiable assault'.[6] If the assault on the child included or consisted of (a) a blow to the head; (b) shaking; or (c) the use of an implement[7] this was unjustifiable.[8]

All forms of corporal punishment have been abolished in schools, residential establishments, by foster carers, child minders and other bodies regulated by the Care Inspectorate.[9]

Section 1 of the Children (Equal Protection from Assault) (Scotland) Act 2019 states:

> '*Abolition of defence of reasonable chastisement*
>
> (1) The rule of law, that the physical punishment of a child in the exercise of a parental right or a right derived from having charge or care of the child is justifiable and is therefore not an assault, ceases to have effect.'

In simple terms, the defence of 'reasonable chastisement' is no longer available to a parent who has been charged with assaulting his or her child. The Act, as its name suggests, gives the child who is a victim of assault, equal protection under the law as any other person. It should be noted that the 2019 Act does not ban smacking; it equalises the protection given to all victims of assault – child or adult.

1 Children (Scotland) Act 1995, s 2(1)(b).
2 *A v United Kingdom* (1999) 27 EHRR 611.
3 Children and Young Persons (Scotland) Act 1937, s 12(1).
4 See **Ch 15** below.
5 Now repealed by s 1(2) of the Children (Equal Protection from Assault) (Scotland) Act 2019.
6 Criminal Justice (Scotland) Act 2003, s 51(1).
7 CJ(S)A 2003, s 51(3)(a)–(c).
8 CJ(S)A 2003, s 51(3).
9 See Standards in Scotland's Schools etc. Act, s 16; Residential Establishments – Child Care (Scotland) Regulations 1996 (SI 1996/3256), reg 10(2); Looked After Children (Scotland) Regulations 2009 (SI 2009/210), Sch 5, para 5 and Sch 6, para 6.

Education

11.7 Parents are under a duty to ensure that their children receive a suitable education until they reach 16.[1] In particular, they must ensure that the child attends school.[2] In order to fulfil these specific obligations and fulfil the general statutory responsibility to promote the child's development,[3] a parent has the right to choose a child's education.[4] This right must be exercised in accordance with the welfare principle. Unless the parent has sufficient means to afford private education, the exercise of the right to choose which school a child will attend will be limited. Parents' rights to choose a local authority school which is suitable for the needs of their children have been strengthened as a result of legislation.[5]

It should be noted that the rights and obligations in respect of a child's education vest not only in the parent but also the child's guardian, any person who is liable to maintain the child and any person having care of the child.[6]

It should also be noted that, where a child fails without excuse to attend regularly at school, this is a ground on which the child can be referred to a children's hearing.[7]

1 Education (Scotland) Act 1980, ss 30–31.
2 E(S)A 1980, s 35. The parent is relieved of this obligation if the parent provides the child with effective education by other means, for example, home schooling. A parent's failure, without reasonable excuse, to ensure that a child attends school is an offence.

But see O'*Hagan v Rae* 2001 SLT (Sh Ct) 30 in which it was held that reasonable excuse had to be interpreted in a way to allow a parent to defend herself on the ground that it was not fair in the circumstances that she should face criminal sanctions in respect of her child's truancy over which she had little control. Otherwise there could be a violation of Article 6(2) of the European Convention on Human Rights which provides that: 'Everyone charged with a criminal offence shall be presumed innocent until proved guilty by law.'

3 E(S)A 1980, s 30(1).

4 Where both parents have parental rights any dispute over choice of school etc, can be resolved by a specific issue order under the Children (Scotland) Act 1995, s 11(2)(e): see, for example, *G v G* 2002 Fam LR 120. While the child's welfare is the paramount consideration, the court will give weight to maintaining the status quo. In *CAM v HM* [2012] CSOH 127 the court made a specific issue order that the children should remain at their current primary school and refused their mother's request that she could remove them to another school in the town where she had gone to live after she had separated from their father.

5 E(S)A 1980, ss 28 and 28A–28H (as amended). See Sarah-Jane Kissock *Petition of UT-H* SCOLAG 2012, 418, 197. The right to choose is not absolute:

6 E(S)A 1980, s 135(1), definition of 'parent' for the purposes of the 1980 Act.

7 See Children's Hearings (Scotland) Act 2011, s 67(2)(o) and **Chs 14** and **15** below.

Religion

11.8 In an increasingly pluralistic society, religious toleration is of the first importance. Scots law recognises that in fulfilment of their responsibility for the child's development, parents have a *prima facie* right to choose a child's religion. This right must be exercised in accordance with the child's welfare. Where a parent's or, indeed a child's, religious convictions will result in physical harm to the child, the parent's and the child's wishes will be overridden. For example, while parents are free to decide that a child should be brought up as a Jehovah's Witness, if the child should require a blood transfusion, the law will not countenance the parent's refusal to consent to such treatment.[1]

Scottish courts have accepted that where parents are of different religions, it matters little to the child whether he or she is brought up in one faith rather than another; the matter will be decided in the light of all the circumstances of the case in accordance with the welfare principle. In *McNaught v McNaught*,[2] a mother who was a Protestant had the children of the marriage living with her. In spite of the fact that she had agreed to bring up the children in her husband's Roman Catholic faith, the husband failed to obtain an order that at least his youngest child, should continue to be brought up as a Roman Catholic. As it was otherwise in the child's best interests to be with his mother, she was free to bring up the child as a Protestant since either faith was for the benefit of the child. In *S v S*,[3] the husband was Egyptian and a Muslim: the wife was Scottish and a Protestant. They had three children. After they had separated, the mother, who was the primary carer, began to send the children to the Church of Scotland. The husband objected and sought a specific issue order that the children should be brought up in the Islamic faith to which the mother had agreed at the time of the marriage. In refusing the order on the grounds that it was not in the children's best interests that such an order be made, the sheriff stated: 'Regardless of the religious obligation, if there is any conflict between that obligation and the interests of the children, then the interests of the children must prevail'.[4]

In the past, the courts were adamant that it was in a child's interests to be brought up in a religious faith. In *M'Clements v M'Clements*,[5] the Lord Justice-Clerk (Thomson) said that in his opinion a child 'ought not to be denied the opportunity of being brought up in the generally accepted religious beliefs of the society in which he lives'.[6] In today's society parents would not be in breach of any parental responsibility if they chose to bring up their child as an atheist or agnostic.[7] It is interesting to note in this context that religious instruction is a 'compulsory' element in the curriculum of public, ie education authority, schools.[8]

On reaching 16, a young person can choose his or her own religion.[9] While parents retain the responsibility to guide their child on such matters until the age of 18[10] they have no power to veto the child's choice. A child below 16 may wish to choose a religion different from that of the child's parents. Given their duty to consult the child, the parents may fulfil their statutory responsibilities by agreeing with the child's choice. In these circumstances it is thought that the parents would only be in breach of their parental responsibilities if it would be against the child's interests to change religion. This could arise if the child proposed to join an extreme sect.

1 In such a situation, a person claiming an interest, or a health board, could raise an action for a specific issue order under s 11(2)(e) of the C(S)A 1995 for the right to

consent to medical treatment: see para **12.4**. In practice an application would be made for a permanence order and the local authority could consent to the child having medical treatment: Adoption and Children (Scotland) Act 2007 Part 2 discussed at paras **13.13** and **14.7**.

2 1955 SLT (Sh Ct) 9.

3 2012 Fam LR 148; GWD 37-739.

4 Ibid at para 147.

5 1958 SC 286.

6 Ibid at 289.

7 Cf *MacKay v MacKay* 1957 SLT (Notes) 17, per the Lord President (Clyde): '... it would be almost impossible for a court in Scotland to award the custody to an atheist with the prospect of the child being brought up without the solace and guidance of any religious teaching at all'.

8 Education (Scotland) Act 1980, ss 8–10. Parents can elect that their child should not take part in religious observance or education: s 8(1). Religious observance can only be discontinued after a poll of local government electors: E(S)A 1980, s 8(2).

9 The parental responsibility and parental right ceases when the child is 16: C(S)A 1995, ss 1(2)(a) and 2(7).

10 The parental responsibility to give guidance lasts until the child is 18: C(S)A 1995, s 1(2)(b).

Medical procedures

11.9 In fulfilment of their responsibility to safeguard and promote their children's health,[1] parents have the *prima facie* right to consent to medical treatment on the child's behalf.[2] The exercise of this right by parents is subject to the welfare principle. There is very little Scottish authority on the point, but English decisions are instructive.

In *Re D (a minor)*[3] for example, a mother consented to the sterilisation of her mentally disabled daughter who had reached the age of puberty. Before the operation took place the child was made a ward of court.[4] The court overrode the mother's decision on the ground that the operation was not in accordance with the welfare of the child. Heilbron J based her decision on the grounds that, although mentally disabled, the child probably had sufficient capacity to enter into marriage; there was no evidence that she was promiscuous; and any unwanted pregnancy could be terminated. In those circumstances, the proposed operation was not in the child's interests. On the other hand, in *Re B (a minor)*,[5] the House of Lords held that a sterilisation operation could be carried out on a mentally disabled girl of 17 who had a mental age of five. Pregnancy and childbirth would have been physically and mentally disastrous for the young woman, therefore it was in her best interests that the operation go ahead.[6]

The right to consent implies the right to refuse consent to medical treatment. This right must again be exercised in accordance with the welfare principle. In *Re B (a minor)*[7] the Court of Appeal overrode the parents' refusal to consent to an operation to remove an intestinal blockage from their new born infant who had Down's Syndrome. The parents had taken the view that, since the child was mentally disabled, it was better for the child to die as a result of the blockage rather than live. The court held that this purported exercise by the parents of their *prima facie* right to withhold consent was not in accordance with the child's welfare and the child had the prospect of a happy life. In the circumstances, the court overrode the parents' decision and consented to the operation on behalf of the child.[8] In *E v Northern Care Alliance NHS Foundation Trust* and *F v Somerset NHS Foundation Trust*,[9] two capacitous minors, one aged 16, the other 17, and both Jehovah's Witnesses, refused consent for blood transfusions should they be necessary in the course of surgical interventions. Both NHS Trusts applied for a declaration that would allow the administration of blood products if required. The court granted the declaration. The minors appealed on the basis that the starting point should be a strong presumption in favour of the minors' capacitous decisions. The Court of Appeal held that there was no such presumption in respect of a mature young person's decision and the court had to act upon its objective assessment of the young person's best interests, even where that conflicted with the views of the young person.[10]

Where the proposed treatment is generally accepted as therapeutic, it is thought that a parent's consent to such treatment on a child will be upheld as a valid exercise of the parent's *prima facie* right since it would be in the child's best interests to consent. Conversely, where a parent refuses to consent to therapeutic medical treatment on a child, the purported exercise of *the prima facie* right will be overridden as it would be against the child's interests not to have the benefit of the treatment.[11] In *Re A*,[12] the Court of Appeal took the view that *prima facie* a court cannot sanction an operation that is clearly against the interests of a child. This case concerned conjoined twins both of whom would die unless separated; but it was also clear that one would undoubtedly die a short time after the operation. In these unique circumstances, the court held that in applying the welfare principle, it had to choose the lesser of two evils and the least detrimental choice was to allow the operation to go ahead since it allowed one of the twins the chance to live. See also *NHS Trust v B*,[13] in which a court ordered that an NHS Trust could administer a blood transfusion to a young child if required during a surgical procedure against the wishes of the parents who were Jehovah's Witnesses. From time to time, cases arise where a child's medical condition is such that he or she is receiving palliative care only. The medical team may deem that it is no longer in the baby or child's best interest to continue with the palliative treatment and, against the wishes of the parents, a withdrawal of treatment is sought by the NHS Trust.[14]

Re A (above) was a case where the procedure was clearly against the interests of the twin who was going to die when separated from her sister. But what of procedures which, if not clearly in the child's best interests, are not clearly against the child's interests? If an analogy be taken from the law on blood tests and DNA profiling,[15] *Docherty v McGlynn*[16] suggests that a medical procedure can be carried out on a child provided it is not positively *against* the child's interests to do so.[17] Further, it is submitted that, in Scots law, parents can lawfully consent to medical procedures on their children which, while not in the child's best interests, are not positively against the child's interests. These would include, for example, non-therapeutic circumcision of male infants;[18] the taking of blood samples from healthy children for the purposes of medical research; and the donation of regenerative tissue, for example bone marrow.[19] However, it is expressly provided that a parent cannot consent on behalf of a child to the storage of the child's gametes under the Human Fertilisation and Embryology Act 2008.[20]

When a child reaches 16, the child can consent to surgical, medical or dental treatment or procedures on his or her own behalf.[21] Given the importance of patient autonomy, this must include the right to refuse medical treatment. As we have seen,[22] a child under 16 may have capacity to consent by virtue of s 2(4) of the Age of Legal Capacity (Scotland) Act 1991. The 1991 Act does not expressly stipulate that parents lose their right to consent on behalf of a child who has s 2(4) capacity. Where the proposed medical treatment is unarguably therapeutic, there is no difficulty if the parents and the child both consent. If the child has s 2(4) capacity, the child's consent is sufficient – even if the parents would not consent. The difficulty arises if the child has s 2(4) capacity and refuses to consent. Can the parents override their child's refusal and consent on the child's behalf? Conversely, if a child with s 2(4) capacity consents to medical treatment which is not unarguably therapeutic, can the parents veto the child's decision: for example, if the child consents to a termination of pregnancy or to donate non-regenerative tissue?

There are two possible views. The first is that when the child has s 2(4) capacity then the parents lose their right to consent as the right is no longer needed. The parent consents as the child's legal representative. Section 15(5) of the C(S)A 1995, provides that a parent can only consent as a legal representative when the child has no capacity to consent to a legal transaction; once a child has s 2(4) capacity under the ALC(S)A 1991, the parent must cease to act as the child's legal representative in relation to medical procedures.[23]

The second is that as the parents retain the parental responsibility to give direction to the child until the child is 16[24] – and guidance until the child is 18[25] – the parents cannot simply be ignored. However, the child with capacity may not wish his or her confidential information to be shared with the parents by the medical practitioner. This may be the case, for example, where a girl under the age of 16 wishes to seek advice on contraception or have a termination without the knowledge of her parents. In the case of *Gillick v West Norfolk and Wisbech Area Health Authority*,[26] an English appeal to the House of Lords held that, in exceptional circumstances, a parent need not be informed when a girl under 16 seeks contraceptives or contraceptive advice from a doctor.

There are two threads of reasoning in the speeches of the majority. Lord Scarman took the view that parental rights exist only in so far as a child lacks the capacity to take decisions for him or herself; thus, when a girl has sufficient understanding, intelligence and maturity to make decisions in relation to, *inter alia*, sexual matters, the parent's rights cease: 'I would hold that as a matter of law the parental right to determine whether or not their minor child below the age of 16 will have medical treatment terminates if and when the child achieves a sufficient understanding and intelligence to enable him or her to understand fully what is proposed.'[27] This supports the first view discussed above. Lord Scarman goes on to say that: 'It will be a question of fact whether a child seeking advice has sufficient understanding of what is involved to give a consent valid in law.' It is difficult to see how this will be determined, particularly in relation to sexual matters. Parents may argue that a child has not reached that degree of maturity when the child's proposed course of conduct appears to be contrary to the parents' concept of what is in the best interests of the child.

Lord Fraser, on the other hand, did not deny that the parents had a *prima facie* right to be informed. However, he maintained that there could be exceptional circumstances where this was not necessary, ie when:

(1) the child understands the advice on the nature and effect of contraceptives;

(2) the child has been strongly advised to consult her parents but has refused;

(3) the child is likely to have or continue to have sexual intercourse without contraceptive treatment;

(4) the child's physical and/or mental health would suffer without contraceptive advice or treatment; and

(5) it is in the child's best interests to be prescribed contraceptives without the parents' knowledge or consent.

Whether an exceptional case has arisen could, in his Lordship's opinion, safely be left to the clinical judgment of the doctor concerned.[28]

It should be noted that before Lord Fraser's exception applies, the proposed course of treatment must be in the child's best interests.

Gillick was, of course, an English decision and is not binding on Scottish courts. The legal basis for the law in Scotland is s 2(4) of the ALC(S)A 1991 where the matter is ultimately one of construction of s 2(4). To the extent that the House of Lords rejected the contention that parents have a right to veto such treatment, this is important. There is no 'best interests' principle written into s 2(4), but parents should discuss with their child the implications of a course of action which the child may choose which they may later regret. In the Scottish context of the prescription of contraceptives to a girl under 16, her parents have a statutory obligation to proffer advice, to discuss, for example, whether it is in her long-term interests to enter sexual relationships at an early age. If they persuade her that this is not in her interests, then no further difficulties arise; but if they do not, they cannot prevent her obtaining contraceptives if she has s 2(4) capacity. In the case of a sexually active girl who is determined to continue to have sexual intercourse, it is thought that the Scottish courts would accept that it was not against her interests to be prescribed contraceptives without her parents' consent.

In respect of other medical procedures if, for example, a 14-year-old girl who has been deemed to have s 2(4) capacity by a qualified medical practitioner, sought termination of a pregnancy then it could be argued that her parents have the right to be informed in order to discuss with her the alternatives to termination and the possible long-term effect on her of having a termination. However, it is the writer's view that, with s 2(4) capacity comes the right to confidentiality of personal and private medical data and the sharing of such data with parents without the child's consent may breach professional duty and practice.[29] Where there is discussion between a child who has capacity under s 2(4) and her parents after which the child is still determined to have the termination it is thought that any purported veto by her parents would be ineffective. Similarly, where a child with s 2(4) capacity refuses life-saving treatment, for example, a 15-year-old who has a terminal condition, then the decision of the child should be respected. This position is part of the British Medical Association professional guidance which states: 'a competent refusal cannot be overridden by any other person, carer or court, even if that treatment is necessary to save or prolong life'.[30] There is a paucity of Scots case law in this area[31] and opinions continue to differ.

1 Children (Scotland) Act 1995, s 1(1)(a).
2 This is by virtue of their responsibility and right to act as the child's legal representative: C(S)A 1995, ss 1(1)(d) and 2(1)(d).
3 [1976] 1 All ER 326, [1976] Fam 185.
4 The term 'ward of court' relates to English law (Children Act 1989). Where a child is made a ward of court, responsibility for major decisions in relation to the child is under the inherent jurisdiction of the High Court. No important decision can be taken without the permission or consent of the court. Day-to-day decisions can continue to be made by an individual or a local authority that has care of the child.
5 [1988] AC 199, [1987] 2 WLR 1213.

6 The court indicated that before such an operation was to be performed, the consent of the court should always be obtained: [1987] 2 WLR 1213 at 1218, per Lord Templeman. In Scots law this could be done by an application under C(S)A 1995, s 11(1). Given that consent can only be given where it is in the child's best interests to do so, it could be argued that the consent of the court is otiose: however, it is thought that it would nevertheless be prudent to obtain the court's approval in such a sensitive area.

7 [1981] 1 WLR 1421, CA.

8 See also *Re C* [2000] Fam 48 where the court overrode the parents' refusal to allow their child to be tested for HIV.

9 [2022] 2 WLR 395.

10 See *Finlayson, Applicant* 1989 SCLR 601 where a ground for the, then, equivalent of a compulsory supervision order was established where parents refused medical treatment for their haemophiliac son even though they were genuinely concerned that the child might be infected with AIDS as a result of the treatment. The child's physical condition had deteriorated as a result of non-treatment.

11 *Re C* [2000] Fam 48 (parents refused consent to have their baby tested for HIV).

12 [2001] 2 WLR 480.

13 [2014] EWHC 3486 (Fam).

14 See: *Great Ormand Street Hospital for Children NHS Foundation Trust v Yates* [2017] EWHC 1909 (Fam) and *Evans v Alder Hey Children's NHS Foundation Trust* and *Manchester University NHS Foundation Trust v Fixsler* [2021] EWHC 1426 (Fam).

15 Discussed at para **9.3.**

16 1983 SLT 645.

17 See: *JS v Decision of a Children's Hearing* [2021] SC EDIN 1, where the sheriff varied a Compulsory Supervision Order to include a measure that would allow a DNA test to be done on a young child, where the mother's consent was not forthcoming.

18 Non-therapeutic male circumcision is generally assumed to be lawful where it is deemed to be in the child's best interests; valid consent has been given; and it is performed by a competent person. Female circumcision cannot lawfully be carried out in the United Kingdom: Prohibition of Female Genital Mutilation (Scotland) Act 2005; Female Genital Mutilation (Protection and Guidance) (Scotland) Act 2020; Prohibition of Female Circumcision Act 1985. See: *Re B and G (Children) (No 2)* [2015] EWFC 3.

19 The donation of non-regenerative tissue, for example a kidney, would be against the child's, ie the donor's, interests: consequently a parent cannot consent to this procedure on behalf of a child. However, if the child had capacity under s 2(4) of the Age of Legal Capacity (Scotland) Act 1991, it would appear that the child could consent.

20 C(S)A1995, s 15(7).

21 ALC(S)A 1991, s 1(1)(b).

22 For discussion, see para **10.2.**

23 For full discussion see *Wilkinson and Norrie*, paras 8.50 ff. See also, Alison Cleland, *Children's Rights in Scotland* (3rd edn, W Green), Ch 10 (Medical Treatment).

24 C(S)A 1995, s 1(1)(b)(i) and (2)(a).

25 C(S)A 1995, s 1(1)(b)(ii) and (2)(b).
26 [1986] AC 112.
27 Ibid at 189.
28 Ibid at 174.
29 See s 208 of Data Protection Act 2018 and British Medical Association professional guidelines and codes of practice.
30 See BMA publication, *Children and young people: toolkit for doctors* (published 2021).
31 See *Houston, Applicant* 1996 SCLR 943.

Looking after children

11.10 Ensuring that a child receives medical care is only one aspect of a parent's responsibility to safeguard and promote the child's health, development and welfare.[1] Apart from alimenting the child,[2] parents should give their children love and affection and provide them with opportunities to play and socialise with other families.[3] Parents must ensure the safety of their children and that their children are looked after in the parents' absence.

Where a parent abandons, neglects or ill-treats his or her child, this may result in the child being referred to a children's hearing where a compulsory supervision order may be imposed.[4] The parents may also be liable to criminal sanctions under s 12(1) of the Children and Young Persons (Scotland) Act 1937. In *Locality Reporter, Stirling v S*,[5] a mother slapped her child on the side of the head causing the child's head to move. The mother was charged under s 12 of the 1937 Act and, while the sheriff found that the mother's conduct had been deliberate, her hitting of the child did not amount to a contravention of s 12 because it was not an act 'likely to cause [the child] unnecessary suffering or injury to health'. Wilful abandonment is a question of fact and degree depending on the period during which the children have been left and the steps, if any, which were taken for their care.[6] Merely to leave a child unattended is not wilful neglect: it will depend on all the circumstances of the case including the age of the child, the age of any babysitter, the time the child was left alone and the reason why the child was left unattended. But it is neglect if a very young child is left alone for a substantial period and, through the absence of care, is likely to experience unnecessary suffering.[7]

Parents must also be prepared to give their children direction and guidance whenever it is in the child's interests to do so.[8] This clearly covers a wide range of issues, for example recreational pursuits, educational opportunities, career opportunities, etc. In practice this will merge with the parent's obligation to consult the child on any major decision which will affect the child, for example moving house or changing school.[9]

---

1 Children (Scotland) Act 1995, s 1(1)(a).
2 On aliment, see **Ch 10.**
3 For full discussion, see *Wilkinson and Norrie*, paras 8.22 ff.
4 Discussed in **Ch 15.**
5 [2018] SC STI 37; 2019 Fam LR 2.
6 *M v Orr* 1995 SLT 26.
7 *H v Lees; D v Orr* 1994 SLT 908 (In *H* case not neglect when mother was intoxicated and unable to look after baby for several hours when no evidence that child required food or changing during that period); (In *D* case not neglect when father left 13-year-old son alone for several hours); *M v Normand* 1995 SLT 128 (not neglect merely to leave a child of 20 months sleeping unattended in a car for 45 minutes: there must be circumstances which suggest that the child would be likely to experience unnecessary suffering).
8 C(S)A 1995, s 1(1)(b).
9 On the duty to consult, see para **11.2**.

Names

11.11 A name is one of the most fundamental elements of a person's sense of self and it has been argued that parents therefore have the responsibility to name their child.[1] Whose surname a child takes is not governed by law. It might be seen as traditional for a child to take the surname of the father, especially where the parents are married or civil partners; or to double-barrel a surname where the parents are cohabitants or living separately. Difficulties arise when parents separate and one parent wishes to change the child's surname. Conflict can arise if the parent with primary care of the child decides unilaterally to change the child's surname, say, from the father's surname to the mother's surname, or to the surname of a new partner or spouse. A credible case can be made for such a change of surname, for example, to help the child feel part of a new family set-up.

However, the retention of a child's original surname is a valuable link in maintaining the child's relationship (usually) with his or her father. This is particularly important if the child and the father had built up a close relationship prior to the breakdown of the parents' relationship. Unless there was persuasive evidence of genuine distress to the child in being known by his or her original surname, as opposed to inconvenience for the parent who wishes to change it, in such circumstances it is submitted that it would be contrary to the child's interests to alter the surname. Conversely, if the child had had little contact with, for example, the father there may be a strong case that a change of surname to that of the mother or a step-parent would be in the child's best interests as this would strengthen the relationship with their step parent. In *MRG v MD*,[2] separating parents both sought specific issue orders that the two children would be known by their respective surnames (the father's surname was recorded on both birth certificates). Both parents continued to play a significant role in the lives of their children post-separation. Sheriff Holligan, recognising that there is little, if any, modern case authority dealing with name change, commended the parents for resolving the issue by agreeing to use both surnames in recognition of the input that both parents had in the lives of their children.

The decision in *MRG v MD* establishes that the giving of a surname to a child (and, by extension, the changing of the child's surname) falls within the scope of s 1 and s 2 of the Children (Scotland) Act 1995 as it concerns the welfare of the child. However, in exercising such responsibility, one parent does not have to consult the other: a child's surname can be changed unilaterally, if only informally, by one of the parents. If the other parent maintains that the change of name is against the child's interests the court has jurisdiction to consider the issues under s 11(1) and s 11(2)(e) of the 1995 Act.[3]

1 *Wilkinson and Norrie*, paras 8.61 ff.

2 2018 Fam LR 2.

3 *M v C* 2002 SLT (Sh Ct) 82 (After divorce the mother changed the child's surname to her own. The father successfully raised a specific issue order and the court ordered that the child's surname revert to that of the father.)

Contact

11.12 We have been considering specific examples of the nature of parental responsibilities and parental rights where the child is living with the parents.[1] A parent who is not living with his or her child has the responsibility to maintain personal relations and direct contact with the child on a regular basis[2] and the parent enjoys the corresponding right to maintain the relationship and have direct contact with the child.[3] As with the other parental rights, the right to contact is a *prima facie* right in the sense that it must be exercised in accordance with the welfare principle. This is not inconsistent with Article 8 of the European Convention on Human Rights which provides that: 'Everyone has the right to respect for his private and family life, his home and his correspondence.' Although the European Court of Human Rights has held[4] that 'the mutual enjoyment by parent and child of each other's company constitutes a fundamental element of family life', it is recognised that the right of a parent to see his or her child cannot be absolute. In particular, it must be balanced against the rights of others, including the child. If a court deprived a parent from exercising his or her right of contact because it was against the child's best interests to do so that would not violate Article 8 provided the parent's interests had been taken into account.[5] In *A v A*,[6] the court held that where the exercise of contact by a parent with the child would not be in the child's best interests, the court ought not to make a contact order.

It is interesting to note that, before the Children (Scotland) Act 1995 came into force, Scottish courts insisted that a father was not entitled to have contact with his child unless he could show that it was positively in the child's best interests to do so.[7] The onus lay on the father to provide such evidence: there was no presumption that contact would be in the best of the child.[8] The position can be summarised as follows:

> 'The father's application for access [contact] was made by him on his own admission, because he is the father. He gave no other reason for his application. A father does not have an absolute right to access to his child. He is only entitled to access if the court is satisfied that it is in the best interests of the child.'[9]

Before an application for contact was successful, the parent had to prove that contact was positively in the child's best interests: the fact that contact was not against the child's interests was not enough. In these circumstances, the right to contact was a right without substance.[10]

The C(S)A 1995 not only gives parents the right to have contact with their children but also imposes an *obligation* upon them to do so. The rationale for such an obligation is that *prima facie* it is in the interests of children to have a continuing relationship with the parent who does not live with them in the same household. The opportunity was therefore open for the courts to assert that there is now a presumption that contact is in a child's best interests and that a parent should only be denied contact if it is established that contact would be contrary to the interests of the child. Nevertheless, in *White v White*,[11] the Inner House of the Court of Session held that there was no presumption that contact with a parent was in the best interests of the child. On the other hand, the court rejected the idea that disputed contact cases should be resolved by considerations of onus of proof. Instead, the Lord President (Rodger) favoured 'a third way'. The welfare of the child was always the paramount consideration but in determining what was in the child's best interests:

> 'the court should have regard to the general principle that it is conducive to a child's welfare to maintain personal relations and direct contact with his absent parent. But the decision will depend on the facts of the particular case and, if there is nothing in the relevant material on which the court, applying that general principle, could properly take the view that it would be in the interests of the child for the order to be granted, then the application must fail'.[12]

---

1 Children (Scotland) Act 1995, ss 1 and 2.
2 C(S)A 1995, s 1(1)(c).
3 C(S)A 1995, s 2(1)(c).
4 *B v United Kingdom* (1988) 10 EHRR 87. The right includes families where the parents are unmarried: *Marckx v Belgium* (1979) 2 EHRR 330.
5 *White v White* 2001 SLT 485. This principle can also be found in: *R v R* 2021 CSOH 69 (where the father had a serious cardiac condition which required an additional adult to be present during his contact with the child).
6 [2020] 10 WLUK 613.
7 *Crowley v Armstrong* 1990 SCLR 361; *Sanderson v McManus* 1997 SC (HL) 55 (note

that, in this case, the action was raised in 1993 – prior to the C(S)A 1995 Act coming into force).

8 *O v O* 1995 SLT 238. But see the dissenting judgment of Lord McCluskey in an Extra Division in *Sanderson v McManus* 1995 SLT 750.

9 *Porchetta v Porchetta* 1986 SLT 105 at 105, per Lord Dunpark. The word '[contact]' has been added.

10 For full discussion of the pre-C(S)A 1995 position, see Joe Thomson 'Whither the "Right" of Access'? 1989 SLT (News) 109.

11 2001 SLT 485.

12 Ibid at 491. Lord Rodger had argued at 489 that courts should have regard to 'the common conception of what will, generally speaking, be in the interests of the children so far as contact is concerned', ie that it is usually in the child's welfare to retain contact. See also *Sanderson v McManus* 1997 SC (HL) 55 where the natural link between a father and his child was described as being of 'intrinsic value' and *NJDB v JEG* [2010] CSIH 83; 2011 SC 191.

Chapter 12

Actions in relation to parental responsibilities and parental rights

INTRODUCTION

12.1 A mother automatically has parental responsibilities and parental rights in relation to her child.[1] The child's father will also automatically have parental responsibilities and parental rights if: (i) he was married to the child's mother at the date of conception or subsequently; or (ii) he has been registered as the father of the child.[2] Where the child was born as a result of assisted reproduction, the mother's partner will automatically have parental responsibilities and parental rights if: (i) she was the mother's spouse or civil partner; or (ii) she has been registered as the child's second female parent.[3] It is possible for other persons to acquire parental responsibilities and parental rights as a result of an application to the court under s 11 of the Children (Scotland) Act 1995. For example, unless he has obtained parental responsibilities and parental rights under an agreement with the child's mother,[4] the father of a child who does not automatically have parental responsibilities and parental rights can only obtain these by virtue of a s 11 order. On divorce or dissolution, the court has power to regulate the parental responsibilities and parental rights of the parties in relation to any children of the marriage or civil partnership. The purpose of this chapter is to discuss the procedures which are applicable and the principles which are applied in litigation relating to parental responsibilities and parental rights.

1 Children (Scotland) Act 1995, s 3(1)(a), discussed at para **11.3**.
2 C(S)A 1995, s 3(1)(b), discussed at para **11.3**. The registration must be on or after 4 May 2006.
3 C(S)A 1995, s 3(1)(c) and (d).
4 C(S)A 1995, s 4, discussed at para **11.3**.

TITLE TO SUE

(1) Independent applications in relation to parental responsibilities and parental rights

12.2 The Court of Session and the sheriff court have the power to make any order in relation to parental responsibilities and parental rights as it thinks fit.[1] An application can be brought by the following persons:

(a) A person who does not have and never has had parental responsibilities and parental rights in relation to the child, but claims an interest.[2] In other words, any person claiming an interest can bring an application. An interest can be a genetic or emotional tie between the applicant and the child. Applicants include the father of a child,[3] the child's second female parent who does not automatically have parental responsibilities and parental rights, a step-parent[4] or the child's grandparents.[5] In addition, a person with an interest in the outcome of the specific application as it relates to the welfare of the child also has title to sue. For example, a Health Board could apply under this provision for the right to consent to medical treatment on behalf of a child whose parents were refusing to consent.

It is expressly enacted that a child has title to sue in respect of the fulfilment of parental responsibilities and parental rights *vis-à-vis* him or herself.[6] If a child wished to live elsewhere than at home, or the child was unhappy with parental decisions relating to the child's education, etc, or was concerned about how his or her property was being administered, the *child* could apply under s 11(1) of the Children (Scotland) Act 1995 for a ruling by the court. A local authority has no title to sue under s 11 for an order in relation to parental responsibilities and parental rights.[7] If the local authority wishes to have parental responsibilities and/or parental rights, it must apply for a permanence order under Part 2 of the Adoption and Children (Scotland) Act 2007.[8] If a social worker considered the child to be in need of a compulsory supervision order, the case should be referred to the Children's Reporter.[9]

(b) Any person who has parental responsibilities or parental rights in relation to a child.[10] If, for example, both parents have parental responsibilities and parental rights but cannot agree on an issue, for example, the child's religion or education, etc, either parent could apply under s 11(2)(e) of the 1995 Act for a ruling by the court on the matter.

(c) Any person who has had parental responsibilities or parental rights in relation to the child.[11] If, for example, a parent has been deprived of his or her parental responsibilities and parental rights by a s 11(1)(a) order, for example, as a result of a serious addiction problem that has significantly affected the child, that parent could apply for parental responsibilities and parental rights when he or she has successfully addressed the addiction and wishes to resume responsibilities towards his or her children. But persons deprived of parental responsibilities and parental rights by the following orders have no title to raise an action under s 11(1)(a) and (b) and s 11(2):[12]

(i) when the parental responsibilities and rights have been extinguished as a result of an adoption order. This means that if a child has been adopted the natural mother or father cannot seek parental responsibilities and parental rights under s 11 of the 1995 Act. There is one exception, namely, with leave of the court, the parent can apply for a contact order in relation to the adopted child;[13]

(ii) when the parental responsibilities have been extinguished by virtue of a parental order under s 54 of the Human Fertilisation and Embryology Act 2008;[14] or

(iii) where the parental responsibilities and rights have vested in a local authority as a result of a permanence order. In this situation, the parent can apply to have the permanence order varied or revoked.[15]

In these three situations, decisions have been made for the long-term future of the child and the parents' interests will have been taken into account on making the relevant order. It would defeat the certainty inherent in adoption and permanence orders if the whole procedure could be undermined by applications under s 11 of the Children (Scotland) Act 1995 for parental responsibilities and parental rights by parents who had recently been denuded of these responsibilities and rights as a consequence of such orders.

1 Children (Scotland) Act 1995, s 11(1)(a), (b) and s 11(2). The court can also make any order relating to the guardianship of the child and the administration of the child's property: C(S)A 1995, s 11(1)(c) and (d).
2 C(S)A 1995, s 11(3)(a)(i).
3 *A v S* 2014 4 WLUK 453.
4 This would include the parent's cohabitant. The fact that it is a same sex cohabitation is irrelevant to the preliminary issue of title to sue as opposed to the merits of the case. In *X v Y* 2002 GWD 12-344 the sheriff took the view that a parent's same sex cohabitant was not a member of the child's family and could not apply. This decision is wrong. Cf the decision in *W v M, M v W* (2002) Sh Ct, where same sex cohabitants obtained parental responsibilities and rights in relation to each other's children. In *Telfer v Kellock* 2004 SLT 1290, the Lord Ordinary (Lady Smith) held that a child was a member of the family of the child's mother's lesbian partner who had accepted the child as a child of the family. Siblings have also applied for parental responsibilities and rights in respect of other siblings, for example contact: it is thought that such actions are competent: *E v E* 2004 Fam LR 115: cf *D v H* 2004 Fam LR 41.
5 *D v Grampian Regional Council* 1994 SLT 1038 (IH); approved 1995 SLT 519, HL.
6 C(S)A 1995, s 11(5): we are assuming the child has legal capacity to sue (s 2(4A) Age of Legal Capacity (Scotland) Act 1991: see **Ch 10**.
7 C(S)A 1995, s 11(5). It can make representations to the court that it would be against a child's interests to award parental responsibilities and rights to the applicant: *McLean v Dorman* 2001 SLT (Sh Ct) 97.
8 On permanence orders, see paras **13.13** and **14.7**.
9 On compulsory supervision orders, see **Ch 15**.
10 C(S)A 1995, s 11(3)(a)(ii).
11 C(S)A 1995, s 11(3)(ab).The application must be for an order other than a contact order.
12 C(S)A 1995, ss 11(4)(a), (c) and s 11A.
13 C(S)A 1995, s 11 (3)(aa).
14 Discussed at para **13.15**.
15 C(S)A 1995, s 11A.

(2) Ancillary actions in relation to parental responsibilities and parental rights

12.3 We have been considering the question of title to sue when a person brings an application relating to parental responsibilities and parental rights independently of other proceedings. In addition, the courts have the power under the Children (Scotland) Act 1995 to make s 11 orders in any action of divorce or dissolution, judicial separation or declarator of nullity of marriage or civil partnership.[1] Even if no application has been made, the court must consider whether to make a s 11 order in the light of such information as is before the court, relating to the arrangements or proposed arrangements for the upbringing of any child of the family.[2] In other words, a court requires to be satisfied that arrangements are in place for any child before the granting of a s 11 order. A child of the family is *either* a child of both parties to the action *or* any other child (other than a child placed with them as foster parents by a local authority) who has been treated by both of them as a child of the family.[3] A child is a person below the age of 16.[4]

The court can postpone granting decree in the principal action if it feels unable to make a s 11 order without further consideration and there are exceptional circumstances which make it desirable in the interests of the child to delay granting decree until the court is able to exercise its s 11 powers.[5] In these circumstances, the court[6] can, for example, appoint a child welfare reporter[7] or a curator *ad litem*[8] to undertake enquiries and provide a report to the court.[9] The report will often contain recommendations with regard to the residence of the child and while the decision is that of the court alone, in practice the recommendations will often be followed. It should be noted that there is an increasing move towards parties agreeing to take part in ADR (alternative dispute resolution) in an attempt to resolve family conflicts without the need for court intervention.[10] Family mediation is not compulsory but in any family action in which an order in relation to parental responsibilities and parental rights is in issue, the sheriff may, at any stage of the action, refer that issue to an accredited mediator.[11]

Where the court considers that a s 11 order should be made, it can make the order even if there was no application for such an order; moreover, the court can make a s 11 order even if it declines to make an order in respect of the principal action.[12] Thus, for example, if one spouse or civil partner brings an action of divorce or dissolution against the other, the court could order that their children should reside with one of the parties, even though the court refuses to grant the divorce or dissolution.

1 Children (Scotland) Act 1995, s 12(1). Ancillary orders are also possible in actions for declarator of parentage: *Robb v Gillan* 2004 Fam LR 120; *Y v M* 2013 GWD 27-550.

2 C(S)A 1995, s 12(1).
3 C(S)A 1995, s 12(4)(a) and (b). But the court cannot order aliment for such a child unless the child was also accepted as a child of the family: FL(S)A 1985, ss 1(1)(d) and 2(2)(a).
4 C(S)A 1995, s 12(3).
5 C(S)A 1995, s 12(2).
6 See Act of Sederunt (Sheriff Court Ordinary Cause Rules) 1993, Sch 1, Chapter 33, OCR 33.21 (child welfare reporters); OCR 33.21A (local authority).
7 The role of a child welfare reporter is to seek the views of the child and report these back to the court and to undertake enquiries and report to the court (OCR 33.21).
8 The role of a curator *ad litem* (in relation to s 11 actions) is represent and protect the interests of the child who lacks capacity. Note that curators *ad litem* are appointed in other legal actions, for example, to represent and protect the interests of an adult with incapacity (OCR 33.26).
9 See C(S)A 1995, s 101A (Register for child welfare reporters) and s 101B (Register of curators *ad litem* for the purposes of s 11D). Note that at the time of writing (July 2022), these sections are not yet in force.
10 ADR comprises: mediation; arbitration; negotiation and collaborative law. Discussion of ADR is outside the scope of this book. See Children (Scotland) Act 2020, s 24 in relation to the duty on the Scottish Government to arrange a pilot scheme for 'mandatory alternative dispute resolution meetings'. Although this section came into force in January 2021, at the time of writing (July 2022) the pilot scheme is not yet set up.
11 OCR 33.22 (see fn 6 above).
12 C(S)A 1995, s 11(3)(b).

THE NATURE OF S 11 ORDERS

12.4 Whether a s 11 order is sought in an independent action or as an ancillary action, the court has the power to make any order in relation to parental responsibilities and parental rights as it thinks fit.[1] Without prejudice to the generality of this power, the Children (Scotland) Act 1995, s 11(2) specifies the following orders.

(a) An order depriving a person of some or all of his or her parental responsibilities and parental rights. For example, if one person is convicted of sexual abuse of his or her children, the other party could apply under s 11(2)(a) for an order depriving the first party of his or her parental responsibilities and parental rights.

(b) An order: (i) imposing upon a person parental responsibilities; or (ii) giving a person parental rights. The person must be aged

16 or over unless that person is a parent of the child.[2] This is the provision under which a person who does not have parental responsibilities and parental rights can obtain them: for example, a father who does not automatically have parental responsibilities and parental rights,[3] a step-parent, or the child's grandparent.

(c) An order regulating the arrangements as to: (i) with whom a child under 16 is to live; or (ii) if with different persons alternately or periodically, with whom and during what periods a child under 16 is to live. This is known as 'a residence order'. This order can be used where, for example, the child's parents separate or divorce and the court wishes to regulate the residence of their child. This could be, for example, that the child lives with one parent for five days per week and with the other parent for two days. Because the court can make any order 'it thinks fit', residence need not be awarded to one or other parent but to a third party, for example the child's grandparent. It should be noted that a child can apply for a residence order.[4]

(d) An order regulating the maintenance of personal relations and direct contact between a child under 16 and a person with whom the child is not living. This is known as 'a contact order'. This order can be used where, for example, the child's parents separate or divorce and one parent obtains a residence order. The other parent can apply for a contact order to maintain his or her personal relationship with the child. It is also the way in which a father who does not automatically have parental responsibilities and parental rights or grandparents who have successfully applied for the parental right of contact can exercise that right. A child can also apply for a contact order.[5] A contact order can be varied on a change of circumstances. An appeal court will only intervene if the order was one which no reasonable judge could reach: its function is not to determine what is in the best interests of the child.[6]

(e) An order regulating any specific question which has arisen in respect of parental responsibilities and parental rights, guardianship or the administration of a child's property. This is known as 'a specific issue order'. The scope of such orders is potentially very wide. Consider the following examples:

(i) The parents cannot agree on the education[7] or religion of their child. An application could be made for a specific issue order to resolve the impasse.

(ii) A child is unhappy with the parents' choice of school, or the decision for the family to move house to another country. The child could apply for a specific issue order asking the court to resolve the matter.

(iii) One parent wishes to take the child to a different country for an extended or prolonged period resulting in the frustration of the other parent's right of contact with the child. Either parent can apply for a specific issue order to resolve the matter.[8]

(f) An interdict to stop any conduct which purports to be done in fulfilment of parental responsibilities or to be an exercise of parental rights relating to a child or the administration of the child's property. Again, the scope of this provision is potentially very wide. Consider the following examples:

(i) The parents of a 14-year-old girl with s 2(4) capacity[9] consent on her behalf to the termination of their daughter's pregnancy even though the girl refuses to consent. The girl or a nurse or a doctor could apply for an interdict prohibiting the operation going ahead until the court has made a specific issue order as to the legality of the operation.

(ii) The parents enter into the sale of a house owned by their 12-year-old child. The child could apply for an interdict preventing the sale going ahead until the court has determined whether the sale was in the child's interests.

(g) An order appointing a judicial factor to manage a child's property or remitting the matter to the Accountant of Court.

(h) An order appointing or removing a person as guardian of the child.[10]

In practice, the most common orders are residence orders, contact orders, specific issue orders and orders giving or depriving persons of parental responsibilities and parental rights. A s 11 order includes an interim order,[11] the variation of an order or the discharge of an order.[12] For the purpose of s 11 of the 1995 Act, a child is a person below 18, except in the case of residence and contact orders when the child must be below 16.[13] If in the course of s 11 proceedings[14] the court considers that a ground for referral exists,[15] it may refer the case to the Children's Reporter who can arrange a children's hearing to consider whether or not the child is in need of a compulsory supervision order.[16]

It will be clear that often more than one person will have parental responsibilities and parental rights in respect of a child.[17] Where this is the case, each can exercise a parental right without the consent of the other(s).[18]

What then is the effect of a s 11 order on a person's parental responsibilities and parental rights? Consider the following example:

> A and B are married. Both have parental responsibilities and parental rights in respect of their child, C. A and B divorce. A obtains a residence order in respect of C. B is awarded a contact order in respect of C. How do these orders affect A and B's parental responsibilities and rights?

By s 11(11) of the 1995 Act, an order has the effect of depriving a person of parental responsibilities and parental rights[19] only in so far as the order expressly so provides and only to the extent that it is necessary to do so to give effect to the order. Thus, in the example, the residence order will not deprive B of *any* parental responsibilities and parental rights unless this is expressly stipulated in the order. Despite not being deprived of responsibilities and rights, B cannot act in any way which would be incompatible with the residence order.[20] So even though B has still the *prima facie* parental right of residence in relation to C, B cannot insist that the child live with B rather than with A during the periods stipulated in the residence order, namely, that C is to live with A. Similarly, A retains the full complement of parental responsibilities and rights but cannot prevent B from seeing C at the times stipulated in the contact order. If the court took the view that A and B would not act sensibly, it could in the residence order expressly deprive B of the s 2(1)(a) right 'to have the child living with him', and in the contact order expressly deprive A of the right to have contact with C during the period B is to have contact with C. The court is enjoined *not* to do so unless satisfied that it would be better for the child to make such orders than that no order to that effect be made at all.[21]

The importance of s 11(11) cannot be over-emphasised. The C(S)A 1995 takes the view that a child should have the benefit of the support and guidance of *both* parents. A s 11 order should have the minimal effect on the parents' existing parental responsibilities and parental rights. Indeed, if a child's parents agree on the steps to be taken in respect of the child's upbringing after they separate or divorce,[22] there should be no need for a s 11 order as the court *cannot* make a s 11 order unless satisfied that it is better for the child to make the order than that none should be made at all.

Even if a s 11 order is made and a person is expressly deprived of a parental responsibility or parental right, this must be the *minimum* necessary to give effect to the order. If in the example, B is deprived of the parental right to have C live with him or her,[23] B still retains the right to determine C's upbringing[24] or act as C's legal representative:[25] these rights continue to be exercised *along with* A, who also retains parental responsibilities and parental rights.

Where a residence order is made which requires a child to live with a person who does not have pre-existing parental responsibilities and parental rights in relation to the child, the effect of the order is to give that person the parental responsibilities in s 1(1)(a), (b) and (d) and the parental rights in s 2(1)(b) and (d) of the 1995 Act for as long as the order is in force.[26] So, in the example, if residence was awarded to C's grandmother, she would have the relevant responsibilities and rights as a result of the residence order.[27] Unless A or B was expressly deprived of parental responsibilities and parental rights in the residence order, they would continue to fulfil their responsibilities and exercise their rights *along with* C's grandmother, provided they did not act in any way that was incompatible with the order.[28]

The C(S)A 1995 adopts a minimalist approach to orders relating to parental responsibilities and parental rights. No s 11 order can be made unless the court is satisfied that it is better for the child to make an order than that none should be made at all.[29] This is particularly pertinent where a residence order or a contact order is sought when a relationship breaks down. In these circumstances, the parties are to be encouraged to reach agreement, if possible, without resort to court proceedings, and, if necessary, through mediation services, on how their children are to be brought up after the breakdown. Where there is such an agreement, there will be no change to the parental responsibilities and parental rights held by each party. There will be no need for a residence or contact order; indeed, the court *cannot* make the orders.[30] But to achieve this objective the parents must put the interests of their children first and recognise the importance of the children's need to retain personal relationships with both parents after the breakdown of a marriage.

---

1 Children (Scotland) Act 1995, s 11(1) and (2).

2 'Parent' means the genetic mother or father subject to Chapter 3 of the Adoption and Children (Scotland) Act 2007, the Human Fertilisation and Embryology Act 1990, ss 27–30 and Part 2 of the Human Fertilisation and Embryology Act 2008.

3 There is no reason in principle why the court cannot make such an order even if the applicant could not immediately discharge his parental responsibilities and rights: *T v A* 2001 SCLR 647.

4 C(S)A 1995, s 11(5).

5 Ibid.

6 *M v M* 2002 SC 103; *NJDB v JEG* [2010] CSIH 83; *S v S* [2012] CSIH 17 (Appeal rejected on the basis that 'the high threshold for appellate intervention has not been met and that the appeal must fail'); *A v S* [2014] 4 WLUK 453; *LRK v AG* [2019] SAC (Civ) 33.

7 *G v G* 2002 Fam L R 120.

8 *Shields v Shields* 2002 SLT 579; *Fourman v Fourman* 1998 Fam LR 98; *MCB v NMF* [2018] CSOH 28; *MK(AP) v TDD* [2019] SC LER 66.

9 That is, capacity to consent to medical treatment by virtue of the Age of Legal Capacity (Scotland) Act 1991, s 2(4), discussed at para **10.2**.

10 On guardianship, see para **11.3**. In *L v H* 1996 SC 86 the father of an illegitimate child applied for guardianship so that he would become a relevant person who would then have the right to attend a children's hearing in respect of the child. The application was refused on the basis that guardianship was for the benefit of the child – not for the benefit of the guardian. But see: *Principal Reporter v K* [2010] UKSC 56.

11 C(S)A 1995, s 11(13).

12 Ibid.

13 C(S)A 1995, ss 15(1), 11(2)(c) and (d).

14 Children's Hearings (Scotland) Act 2011, s 62. The child must normally be below 16.

15 On grounds for referral, see para **15.7**. The provision does not apply where the ground for referral is that the child has committed an offence: CH(S)A 2011, s 67(2)(j).

16 CH(S)A 2011, s 66. For full discussion, see **Ch 15.**

17 For full discussion, see para **11.3**.

18 C(S)A 1995, s 2(2). But a parent cannot take a child out of the United Kingdom without the consent of any other person with parental responsibilities and rights: C(S) A 1995, s 2(3) and (6).

19 However, the court can revoke a s 4 or s 4A agreement if necessary: C(S)A 1995, s 11(11). On s 4 and s 4A agreements, see para **11.3**.

20 C(S)A 1995, s 3(4).

21 C(S)A 1995, s 11(7)(a).
22 Discussed at para **12.5**.
23 C(S)A 1995, s 2(1)(a).
24 C(S)A 1995, s 2(1)(b).
25 C(S)A 1995, s 2(1)(d).
26 C(S)A 1995, s 11(12). These are known as 'relevant responsibilities and rights'.
27 Subject to any provision in the order that she was *not* to have any relevant responsibility or right.
28 C(S)A 1995, s 3(4).
29 C(S)A 1995, s 11(7)(a). There must be evidence that it would be better for the child that an order should be made: *Q v P* 2016 Fam LR 54; *MCB v NMF* [2018] CSOH 28; *G v G* [2014] CSOH 88; *H v H* [2015] 4 WKUK 46.
30 C(S)A 1995, s 11(7)(a).

THE WELFARE PRINCIPLE

12.5 In considering whether to make a s 11(1) order and, if so, the nature of the order, the court has to exercise discretion. In so doing s 11(7)(a) of the 1995 Act provides that the court:

> 'shall regard the welfare of the child concerned as its paramount consideration and shall not make any such order unless it considers that it would be better for the child that the order be made than that none should be made at all'.

We have discussed the minimum intervention aspect of this provision in the preceding section. In this section we shall explore the welfare principle in some detail.

It is a fundamental tenet of the 1995 Act that decisions relating to parental responsibilities and parental rights should be child centred. Not only is the child's welfare the paramount consideration in s 11 proceedings but, by s 11(7)(b), the court is also enjoined so far as practicable, taking account of the child's age and maturity, to do the following:[1]

(i) give the child an opportunity to indicate whether the child wishes to express any views;

(ii) if the child so wishes, give the child an opportunity to express his or her views; and

(iii) have regard to such views as the child may express.

The court has a duty[2] 'so far as practicable' to give the child the opportunity to express his or her views and have regard to such views. This duty to consult continues throughout all the proceedings until a final order is made.[3] At the time of writing (July 2022) a child aged 12 or over is presumed to be of sufficient age and maturity to form a view,[4] but the views of a child below that age can be taken into account if the child *in fact* is of sufficient age and maturity.[5] In giving his or her views, the child does not have to be legally represented if he or she does not wish to be.[6] Thus, the views of the child at the centre of the proceedings must be fed into the court's decision-making process.[7] It is then for the court to have regard to the views expressed by the child. The court will accord weight to the child's views. For example, in *X v Y*,[8] the views expressed by a child were not accepted by the sheriff as being 'the child's genuine view, independently formed'.

Difficulties can arise if the child requests that his or her views be kept confidential. The parties are entitled to a fair hearing under Article 6 of the European Convention on Human Rights. This usually involves disclosure of the evidence that the court has taken into account in reaching its decision. However, from time to time, situations can arise where the views of the child require to be kept confidential and only the sheriff has sight of them. For example, where parents are disputing residence and contact arrangements for a child, the sheriff may appoint a child welfare reporter to take the views of the child. In situations where the child may be reluctant to express his or her views due to anxiety or fear of the consequences should the parents find out, it is possible to submit the child's views to the sheriff alone, without those views becoming a part of the court process. This is facilitated by lodging the document containing the child's views (or the part of the child's views that he or she does not want shared) with the court in compliance with Chapter 33.20 of the Ordinary Cause Rules.[9] The court will maintain the confidentiality of the child's views only where it considers that there is a real possibility of significant harm to the child. The interests of the child have to be balanced against the interests of the other parties, so non-disclosure should be the exception rather than the rule.[10] However, it is the *court's* view of what is in the child's best interests which will ultimately prevail. The views of the child will be considered along with all other factors before the court.

Although under s 11(7)(a) the welfare principle is the paramount consideration, s 11(7A) provides that in carrying out this duty the court must have regard to the matters listed in s 11(7B). These are:

(a) the need to protect the child from abuse or the threat of abuse which might affect the child;

(b) the effect such abuse or the risk of such abuse may have on the child;

(c) the ability of the abuser to care for or otherwise meet the needs of the child; and

(d) the effect of any abuse or the risk of any abuse on a person with parental responsibilities (or who would have such parental responsibilities by virtue of an order under s 11(1)) from carrying out these responsibilities.[11]

Abuse is very broadly defined. It includes violence, harassment, threatening conduct and any other conduct giving rise to physical or mental injury, fear, alarm or distress.[12] Importantly, it includes abuse directed at a person other than the child.[13] So in determining under s 11(7)(a) what is in the child's best interests, a court must take into account the fact that the child's parent has been abused even if the abuser has not abused the child. 'Domestic abuse' is also included.[14] It has been held that the abuse, or risk of abuse, does not have to be directed towards the child,[15] (or a third party), nor does it have to be intentional.[16] In other words, the test for the existence of abuse is objective. A person who behaves aggressively when drunk, or under the influence of drugs, engages in abuse even although his or her aggression is unintentional and not directed towards the family. 'Conduct' includes speech and being present at a particular place or area.[17]

These provisions focus on abuse or risk of abuse to the person who has care of the child as well as the direct abuse or possibility of abuse of the child. Because abuse of the carer may affect the quality of his or her care, it is a matter which indirectly affects the child's welfare which must always remain the paramount consideration in s 11 applications. An abuser's ability to care for the child is a relevant factor when he or she has directly abused the child or might carry out abuse on the child. But the fact that the abuser abused his or her spouse or partner when they lived together with their child may not be relevant to the abuser's ability to care for the child. This is particularly important given the width of the definition of abuse which includes any language which could give rise to distress, or the mere presence of a person in a particular place. In *R v R*, [18] the court emphasised that evidence of abuse or the risk of abuse did not in itself give rise to a presumption against granting parental responsibilities and parental rights; and in *SM v AN*,[19] the three-year old child continued to live with the mother, with the father being granted direct contact, despite a finding that the father had been the victim of abusive behaviour by the mother. There was no suggestion here that the child was not well cared for by the mother. However, in *Ahmed v Ahmed*,[20] the court refused a contact order to a father whose abuse towards the mother had a detrimental effect on their son. Once again it is important to remember that, at the end of the day, it is the child's welfare, not whether a parent was an abusive spouse or partner, that is the paramount consideration and the child's views are always to be taken into account.[21]

Nevertheless, it is the welfare principle that must be used to determine the difficult questions that can be raised in s 11 proceedings. It would apply in deciding, in what would be exceptional circumstances, that a parent should be deprived of parental responsibilities and parental rights. The welfare of a child will also be the paramount consideration in determining whether to give parental responsibilities and parental rights to a father or a second female parent who does not automatically have them,[22] or a step-parent or a grandparent of the child. Acute problems can be envisaged in specific issue orders,[23] but again the welfare principle must provide the solutions. An exception is made to this in proceedings relating to a child's property to the extent that the court must endeavour not to affect adversely a person who has 'in good faith and for value, acquired any property of the child concerned, or any right or interest in such property'.[24] This could arise if the child's parents had leased heritable property owned by the child to a *bona fide* tenant when it was not in the child's best interests to do so.

Where the welfare principle was most commonly applied before the enactment of the 1995 legislation was in actions for custody and access. These cases are also illustrative of how it is used in applications for residence and contact orders. The pre-1995 Act decisions must be used with caution given that, under the 1995 Act: (1) the court should not make any order unless it is better for the child to do so than that no order should be made at all;[25] and (2) the court *always* has a duty to consult the child.[26]

Finally, as stated above, when making an order under s 11 of the C(S)A 1995, the court has a duty to give the child the opportunity to express his or her views and to have regard to those views. However, it has long been a concern that little or no attempt is made to explain to the child the meaning and the consequences for him or her of the court's decision – a decision that can significantly affect the child's family life, relationships and ongoing welfare. Section 11F of the C(S)A 1995 (not yet in force at the time of writing (July 2022)) imposes a duty on the court to 'ensure that the decision is explained to the child concerned in a way that the child can understand'.[27] This may be done by an explanation being given to the child by the court or by arranging for a child welfare reporter to speak to the child.[28] See *Patrick v Patrick,*[29] in which Sheriff Anwar wrote a letter to the parties' children to explain to them the decision taken by the court and the reasons for making the decision.

---

1 Children (Scotland) Act 1995, s 11(7)(b)(i), (ii) and (iii).

2 See *LRK v AG* [2021] SAC (Civ) 1, where neither party sought the views of the child and the sheriff had not sought the views of the child because he was too young. The Sheriff Appeal Court criticised the sheriff on the basis that it is the duty of the court to ascertain the views of the child unless a matter of practicability made it impossible to do so. See also: *FBI v MH* [2021] SAC (Civ) 16 for a similar outcome.

3 See: *M v C* [2021] CSIH 14 in which the child was just under five years old. The Sheriff Appeal Court and the Inner House found that the sheriff had failed to apply the correct test in refusing to take the views of the child on the basis that inappropriate information would have to be shared with the child. Lord Malcolm stated, 'If children are of sufficient age and maturity to form and express a view, their voices must be heard unless there are weighty adverse welfare considerations of sufficient gravity to supersede the default position. Careful thought as to how a child's position is to be ascertained will often resolve concerns. The court would require to be in a position to justify the proposition that the welfare issues are such as to render the exercise impracticable'. See also: *Shields v Shields* 2002 SLT 579, where the child was seven years old when the case started and nine years old when the case was finally decided. It had not been considered practicable for the boy to give his views as a seven-year-old, but this did not bar him from giving his views as a nine-year-old. The court stressed that the only proper and relevant test was whether, in all the circumstances, it was practicable to consult the child.

4 Section 1(3)(a) of the Children (Scotland) Act 2020 will repeal (amongst other things) ss 11(7)–(7E) and s 7(10) of the Children (Scotland) Act 1995. The presumption of

age 12 and over (currently in s 7(10)) is to be repealed when s 11ZB comes into force. The presumption will be replaced by the principle that: 'The child is to be presumed to be capable of forming a view unless the contrary is shown.'

5 C(S)A 1995, s 11(10).

6 C(S)A 1995, s 11(9): the presumption in s 11(10) applies to a child's decision under s 11(9).

7 *Shields v Shields* 2002 SLT 579.

8 [2018] SC DUM 54, at para [130].

9 Act of Sederunt (Sheriff Court Ordinary Cause Rules) 1993 No 1956 (s 223) Sch 1. See also *Dosoo v Dosoo* 1999 SLT (Sh Ct) 86.

10 *Re D (minors)* [1995] 4 All ER 385; followed in *McGrath v McGrath* 1999 SLT (Sh Ct) 90; *Dosoo v Dosoo* 1999 SLT (Sh Ct) 86.

11 Sections 11(7A) to (7E) of the Children (Scotland) Act 1995 will be repealed and replaced with similar provisions in s 11ZA ('Paramountcy of the child's welfare, and the non-intervention presumption').

12 C(S)A 1995, s 11(7C)(a), to be repealed and replaced with s 11ZA(4)(a).

13 C(S)A 1995, s 11(7C)(b), to be repealed and replaced with s 11ZA(4)(b)

14 C(S)A 1995, s 11(7C)(c), to be repealed and replaced with s 11ZA(4)(c).

15 See Domestic Abuse (Scotland) Act 2018, s 5 which makes the offence of abusive behaviour towards a partner or an ex-partner aggravated if a child is used to direct the abusive behaviour to party B, or if a child sees, hears, or is present during an incident where A directs abusive behaviour towards B as part of a course of behaviour.

16 *R v R* 2010 GWD 23-442.

17 C(S)A 1995, s 11(7C), to be repealed and replaced with s 11ZA(4).

18 2010 Fam LR 123.

19 [2021] CSOH 60. See also *J v M* 2016 SC 835. See also: *W v G* 2012 GWD 34-692 (Father awarded a residence order even though there had been bouts of violence towards the mother during their volatile relationship and evidence of alcohol and drug abuse. In the course of his judgment the sheriff stated that: 'At the end of the day it comes down to a question of risk. Whilst no one can ever predict with certainty what the future holds for anyone, I am satisfied on the evidence that the pursuer will always put the welfare of [the child] at the top of his list of priorities. I am not satisfied that the defender will always do so': ibid at para 19).

20 2020 Fam LR 68.

21 C(S)A 1995, s 11(7)(b). See also ss 11(7D) and (7E) which oblige the court to consider whether it should make an order where the result of doing so is that two persons – usually the child's parents – will have to co-operate with each other. The inference is that if they can't co-operate the court should not make the order. However, consider where, if such an order were otherwise in the best interests of the child why should the court not make an order even though the parents may find it difficult to co-operate with each other?

22 See: *AY v MM* 2012 GWD 33-674.

23 See: *Q v P* 2016 Fam LR 54; *MCB v NMF* [2018] CSOH] 28; and *MK(AP) v TDD* [2019] SC LER 66.

24 C(S)A 1995, s 11(8).

25 Discussed at para **12.4**.
26 See above.
27 C(S)A 1995, s 11F(2).
28 C(S)A 1995, s 11F(4).
29 [2017] SC GLA 46.

The relevant factors in applying the welfare principle in residence orders

12.6 While the welfare of the child is the paramount consideration, all the factors of the case are considered to the extent that they point to the course of action which is best for the child. As Lord MacDermott explained in *J v C*,[1] the welfare principle connotes:

> 'a process whereby, when all the relevant facts, relationships, claims and wishes of parents, risks, choices and other circumstances are taken into account and weighed, the course to be followed will be that which is most in the interests of the child's welfare …'.[2]

Specific factors are relevant in so far as they pertain to the child's welfare. In determining what is best for the child, a judge will be influenced by a number of factors that will include information about family relationships, the child's sibling relationships, education, the medical needs of the child and the views of the child him or herself. In Scots law there is no 'welfare checklist' to guide a judge on the matters for consideration.[3] When a decision is made by a court, it is generally recognised that an appellate court will not interfere with the decision of the judge at first instance unless the court is satisfied either that the judge exercised his or her discretion upon a wrong principle, or that the decision is so plainly unreasonable that the judge must have exercised his or her discretion wrongly.[4]

It is worthwhile noting the historical development of the welfare principle, At the beginning of the twentieth century, it was the practice of the Court of Session in divorce actions to apply a presumption that the 'innocent' spouse whose conduct was not responsible for the breakdown of the marriage should be granted custody; this presumption was rebuttable on evidence that it would be against the child's welfare to award custody to the innocent spouse.[5] Such a presumption has no place in modern Scots law where the welfare of the child is the paramount consideration in s 11 proceedings and the law of divorce and dissolution is, theoretically at least, based on the non-fault concept of irretrievable breakdown of the relationship.[6] Instead, a person's 'conduct' should only be relevant in so far as it suggests that it would not be in the child's best interests to live with that person. So, for example, the decision to allow a child to live with a parent who has a drug addiction may be considered in keeping with the child's best interests if the parent has support from a community psychiatric nurse service and the addiction is being supported and monitored. However, where the behaviour of a parent with a drug addiction includes, for example, selling drugs from the family home, this puts the child's safety at risk and this behaviour would be relevant in determining the effects on the child's welfare.

It is submitted that a similar approach should be taken when the person seeking residence or contact is LGBTQ+. In the past a parent's sexual orientation has been considered to be an important factor. In *Early v Early*,[7] a lesbian mother lost custody of her child who had lived happily with her for several years. The court held, *inter alia*, that the boy, who was approaching adolescence, required a suitable male role model and could better adjust to his mother's sexuality if he lived with his father and siblings.[8] However, in *Salguiero da Silva Mouta v Portugal*,[9] the European Court of Human Rights held that the decision of a Portuguese court to award custody of a child to his mother simply because she was heterosexual, and the father was homosexual, constituted a violation of the father's rights under Article 8 and unlawful discrimination under Article 14 of the European Convention on Human Rights. The approach evidenced in *Early*[10] can no longer be justified.

In weighing up the factors which determine what is best for the child, in the past the Scottish courts also gave considerable importance to ensuring that a child obtained a religious upbringing. The 'solace and guidance' of a religious faith was regarded as so important for the welfare of a child that on divorce it was difficult for an atheist spouse to obtain custody if the other spouse was prepared to provide a religious environment. In *M'Clements v M'Clements*,[11] for example, an adulterous mother was awarded custody rather than an atheist father because she would give the children a religious upbringing.[12] Where both parties were prepared to offer the child a religious upbringing, there was no bias in favour of any particular Christian denomination and custody was determined by weighing up other factors in accordance with the welfare principle.[13] These cases were decided over 60 years ago. It is submitted that given our increasingly secular society, a religious upbringing is not such an important factor in applying the welfare principle.[14] On the other hand, a child's ethnicity and cultural background are considered relevant.[15]

It is also interesting to note that the Scottish courts have rejected (some decades ago) any presumption that a young child should *prima facie* live with his or her mother. In *Hannah v Hannah*,[16] the Lord Ordinary had proceeded on the basis that it was 'more in accordance with nature' that a child should be removed from the custody of her father and his cohabitant where she had been living for several years after the marriage had broken down and be returned to the mother. In reversing the judge's decision, in the Inner House of the Court of Session Lord Walker observed:

> 'What exactly the Lord Ordinary meant by nature, or what precisely nature has to do with it, I must confess I find difficulty in appreciating as a proper test in matters of this kind. It is not nature but the welfare of the child which is the material matter.'[17]

The evidence established that the child – who had lived with her father for six years – was happy and well adjusted; in these circumstances, the court held that it was in her best interests that custody be awarded to her father.

In *Brixey v Lynas*[18] the sheriff awarded custody to the father of an illegitimate child. The decision was upheld by the Sheriff Principal. Since her birth and throughout the proceedings, the child had been in the care of her mother and was well looked after. In reversing the decisions of the sheriff and Sheriff Principal, the Inner House of the Court of Session held that the child should remain with her mother. In the course of his judgment, Lord Morison took the view that the sheriff had given insufficient weight to:

> 'the practice of the courts in Scotland to recognise as an important factor which has to be fully taken into account in a dispute concerning custody between the mother and father of a very young child, that during his or her infancy the child's need for the mother is stronger than the need for a father'.[19]

At the same time Lord Morison recognised that 'this principle should not be regarded as creating any presumption in favour of the mother, nor, certainly, as a rule of law'.[20] On appeal, the House of Lords held that the contention that a young child should be in the care of his or her mother was neither a presumption nor a principle but rather the recognition of a widely held belief of ordinary people based on nature![21]

It is thought that although the judges overstated the importance of a *mother's* – as opposed to a *parent's* – role in the upbringing of a child, the result in *Brixey* is justified on the basis that the child was thriving in the *de facto* care of her mother. In *Re B (a child)*,[22] the Supreme Court approved the dictum of Lady Hale delivered in the earlier case of *Re G*:[23]

> 'All consideration of the importance of parenthood in private law disputes about residence must be firmly rooted in an examination of what is in the child's best interests. This is the paramount consideration. It is only as a contributor to the child's welfare that parenthood assumes any significance. In common with all other factors bearing on what is in the best interests of the child, it must be examined for its potential to fulfil that aim.'

Acute difficulties arise in relation to relocation cases. This is where a parent who has a residence order wishes to relocate with the child. This may make it difficult, if not impossible, for the other parent to retain contact with the child. To permit relocation therefore goes against the shared parenting philosophy of the Children (Scotland) Act 1995. In England, however, the Court of Appeal in *Payne v Payne*[24] considered that the reasonable proposals of the resident parent seeking to relocate were factors of great weight giving rise in effect to a presumption in favour of a resident parent's wishes. This approach was rejected by the Inner House in *M v M*[25] and the principle that there is no presumption in Scots law in favour of either parent was affirmed in *S v S*[26] and again in *GL v JL*.[27] Instead, the welfare and best interests of the child or children concerned are paramount and fall to be judged without any preconceived leaning in favour of the rights and interests of others. The onus therefore rests on the party seeking relocation to establish to the satisfaction of the court that it would be in the best interests of the child to do so.[28]

It is submitted that one of the factors to be taken into account when determining with whom a child should live is where and with whom the child is currently living or has lived since the parental breakdown. The preservation of the status quo may help to give stability to the child in the face of family disruption and the court has a duty to apply the minimum intervention principle[29] when making a decision relating to the welfare of the child. In *MCB v NMF*,[30] the father wanted the court to grant him a residence order over his child on the basis that it was necessary only in the event of a move to Cyprus by his child's mother.

Other things being equal, it is considered to be in a child's best interests to preserve the status quo and allow the child to live with the parent or person who has looked after the child since the breakdown of the marriage or the relationship.[31] In *AY v MM*, [32] a residence order (along with a declarator of paternity) was granted to the father of a three-year-old child who had been the *de facto* carer of the child for around three years.

It must be stressed that preserving the status quo is only a *prima facie* presumption. If it is established that it is in the best interests of the child to be moved, the courts should not hesitate to do so. In *Hastie v Hastie*,[33] a nine-year-old child had been in the care of his father's mother, ie the child's grandmother, for four years. The grandmother, who was 63, attempted to indoctrinate the child against his mother. In these circumstances, Lord Davidson ordered that the child should live with his mother because this would restore a 'normal' parent child relationship which was in the child's best interests. Given the range of acceptable family set ups, the courts have moved away from what were seen as 'normal' family relationships and have acknowledged that families are no longer limited to the traditional set up of a married different sex couple and their genetic children. In the past, the child's best interests would be considered best served if the child was removed from the residential care of a lesbian or gay parent to live with the heterosexual parent.[34] Other factors, for example if a child was to be removed from a school where he or she was settled, may result in the child residing with a parent who has not hitherto had care and control of the child.[35]

The preservation of the status quo is generally accepted to be in the best interests of the child whether it favours the father or the mother.

That said, in practice, when a marriage, civil partnership or relationship breaks down, the child or children will generally remain in the care of their mother. In most cases, the couple agrees that the child or children should reside with the parent who has retained care since the breakdown. In the majority of cases, this will be the mother. A residence order simply reflects this arrangement.[36] This practice has been reflected in the principle of minimum intervention in s 11(7)(a) of the Children (Scotland) Act 1995 so few residence orders are awarded since it is not in the child's interests to make an order which simply reflects what the parties have already agreed.[37]

A final point. While the court has a duty to give the child the opportunity to express a view in residence disputes, it is for the court to determine with whom the child will reside. While the child may express a preference, the court will have regard to the child's views but the final decision will be taken with the welfare of the child as the paramount consideration.[38]

---

1 [1970] AC 668 at 710–711, HL.

2 In *Campins v Campins* 1979 SLT (Notes) 41 at 42, Lord Cameron emphasised that nothing can override or be superior to the child's welfare.

3 This is a matter about which there is continuing discussion. See Children Act 1989, s 1(3). This is not an exhaustive list. See also, Elaine Sutherland, *The Welfare Test: Determining the Indeterminate*, 2018 Edin L R, Vol 22, pp 94-100.

4 See: *H v H* [2015] CSIH 10 in which an Extra Division of the Court of Session issues a reminder of the steps that should be taken by a party who is dissatisfied with the decision of the court at first instance in residence and contact actions. See also: *Early v Early* 1990 SLT 221*; J v J* 2004 Fam LR 20; *Y v M* 2013 GWD 27-550; *M v M* [2011] CSIH 65; *S v S* [2012] CSIH 17; *A v S* [2014] 4 WLUK 453.

5 *Hume v Hume* 1926 SC 1008.

6 On 6 April 2022, the law relating to so called 'no fault divorce' came into force in England and Wales. See Matrimonial Causes Act 1973, as amended by the Divorce, Dissolution and Separation Act 2020.
See **Ch 6**.

7 1989 SLT 114, approved 1990 SLT 221.

8 In *Hill v Hill* 1990 SCLR 238, a child was returned to his gay father in Canada on the ground that the father was not a danger to the child with whom he had had a good relationship. In *X v Y* 2002 Fam LR 58, a gay father was given contact with his son who had been born as a consequence of AID.

9 2001 Fam LR 2.

10 1989 SLT 114.

11 1958 SC 286.

12 Cf *MacKay v MacKay* 1957 SLT (Notes) 17, where the atheist father was awarded custody on condition that the child's grandmother gave the child religious instruction.

13 *McNaught v McNaught* 1955 SLT (Sh Ct) 9.

14 See *L v L* 2011 [2011] WLUK 876 in which the court held that a father was entitled to further and uninterrupted weekend contact to compensate for the mother collecting the child on a Sunday morning to take her to Catholic mass, then returning to the father afterwards.

15 *Osbourne v Matthan* (No 3) 1998 SC 682; *Perendes v Sim* 1998 SLT 1382.

16 1971 SLT (Notes) 42.

17 Ibid 42 at 43.

18 1994 SLT 847.

19 Ibid at 849.

20 Ibid.

21 *Brixey v Lynas* 1995 SLT 856. This view was endorsed by the House of Lords in *Re G (children)* [2006] UKHL 43 (order in favour of natural mother of children conceived by AID during a lesbian relationship). In the course of his speech, Lord Scott profoundly observed, 'Mothers are special'.

22 [2009] UKSC 5.

23 [2006] UKHL 43 at para 37.

24 [2001] Fam 473.

25 [2011] CSIH 65 [para 52] in which the Inner House stated: 'In particular, the welfare and best interests of the relevant child or children are paramount and must be judged without any preconceived leaning or presumption in favour of the rights and interests of either parent.'

26 2012 Fam LR 32.

27 [2017] CSOH 60. See also, *Donaldson v Donaldson* [2014] CSIH 88.

28 ibid at [para 9]. Lady Wise states that. '... it is neither instructive nor appropriate to try to formulate any list of applicable factor to be applied in considering a case of this sort ... these cases are fact sensitive and scrutiny of the particular circumstances of the dispute and the child concerned is what matters'.

29 C(S)A 1995, s 11(7)(a).

30 [2018] CSOH 28.

31 See: *L v L* 2013 GWD 25-496. Also, in *Senna-Cheribbo v Wood* 1999 SC 328, a two-year-old girl who was being looked after by her paternal grandparents was allowed to remain there in spite of her grandmother's age and diminution in energy; her mother who sought a residence order was simply incapable of coping with a child on a permanent basis.

32 2012 GWD 33-674; [2012] 8 WLUK 64.

33 1985 SLT 146.

34 *Early v Early* 1989 SLT 114; *T, Petitioner* 1997 SLT 724 (IH); and *Salgueiro Da Silva Mouta v Portugal* (2001) Fam LR 2.

35 See: *CAM v HM* [2012] CSOG 127.

36 Statistical information on the number of cases where the child or children live with the mother after divorce, dissolution or separation is not regularly produced. In 2010 the Scottish Government carried out research: *Understanding Child Contact Cases in Scottish Sheriff Courts* (Karen Laing, Graham Wilson, Scottish Government Social Research, 2010). This found that fathers were more likely to be the non-resident parent

than mothers; and, in the vast majority of courts actions relating to child contact, the pursuer was a non-resident father.

37 See para **12.4**; *G v G* 1999 Fam LR 30.

38 C(S)A 1995, s 11(7)(a).

Relevant factors in applying the welfare principle in contact orders

12.7 Before the Children (Scotland) Act 1995 came into force, in actions for access, the Scottish courts insisted that the onus lay on the pursuer to prove that access was positively in the child's best interests.[1] As a result of the 1995 Act,[2] where a person already has parental responsibilities and parental rights, *prima facie* that person has both the duty and the right to maintain personal relations and direct contact with a child who is no longer living with him or her. This responsibility and right to contact remains, even where the child is subject to a residence order in favour of the other parent or another person, unless the person has been expressly deprived of the responsibility and right.[3] In other words, the whole thrust of the 1995 Act is that it is *prima facie* in a child's best interests to have contact with an absent parent as this fosters the child's relationships with both his or her parents. Conversely, the granting of a contact order to a parent with whom the child does not live will be refused if the court finds that contact will be detrimental the child's welfare.[4]

In *White v White*,[5] the Inner House of the Court of Session held that there was no onus of proof on the father to establish that contact was positively in the child's best interests. On the other hand, the application of Article 8 of the European Convention on Human Rights,[6] does not mean automatic enforcement of the right of contact to a parent in the absence of evidence that contact would be *against* the child's interests. Instead the welfare principle should prevail and the common conception that contact between a parent and his or her child is in the child's best interests should form part of the reasons given for the granting of the order.[7] A parent with parental responsibilities and parental rights who is seeking a contact order is not in an advantageous position over the parent with no parental responsibilities and parental rights. A court will apply the welfare principle in deciding if the granting of a contact order is in the best interests of the child.

In contact cases, the views of the children are of particular importance; but where a child says he or she does not wish to see the pursuer, the court should take pains to ensure that the refusal is genuine.[8]

Where a contact order is granted, the parents of the child or children must obtemper the terms of the order. Failure to do so can amount to a contempt of court. In *Blance v Blance,*[9] Lord Stewart stated: 'It is the duty of the person who has care of the child to tell the child, if necessarily firmly, to go with the person to whom access has been granted. In other words, the person having custody should do his or her best to ensure that the access granted is in fact enjoyed … The child should be persuaded, encouraged and instructed but not physically forced to go with the person to whom access has been granted.'[10]

Where a person knowingly or deliberately fails to obtemper a court order for contact, this amounts to a contempt of court for which the punishment can be imprisonment. However, the courts are reluctant to impose a custodial sentence on a parent with whom the child resides as this will, undoubtedly, have a detrimental effect on the welfare of the child.[11]

---

1 *Porchetta v Porchetta* 1986 SLT 105; *Crowley v Armstrong* 1990 SCLR 361; *O v O* 1995 SLT 238; *Sanderson v McManus* 1997 SC (HL) 55.

2 Children (Scotland) Act 1995, ss 1(1)(c) and 2(1)(c).

3 C(S)A 1995, s 11(11); see para **12.4**.

4 *J v M* [2016] CSIH 52; 2016 SC 835 (court refused father's application for a contact order based on the effects on the child of the hostile relationship between the parents. See also: *Ahmed v Ahmed* [2019] 11 WLUK 535.

5 2001 SLT 485.

6 ECHR, Art 8(1): 'Everyone has the right to respect for his private and family life, his home and his correspondence.'

7 However, in *A v S* [2014] 4 WLUK 453, the court emphasised that there was no presumption in favour of contact once the biological father and child relationship had been established. The Sheriff Principal stated that: 'the sheriff's process of reasoning was bereft of articulation of the child's best interests in the context of a potential award of contact in favour of the pursuer'.

8 See: *X v Y* [2018] SC DUM 54, in which the sheriff did not accept the child's view as being 'genuine' and 'independently formed'.

9 1978 SLT 74.

10 Ibid at p 75.

11 See: *M v S* 2011 SLT 918; *G v B* [2011] CSIH 56; *F v H* 2014 GWD 26-515; *SM v CM* [2017] CSIH 1; *TJ v SB* [2018] SAC (Civ) 15. See also: Shona Templeton *Why are contact orders so hard to enforce?* Fam LB 2018, 155.

CONCLUSION

12.8 In theory, any proceedings in relation to parental responsibilities and parental rights are determined by the welfare principle. But in relation to the residence of children whose parents' relationship breaks down, the outcomes today are not so very dissimilar to those of several decades ago. Professor Joe Thomson, in previous editions of this book, quoted from Maidment[1] who produced three findings from a British socio-legal study:

> 'Firstly, about 94 per cent of divorcing parents agree between themselves the arrangements for the care of their children after the divorce. Secondly, about 90 per cent of these arrangements provide for the mother being the main caretaker in that the children live with her. Thirdly, the court, which need not but usually is asked to confirm the private consensual arrangements, rarely disturbs parents' agreements and almost invariably preserves the residential status quo of the child …'.

Whatever the theoretical powers of the court, the judge will generally 'rubber stamp' the arrangements which have been negotiated by the parties where it is in the child's best interests to do so. Preserving the status quo is thought to be conducive to the child's welfare as it does not disturb the continuity of the child's relationship with the *de facto* caring parent.

Unless a parent has been deprived of his or her parental responsibilities and parental rights, the parent with whom the child does not reside can continue to exercise his or her rights and fulfil his or her responsibilities in relation to the upbringing of the child. The non-residential parent has the right to maintain contact[2] with the child. In most cases, the parents will have agreed with which parent the child or children will live and the terms of contact arrangements with the non-residential parent and the child or children.

There is growing evidence that children will make a better recovery from the traumatic effects of the breakdown of their parents' relationship when they can sustain an emotional tie with both parents. As a consequence of the principle that no s 11 order should be made unless it is better for the child to make the order than that none be made at all, and that when such orders are made, they should have the minimum effect on a parent's existing responsibilities and rights, the C(S)A 1995 has given Scots law the framework to achieve this end. There is some evidence that many family law practitioners and parents have taken the opportunity to make this aspiration an everyday reality.

Nevertheless, there are still cases where residence and contact matters are bitterly disputed between parents resulting in protracted proceedings; these long proofs are not in the interests of the children involved. They are also extremely expensive and can exacerbate the poor relationship between the parties. In *NJDB v JEG*,[3] the Lord President (Hamilton) described such proceedings as a 'highly unsatisfactory' state of affairs and reminded professional advisers of their duty to their clients and the court to attempt to obtain an expeditious disposal by taking steps to identify and concentrate on, and only on, what is in the best interest of the children at the centre of the case. When the case proceeded to the Supreme Court[4] Lord Reed was highly critical of the length of time the dispute had lasted and the costs involved. He focused on the lack of judicial control over the process due to the extensive pleadings of both parties which then resulted in an extensive proof. In his view: 'The glacial pace of the proceedings was itself inimical to the best interests of the child… the proceedings have overshadowed the life of this young child, perpetuating and deepening the conflict between his parents which has caused him such distress.'[5]

As stated above, the ultimate sanction for failing to obtemper a court order for residence or contact is a finding of contempt of court and possible imprisonment. These are hardly conducive to the child's welfare. This reinforces the benefits to the child and to the parents of working to achieve an agreement on child related issues and at all costs avoid litigation.[6]

---

1 Maidment *Child Custody and Divorce* (1984, Croom Helm), p 68. (Note: (i) that the quoted percentages date back to the mid-1980s; and (ii) the breakdown of relationships would now include dissolution of a civil partnership and separation of cohabitees.)

2 Children (Scotland) Act 1995, s 2(1)(c).

3 2010 CSIH 83.

4 [2012] UKSC 21, 2012 SC (UKSC) 293.

5 Ibid at para 21.

6 See para **12.7**.

Chapter 13

Adoption and Permanence Orders

ADOPTION

13.1 Adoption is the legal process by which the relationship of parent and child is created by the order of a court and, as a consequence, the legal relationship between the biological parents and their child is severed permanently. The law relating to adoption was found in the Adoption (Scotland) Act 1978. With the exception of a few sections,[1] the 1978 Act has been repealed and replaced with the Adoption and Children (Scotland) Act 2007.[2] The effect of an adoption order is to vest parental responsibilities and parental rights in relation to the child in the adoptive parent or parents.[3] An adopted child is treated in law as the child of the adopter, as if he or she had never been the child of any person[4] other than the adoptive parent or parents.[5] Thus the parental responsibilities and parental rights of the biological parents towards their child are extinguished when the child is adopted and the child's rights are enforceable against the adopters and not the biological parents. Parental responsibilities and parental rights[6] vested in the adoptive parents will come to an end when the child reaches 16 (18 in relation to the parental responsibility to provide guidance) but the child will remain the legal child of the adoptive parents for the duration of the child's life. Adoption is therefore a radical interference with the rights of children and their biological parents to respect for private and family life under Article 8 of the European Convention on Human Rights. Accordingly, the procedure must carefully balance the interests of those persons if a violation of Article 8 is to be avoided. This matter was addressed in the case of *S v L*,[7] in which the biological mother appealed the decision of the Inner House to grant an adoption order. In granting the order, the court required the mother's consent to be dispensed with under s 31(3)(d) of the 2007 Act. The mother claimed that the court's reading of s 31(3)(d) failed to respect the parent's Article 8 (ECHR) rights. Lord Reed stated:

> '[Sec] 31(3)(d) empowers the court to dispense with the parent's consent only if it is satisfied that the welfare of the child "requires" it. The word "requires" imposes a high test. That is so as a matter of ordinary English: to say that something is required means that it is not merely desirable or reasonable, but that it is necessary.'[8]

Lord Reed goes on:

> 'There must, in other words, be an overriding requirement that the adoption proceed for the sake of the child's welfare, which remains the paramount consideration. The court must be satisfied that the interference with the rights of the parents is proportionate: in other words, that nothing less than adoption will suffice.'[9]

There are exceptions to the general principle that on adoption the child is no longer regarded as the legal child of his or her parents. In determining prohibited degrees of relationship for the purpose of the law of marriage, civil partnership and incest, the child remains the child of his or her parents;[10] in addition, an adopted child cannot marry an adoptive parent.[11] Adoption does not affect the law on nationality or citizenship.[12] Similarly, adoption does not affect a child's entitlement to a pension which was in payment at the time of the adoption.[13] Finally, while as a general rule an adopted child is treated for the purposes of the law of succession as the child of the adopters and no other person,[14] the child retains rights in relation to a parent's estate if the adoptive parent died before the commencement of the Succession (Scotland) Act 1964 and the parent dies after the commencement of the Law Reform (Miscellaneous Provisions) (Scotland) Act 1966.[15]

In spite of these exceptions, it must be emphasised that the effect of an adoption order on the child's relationship with his or her biological parents is drastic and permanent. Put simply, the parents lose all parental responsibilities and parental rights when their child is adopted. In particular it should be noted that under ss 11(4)(a) and 11A of the Children (Scotland) Act 1995, the parent loses the right to apply for parental responsibilities and parental rights, including contact, after a child has been adopted or is subject to a permanence order.[16]

Traditionally, adoption was considered as a way of providing a home for a newborn infant, usually with a childless couple. However, increasingly, adoption is serving as a long-term solution for children in need.[17] In these circumstances, adoption orders should not be made without the agreement of the parents unless they have clearly forfeited their *prima facie* parental responsibilities and parental rights to bring up their child.

Scotland's Adoption Register was established in 2011 and supports adoption agencies to facilitate adoption.[18] Individuals and couples who have been approved to adopt but not matched with a child within three months are referred to the Register. Both prospective adopters and social workers seeking to match children can register online profiles with the aim of identifying suitable matches.

---

1 Adoption (Scotland) Act 1978, Pt IV.

2 See generally *Wilkinson and Norrie* , Ch 21. See also, Morag Jack, *Adopting Children in Scotland* (5th edn, 2016, W Green).

3 Adoption and Children (Scotland) Act 2007, s 28(1).

4 But see AC(S)A 2007 s 35(1)(a) which states that where a member of 'relevant couple' is granted an adoption order, this does not affect any parental responsibilities and parental rights which were vested in the other member of the relevant couple immediately before the making of the order.

5 AC(S)A 2007, s 40(1) and (4). Where the person adopting a child is a member of a relevant couple with the child's birth parent the effect of the adoption order is to treat the child as the child of the couple and not the child of any other person except the adopter and the other member of the couple: AC(S)A 2007, s 40(2) and (3). On relevant couples see para **13.4**.

6 Children (Scotland) Act 1995, ss 1 and 2.

7 [2012] UKSC 30.

8 Ibid at para [32].

9 Ibid at para [34].

10 AC(S)A 2007, s 41(1).

11 Adoptive siblings can marry: AC(S)A 2007, s 41(2). For full discussion, see para **2.6**.

12 AC(S)A 2007, s 41(3).

13 AC(S)A 2007, s 42.

14 Succession (Scotland) Act 1964, s 23(1). See *Cameron v MacIntyre's Executor* 2006 SLT 176. The adopted child inherits by virtue of the provisions in the 1964 Act, not by virtue of s 40 of the AC(S)A 2007: AC(S)A 2007, s 44.

15 Law Reform (Miscellaneous Provisions) (Scotland) Act 1966, s 5.

16 See para **12.2** above.

17 See Chs 14 and 15.

18 See https://scotlandsadoptionregister.org.uk for more information.

ADOPTION AGENCIES

13.2 It is the duty of every local authority to establish and maintain a comprehensive adoption service to meet the needs of all those who are or would be affected by an adoption – in particular the child, the parents, the rest of the child's family and the adoptive parents.[1] The facilities to be provided include arrangements for assessing children and prospective adopters, placing children for adoption and giving information.[2] The adoption service must also provide adoption support services which include counselling, guidance and any other assistance in relation to the adoption process that the local authority considers appropriate in the circumstances of a particular case.[3] In doing so, the local authority must have regard to the other social services that it provides so that help can be given in a co-ordinated manner.[4] Where a local authority does not have an adoption service it may use the services of registered adoption services.[5] For the purpose of the Adoption and Children (Scotland) Act 2007, an 'adoption agency' includes both the local authority adoption service and a registered adoption service.[6]

It is a fundamental tenet of the AC(S)A 2007 that all the preliminary arrangements for an adoption should be made by an adoption agency. It is a criminal offence for a person other than an adoption agency to make arrangements for the adoption of a child or place a child for adoption.[7] The person who makes the placement and the person who receives the child, knowing the placement is with a view to adoption, can be prosecuted.[8]

There is one exception where arrangements made by persons other than an adoption agency are lawful. A private person can place a child for adoption where the proposed *adopter* is the child's parent or, where the parent is a member of a relevant couple, the other member of the couple, or any other relative of the child.[9] Thus, for example, a mother can place her child for adoption by her sister, ie the child's aunt.

1 Adoption and Children (Scotland) Act 2007, s 1(1) and (2).
2 AC(S)A 2007, s 1(4).
3 AC(S)A 2007, s 1(5). Except when the services need to be provided as a matter of urgency, on a request for such services the local authority will make an assessment of the needs of the person for such services: AC(S)A, ss 9, 10 and 11. The local authority has the power to provide the person entitled to the services with a payment instead of the service: AC(S)A 2007, s 12.

4 AC(S)A 2007, s 2(1)(a). It must also have regard to any registered adoption service provided in the local authority area: AC(S)A, s 2(1)(b), for example: *Scottish Adoption* or *Adoption UK*.
5 AC(S)A 2007, s 2(2).
6 AC(S)A 2007, s 119(1).
7 AC(S)A 2007, s 75(1).
8 AC(S)A 2007, s 75(3).
9 AC(S)A 2007, s 75(2). On relevant couples, see para **13.4**.

WELFARE OF CHILDREN

13.3 Where a court or adoption agency is coming to a decision relating to the adoption of a child it must have regard to all the circumstances of the case and is to regard the need to safeguard and promote the welfare of the child throughout the child's life as the paramount consideration.[1] So far as is reasonably practicable to do so, they must have regard in particular to:

(i) the value of a stable family unit in the child's development;

(ii) the child's ascertainable views regarding the decision taking into account the child's age and maturity;

(iii) the child's religious persuasion, racial origin and cultural and linguistic background; and

(iv) the likely effect on the child, throughout the child's life, of making the adoption order.[2]

At the time of writing (July 2022), a child aged 12 or over is presumed to be of sufficient age and maturity to form a view to which the court or adoption agency must, so far as is reasonably practicable, have regard.[3] This principle is to be repealed and replaced with a new s 14(4A), 14(4B) and 14(4C) which will place a duty on a court or adoption agency to give the child an opportunity to express his or her views in a manner that the child prefers or a manner suitable to the child's needs.[4] Therefore, regardless of age, the court or adoption agency must give the child an opportunity to express his or her view unless the child is shown to be incapable of doing so.[5] All children are presumed to be capable of forming a view unless the contrary is shown.[6]

Thus, at *every* stage of the adoption procedure when a court or adoption agency makes a decision which involves a degree of discretion – as opposed to a finding of fact – the welfare of the child *throughout his or her life* is the paramount consideration and the views of the child must be fed into that decision-making process.[7] Problems can arise where the child requests that his or her views should be treated as confidential. This should only be granted by the court in exceptional circumstances where there is a risk of significant harm to the child.[8]

Before placing a child for adoption, an adoption agency *must* consider whether or not adoption is the best way to meet the needs of the child or whether there is some better, practical alternative: if there is a practical alternative,[9] the adoption agency must not make arrangements for the adoption of the child.[10] In *X v Y*,[11] the adoption order was refused. The sheriff made it clear that neither the social worker nor the curator had demonstrated in their reports discussion of alternatives to adoption and, consequently, the court was 'left not knowing what the recommendation of the social worker and curator/reporting officer would have been had they done so'.[12] An alternative to adoption may be for the step parent to apply for parental responsibilities and parental rights over the child.[13] As in the case of *X v Y*, these would be exercised jointly with the birth parents. Similarly, if the prospective adopters are relatives of the child, for example the child's grandparents, uncle or aunt, it may be better for the child that they apply for parental responsibilities and parental rights rather than distort the natural relationships through the adoption process.

In placing a child for adoption, an adoption agency must have regard, so far as is reasonably practicable, to the views of the child's parents, guardians and other relatives.[14] Nevertheless, the child's welfare is the paramount consideration[15] and the adoption agency should give effect to the family's views only when it is consistent with the child's welfare to do so. Only children who are under 18[16] and who have not been married or registered a civil partnership[17] can be adopted in Scots law. An adopted child can be adopted again.[18] Where the child is aged 12 or over, an adoption order cannot be made without the child's consent.[19] However, in reaching any decision, the views of a child of any age must be given due consideration by a court or adoption agency.[20]

1 Adoption and Children (Scotland) Act 2007, s 14(2) and (3).
2 AC(S)A 2007, s 14(4).

3 AC(S)A 2007, s 14(4)(b) and s 14(8). This is without prejudice to the need for the consent of a child aged 12 or over to the adoption order: AC(S)A 2007, s 32.
4 AC(S)A 2007, s 14(4A), as amended by s 2(2)(c) of the Children (Scotland) Act 2020.
5 AC(S)A 2007, s 14(4B), as amended by s 2(2)(c) of the Children (Scotland) Act 2020.
6 AC(S)A 2007, s 14(4C), as amended by s 2(2)(c) of the Children (Scotland) Act 2020.
7 See: *X v Y* 2015 Fam LR 41, where the 14-year child expressed a view that he wished to be adopted by his stepmother. The boy's biological mother did not give her consent to the adoption. The sheriff stated that: 'Being [the views] of a 14-year old, they carry considerable weight. However, while the basis for his views in preferring one regime to another might provide a powerful motive for him in consenting to adoption, it is not a particularly strong reason to divest the respondent [mother] of her legal attachment to him'. In this case, the court granted parental responsibilities and parental rights to the stepmother.
8 For discussion, see para **12.5**.
9 AC(S)A 2007, s 14(6).
10 AC(S)A 2007, s 14(7).
11 2015 Fam LR 41.
12 Ibid at para [7].
13 Children (Scotland) Act 1995, ss 1 and 2. Application would be made under C(S) A 1995, s 11. See **Ch 12**.
14 AC(S)A 2007, s 14(5).
15 AC(S)A 2007, s 14(3). The *child's* religious persuasion, racial origin and cultural and linguistic background are factors to be fed into the welfare principle: AC(S)A 2007, s 14(4)(c).
16 AC(S)A 2007, s 119. An adoption order can be made in respect of a person aged 18 or over, if the application was made before the person was 18: AC(S)A 2007, s 28(4). See: Kenneth Norrie, *Adoption of adults: Conceptually competent but practically pointless*, Fam LB 2018, 156, 2–5.
17 AC(S)A 2007, s 28(7).
18 AC(S)A 2007, s 28(6).
19 AC(S)A 2007, s 32(1). The court may dispense with the child's consent if satisfied that the child is incapable of giving consent: AC(S)A 2007, s 32(2).
20 AC(S)A 2007, s 14(4)(b), but note the pending changes to this section. See fns 4, 5 and 6 above. It is interesting to note that in a pre-2007 Act case, *C, Petitioners* 1993 SLT (Sh Ct) 8, it was held to be impracticable to ascertain the views of a six-year-old child when the prospective adopters refused to allow her to be interviewed since they did not wish her to know that she was adopted: the prospective adopters were the child's birth mother and stepfather.

PROSPECTIVE ADOPTERS

13.4 A relevant couple can apply to adopt a child jointly. A couple is 'relevant' if its members:

(a) are married to each other;

(b) are civil partners of each other; or

(c) are living together as if husband and wife in an enduring family relationship.[1]

Each member of the relevant couple must be 21 or over and neither must be the parent of the child.[2]

A spouse or civil partner who is not the child's parent and is 21 or over can adopt a child alone if the court is satisfied that the other spouse or civil partner cannot be found, or that the spouses or civil partners have separated and are living apart and the separation is likely to be permanent, or the other spouse or civil partner is by reason of ill health (whether physical or mental) incapable of making an application for an adoption order.[3] A member of a relevant couple (by virtue of living together as spouses) who is not the child's parent and is 21 or over can adopt a child alone if the court is satisfied that the other member of the couple is by reason of ill health (whether physical or mental) incapable of making an application for an adoption order.[4]

Where a person is a member of a relevant couple and the other member of the couple is a parent of the child, then that person can adopt the child alone provided that person is 21 or over and the parent is 18 or over.[5] Here the effect of the adoption order is that the child is to be treated as the child of the couple concerned and as not being the child of any person other than the adopter and the other member of the couple, ie the child's parent.[6] The adoption order does not affect the parental responsibilities and parental rights which immediately before the order were vested in the member of the couple who is the child's parent; similarly that parent's duty to aliment the child is not extinguished.[7] However it is important to note that the parental responsibilities and parental rights of the child's other parent are extinguished by the adoption order as is his or her duty to aliment the child.[8]

Where a person is not a member of a relevant couple and is 21 or over he or she can adopt the child alone.[9] However, if that person is the natural parent of the child, before the application can go ahead the court must be satisfied that:

(a) the other natural parent is dead; or

(b) the other natural parent cannot be found; or

(c) by virtue of provisions in the Human Fertilisation and Embryology Acts 1990 and 2008 there is no other parent;[10] or

(d) the exclusion of the other natural parent from the application for adoption is justified on some other ground.[11]

The situations where a natural parent will wish to adopt his or her child alone will be rare. It could arise, for example when a father has no parental responsibilities or parental rights and decides to adopt his child after the death of the mother.

---

1 Adoption and Children (Scotland) Act 2007, s 29(3). Since the introduction of same sex marriage any reference in an enactment to persons living together as if they were in a civil partnership ceases to have effect: Marriage and Civil Partnership (Scotland) Act 2014 s 4(4). By s 4(1) CP(S)A 2014, 'husband and wife' refers to same sex spouses and therefore same sex couples can be a relevant couple. It is difficult to see how a couple will establish that they live in 'an enduring family relationship'. The statutory implication seems to be that the relationship of spouses or civil partners need not be enduring!

2 AC(S)A 2007, s 29(1). Parent means a parent who has any parental responsibilities or parental rights in relation to the child: AC(S)A 2007, s 29(4). A member of the couple must be domiciled in part of the British Isles or each member of the couple has been habitually resident in part of the British Isles for at least one year ending with the date of the application: AC(S)A 2007, s 29(2).

3 AC(S)A 2007, s 30(4). Parent means a parent who has any parental responsibilities or parental rights in relation to the child: AC(S)A 2007, s 30(8).

4 AC(S)A 2007, s 30(5). If, of course, the couple had separated they would not qualify as a relevant couple. Parent means a parent who has any parental responsibilities and rights in relation to the child: AC(S)A 2007, s 30(8).

5 AC(S)A 2007, s 30(3). Parent means a parent who has any parental responsibilities or parental rights in relation to the child: AC(S)A 2007, s 30(8).

6 AC(S)A 2007, s 40(2)(b) and (3).

7 AC(S)A 2007, s 35(1).

8 AC(S)A 2007, s 35(2). Where the duty arises under a deed or arrangement which constitutes a trust or expressly provides that the duty is not to be extinguished by the making of an adoption order, then the duty will not be extinguished: AC(S)A 2007, s 35(3).

9 AC(S)A 2007, s 30(1) and (2)

10 Human Fertilisation and Embryology Act 1990, s 28 (disregarding s 28(5A) to (5I)) or HFEA 2008, ss 34 to 47 (disregarding ss 39, 40 and 46).

11 AC(S)A 2007, s 30(7).

PROCEDURE

13.5 Where the child was placed with the applicants by an adoption agency[1] or where the applicant is a parent, step-parent or relative of the child, the child must be at least 19 weeks old before an adoption order can be made and have lived with the applicant at all times during the preceding 13 weeks.[2] If a child was not placed with the applicants by an adoption agency and the applicants are not related to the child, the child must be at least 12 months old before an adoption order can be made and have lived with the applicants at all times during the preceding 12 months.[3] For example, this would apply where foster carers want to adopt a child who has been looked after by them.

Where a child has not been placed with the applicants by an adoption agency, the applicants must give notice to the local authority within whose area the child has his or her home of their intention to adopt the child. The notice must be given at least three months before the date of the order. During that period the local authority investigates the suitability of the adoptive parents, etc, and makes a report to the court.[4] Where a child has been placed by an adoption agency, the adoption agency submits a report to the court on the suitability, etc, of the adoptive parents.[5] An adoption order will not be made unless the court is satisfied that the applicants have afforded the adoption agency or the local authority sufficient opportunities to see the child in the home environment.[6]

Where the child has been placed with the 'prospective adopters'[7] by an adoption agency and the child's parents have consented to the placement, the parents cannot remove the child without the leave of the adoption agency or the appropriate court.[8] Where an application for an adoption order is made by a person with whom the child has had his or her home for the preceding five years, no person can remove the child from the applicant's home while the application is pending unless the prospective adopters consent, the appropriate court grants leave for the removal of the child, the child is arrested, or the removal is authorised by virtue of an enactment.[9] This protection extends to foster carers who decide to adopt a child who is being looked after by a local authority but who has lived with the applicants for the preceding five years.[10]

An application for an adoption order can be made to the Court of Session or the sheriff court of the sheriffdom where the child is.[11] The proceedings are heard in private.[12] A curator *ad litem* must be appointed with the duty of safeguarding the child's interests; in particular it is the curator's duty to provide the court with a comprehensive report dealing with all the circumstances of the adoption application.[13] Thus, the court will have an independent assessment of whether the adoption will be in the best interests of the child.

---

1 Adoption and Children (Scotland) Act 2007, s 119(1).
2 AC(S)A, s 15(1), (2) and (3).
3 AC(S)A 2007, s 15(1) and (4).
4 AC(S)A 2007, ss 18 and 19.
5 AC(S)A 2007, s 17.
6 AC(S)A 2007, s 16.
7 AC(S)A 2007, s 20(1).
8 AC(S)A 2007, s 20.
9 AC(S)A 2007, s 22. Similar protection exists for the period during which a prospective adopter has given notice of intention to adopt a child to a local authority but before the application is made: the child must have lived with the prospective adopters for the preceding five years: AC(S)A 2007, s 21.
10 AC(S)A 2007, s 23.
11 AC(S)A 2007, s 118.
12 AC(S)A 2007, s 109.
13 AC(S)A 2007, s 108(a). A reporting officer must also be appointed for witnessing agreements etc: AC(S)A 2007, s 108(b). The same person can be both curator *ad litem* and reporting officer.

PARENTAL CONSENT

13.6 It is a fundamental principle of the law of adoption that an adoption order cannot be made unless the court is satisfied that each parent or guardian of the child 'understands what the effect of making an adoption order would be and consents to the making of the order (whether or not the parent or guardian knows the identity of the persons applying for the order)'.[1] For this purpose, parent means a parent who has *any* parental responsibilities or parental rights in relation to the child.[2] The following are examples:

(1) The mother and father are married at the child's conception or subsequently: both have parental responsibilities and parental rights and are parents.[3]

(2) The mother is unmarried: she has parental responsibilities and parental rights and is a parent.[4]

(3) The parents are not married and the father has not been registered as the father of the child: the mother is a parent, but the father has no parental responsibilities and parental rights and is not a parent.[5]

(4) The parents are not married but the father has obtained a contact order under s 11(2)(d) of the Children (Scotland) Act 1995: he has the parental responsibility and parental right to contact with his child and is a parent.[6]

(5) The mother and father are married at the child's conception but both have been deprived of parental responsibilities and rights under s 11(2)(a) of the C(S)A 1995: neither has parental responsibilities and parental rights, therefore neither is a parent.[7]

A guardian is a person appointed to be the child's guardian by deed or will or court order.[8] The agreement of a person, other than the child's mother or father, who has parental responsibilities and parental rights is *not* required unless that person has been appointed to be the child's guardian. A mother's agreement is ineffective if given less than six weeks after the child's birth.[9]

1 Adoption and Children (Scotland) Act 2007, s 31(2)(a).
2 AC(S)A 2007, s 31(15)(a). 'Parent' also means a parent who, by virtue of a permanence order which does not include provision granting authority for the child to be adopted, has no parental responsibilities and parental rights: AC(S)A 2007, s 31(15)(b). On permanence orders, see paras **13.13** and **14.7**.
3 Children (Scotland) Act 1995, s 3(1)(a) and (b).
4 C(S)A 1995, s 3(1)(a).
5 C(S)A 1995, s 3(1)(b).
6 On C(S)A 1995, s 11(2)(d), see para **12.4**. The father would also be a parent if he obtained the parental responsibilities and parental rights by agreement with the mother: C(S)A 1995, s 4, discussed at para **11.3**.
7 On C(S)A 1995, s 11(2)(a), see para **12.4**.
8 AC(S)A 2007, s 119. On guardianship, see para **11.3**.
9 AC(S)A 2007, s 31(11).

Dispensing with parental consent

13.7 As we have seen, the consent of the child's parent or guardian is necessary before an adoption order can be made. However, under s 31(2)(b) of the Adoption and Children (Scotland) Act 2007 the court has the power to dispense with their parents' consent in certain circumstances; these will be discussed in this section.

It is a feature of the law of adoption in Scotland that dispensing with parental consent involves the court in a two-stage process.[1] Stage one is that the court must be satisfied that a ground for dispensation exists. This is primarily a question of fact. If that ground is established, the court must then consider stage two, namely, whether the consent of the parent or guardian *should* be dispensed with on that ground. In reaching the decision at stage two, the court must apply the welfare principle in s 14(2) of the AC(S)A 2007, ie the welfare of the child is the paramount consideration. But it must be emphasised that s 14(2) is only relevant at this second stage, ie *after* the ground has been established. But, as we shall see,[2] the 2007 Act includes a 'welfare' ground which appears to conflate the two stages. Not surprisingly, this ground has caused considerable controversy. We shall consider the grounds in turn.

1 *L v Central Regional Council* 1990 SLT 818. See also *Lothian Regional Council v A* 1992 SLT 858.
2 See para **13.12**.

Parent or guardian is dead[1]

13.8 When the parent or guardian is dead, he or she cannot give consent. Therefore, there is no need to dispense with their consent. Moreover, when a parent is dead, he or she cannot have parental responsibilities and parental rights and accordingly is not a parent within the definition of 'parent' in s 31(15) of the AC(S)A 2007. For these reasons, the death of a parent or guardian cannot technically be a ground for dispensing with their consent. In these circumstances, we must conclude that this provision has been included for the avoidance of any doubt.

1 AC(S)A 2007, s 31(3)(a).

Parent or guardian cannot be found or is incapable of giving consent[1]

13.9 Whether a parent or guardian cannot be found is usually decided on the information contained in the report of the curator *ad litem* and the court productions. The court must be told what steps were taken to find the parent or guardian and, in particular, it is important to 'follow up' evidence that relatives or friends may still be in contact with the missing person.[2] Evidence of incapacity to give agreement will usually be a medical report on the parent's or guardian's physical or mental condition.

Once the ground is established, the court must apply s 14(3) of the Adoption and Children (Scotland) Act 2007 to determine whether consent *should* be dispensed with on that ground. Consider the following examples:

Example 1

A parent is unconscious in hospital after a road accident. Clearly the s 31(3)(b) ground is established as the parent is incapable of giving consent. The medical prognosis is that the parent is likely to regain consciousness within a month. This evidence is relevant to the second stage, ie whether the court should dispense with the parent's agreement on the ground that he or she is incapable of giving it. The issue is determined by s 14(3) of the 2007 Act. Since it is *prima facie* in a child's best interests to be brought up by his or her parent(s), giving paramount consideration to the welfare of the child, it is thought that the court should not dispense with the parent's agreement and the adoption order should therefore not be made at that time.

Example 2

A parent is unconscious in hospital after a road accident. Clearly the s 31(3)(b) ground is established as the parent is incapable of giving consent. The medical prognosis is that the parent is severely brain damaged and unlikely to regain consciousness. This evidence is relevant to the second stage, ie whether the court should dispense with the parent's agreement on the ground that he or she is incapable of giving it. The issue is determined by s 14(3) of the 2007 Act. Giving paramount consideration to the welfare of the child and the circumstances of the parent, it is thought that the court would dispense with the parent's agreement on this ground and make the adoption order.

---

1 AC(S)A 2007, s 31(3)(b).
2 In *S v M* 1999 SC 388 no steps were taken to contact the mother's father in an attempt to find her: since not all reasonable steps had been taken to find her, the inference could not be drawn that she could not be found. This case was cited in the English case of *West Sussex CC v Alma* [2016] 4 WLR 129 in which parental consent to adoption was dispensed with on the basis that all reasonable steps had been taken to identify the parents.

Inability to discharge parental responsibilities and parental rights[1]

13.10 This ground, commonly referred to as the 'incapacity ground', is concerned with parents who have parental responsibilities and parental rights. However, it does not apply to those parents whose only parental responsibilities and parental rights are the responsibility of maintaining personal relations and direct contact with the child and the right to do so.[2] Accordingly, when a parent has merely contact responsibilities and rights, the failure to have contact cannot trigger s 31(4) and another ground must be used to dispense with the parent's consent.

Where a parent has parental responsibilities and parental rights beyond contact responsibilities and rights, then s 31(4) applies if in the opinion of the court (i) the parent is unable satisfactorily to discharge those responsibilities and exercise those rights, and (ii) the parent is likely to continue to be unable to do so. It will be noticed that the crucial issue is the parent's *inability* to discharge the rights and duties satisfactorily; there is no implication of blame. That said, where a parent has abused or neglected a child, it is thought that the court is entitled to infer from these facts not only that the parent was unable satisfactorily to discharge parental responsibilities and parental rights but the abuse or neglect are also relevant to the question of whether the parent will be able satisfactorily to discharge them in the future.[3] In considering whether the parent is likely to be able to continue to discharge parental responsibilities and parental rights, the court is engaged essentially in a fact-finding exercise. For example, in *BH v CH*,[4] the parents appealed against the decision of the sheriff to grant an adoption order on the basis that the sheriff had failed to apply the relevant statutory tests. The Sheriff Appeal Court held that the sheriff had made sufficient findings in fact to support the relevant statutory tests. This included consideration of alternatives to the making of the adoption order.

The ground applies even although the parent's parental responsibilities and parental rights have been curtailed or suspended by the terms of a compulsory supervision order.[5] The ground is concerned with whether the parent is unable satisfactorily to discharge his or her parental responsibilities and parental rights and is not restricted as to how he or she has, in fact, treated the child in the past.

The court must also be satisfied that the parent is likely to continue to be unable satisfactorily to discharge parental responsibilities and parental rights in the future. It is difficult to assess future parenting abilities and the court needs to be very clear about the process of consideration and the reasons founded upon to dispense with parental consent under s 31(4)(c). In *LO v N*, [6] the Inner House upheld a mother's appeal that the sheriff and Sheriff Principal erred by failing to apply the relevant fact-finding tests, had been confused about the application of the law and had not given proper consideration to the alternatives to adoption.[7] In *AV v AJF*,[8] Lady Wise granted the adoption order, finding, on the evidence, that the condition in s 31(4) was satisfied. Lady Wise then considered the next stage, namely, the various welfare considerations contained in s 14 of the 2007 Act, stating:

> 'Each of these factors must be considered in light of the requirements of necessity and proportionality bearing in mind the authoritative statements that adoption is an order of last resort.'[9]

It may be difficult to assess the 'parenting abilities' of a person with whom children have not resided for a considerable time, or to establish the parents' future ability. However, in *M v R*,[10] Lord Glennie, while accepting that it involved some suspension of disbelief, thought that 'the proper approach is for the court to assess the parents' parenting abilities by assuming that the child will return to live with the birth parents; and asking whether, in such circumstances, the parents can satisfactorily discharge their parental responsibilities and exercise their parental rights'.[11] It must be an inability of enduring significance. Thus, if a parent's inability was due to drug addiction, the ground of dispensation would not be satisfied if the parent had recovered after successfully undergoing treatment and was now able to look after the child.

Even if the incapacity ground is established, the court must apply s 14(3) of the 2007 Act to determine whether the agreement *should* be dispensed with. However, as the court must be satisfied that the parent is likely to continue to be unable satisfactorily to discharge parental responsibilities and parental rights in order for the ground to be established, it is submitted that circumstances will be rare when it will not be in the child's best interests to dispense with the parent's consent on this ground.

---

1 AC(S)A 2007, s 31(4).
2 AC(S)A 2007, s 31(4)(a).
3 *D Petitioner* 2012 SLT (Sh Ct) 73. See also, *CEC v EAH, DEH v WD* [2018] SC EDIN 29; 2018 WL 02365806. This is an application for a permanence order. At para [158] the sheriff makes reference to non-accidental injuries sustained by the child 'clearly establishes that it was seriously detrimental to [the child's] welfare that he continues to reside with [the father].
4 [2019] SAC (Civ) 7. See also, *S, Petitioner* [2014] CSIH 42 and *JA v JC* [2018] SAC (Civ) 6.
5 It is thought that the Lord Ordinary was wrong when he opined in *M v R* [2012] CSOH 186 that the ground was not available in these circumstances.
6 [2017] CSIH 14.
7 See *X v Y* 2015 Fam LR 41.
8 [2017] CSOH 103.
9 Ibid, at para [92].
10 [2012] CSOH 186.
11 Ibid, at para [74].

Absence of parental responsibilities and parental rights as a result of a permanence order[1]

13.11 As we shall see[2] a local authority has the power to apply for a permanence order when the child's residence with the parent is or is likely to be seriously detrimental to the welfare of the child.[3] The effect of a permanence order is to transfer to the local authority the parent's parental right to regulate the child's residence[4] and any other parental responsibilities and parental rights as the court considers appropriate.[5] This ground arises when the parent has *no* parental responsibilities and parental rights by virtue of a permanence order (which does not contain authority to adopt)[6] being made and the court is satisfied that it is unlikely that such responsibilities will be imposed on, or such rights given to, the parent.[7] Given that before a permanence order can be made, the parental environment must be found to be seriously detrimental to the child's welfare and that for the ground to be established the court must be satisfied that it is unlikely that the parent will regain parental responsibilities and parental rights,[8] it is thought that it will almost always be in the child's best interests to dispense with the parent's consent on this ground.

---

1 AC(S)A 2007, s 31(5).
2 See paras **13.13** and **14.7**.
3 AC(S)A 2007, s 80 and s 84(5)(c)(ii).
4 This is known as the 'mandatory provision'; see Children (Scotland) Act 1995, s 2(1)(a) and see AC(S)A 2007, s 81.
5 These are known as the 'ancillary provisions'; see C(S)A 1995, ss 1 and 2 and see AC(S)A 2007, s 82.
6 AC(S)A 2007, s 31(6).
7 AC(S)A 2007, s 31(5).
8 AC(S)A 2007, s 31(5)(b).

The child's welfare

13.12 Section 31(3)(d) of the Adoption and Children (Scotland) Act 2007 provides that where neither s 31(4) (inability to discharge parental responsibilities and parental rights) nor s 31(5) (absence of parental responsibilities and parental rights as a result of a permanence order) applies the consent of a parent or guardian can be dispensed with if 'the welfare of the child otherwise requires the consent to be dispensed with'.[1]

Accordingly, s 31(3)(d) is triggered when: (a) consent cannot be dispensed with under s 31(4) because the court takes the view that the parent might *become* able to discharge parental responsibilities and exercise parental rights; or (b) consent cannot be dispensed with under s 31(5) because the court takes the view that it is likely that parental responsibilities will be imposed on or parental rights given to the parent. If this is so, then having failed to establish a s 31(4) or (5) ground, the court can dispense with parental consent if the child's welfare requires it.

This would mean that if s 31(3)(d) could be used to dispense with parental consent whenever adoption was in the child's best interests in accordance with the welfare principle in s 14(3), a competent and reasonably capable parent could have her consent dispensed with if adoption were a better option for the future of the child. It has been argued that this could amount to an infringement of the parent's Article 8 right to respect for private and family life.[2]

In *S v L*[3] the Supreme Court held that when properly construed, s 31(3)(d) was not an infringement of Article 8. Lord Reed explains:[3]

> 'It follows that legislation authorising the severing of family ties between parents and their children will not readily be construed as setting anything less than a test of necessity. Section 31(3)(d), in stipulating that the welfare of the child must "require" that parental consent be dispensed with, is consistent with such a test. There must, in other words, be an overriding requirement that the adoption proceed for the sake of the child's welfare, which remains the paramount consideration. The court must be satisfied that the interference with the rights of parents is proportionate: in other words, that nothing less than adoption will suffice. If the child's welfare can be equally well secured by a less drastic intervention, then it cannot be said that the child's welfare "requires" that consent to adoption be dispensed with. That requirement is consistent with section 28(2), which prohibits the court from making an adoption order unless it considers that it would be better for the child that the order be made than not.'[4]

Put another way, the scope of s 31(3)(d) is restricted to the situation where the child's welfare *requires* the court to dispense with the parent's consent because adoption is the best way to protect the child from a positively harmful situation and not merely a better outcome than continuing to remain a member of the child's existing family.[5]

---

1 Adoption and Children (Scotland) Act 2007, s 31(3)(d).

2 See, for example, *Olsson v Sweden* (1988) 11 EHRR 259; *Ka v Finland* [2003] 1FLR 696; *Buchberger v Austria* (2003) 37 EHRR 13; *Haase v Germany* (2004) 40 EHRR 19.

3 [2012] UKSC 30. See **13.1** above.
4 Ibid at para [34].
5 The welfare ground was used in *M v R* [2012] CSOH 186. See also, *X v Y* 2015 Fam LR 41.
6 For a comprehensive discussion, see Kenneth Norrie, *Welfare and the new grounds for dispensing with parental consent to adoption*, 2008 SLT 213, and Janys Scott, *Welfare and the new grounds for dispensing with parental consent to adoption – a reply*, 2009 SLT 17.

PERMANENCE ORDERS

13.13 We've seen that the effect of an adoption order is permanently to remove parental responsibilities and parental rights held by the birth parents and to grant those responsibilities and rights to the adoptive parents. An adoption order lasts for the lifetime of the child.[1] A permanence order can last throughout the child's childhood,[2] and is granted where a court regards the need to safeguard and promote the welfare of the child as the paramount consideration. In certain cases, a court may grant a permanence order and an adoption order together. This is known as a 'permanence order with authority for adoption'.[3] By s 80 of the Adoption and Children (Scotland) Act 2007, a local authority can apply for a permanence order. A permanence order consists of a mandatory provision under which the parental right to provide guidance appropriate to a child's stage of development[4] and the parental right to regulate the child's residence[5] vest in the local authority.[6] The order may contain a range of ancillary orders vesting other parental responsibilities and parental rights in the local authority or a third party.[7] Most importantly an ancillary order can be made extinguishing the parent's parental responsibilities and parental rights.[8] In so doing the court must ensure that that each parental responsibility and parental right vests in a person.[9] However, even if all the parent's parental responsibilities and parental rights have been extinguished by the permanence order, the parent retains the right to refuse to consent to the adoption of the child unless the court can dispense with parental consent under s 31(5) (or arguably s 31(3)(d)).[10]

Before the court can make a permanence order, it must be satisfied either (a) that no one has the right to have the child living with them, or (b) where there is such a person, the child's residence with that person is or is likely to be seriously detrimental to the welfare of the child.[11] The test under s 84(5)(c)(ii) has become known as the 'threshold test'. It cannot be over emphasised that before a permanence order can be made, the threshold test must be met, namely, that the child's residence with the parent is likely to be *seriously* detrimental to the welfare of the child. It is not sufficient that it would be better for the child to be removed from the care of the parents. In *West Lothian Council v MB*,[12] the Supreme Court allowed the parents' appeal on the basis, amongst other things, that the threshold test had not been met. Lord Reed stated that: 'It follows that decisions … as to a future likelihood of harm cannot be based merely on allegations or suspicions: a conclusion that harm is likely must be based on findings in fact.'[13] Lord Reed went on to say that: 'The requirement in the threshold test that residence with the parent should not be merely detrimental to the welfare of the child, but 'seriously' detrimental is also of crucial importance.'[14] It should be noted that it is for the local authority – the party bringing the application for a permanence order – to provide the court with factual evidence that will satisfy the test in s 84(5)(c).[15]

Only once the threshold test has been met will the court then consider the remaining tests. Those are: (i) in considering whether or not to grant the permanence order (and any provisions), the court must regard the need to safeguard and promote the welfare of the child throughout childhood as the paramount consideration;[16] and (ii) that no order should be made unless the court considers that it would be better for the child that the order be made than that it should not be made.[17]

The timing of the application of the threshold test is an important factor to be taken into account when a court is making a decision on the granting of a permanence order. In *City of Edinburgh Council v GD*,[18] the Lord President stated that: 'The obvious time [for applying the threshold test] is at the point at which the sheriff makes a final decision on the permanence order and the authority to adopt.'[19] It is submitted that the application of the threshold test at the point where the final decision is made on the permanence order may benefit the parent who has successfully addressed, for example, a serious addiction, lifestyle or parenting issue and where the court is satisfied that the child's residence with that parent will not be seriously detrimental to the welfare of the child.[20]

A permanence order cannot be made in respect of a child aged 12 or over unless the child consents.[21] The court has a duty to take account of the views of the child before making a permanence order.[22] At the time of writing (July 2022), s 84(5) and s 84(6) of the 2007 Act remain in force. When s 2(3) of the Children (Scotland) Act 2020 comes into force, amendments will be made to s 84(5); and s 84(6) – the presumption that a child aged 12 and over is of sufficient age and maturity to form a view – will be repealed.[23] In addition to the court having regard to the child's views, it must also have regard to the child's religious persuasion, racial origin and cultural and linguistic background, and the likely effect on the child if the order is made.[24] A permanence order can be made in respect of a child who has been adopted but not if the child is or has been married or is or was a party to a civil partnership.[25]

When applying for a permanence order, the local authority can also make a request to the court for a provision granting authority for the child to be adopted (see above).[26] Before such authority can be granted, the court must be satisfied that the child has been or is likely to be placed for adoption.[27] The parents of the child must understand the effect of making an adoption order and consent to such an order being made in respect of the child.[28] But the court can dispense with parent's consent on exactly the same grounds as the court can use to dispense with parental consent to an adoption order itself.[29] The court can rely on the same body of evidence in deciding whether to grant authority to adopt as it relied on in deciding to make the permanence order.[30]

Even although a ground exists, the court should only dispense with the parent's consent if the welfare test in s 14(3) is satisfied as an order granting authority for adoption is a decision relating to the adoption of the child.[31] Since a permanence order can only be made when the child's residence with the parent is or would be likely to be seriously detrimental to the child's welfare, in most cases grounds will exist to dispense with the parent's consent. If the authority to adopt is granted in the permanence order, then there is no need to obtain or dispense with the parent's consent to the adoption order itself.[32] Where a permanence order is in force without a provision granting authority for the child to be adopted, the local authority can apply to have the order amended to include such authority.[33] The permanence order comes to an end once the adoption order has been made.[34]

Adoption orders and permanence orders are important elements of the law in force to support children who are faced with familial difficulties and for whom long-term care is necessary to ensure their welfare and allow them to thrive in kinship, foster or adoptive families.[35]

1 Adoption and Children (Scotland) Act 2007, s 14(3).
2 AC(S)A 2007, s 84(4).
3 AC(S)A 2007, s 80(2)(c) and s 83.
4 Children (Scotland) Act 1995, s 1(1)(b)(ii).
5 C(S)A 1995, s 2(1)(a).
6 AC(S)A 2007, s 81.
7 AC(S)A 2007, s 82.
8 AC(S)A 2007, s 82(1)(c) and (d).
9 AC(S)A 2007, s 80(3).
10 AC(S)A 2007, s 31(15)(b).
11 AC(S)A 2007, s 84(5)(c)(i) and (ii).
12 [2017] UKSC 15. See also, *West Lothian Council v M* [2016] CSOH 50.
13 Ibid, at para [22].
14 Ibid, at para [27].
15 See *North Lanarkshire Council v KR* [2017] SAC (Civ) 38.
16 AC(S)A 2007, s 84(4).
17 AC(S)A 2007, s 84(3).
18 [2018] CSIH 52. In this case the sheriff had based his decision on the information before the court at the time of the decision. The Sheriff Appeal Court disagreed and held that the threshold test should be applied at the time the child was taken into care. The parent appealed the decision of the SAC.
19 Ibid, at para [30].
20 *City of Edinburgh Council for Permanence Orders in Respect of Children AB and CD v WX and YZ* [2014] SC LIV 2. In this case, the sheriff was satisfied that the mother had been able to turn her life around and, consequently, did not make permanence orders in respect of the two children. The sheriff stated: 'Having weighed everything up as carefully as I can, I have come to the view, although not without hesitation, that the Council falls short of satisfying me that the children's residence with their mother is likely to be seriously detrimental to their welfare. I have come to the conclusion that the serious detriment test is not satisfied, and that this is not a case where a Permanence Order would be justified. The test for making a Permanence Order is a high one, and I am not persuaded that the correct course of action for these children is to make such an order.' Para [61].
21 AC(S)A 2007, s 84(1). The child's consent is not required if the child does not have the capacity to consent: s 84(2).
22 *City of Edinburgh Council for Permanence Orders in Respect of Children AB and CD v WX and YZ* [2014] SC LIV 2, paras [41]–[43].
23 See Children (Scotland) Act 2020, s 2(3). The new s 84(5B) will state: 'The child is to be presumed to be capable of forming a view unless the contrary is shown.'

24 AC(S)A 2007, s 84(5)(b)(ii) and (iii).
25 AC(S)A 2007, s 85.
26 AC(S)A 2007, s 80(2)(c) and s 83.
27 AC(S)A 2007, s 83(1)(b).
28 AC(S)A 2007, s 83(1)(c)(i).
29 Discussed above paras **13.ff**. The necessity criterion must be satisfied before the court can dispense with consent on the welfare ground in s 83(2)(d): see para **13.12**.
30 *S v City of Edinburgh Council* [2012] CSIH 95, 2013 SCLR 534.
31 *City of Edinburgh Council Ptrs* 2010 GWD 25-472.
32 AC(S)A 2007, s 31(7).
33 AC(S)A 2007, s 93. The consent of the parent is necessary or have been dispensed with on the same grounds as in the case of the adoption order itself.
34 AC(S)A 2007, s 102.
35 See further on permanence orders, para **14.7**.

PERMANENCE ORDER WITH AUTHORITY FOR ADOPTION

13.14 If the child is the subject of a permanence order with authority for adoption or the relevant parental consents have been obtained or dispensed with, the court can then proceed to make the adoption order. It will do so having regard to s 14(3) of the 2007 Act, namely, that the court is to regard the need to safeguard and promote the welfare of the child throughout the child's life as the paramount consideration. However, the court must not make an adoption order unless it considers that it would be better for the child that the order be made than if it was not.[1] For example, in *BH v CH*,[2] the sheriff had been correct in, first, determining that the consent of the parent should be dispensed with, then making a decision about what (if any) order should be made to safeguard and promote the welfare of the child throughout the child's life and whether it would be better for the child that the order is made than it should not be made'.[3] In *X v Y*,[4] the sheriff did not grant the adoption order in favour of the stepmother on the basis that the 14-year-old boy (who lived with his father and stepmother) was already in a stable family and it would not be better for the child to make the order than not.[5]

1 AC(S)A 2007, s 28(2).
2 [2019] SAC (Civ) 7). See also *T, Petitioner* 1997 SLT 724 where the Inner House made an adoption order in favour of a male nurse who was living with his same sex cohabitant. The child had been rejected by his mother and it was in his best interests

to be cared for by the applicant and his partner. (Their sexual orientation was not important in the circumstances.)

3 Ibid, at para [36].

4 2015 Fam LR 41.

5 See *North Lanarkshire Council v KR* 2020 SCLR 1, at para [69].

Post-adoption contact

13.15 Adoption extinguishes the parental responsibilities and parent rights of the birth parents.[1] By definition, this extinguishes the right of the birth parent to maintain personal relations and direct contact with the child on a regular basis.[2] By s 28(3) of the AC(S)A 2007 the court has power to attach any terms or conditions to the order as it thinks fit. This discretion is governed by the welfare principle in s 14(3) of the 2007 Act. This power can be used to allow the child to have contact with his or her birth family after the adoption if the court considers this to be in the best interests of the child. In *AV v AJF*,[3] the natural parents were granted indirect contact with the children to be agreed between the parties. In *AB & CD v LM*,[4] the Sheriff Appeal Court upheld the sheriff's refusal to grant post-adoption indirect contact, the sheriff having found that: 'There was no evidence of any lasting memory. [The child] is too young to express any view. Any reinstatement of contact would be likely to cause some confusion with no evidence of benefit to the child.'[5] The debate on the benefits or otherwise of post-adoption contact for the child, the birth parents and the adoptive parents is ongoing. The discussion is outwith the scope of this book but there exist many excellent articles on this matter.[6]

Adoption orders are registered in the Adopted Children Register. On reaching 16 an adopted person is entitled to obtain information in respect of his or her birth; counselling services are available for adopted persons who have received such information.

1 Adoption and Children (Scotland) Act 2007, s 35(2).

2 Children (Scotland) Act 1995, s 2(1)(b).

3 [2017] CSOH 103. See also, *City of Edinburgh Council v T* [2021] 7 WLUK 554.

4 2019 Fam LR 60.

5 Ibid, at para [40].

6 For example, see Woolfson and Adam, *Adoption: when should contact continue?* JLSS 2014 (Oct).

Surrogacy

13.16 It should be stated at the start of this section on surrogacy that, at the time of writing (July 2022), the Law Commission (for England and Wales) and the Scottish Law Commission are currently overseeing the reform of the law of surrogacy.[1]

Surrogacy involves a couple or an individual (intended parent(s)) engaging the services of a woman (the surrogate) to undergo pregnancy. The intention from the outset is that the child who is born will then be raised within the family of the intended parent(s).

When a child is born as a result of a surrogacy arrangement, as per the law on legal parenthood, the woman who gives birth to the child, ie the surrogate, will be the child's legal mother[2] and the child's legal father will be the surrogate's spouse or civil partner if she has one.[3] The surrogate will be registered as the child's mother even if she is not biologically related to the child.[4] Legal parental status and parental responsibilities and parental rights can be transferred to the intended parent(s) by application for a parental order under s 54 (two applicants) or s 54A (one applicant) of the Human Fertilisation and Embryology Act 2008 (see below). An application for a parental order must be made within the period of six months beginning with the day on which the child is born[5] and, at the time the application is made, the child must be living with the applicant(s).[6] The effect of the order is that the child is to be treated in law as the child of the applicant(s).[7]

Surrogacy is typically used by heterosexual couples where the woman, for whatever reason, is unable to carry a child throughout pregnancy or by same sex male couples.[8] Surrogacy can also be used by single persons – male or female.[9] Under UK law, where an application for a parental order is made under s 54, the gametes of at least one of the applicants must have been used to bring about the creation of the embryo.[10] Where an application for a parental order is made under s 54A, the gametes of the applicant must have been used to bring about the creation of the embryo.[11] An interesting legal situation arose in *Re X (Parental death of intended parent prior to birth)*[12] in which Mr and Mrs Y entered a surrogacy agreement with Mr and Mrs Z in which the gametes of Mr Y and Mrs Z were used to create the embryo. The intention was that Mr and Mrs Y would apply for a parental order under s 54 of the 2008 Act. When Mrs Z was five months pregnant,

Mr Y died. Under strict interpretation of s 54, a parental order could be granted only where the application was made by a couple (one of whose gametes had been used). Under a strict interpretation of s 54A, Mrs Y was unable to apply for a parental order because her gametes had not been used in the creation of the embryo (the gametes were those of her deceased husband). In this case, the court was satisfied that Articles 8 and 14 of the European Convention on Human Rights were relevant to the decision which allowed the court to interpret the 2008 Act sufficiently widely to be 'read down' in a way that was compliant with the ECHR.

There are two types of surrogacy: 'gestational' surrogacy where the surrogate is not biologically related to the child she is carrying and 'traditional surrogacy' where the surrogate is biologically related to the child she is carrying because her egg was used to create the embryo. In gestational surrogacy arrangements, the egg of the intended mother or a donor egg will be used. As stated above, in both gestational and traditional surrogacy arrangements, at least one of the intended parents must be biologically related to the child for a parental order to be granted.[13]

Before the making of a parental order, the court must be satisfied that the surrogate and any other person who is the parent of the child give their consent.[14]

Parental orders cannot be granted until the child is at least six weeks old; any agreement by the surrogate mother is ineffective if given within six weeks of the birth.[15] The court must also be satisfied that no money or other benefit (other than for expenses reasonably incurred) has been given or received by the applicants for, or in consideration of, the making of the order, the parental agreement, the handing of the child over to the applicants, or the making of arrangements in respect of the order.[16]

The Commissions are expected to publish a joint Report with recommendations for reform of surrogacy law and a draft Bill in autumn 2022.

---

1 Law Commission for England and Wales and Scottish Law Commission (2019) "Building families through surrogacy: a new law." Available at: www.scotlawcom.gov.uk/files/1015/5980/7782/Joint_consultation_paper_on_Building_families_through_surrogacy_-_a_new_law_LCCP_244_SLCDP_167.pdf.

2 Human Fertilisation and Embryology Act 2008, s 33 and Children (Scotland) Act, s 3(1)(a).
3 HFEA 2008, s 35 and C(S)A 1995, s 3(1)(b)(i) and (ii) and Law Reform (Parent and Child) (Scotland) Act 1986, s 5(1)(a).
4 HFEA 2008, s 33(1).
5 HFEA 2008, s 54(3) and s 54A(2). But see *Re X (A Child) (Surrogacy: Time Limit)* (2015) 1 FLR 39 and *Re X (Children) (Parental Orders: Time Limit)* [2022] EWHC 198 (Fam).
6 HFEA 2008, s 54(4) and s 54A(3).
7 HFEA 2008, s 54(1) and s 54A(1).
8 HFEA 2008, s 54 allows for two applicants to apply for a 'parental order'.
9 HFEA 2008, s 54A allows for the application for a parental order by one applicant who must be aged 18 or over at the time of the making of the order: s 54A(4). Section 54A was added by the Human Fertilisation and Embryology Act 2008 (Remedial) Order 2018/1413. It came into force in January 2019.
10 HFEA 2008, s 54(1)(b).
11 HFEA 2008, s 54A(1)(b).
12 [2020] EWFC 39.
13 The intended father supplying the sperm or the intended mother supplying the ovum.
14 HFEA 2008, s 54(6) and s 54A(5). See: *Re AB (Surrogacy: Consent)* [2016] EWHC 2643 in which the surrogate refused to consent to the making of the parental order. No parental order was granted, even though it was considered to be in the children's best interests to grant the order.
15 HFEA 2008, s 54(7) and s 54A(6).
16 HFEA 2008, s 54(8) and s 54A(7). But see [2016] EWFC 33 in which payment for 'recuperation holidays' was considered 'reasonable expenses'.

Chapter 14

Children: Responsibilities and powers of local authorities

INTRODUCTION

14.1 Although family autonomy may be regarded as a hallmark of a democratic society, it is accepted that a modern state should provide general services in relation to health, education, housing and leisure which indirectly benefit all children and families. But it has also been recognised that a local authority should make provision through its social work agencies for the assistance, support and protection of children who are vulnerable when the family of which they are part is or becomes dysfunctional. At one extreme, this provision may simply take the form of advice, support and guidance to the family; at the other, it might involve the compulsory removal of a child from the family.

Where a child is compulsorily removed from the family, two points must be stressed. First, not only are some or all parental responsibilities and parental rights being overridden but, in an extreme situation, the child may also be deprived of liberty. Clearly, serious human rights issues arise under Article 5 (right to liberty and security of person) and Article 8 (right to respect for private and family life) of the European Convention on Human Rights.[1] Article 5(d) of the ECHR recognises that the detention of a child can be justified if it is made by lawful order 'for the purpose of educational supervision or to bring him before a competent legal authority'. To avoid violations of these Articles, it is therefore important that the law should provide procedural safeguards to ensure that these interests are adequately represented before a decision is made which would deprive parents of their child and the child of his or her family – even if, ultimately, this step must be taken to secure the welfare of the child. This, in turn, can raise human rights issues, in particular Article 6 of the European Convention (right to a fair and public hearing). In short, the procedures must satisfy the minimum standards of a fair hearing set down in Article 6, which provides as follows:

'(1) In the determination of his civil rights and obligations or of any criminal charge against him, everyone is entitled to a fair and public hearing within a reasonable time by an independent and impartial tribunal established by law. Judgment shall be pronounced publicly but the press and public may be excluded from all or part of the trial in the interests of morals, public order or national security in a democratic society, where the interests of juveniles or the protection of the private life of the parties so require, or to the extent strictly necessary in the opinion of the court in special circumstances where publicity would prejudice the interests of justice.

(2) Everyone charged with a criminal offence shall be presumed innocent until proved guilty according to law.

(3) Everyone charged with a criminal offence has the following minimum rights:

(a) to be informed promptly, in a language which he understands and in detail, of the nature and cause of the accusation against him;

(b) to have adequate time and facilities for the preparation of his defence;

(c) to defend himself in person or through legal assistance of his own choosing or, if he has not sufficient means to pay for legal assistance, to be given it free when the interests of justice so require;

(d) to examine or have examined witnesses against him and to obtain the attendance and examination of witnesses on his behalf under the same conditions as witnesses against him; and

(e) to have the free assistance of an interpreter if he cannot understand or speak the language used in court.'

The second point which must be stressed is that although a large degree of discretion must be given to social work agencies, their decisions in relation to a child may have serious consequences for the child and the child's family. It is therefore crucial that the parameters within which this discretion can lawfully be exercised are clearly laid down and monitored.

The law relating to the responsibilities and powers of local authorities is governed by provisions in the Social Work (Scotland) Act 1968, the Children (Scotland) Act 1995, the Children's Hearings (Scotland) Act 2011 and the Children and Young Persons (Scotland) Act 2014.[2]

It seems logical to look at each Act whilst remembering that the responsibilities and duties of local authorities have a wide and integrated scope.

1 Convention for the Protection of Human Rights and Fundamental Freedoms (Rome, 4 November 1950; 213 UNTS 221; TS 71 (1953); Cmd 8969). Most, but not all, of the 1950 Convention has been incorporated into United Kingdom law as Sch 1 to the Human Rights Act 1998.
2 See generally *Wilkinson and Norrie*, Chs 15–20.

THE RESPONSIBILITIES AND DUTIES OF LOCAL AUTHORITIES

14.2 In relation to children and families, local authorities across Scotland have a range of statutory duties that they must carry out to ensure provision of appropriate support services to persons living within each local authority area.

Section 12 of the Social Work (Scotland) Act 1968 imposes a duty on all local authorities to make available advice, guidance and assistance to persons living in each local authority area. Assistance can be given to a relevant person,[1] ie, a person aged 18 or over.[2] Generally, assistance is given in kind but, in exceptional circumstances constituting an emergency, assistance can be given in cash. Assistance may also be given in cash if to do so would avoid the local authority incurring greater expense in giving assistance to the person in some other way either then or in the future,[3] for example, giving a parent cash to avoid the child having to be looked after in local authority accommodation. In this way, by helping adult members of a family, the local authority indirectly helps the child in need.

In the main, there are two categories of children with whom a local authority comes into contact. The first is a 'child in need'[4] defined as a child who is in need of care and attention because:

(i) he or she is unlikely to achieve or maintain, or to have the opportunity of achieving or maintaining, a reasonable standard of health or development unless there are provided for him or her, under or by virtue of [Part II of the Act], services by a local authority;

(ii) he or she is disabled; or

(iii) he or she is affected adversely by the disability of another person in his or her family; or

(iv) because the child is 'looked after' by a local authority.[5]

In relation to a 'child in need', s 22(1) of the Children (Scotland) Act 1995 sets out that a local authority, by providing a range and level of services appropriate to the children's needs, shall:

(a) safeguard and promote the welfare of children[6] in their area who are in need; and

(b) so far as is consistent with that duty, promote the upbringing of such children by their families.

In *Crossan v South Lanarkshire Council*,[7] it was held that this provision amounted to a *general* duty to provide services with the detailed nature and extent of those services being left to the local authority's discretion; it does not oblige local authorities to provide services to individual children in respect of their individual needs. However, the local authority has a discretion – not an enforceable obligation – to provide services for a particular child and members of the child's family if it will safeguard or promote the child's welfare to do so.[8] The services may include giving assistance in kind or, in exceptional circumstances, cash. In providing childcare services, the local authority should, so far as is practicable, have regard to the child's religious persuasion, racial origin and cultural and linguistic background.[9]

Information about the relevant services available for children in each local authority area is to be published by the local authority.[10] There is an emphasis on co-operation between the local authority, the health boards, national health trusts and other local authorities in the provision of appropriate services.[11] Among its services, a local authority should provide help for physically and mentally disabled children[12] and daycare for pre-school age children.[13]

The second category of child with whom a local authority comes into contact is a 'looked after' child.[14] This is a child:

(a) for whom the local authority is providing accommodation under s 25 of the 1995 Act;

(b) who is subject to a compulsory supervision order[15] or an interim compulsory supervision order[16] and in respect of whom it is the implementation authority (within the meaning of the Children's Hearings (Scotland) Act 2011;

(c) who is subject to an order in accordance with which, by virtue of regulations made under s 33(1) of the C(S)A 1995 Act or s 190 of the CH(S)A 2011, it has responsibilities as respects the child; or

(d) in respect of whom a permanence order has, on the application by them under s 80 of the Adoption and Children (S) Act 2007, been made and has not ceased to have effect.

All children who have a measure of intervention by a local authority are considered to be 'looked after' children. Children who have a measure of intervention and may, consequently, live away from the family home, for example, in kinship or foster care, are considered to be 'looked after and accommodated' children.

Under s 25 of the C(S)A 1995, a local authority *may* provide accommodation for any child within its area if it considers that it would safeguard or promote the child's welfare to do so.[17] A local authority *must* provide accommodation for any child, residing or found in its area, if it appears to the local authority that the child requires accommodation because:

(a) no one has parental responsibility[18] for the child;

(b) the child is lost or abandoned; or

(c) the person who has been caring for the child is prevented, whether or not permanently and for whatever reason, from providing the child with suitable accommodation or care.[19]

A 'child' for these purposes is a person who has not attained 18.[20] Before providing a child with accommodation, the local authority, so far as practicable, must have regard to the child's views (if the child wishes to express them) taking account of the child's age and maturity; a child aged

12 or over is presumed to be of sufficient age and maturity to form a view, though the views of younger children should be considered if they *in fact* have sufficient maturity.[21]

It is the policy of the C(S)A 1995 to enable children in need to be supported at home rather than in local authority accommodation. Accordingly, a local authority cannot provide accommodation for a child if any person with parental responsibilities and the parental rights mentioned in s 2(1)(a) and (b) of the 1995 Act[22] objects *and* is willing and able to provide or arrange accommodation for the child.[23] Any such person can remove the child from local authority accommodation at any time.[24] But a child cannot be removed from local authority accommodation if the child is 16 or over and agrees to remain in the local authority accommodation.[25] Where the child is subject to a residence order[26] the child cannot be removed by a person with parental responsibilities and parental rights if the person in whose favour the residence order was made agrees that the child should be looked after in accommodation provided by the local authority.[27] Where a child has been provided with accommodation by a local authority for a continuous period of six months or more, any persons with the relevant parental responsibilities and parental rights cannot remove the child without having given the local authority at least 14 days' notice in writing of their intention to do so.[28]

The accommodation provided by the local authority can be with foster carers, the child's relatives (known as 'kinship care') or any other suitable person but the child cannot be accommodated with any persons who have parental responsibilities or with whom the child has been living.[29] In so far as placement with a kinship carer is concerned, under reg 11(2) of the Looked After Children (Scotland) Regulations 2009,[30] the local authority must be satisfied, amongst other considerations, that the placement is in the best interests of the child, the placement of the child with that particular kinship carer is in the best interests of the child and an assessment of the suitability of the kinship carer,[31] has been carried out. A kinship carer is eligible to receive support in the form of counselling, advice or information; financial support or support in kind; and provision of local authority services on a subsidised basis.[32] The child can also be maintained in a residential establishment or other appropriate place.[33]

When a local authority is looking after a child for whom it is providing accommodation, the authority must act to promote and safeguard the child's welfare: this is the paramount consideration.[34] The local authority must also make use of the services available for children who are being cared for by their parents.[35] The services of 'corporate parents', for example a health board, can be used.[36] The authority must take steps to promote personal relationships and direct contact between the child and any person with parental responsibilities provided it is practicable and appropriate to do so.[37] The local authority also has a duty to take steps to promote, on a regular basis, personal relations and direct contact between the child, the child's sibling(s) or 'any other person with whom the child has lived and with whom the child has an ongoing relationship with the character of a relationship between siblings'.[38] In reaching any decision in relation to the child, the local authority, so far as is reasonably practicable, must ascertain the views of the child,[39] the child's parents, any person with parental rights who is not a parent of the child and any other person whose views the authority considers relevant.[40] In addition to the child's views and those of the other persons described above, the child's religious persuasion, racial origin, and cultural and linguistic background must all be regarded by the local authority in making its decision.[41] In addition the local authority must have regard to the general principle that its functions should be exercised in relation to children and young people in a way which is designed to safeguard, support and promote their wellbeing.[42] The wellbeing factors set out in s 96(2) of the Children and Young People (Scotland) Act 2014 have become known as the 'SHANARRI' principles.[43] These are used to assess the wellbeing of the child or young person. In short, all these factors must be fed into the welfare principle which is the paramount consideration.[44] The authority can depart from the welfare principle only if it is necessary for the protection of the public from serious harm.[45] When a child is being looked after by a local authority, the child's case must be reviewed periodically.[46]

It is important to emphasise that this duty to look after the child arises not only when the child has been provided with accommodation under s 25 of the C(S) A 1995, but also when the child is in local authority accommodation as a result of a compulsory supervision order[47] or any order, warrant or authorisation made under the Children's Hearings (Scotland) Act 2011 as a result of which the local authority has responsibilities in respect of the child.[48]

When a child who is at least 16 ceases to be looked after by a local authority, the authority must provide the young person with continuing care.[49] In addition, when the child is at least 16 but not yet 19, and was, on his or her sixteenth birthday or at any subsequent time, looked after by a local authority, the local authority is under a duty to provide the young person with advice, guidance and assistance when the young person leaves local authority accommodation.[50] Between the ages of 19 and 26, the person can apply to the local authority for such advice, guidance and assistance; and the local authority may grant the application unless satisfied that the young person's welfare does not require it.[51] This may include assistance in kind or cash.[52] The local authority can also make grants to help such a person meet expenses in relation to education and training,[53] and can contribute towards the costs of the person's maintenance and accommodation in any place where the person is, or is seeking, employment or receiving education or training until the person is 26.[54] These 'after-care' provisions are important as they help the person make the difficult transition from the local authority environment to independence as an adult in the general community. The C(S)A 1995 also provides for short-term refuges for children at risk of harm.[55] When a *child* requests refuge and it appears to the local authority (or the manager of a registered residential establishment) that the child is at risk of harm, the local authority may provide the child with accommodation for a period of up to seven days or, in exceptional circumstances, 14 days.[56] During that period the local authority can determine what further steps should be taken to safeguard and promote the welfare of the child.[57]

Under Part 3 of the Children and Young People (Scotland) Act 2014, every three years a local authority and the relevant health board must prepare a children's services plan for the area of the local authority.[58] This plan is to be used so that children's services in the area are provided in the way that: (i) best safeguards, supports and promotes the wellbeing of children in the area; (ii) ensures that any action to meet needs is taken at the earliest appropriate time and that where appropriate, action is taken to prevent needs arising; (iii) is most integrated from the point of view of the recipients; and (iv) constitutes the best use of available resources.[59] The purpose of a children's service plan is to set out how each local authority will deliver services that will best safeguard, support and promote the wellbeing of children in the area. It is through the comprehensive and efficient delivery of such services that each child in that local authority area will not become a 'child in need'.[60]

It is worth knowing that it was the intention of the Scottish Government to introduce a, so called, Named Person Service under Part 4 of the CYP(S) A 2014. Briefly, the intention of Part 4 was that each local authority would make available a named person service to children and young persons in its area.[61] The functions of the named person were to:[62]

(i) advise, inform or support the child or young person or their parent;

(ii) help the child or young person or their parent to access a service or support; or

(iii) discuss or raise, a matter about the child or young person with a service provider or relevant authority.

One of the central and necessary features of the named person service was its information sharing provisions. These, along with other matters, were challenged by a coalition of concerned parents and religious groups.[63] The UKSC held that the information sharing provisions that were integral to the implementation of the named person service were incompatible with the rights of children, young persons and parents under Article 8 of the European Convention on Human Rights, namely, that: 'Everyone has the right to respect for his private and family life, his home and his correspondence.'

On the basis of the successful challenge, the Scottish Government decided to repeal Parts 4 and 5 of the 2014 Act. The Scottish Government stated: 'While our commitment to these policies is unabated, we no longer believe that legislation to underpin the delivery of a named person service and child's plans is necessary and … we are giving notice of our intention to seek to repeal Parts 4 and 5 of the Children and Young People (Scotland) Act 2014 … in due course.'[64]

---

1 Note that a 'relevant person' mentioned in s 12(2) of SW(S)A 1968 does *not* have the same meaning as a 'relevant person' in terms of s 200 of the Children's Hearings (Scotland) Act 2011.

2 SW(S)A 1968, s 12(2).

3 SW(S)A 1968, s 12(2). Giving assistance in kind or cash is also subject to the provisions in s 12(3), (4) and (5) of the 1968 Act.

4 C(SI)A 1995, s 93(4)(a).
5 C(S)A 1995, s 17(6), and below.
6 A child is a person under 18: Children (Scotland) Act 1995, s 93(2)(a).
7 2006 SLT 441. Here, a father challenged the refusal of a local authority to pay for after school and out of school care for his disabled child. The father claimed that the local authority was under an obligation to pay such fees. The Outer House held that a local authority had a discretion, not an obligation, in terms of s 27(3) of C(S)A 1995 and its decision was not unreasonable.
8 C(S)A 1995, s 22(3)(a).
9 C(S)A 1995, s 22(2).
10 C(S)A 1995, s 20.
11 C(S)A 1995, s 21.
12 C(S)A 1995, s 23.
13 C(S)A 1995, s 27.
14 C(S)A 1995, s 17(6).
15 Children's Hearings (Scotland) Act 2011, s 83
16 CH(S)A 2011, s 86.
17 C(S)A 1995, s 25(2).
18 On parental responsibilities and parental rights, see **Ch 11.**
19 C(S)A 1995, s 25(1).
20 C(S)A 1995, s 93(2)(a). A local authority *may* provide accommodation for a person in its area aged between 18 and 21 if it would safeguard or promote that person's welfare to do so: C(S)A 1995, s 25(3).
21 C(S)A 1995, s 25(5).
22 On parental rights, see **Ch 11**.
23 C(S)A 1995, s 25(6)(a).
24 C(S)A 1995, s 25(6)(b).
25 C(S)A 1995, s 25(7)(a).
26 On residence orders, see para **12.4**.
27 C(S)A 1995, s 25(7)(b).
28 C(S)A 1995, s 25(7).
29 C(S)A 1995, s 26(1)(a).
30 SSI 2009/210.
31 Ibid, reg 10(3).
32 CYP(S)A 2014 Part 13, s 73(1).
33 C(S)A 1995, s 26(1)(b) and (c).
34 C(S)A 1995, s 17(1)(a). This includes the duty to provide the child with advice and assistance to prepare the child for when he or she is no longer looked after by the local authority: s 17(2).
35 C(S)A 1995, s 17(1)(b).
36 CYP(S)A 2014. For a full list of corporate parents, see Sch 4 to the 2014 Act. See also CYP(S)A 2014, s 56.
37 C(S)A 1995, s 17(1)(c).
38 C(S)A 1995, s 17(1)(d) and s 17(1A). Section 17(1B) states that: 'two people are siblings if they have at least one parent in common'. A sibling-like relationship is one

where, for example, the child has built up a relationship with a peer member of a foster family in which the child has resided.

39 Note that there is no presumption of 'age 12 and over' in s 17(4). The duty on the local authority is to 'have regard so far as practicable to the views of the child ... taking account of his [or her] age and maturity'.

40 C(S)A 1995, s 17(3).

41 C(S)A 1995, s 17(4)(c).

42 C(S)A 1995, s 23A.

43 The SHANARRI assessment principles are that the child is: Safe, Healthy, Achieving, Nurtured, Active, Respected, Responsible and Included.

44 C(S)A 1995, s 17(1)(a).

45 C(S)A 1995, s 17(5).

46 C(S)A 1995, s 31(1). Where a child is being looked after by a local authority, any natural person who has parental responsibilities must inform the local authority of any change of address: C(S)A 1995, s 18(1).

47 See **Ch 15**.

48 See **Ch 15**.

49 C(S)A 1995 s 26A.

50 C(S)A 1995, s 29(1).

51 C(S)A 1995, s 29(2).

52 C(S)A 1995, s 29(3). The local authority must carry out an assessment of the young person's needs: C(S)A 1995, s 29(5).

53 C(S)A 1995, s 30(1)(a).

54 C(S)A 1995, s 30(1)(b).

55 C(S)A 1995, s 38.

56 C(S)A 1995, s 38(5).

57 A local authority is also under an obligation to safeguard and promote the welfare of a child if the authority receives notice from the managers of a hospital in its area that the parents of a child in the hospital have not been in contact with their child for a continuous period of three months or more (or it is likely that there will be no contact with the child for three months or more taking into account any preceding period of absence of parental contact). On receipt of such notice the local authority must consider what further steps, if any, it should institute under the C(S)A 1995 to safeguard and promote the child's welfare: see C(S)A 1995, s 36.

58 CYP(S)A 2014, s 8.

59 CYP(S)A 2014, s 9.

60 C(S)A 1995, s 93(4)(a) and see above.

61 CYP(S)A 2014, s 19 and s 21.

62 CYP(S)A 2014, s 19(5). (Note that Parts 4 and 5 of the Children and Young People (Scotland) Act 2014 are to be repealed.)

63 *The Christian Institute and others v The Lord Advocate (Scotland)* [2016] UKSC 51.

64 See: *Scottish Government response to the GIRFEC Practice Development Panel's recommendations* at: www.gov.scot/publications/getting-right-child-girfec-practice-development-panel-report-scottish-government-response/ (accessed April 2022). Note that the intention to repeal applies to Parts 4 and 5 of the CYP(S)A 2014 only.

THE POWERS OF LOCAL AUTHORITIES

14.3 We have seen that when children are in need, a major objective of the Children (Scotland) Act 1995 is that local authorities should provide services to support children in their family environment.[1] The 1995 Act also gives a local authority the right to apply to the sheriff for a range of court orders to help the local authority fulfil its obligations in respect of children. These orders are discussed in this section.

1 Children (Scotland) Act 1995, s 22(1)(a) and (b).

The court's duty to consult the child

14.4 At the outset, it is important to appreciate that in determining any matter relating to the child, the welfare of the child throughout his or her childhood is the paramount consideration of the court.[1] Where a local authority applies to a sheriff for an assessment order,[2] a child protection order,[3] an exclusion order,[4] or a permanence order,[5] the sheriff must, so far as is practicable and taking into account the age and maturity of the child concerned, give the child an opportunity to indicate whether he or she wishes to express a view. If the child wishes to express a view, the sheriff must give him or her the opportunity to express that view; and have regard to the view expressed.[6] At the time of writing (July 2022), a child of 12 years of age or more is presumed to be of sufficient age and maturity to form a view, but younger children's views must also be heard if they *in fact* have sufficient age and maturity.[7] It should be noted that s 16(2) of the Children (Scotland) Act 1995 is due to be substituted with a new s 16(2), (2A) and (2B) when s 1 of the Children (Scotland) Act 2020 comes into force. Section 16(2B) states: 'The child is to be presumed to be capable of forming a view unless the contrary is shown.'[8] The importance of the duty to give the child the opportunity to express his or her views cannot be over-emphasised. It is a central policy of the Children (Scotland) Act 1995 that the child at the centre of the judicial proceedings should have the opportunity to state his or her views and that these are fed into the sheriff's decision-making process, which is ultimately governed by the welfare principle, the paramount consideration. A sheriff can only depart from the welfare principle if this is necessary for the protection of the public from serious harm.[9] Consonant with the underlying philosophy of the 1995 Act – that help for a child in need should take place within the child's own family environment – the sheriff should not make any order unless satisfied that it would be better for the child that the order be made than that none should be made at all.[10]

1 Children (Scotland) Act 1995, s 16(1).
2 See para **14.5**.
3 See para **14.6**.
4 See para **14.7**.
5 See para **14.8**.
6 C(S)A 1995, s 16(2).
7 C(S)A 1995, s 16(2). The court should not grant a child's request that his or her views should be kept confidential unless there is a risk of serious harm to the child should they become known. For discussion, see para **12.5**.
8 This means that when the new s 16(2), (2A) and (2B) come into force, there will be no presumption of age 12 years of age or more.
9 C(S)A 1995, s 16(5).
10 C(S)A 1995, s 16(3).

Child assessment orders

14.5 In order to safeguard and promote the welfare of children, a local authority may require access to a child in order to make an assessment of the child's needs. After the assessment is made, the local authority can determine what steps should be taken to help the child by way of provision of services or taking further proceedings under the Children's Hearings (Scotland) Act 2011.

If the local authority social workers experience difficulties in seeing the child, for example if the child's parents or family deny access to the child, the local authority can apply to a sheriff for a child assessment order.[1] The purpose of this order is to assess the state of the child's health or development or the way in which the child has been treated or neglected. For the purpose of a child assessment order, a child is a person who is under 16 years of age.[2] Before an order can be made the sheriff must be satisfied that:

(a) the local authority has reasonable cause to suspect that the child is suffering or is likely to suffer *significant* harm as a result of the way the child is being treated or neglected;

(b) that an assessment is necessary in order to establish whether there is reasonable cause to believe that the child has been or is being so treated or neglected; and

(c) the local authority is unlikely to be able to make such an assessment unless the order is made.[3]

The welfare of the child throughout the child's childhood is the paramount consideration.[4] The duty of the court to consult the child applies in proceedings for an assessment order[5] and the sheriff must also be satisfied that it is better to make the order than that none should be made at all.[6]

The sheriff must specify the date on which the assessment is to begin and the period during which the child is to be assessed.[7] This period must begin no later than 24 hours after the order is granted and should not exceed three days.[8] An assessment order cannot be renewed. The person who has the child must produce the child, allow the assessment to be carried out and comply with any directions in the order relating to contact.[9] The assessment is carried out by an authorised person, ie, an officer of a local authority or a person authorised by that officer, for example a doctor or social worker.[10] The sheriff has the power to order the child to be taken to any place for the purpose of making the assessment, for example a hospital, and can authorise the child to be kept there for a specified period. During that time, the court can make directions for the child to have contact with any person, for example the child's parents. The assessment may involve the medical examination of the child. If the child is under 16 but has capacity to consent under s 2(4) of the Age of Legal Capacity (Scotland) Act 1991,[11] the child's rights are preserved by s 186 of the CH(S)A 2011. Thus, the child with s 2(4) capacity could refuse to consent to a medical examination.

The order lasts for a maximum period of three days. It may be for this reason that the CH(S)A 2011 does not expressly provide an appeals procedure for such orders. This may appear odd given that the child can be removed from home for the purposes of the assessment. However, it is thought that the normal appeals procedure from an order of a sheriff is available but, given the time constraints, an appeal would only be possible where the assessment was not to take place until several weeks after the proceedings in court.

After the assessment has taken place, the local authority will be in a position to determine what steps should be taken to help the child. These could include further orders under the C(S)A 1995 or the CH(S)A 2011, referral of the case to a Reporter to arrange a children's hearing[12] or, if practicable, support for the child at home through the provision of services.[13]

By s 36(3) of the CH(S)A 2011, where an application is made for a child assessment order, if the sheriff considers that the conditions exist for making a child protection order, the sheriff may grant a child protection order instead.[14]

1 Children's Hearings (Scotland) Act 2011, s 35(1).
2 CH(S)A 2011, s 199(1). Also included is a child between 16 and 18 who is subject to a compulsory supervision order: on compulsory supervision orders, see **Ch 15**.
3 CH(S)A 2011, s 36(2).
4 CH(S)A 2011, s 25.
5 CH(S)A 2011, s 27. Note that changes will be made to s 27 of C(S)A 1995 when s 3 of the Children (Scotland) Act 2020 comes into force – primarily, the removal of the presumption of age 12 or over, currently in s 27(4) of the C(S)A 1995.
6 CH(S)A 2011, s 29(1)(a) and (2).
7 CH(S)A 2011, s 35(4).
8 CH(S)A 2011, s 35(5).
9 CH(S)A 2011, s 35(3).
10 CH(S)A 2011, s 35(2).
11 Discussed at para **10.2**.
12 On children's hearings, see **Ch 15**.
13 Children (Scotland) Act 1995, s 22(1)(a) and (b).
14 On child protection orders, see, also, para **15.2**.

Exclusion orders

14.6 The philosophy underlying an exclusion order is simple – that where a child is, or is likely to suffer significant harm as a result of the conduct, or reasonably apprehended conduct, of a 'named person'[1] it is better for that person to leave the home environment than the child be removed from home. This is consonant with the aim of the Children (Scotland) Act 1995 that, so far as it is consistent with the local authority's duty to safeguard and promote the child's welfare, a child should be brought up by his or her own family.[2]

A local authority can apply to a sheriff for an order excluding any person named in the order (a 'named person') from the child's family home.[3] A child for the purpose of an exclusion order is a person below 16.[4] Family home means any house, caravan, houseboat or other structure used as a family residence. It includes any garden or other ground or building attached to, or usually occupied with, the home.[5] The family home is the place in which the child ordinarily resides with a person who has parental responsibilities[6] in relation to the child, or who ordinarily has charge of or control over the child.

The sheriff *may* grant an exclusion order if the following conditions are satisfied:

(a) that the child has suffered, is suffering, or is likely to suffer, *significant* harm as a result of any conduct, or any threatened or reasonably apprehended conduct,[7] of the named person;

(b) that the making of an exclusion order against the named person—

  (i) is *necessary* for the protection of the child, irrespective of whether the child is for the time being residing in the family home; and

  (ii) would better safeguard the child's welfare than the removal of the child from the family home; and

(c) that, if an order is made, there will be a person specified in the application who is capable of taking responsibility for the provision of appropriate care for the child and any member of the family who requires care and who is, or will be, residing in the family home (an appropriate person).[8]

Although condition (b) prescribes that the test is 'necessary', unlike the position under s 4 of the Matrimonial Homes (Family Protection) (Scotland) Act 1981,[9] in an application for an exclusion order under the C(S)A 1995, the welfare of the child *is* the paramount consideration.[10] Moreover, in determining whether an exclusion order should be made, the sheriff has a duty to consult the child.[11] In addition, the sheriff cannot make an order unless satisfied that making the order is better than that none should be made at all.[12]

It is difficult to give the appropriate weight to the statutory conditions for an exclusion order within the context of the paramount consideration being the welfare of the child. For if the welfare of the child is indeed paramount, some, at least, of the statutory conditions would be redundant. There are very few reported decisions on this matter.[13] What is clear is that an exclusion order can be made even where the child is not residing in the family home at the time of the application thus avoiding the problems initially experienced in relation to exclusion orders under s 4 of the 1981 Act.[14]

An exclusion order cannot be finally determined unless the named person has been afforded an opportunity of being heard or represented before the sheriff, and the sheriff has considered the views of any person on whom notice of the application has been served.[15] If the sheriff is satisfied that the conditions in s 76(2) of the C(S)A 1995 are met but the conditions in s 76(3) are not fulfilled, ie, the named person has not been heard, the sheriff may grant an interim order which will have the effect of an exclusion order pending a hearing before the sheriff within a period to be specified in rules.[16] At that hearing, the sheriff can confirm or vary the interim order until the case is finally determined.[17] An interim order can be made – even if the conditions in s 76(3) of the 1995 Act are met – at any time before the final determination of the case. Since an exclusion order is defined as including an interim exclusion order,[18] the obligation to consult the child applies in proceedings for such an order.

As a consequence of provisions similar to those in s 4 of the Matrimonial Homes (Family Protection) (Scotland) Act 1981,[19] the sheriff is enjoined *not* to make an exclusion order if it appears to the sheriff that it would be unjustifiable or unreasonable to grant the order having regard to all the circumstances of the case[20] including:

(1) the conduct of the members of the child's family (whether in relation to each other or otherwise);

(2) the respective needs and financial resources of the members of the family; and

(3) the extent, if any, to which the family home and any relevant item in that home is used in connection with a trade, business or profession by any member of the family.[21]

Other relevant factors in this context are whether the named person must reside in the family home because it is or is part of an agricultural holding or is let to the named person by an employer as an incident of employment. As with s 4 of the 1981 Act, it is difficult to envisage situations where it would be unjustifiable or unreasonable to grant an exclusion order when *ex hypothesi* the sheriff is satisfied that the condition in s 76(2)(b)(i) of the C(S)A 1995 is met, ie the order is *necessary* for the protection of the child.[22] *A fortiori* this would appear to be the case, when we remember that the welfare of the child is the paramount consideration in determining whether or not to make an exclusion order under the 1995 Act.[23]

If in an application for an exclusion order, the sheriff considers that the conditions for a child protection order under Part 5 of the Children's Hearings (Scotland) Act 2011 are satisfied, the sheriff *may* make a child protection order rather than an exclusion order if it is in the child's best interests to do so.[24]

The effect of an exclusion order is to suspend the named person's rights of occupancy[25] (if any) in the family home and to prevent the named person from entering the home except with the express permission of the *local authority* which applied for the order. A wide range of ancillary orders is available;[26] these include:

(a) a warrant for the summary ejection of the named person from the home;

(b) an interdict prohibiting the named person from entering the home without the express permission of the local authority;

(c) an interdict preventing the named person removing any relevant item from the home (ie an item reasonably necessary to enable the home to be used as a family residence) except where express permission has been given;

(d) an interdict prohibiting the named person from entering or remaining in a specified area in the vicinity of the home;

(e) an interdict prohibiting the named person from taking any step specified in the interdict in respect of the child, for example meeting the child at school or telephoning the child; and

(f) an order regulating contact between the child and the named person.[27]

With the exception of an interdict prohibiting the named person from entering the home, the sheriff cannot make any of these ancillary orders if the named person satisfies the sheriff that it is unnecessary to do so.[28] A contact order can be made by the sheriff *ex proprio motu*[29] if it is in the best interests of the child to do so.[30] But it must be remembered that, unless the named person is interdicted from seeing the child, if the named person has parental responsibilities and parental rights he or she will retain the responsibility and right to have contact with the child on a regular basis and a contact order is strictly not necessary.[31] The local authority may, at any time during which an exclusion order is in force, apply to the sheriff to have a power of arrest attached to any interdict granted by the sheriff.[32] This power applies to an interim exclusion order as well as a final order. The detailed provisions in respect of powers of arrest are to be found in s 78 of the C(S)A 1995.

A final exclusion order ceases to have effect six months after being made[33] unless the sheriff directed that it should end earlier or any permission given by a third party to the spouse or partner of the named person to occupy the home is withdrawn.[34] 'Partners' are persons who live together as if they were husband and wife.[35]

On the application of the local authority or the named person or an appropriate person (ie, a person who has responsibility for the care of the child) or the spouse or partner of the named person (if not excluded from the home or if not an appropriate person), the sheriff may vary or recall an exclusion order or any ancillary order;[36] the welfare of the child is, of course, the paramount consideration. If the exclusion order is recalled, it ceases to have effect.[37]

An exclusion order cannot be renewed. It only allows a breathing space of six months to enable appropriate steps to be taken by the local authority for the long-term support of the child. But because the time limits are so tight it was held in *Glasgow City Council v H*[38] that after an interim exclusion order had lapsed, a fresh application for an exclusion order was not an abuse of process. The crucial role given to local authorities in relation to exclusion orders can be seen as an aspect of their general obligations under the C(S)A 1995 to safeguard and promote the welfare of children in need.

1 Children (Scotland) Act 1995, s 76(1).
2 C(S)A 1995, s 22(1)(b).
3 C(S)A 1995, s 76(1).
4 C(S)A 1995, s 93(2)(b).
5 C(S)A 1995, s 76(12).
6 On parental responsibilities, see **Ch 12**.
7 For example, it may be reasonably apprehended that a Sch 1 offender will repeat similar offences if he or she has repeated them in the past and refused to acknowledge his or her guilt, as in *Russell v W* 1998 Fam LR 25. On Sch 1 offences, see the Criminal Procedure (Scotland) Act 1995, Sch 1, and para **15.7**.
8 C(S)A 1995, s 76(2).
9 Discussed at para **5.9**.
10 C(S)A 1995, s 16(1).
11 C(S)A 1995, s 16(2). Note that s 16(2) will be repealed and replaced with s 16(2), (2A) and (2B) on the coming into force of s 1 of the Children (Scotland) Act 2020. The new s 16(2), (2A) and (2B) will repeal the presumption that a child aged 12 and over shall be of sufficient age and maturity to form a view.
12 C(S)A 1995, s 16(3). This provision appears to make little sense in the context of exclusion orders: *sed quaere*.
13 There is a paucity of reported decisions on C(S)A 1995, s 76. It would appear to be little used. See, however, *Russell v W* 1998 Fam LR 25 and *Glasgow City Council v H* 2004 SC 189.
14 For discussion, see para **5.9**.
15 C(S)A 1995, s 76(3).
16 C(S)A 1995, s 76(4) and see C(S)A 1995, s 91(3)(e).
17 C(S)A 1995, s 76(5).
18 C(S)A 1995, s 76(12).
19 Discussed at para **5.9**.
20 C(S)A 1995, s 76(9).
21 C(S)A 1995, s 76(10).
22 A possible scenario is when other orders are available under the C(S)A 1995 or CH(S)A 2011 that would equally protect the child.
23 Cf the Matrimonial Homes (Family Protection) (Scotland) Act 1981, s 4.
24 C(S)A 1995, s 76(8). See also, s 37 to s 39 of the Children's Hearings (Scotland) Act 2011. On child protection orders, see para **15.2**.
25 C(S)A 1995, s 77(1). On occupancy rights, see **Ch 5**.
26 C(S)A 1995, s 77(2).
27 C(S)A 1995, s 77(3).
28 C(S)A 1995, s 77(4).
29 A decision made on the court's own initiative.
30 C(S)A 1995, s 77(6).
31 See generally **Ch 11**.
32 C(S)A 1995, s 78.
33 C(S)A 1995, s 79(1). Interim orders also cease after six months: *Glasgow City Council v H* 2004 SC 189.

34 C(S)A 1995, s 79(2)(a) and (c).This provision does not appear to have been amended to include civil partners.
35 C(S)A 1995, s 79(4). Husband and wife include same sex spouses as a result of the Marriage and Civil Partnership (Scotland) Act 2014, s 4(1). Therefore, same sex couples are included.
36 C(S)A 1995, s 79(3).
37 C(S)A 1995, s 79(2)(b).
38 2004 SC 189.

Permanence orders

14.7 A local authority has a duty to endeavour to support a child who is in need within the child's own family environment.[1] However, situations may arise when it is neither practicable nor conducive to the child's welfare to do so. The child's case may be passed to a Reporter to refer the matter to a children's hearing to determine whether the child is in need of a compulsory supervision order.[2] As discussed in Chapter 13, the local authority could apply to the court for a permanence order[3] vesting parental responsibilities and parental rights in respect of the child in the local authority.[4] A permanence order consists of: (a) the mandatory provision; (b) such of the ancillary provisions as the court thinks fit; and (c) if the appropriate conditions are satisfied, a provision granting authority for the child to be adopted.[5]

The mandatory provision vests in the local authority the parental responsibility to provide guidance appropriate to the child's stage of development *and* the parental right to regulate the child's residence.[6] These are the parental responsibility in s 1(1)(b)(ii) and the parental right under s 2(1)(a) of the C(S)A 1995 respectively. The responsibility to provide guidance lasts until the child reaches the age of 18 and the right to regulate the child's residence lasts until the child reaches the age of 16.[7] When the order is made the parent's s 2(1)(a) right in relation to the child is extinguished.[8]

The ancillary provisions are provisions:

(i) vesting in the local authority such of the responsibilities to safeguard and promote the child's health, development and welfare, to provide guidance to the child and to act as the child's legal representative; and such of the parental rights to control, direct or guide the child's upbringing, and to act as the child's representative as the court considers appropriate;[9]

(ii) vesting such of the C(S)A 1995 s 1 parental responsibilities and such of the parental rights mentioned above in a person other than the local authority as the court thinks appropriate.[10] Where parental responsibilities and parental rights vest in the local authority under s 82(1)(a), or another person under s 82(1)(b), and the parent still retains parental responsibilities and parental rights, they can each exercise their parental rights without the consent of the other;[11]

(iii) extinguishing any parental responsibilities and parental rights which immediately before the order was made vested in the child's parent or guardian but which by virtue of s 82(1)(a) or (b) now vest in the local authority or another person.[12] It will be clear that making an ancillary order to extinguish a parent's parental responsibilities and rights is a serious inroad into the parent's right under Article 8 to respect for family life and must be necessary to protect the child from serious harm;[13]

(iv) specifying arrangements for contact between the child and his or her family where it is in the child's best interests to do so;[14] and

(v) determining any question in relation to any parental responsibilities and parental rights and any other aspect of the welfare of the child.[15]

The conditions for an order granting authority for adoption and the effect of granting such authority have already been discussed.[16]

It will be clear that the effect of a permanence order is that the child is likely to be removed from home and the local authority will have the right to make the major decisions in relation to the upbringing of the child. In doing so, the local authority must act in accordance with the principles already discussed in the context of the provision of accommodation for children being looked after by the authority.[17] In addition the court can also make an ancillary order extinguishing the child's parents' parental responsibilities and parental rights in respect of the child. If a permanence order is made it revokes any existing order relating to parental responsibilities and parental rights.[18]

Given the potentially drastic effects of such an order on both the child and the parents, the court can make the order only if one of the following grounds can be established:

(a) that there are no persons who have the parental right to have the child living with them;[19] or

(b) where there is such a person, the child's residence with that person is, or is likely to be, seriously detrimental to the welfare of the child.[20] It cannot be emphasised too much that this ground will only be satisfied if it would be *seriously* detrimental to the welfare of the child to remain at home with his or her parent. It is not enough that it would be in the child's best interests to be removed from home.[21]

Even when one of the grounds exists, there are further conditions which must be satisfied before a permanence order can be made. The need to safeguard and promote the child's welfare throughout childhood is the paramount consideration in considering whether to make an order and what provision the order should contain.[22] Moreover the court cannot make a permanence order unless it considers that it would be better for the child that the order be made than that it should not be made.[23] The views of the child must be taken into consideration[24] and the court should have regard to the child's religious persuasion, racial origin and cultural and linguistic background as well as the likely effect on the child of making the order.[25] There is no hierarchy among these conditions: all of them have a bearing on whether a permanence order should be made.[26]

Where the child is aged 12 or over, a permanence order cannot be made unless the child consents.[27] While a permanence order can be made in respect of a child who is adopted, it cannot be made in respect of a child who is or has been married or is or has been a civil partner.[28]

In proceedings for a permanence order, the court must allow representations from the local authority, the child, the child's parents and any person who claims an interest.[29] These persons can also apply for the variation of ancillary provisions in a permanence order[30] but, apart from a local authority, they must obtain the leave of court to do so.[31] Leave must be granted if there has been a material change of circumstances or that for any other reason it is proper to allow the application to be made.[32]

A local authority and any of these persons with leave of court can apply to have a permanence order revoked. The court will revoke the order if satisfied it is appropriate to do so in all the circumstances of the case including in particular any material change of circumstances directly relating to any of the order's provisions and any wish by the parents to have their parental responsibilities and parental rights reinstated.[33] If the court revokes a permanence order, it must consider whether or not to make an order under s 11 of Children (Scotland) Act 1995 imposing parental responsibilities on and giving parental rights to any person, for example a step-parent of the child or a person who claims and interest.[34]

---

1 Children (Scotland) Act 1995, s 22(1)(b).
2 On compulsory supervision orders, see **Ch 15**.
3 Adoption and Children (Scotland) Act 2007, s 80(1).
4 For more details of the process of seeking a permanence order, see para **13.13**.
5 AC(S)lA 2007, s 80(2).
6 AC(S)A 2007, s 81(1).
7 AC(S)A 2007, s 81(2).
8 AC(S)A 2007, s 87.
9 AC(S)A 2007, s 82(1)(a).
10 AC(S)A 2007, s 82(1)(b).
11 AC(S)A 2007, s 91.
12 AC(S)A 2007, s 82(1)(c) and (d).
13 *West Lothian Council v MB* [2017] UKSC 15
14 AC(S)A 2007, s 82(1)(e).
15 AC(S)A 2007, s 82(1)(f).
16 See **Ch 13**.
17 Children (Scotland) Act 1995, s 17.
18 AC(S)A 2007, s 88.
19 AC(S)A 2007, s 84(5)(c)(i).
20 AC(S)A 2007, s 84(5)(c)(ii). See *W v Aberdeen Council* [2012] CSIH 37,2013 SC 108.
21 See: *North Lanarkshire Council v KR* 2020 SCLR 1, at para [69] in which Lord Menzies stated: '... the test for severing the relationship between parent and child is very strict – and properly so. But it is not an insurmountable test; where a court has identified all the available options for the care of a child, and carefully assessed the merits and demerits of all of these, and concluded that a permanence order with authority to adopt is the option which best safeguards and promotes the welfare of the child throughout the child's life, then that is the order which the court must make'.

22 AC(S)A 2007,s 84(4). See *East Lothian Council, Petitioner* [2018] 12 WLUK 617. In *Dumfries and Galloway Council Petitioner* 2013 GWD 31-628, the sheriff said at para [20] ' if the order sought would best promote and safeguard the child's welfare it is difficult to see how it would not be necessary to make the order unless, of course, what the order sought to achieve would happen without it. Not to do so would be to disregard the paramountcy of the child's welfare. So in that sense, the section 84(4) welfare test is one of necessity'.

23 AC(S)A 2007, s 84(3). See *East Lothian Council, Petitioner* [2018] 12 WLUK 617 at paras [190]–[196].

24 AC(S)A 2007, s 84(5)(a) and (b)(i). Note that s 84(5) will be amended; and s 84(6) will be repealed when s 2(3) of the Children (Scotland) Act 2020 comes into force.

25 AC(S)A 2007, s 84(5)(b)(ii) and (iii).

26 *W v Aberdeenshire Council* {2012] CSIH 37, 2013 SC 108

27 AC(S)A 2007, s 84(1). The child's consent is not necessary if the child is incapable of consenting: s 84(2).

28 AC(S)A 2007, s 85(1) and (2).

29 AC(S)A 2007, s 86(1) and (2).

30 AC(S)A 2007, s 92.

31 AC(S)A 2007, s 94(4).

32 AC(S)A 2007, s 94(5).

33 AC(S)A 2007, s 98.

34 AC(S)A 2007, s 100.

Chapter 15

The children's hearings system

INTRODUCTION

15.1 We have been discussing the obligations and powers of a local authority to provide support for children. As we have seen, the local authority should endeavour to safeguard and promote the child's welfare by providing support within the child's home environment. As such, the child and the child's family voluntarily accept the local authority's help through its social work department.[1] However, circumstances can arise where it is not possible to provide support for a child on a voluntary basis and the only way to safeguard and promote the child's welfare is through *compulsory* supervision of the child. Compulsory supervision orders are made by a children's hearing.

Briefly, the Children's Hearings System came into existence as a result of the publication in 1964 of the Kilbrandon Report on *Children and Young Persons*.[2] The remit of the report was:

> 'to consider the provisions of the law of Scotland relating to the treatment of juvenile delinquents and juveniles in need of care or protection or beyond parental control and, in particular, the constitution, powers and procedure of the courts dealing with such juveniles, and to report'.

The Kilbrandon Report concluded, amongst other things, that there are 'underlying similarities' present in 'juvenile delinquents' and 'juveniles in need of care and protection or beyond parental control' and that,

> 'common to all the children concerned, is their need for special measures of education and training, the normal up-bringing processes having, for whatever reason, fallen short'.[3]

In Scots law, the children's hearings system deals with children who are in need of care and protection and children who have committed an offence in the same way and on the basis that the underlying causes are similar and, generally, can be attributed to the dysfunction of the child's family. The approach taken by a children's hearing to all children who are referred to the process is welfarist and not punitive. As with all areas of Scots child law, the welfare of the child is the paramount consideration.[4]

Where a child is in need of compulsory supervision, a children's hearing[5] will make a 'compulsory supervision order'.[6]

A child's case is referred to a children's hearing by a Reporter[7] to the children's panel who acts independently of any local authority. In this chapter we shall examine the operation of this system.[8] As previously stated, it is important to emphasise that, in deciding any matter in relation to a child, the welfare of the child throughout his or her childhood is the paramount consideration of the children's hearing.[9] A children's hearing can only depart from the welfare principle if this is necessary to protect the public from serious harm; even here, the welfare of the child is a primary, as opposed to the paramount, consideration.[10] Moreover, as a general rule when reaching its decision, the children's hearing is under the same obligation to consult the child as a sheriff when making a court order.[11] The children's hearing is also enjoined not to make a compulsory supervision order unless the hearing considers that it would be better for the child if the order were in force than not.[12]

The Scottish Children's Reporter Administration (SCRA) publishes annual statistics detailing data and trends in, for example, the number and types of children's referrals, the ages of the children referred to the Children's Reporter and decisions and outcomes.[13]

---

1 An exception is, of course, a permanence order. See **Chs 13** and **14**.
2 *Report in Children and Young Persons* (The Kilbrandon Report) Cmnd 2306.
3 Ibid, at paras 12–15.
4 Children's Hearings (Scotland) Act 2011, s 25(2).
5 On the constitution of children's hearings, see para **15.6**. The three members of a children's hearing are often referred to as the 'panel'.
6 CH(S)A 2011, s 83.
7 The Children's Hearing (Scotland) Act 2011 refers to 'the Principal Reporter', but this includes other officers of the Scottish Children's Reporter Administration to whom the Principal Reporter's functions are delegated, ie Reporters: CH(S)A 2011, Sch 3, para 10.
8 On the role of the Reporter in the system, see para **15.4** below.

9 CH(S)A 2011, s 25(2).
10 CH(S)A 2011, s 26.
11 CH(S)A 2011, s 27. The effect of s 3(2) of the Children (Scotland) Act 2020 (when it comes into force) will be to repeal s 27(3) and (4) and replace them with a new s 27(3), (4) and (4A). This will include the removal of the presumption that a child aged 12 and over is of sufficient age and maturity to form a view. On the obligation to consult, see para **14.4**.
12 CH(S)A 2011, s 28(1) and (2).
13 For the annual statistics for 2021–2022, see: https://www.scra.gov.uk/2022/06/scras-official-statistics-2021-22/.

EMERGENCY PROCEDURES: CHILD PROTECTION ORDERS

15.2 Situations can arise where it is necessary to act quickly to protect a child from serious ill-treatment by removing the child to a place of safety. This can be done by application to the sheriff court for a child protection order under s 37 and s 38 of the Children's Hearings (Scotland) Act 2011. A child protection order is not a long-term measure. It is an emergency measure designed to remove the child from actual harm or the risk of harm. A Reporter can then consider whether the child is in need of a compulsory supervision order and, if so, arrange a children's hearing. A child for these purposes is a person below 16.[1]

On an application by a local authority or any other person (for example, a social worker)[2] a sheriff *may* make a child protection order if satisfied that:

(a) there are reasonable grounds to *believe*[3] that:

 (i) the child has been or is being treated in such a way that the child is suffering or is likely to suffer significant harm,

 (ii) the child has been or is being neglected and as a result of the neglect the child is suffering or is likely to suffer significant harm,

 (iii) the child is likely to suffer significant harm if the child is not removed to and kept in a place of safety,

 (iv) the child is likely to suffer significant harm if the child does not remain in the place at which the child is staying (whether or not the child is resident there); and

(b) the order is *necessary* to protect the child from that harm or from further harm.[4]

When the applicant is a local authority, a sheriff *may* also make a child protection order if satisfied that:

(a) the local authority has reasonable grounds to *suspect* that:

(i) the child has been or is being treated in such a way that the child is suffering or is likely to suffer significant harm,

(ii) the child has been or is being neglected and as a result of the neglect the child is suffering or is likely to suffer significant harm, or

(iii) the child will be treated or neglected in such a way that is likely to cause significant harm to the child.

(b) the local authority is making enquiries to allow it to decide whether to take action to safeguard the welfare of the child, or is causing those enquiries to be made;

(c) those enquiries are being frustrated by access being unreasonably denied; and

(d) the local authority has reasonable cause to believe that access is required as a matter of urgency.[5]

It should be noted that, theoretically at least, the sheriff has discretion whether or not to make the order. The application must identify the applicant and, where practicable, the child concerned; state the grounds for the application; and be accompanied by supporting evidence.[6] As soon as practicable after the child protection order has been made, the applicant must give notice to the person required to produce the child, each relevant person in relation to the child,[7] the relevant local authority if the local authority is not the applicant, the Reporter and any other person to whom the applicant is required to give notice under rules of court. When the Reporter receives such notice, the Reporter must give notice of the order to any person other than a relevant person whom the Reporter considers to have or recently have had a significant involvement in the upbringing of the child.[8]

The effect of the order is to require any person in a position to do so to produce the child and to authorise the removal of the child to a place of safety[9] (or prevent the child being removed from the place the child is currently being accommodated). It also authorises an assessment of the child's health or development and the way in which the child has been or is being treated or neglected.[10] The order can include an information non-disclosure direction under which the location of the place of safety or any other information is not to be disclosed to any person specified in the order.[11] An applicant's actions in respect of the child are restricted to those acts the applicant believes are necessary to safeguard or promote the welfare of the child.[12]

The sheriff must consider whether to include a contact direction in the order. A contact direction can prohibit contact between the child and the child's parent, or any person with parental responsibilities and any specified person or class of persons; it may also direct contact between the child and such persons subject to any conditions which the sheriff considers appropriate to safeguard and promote the welfare of the child.[13] The applicant may apply for a direction in relation to the fulfilment of parental responsibilities and the exercise of parental rights in relation to the treatment of the child arising out of any assessment authorised by the order or any other matter the sheriff considers appropriate.[14] Such a direction can authorise a medical examination of, and related treatment for, the child, but if the child has capacity under s 2(4) of the Age of Legal Capacity (Scotland) Act 1991,[15] no examination or treatment can take place if the child refuses to consent.[16]

Unless the Reporter has received notice of an application to set aside or vary the child protection order,[17] the Reporter must arrange a children's hearing to determine whether the protection order should continue.[18] This initial children's hearing must take place on the second working day after the order has been made.[19] If satisfied that the conditions for making a child protection order are established, the children's hearing can continue the order and any directions (with or without variations) until a second children's hearing can be arranged to consider whether the child is in need of a compulsory supervision order.[20] If not satisfied that the conditions are met, the children's hearing can terminate the child protection order.[21] If the second children's hearing has not taken place within a maximum of eight working days, then the child protection order comes to an end.[22] It is important to note that the duty to consult the child does *not* arise where the sheriff is deciding whether to make a child protection order.[23]

When a child is removed to a place of safety provided by a local authority, the local authority has the same duties towards the child as if the authority was looking after the child by virtue of s 17 of the Children (Scotland) Act 1995.[24]

An application can also be made by any person to a justice of the peace for an order requiring any person who can do so to produce the child and for authorisation to remove a child to, or prevent the child's removal from, a place of safety.[25] The justice of the peace must be satisfied that the conditions for a child protection order are met and that it is not practicable in the circumstances for an application for a child protection order to be made to a sheriff.[26] This is an emergency procedure; the duty to consult the child does not arise.[27] The authorisation ceases after 12 hours if arrangements have not been made to remove the child to, or prevent the child's removal from, a place of safety.[28] Where these steps have been taken, the authorisation ceases after 24 hours or when an application to a sheriff for a child protection order has been disposed of, if earlier.[29] In other words, it is essential to apply to a sheriff for a child protection order as soon as possible within the 24 hours that the authorisation lasts and that steps are taken to protect the child within 12 hours of the authorisation being granted.

A police constable has the power to remove a child to a place of safety if the grounds for a child protection order are met and the removal of the child is necessary to protect the child from harm and it is not practicable in the circumstances for an application to be made to a sheriff for such an order.[30] As soon as practicable, the constable must inform the Reporter that the child has been removed.[31] A child may not be kept in a place of safety under this provision for more than 24 hours;[32] during that period, the Reporter can apply for a child protection order.

There is no appeal from the sheriff's decision to grant a child protection order or the decision of the initial children's hearing to continue the order. However, an application can be made to a sheriff to terminate or vary the child protection order and directions (if any). This must be done *before* the initial children's hearing has commenced to consider whether the order should be continued.[33] An application can also be made to a sheriff to set aside (or vary) a decision of the initial children's hearing that the order and directions (if any) should continue. This must be done within two working days of the hearing's decision.[34] The application can be brought by the child; a relevant person; any person not being a relevant person who has, or recently has had, a significant involvement in the upbringing of the child; the person who had applied for the child protection order; the person specified in the order to produce the child; the Reporter and any other person prescribed by rules of court.[35] Notice of the application must also be given to these persons.[36] The Reporter can then arrange a children's hearing to provide advice for the sheriff hearing the application.[37]

Before determining the application the sheriff must give the following persons the opportunity to make representations: the applicant; the child; each relevant person; any person who is not a relevant person, ie, who the sheriff considers to have, or recently have had, a significant involvement in the child's upbringing; the applicant for the child protection order; the relevant local authority if not the applicant for the child protection order and the Reporter.[38] The sheriff must make the determination within three working days after the day on which the order was made[39] otherwise the order ceases to have effect.[40] The sheriff will terminate the order if the sheriff is not satisfied that the conditions for a child protection order are not met.[41] If they are met, the order and any directions can be varied or the child protection order can simply be confirmed.[42]

A child protection order ceases to have effect in the following circumstances:

(a) if no attempt has been made to implement the order by the end of 24 hours of a child protection order being made;

(b) where the initial children's hearing does not continue the order;

(c) where an application to have the order terminated or varied is not determined timeously, ie, within three days of the application;

(d) where a sheriff terminates the order;

(e) where the Reporter considers that the conditions for a child protection order are no longer satisfied and the person who implemented the order or the applicant has received notice of the Reporter's decision;

(f) where the Reporter decides not to arrange a second children's hearing to determine whether the child is in need of a compulsory supervision order and the person who implemented the order or the applicant has received notice of the Reporter's decision;

(g) where a child protection order has been continued, on the commencement of a second children's hearing to consider whether the child is in need of a compulsory supervision order;

(h) where a child protection order contains the authorisation to remove the child to a place of safety, the end of eight working days beginning on the day after the day on which the child was removed to the place of safety;[43] or

(i) where the order does not contain such authorisation, the end of eight working days beginning on the day after the day on which the order was made.[44]

Child protection orders have been discussed in considerable detail. The reason for doing so is that these orders deprive the child of his or her family and parents of their child. They are paradigmatic of the tension inherent in any system of child protection law between the autonomy of the family and the obligation of the state to intervene in order to protect a child. Unless the procedures are fair and recognise the interests of the child and the family, there could be a violation of Article 5 (right to liberty), Article 8 (right to respect for private and family life)[45] or Article 6 (right to a fair trial) of the European Convention on Human Rights. In the Children's Hearings (Scotland) Act 2011, the Scottish Parliament has enacted a complex system of strict time limits, hearings and reviews in order to balance these two potentially competing interests. In particular, they ensure that the parents of the child involved are given an opportunity to be heard within a reasonable time of the child being removed.[46]

---

1 Children Hearings (Scotland) Act 2011, s 199(1). Also included is a child between 16 and 18 who is already subject to a compulsory supervision order: CH(S)A 2011, s 199(6) and (7).

2 It is rare for anyone other than a local authority to make an application for a child protection order. See: *In the matter of a Child Protection Order* 2015 SLT (Sh Ct) 9 in which Sheriff Holligan provides written reasons for the decision taken in an application for a child protection order. See para [7] for comment on CH(S)A 2011, s 39.

3 Different considerations apply where an application is made by a local authority – 'reasonable grounds to *suspect*', (CH(S)A 2011, s 38(2)); or by a person – 'reasonable grounds to *believe*', (CH(S)A 2011, s 39(2). 'Reasonable grounds to believe' is more exacting than 'reasonable grounds to suspect'. See para [9] of Sheriff Holligan's written reasons (see fn 2 above).

4 CH(S)A 2011, s 39(2).
5 CH(S)A 2011, s 38(2).
6 CH(S)A 2011, s 37(5).
7 CH(S)A 2011, s 200. See also para **15.5**.
8 CH(S)A 2011, s 43(1) and (2).
9 A place of safety is a residential or other establishment provided by a local authority, a community home, a police station, a hospital or surgery whose management is willing temporarily to receive the child, the dwelling house of a suitable person or any other suitable place the occupier of which is willing to receive the child: CH(S)A 2011 s 202. A child may be kept or detained in a police station only if it is not reasonably practicable to keep or detain the child in a place of safety which is not a police station: steps must be taken to identify a place of safety which is not a police station and transfer the child to that place as soon as is reasonably practicable: CH(S)A 2011, s 189(3).
10 CH(S)A 2011, s 37(2).
11 CH(S)A 2011, s 40.
12 CH(S)A 2011, s 58(1) and (2).
13 CH(S)A 2011, s 41.
14 CH(S)A 2011, s 42.
15 Discussed at para **10.2**.
16 CH(S)A 2011, s 186.
17 CH(S)A 2011, ss 45(1)(c) and 46(1)(c).
18 CH(S)A 2011, ss 45(2) and 46(2). This is known as 'an initial hearing'.
19 CH(S)A 2011, ss 45(3) and 46(3).
20 CH(S)A 2011, s 47.
21 CH(S)A 2011, s 47(1)(b).
22 CH(S)A 2011, s 54.
23 CH(S)A 2011, s 27(2).
24 CH(S)A 2011, s 44. On s 17 of C(S)A 1995, see para **14.2**.
25 CH(S)A 2011, s 55(1).
26 CH(S)A 2011, s 55(2). Note that the justice of the peace must be satisfied that it has not been practicable in the circumstances for the application for a child protection order to be made to or considered by a sheriff: s 55(2)(b).
27 CH(S)A 2011, s 27(2).
28 CH(S)A 2011, s 55(4).
29 CH(S)A 2011, s 55(5).
30 CH(S)A 2011, s 56(1).
31 CH(S)A 2011, s 56(2).
32 CH(S)A 2011, s 56(3).
33 CH(S)A 2011, s 48(3)(a).
34 CH(S)A 2011, s 48(3)(b).
35 CH(S)A 2011, s 48(1) and (2). The Reporter cannot bring an application to have the order terminated as opposed to varied: CH(S)A 2011, s 48(2).
36 CH(S)A 2011, s 49.
37 CH(S)A 2011, s 50.

38 CH(S)A 2011, s 51(2).
39 CH(S)A 2011, s 51(3).
40 CH(S)A 2011, s 51(4).
41 CH(S)A 2011, s 51(5)(a).
42 CH(S)A 2011, s 51(5)(b) and (c).
43 CH(S)A 2011, s 54(c).
44 CH(S)A 2011, s 54(d).
45 *NJ v Lord Advocate* 2013 SLT 347.
46 See *City of Edinburgh Council v C* 2012 GWD 38-758.

COMPULSORY SUPERVISION ORDERS

Information that a child may be in need of a compulsory supervision order

15.3 We have been considering the situation where a child enters the children's hearing system as a result of a child protection order. This is an emergency procedure which should only be used in exceptional circumstances. A child protection order is not intended as a long-term measure. The more usual route for entering the children's hearings system is that the Reporter receives information that a child may be in need of a compulsory supervision order. Any person who considers that a child is in need of 'protection, guidance, treatment or control' and that it might be necessary for a compulsory supervision order to be made in relation to the child may inform a Reporter[1]. A police constable has a duty to inform the Reporter if the constable considers that a child is in need of protection, guidance, treatment or control and that it might be necessary for a compulsory supervision order to be made in relation to the child.[2] Likewise, if a local authority acquires information, for example from social workers or school staff, that a child may be in need of a compulsory supervision order, the local authority must make all necessary inquiries into the child's circumstances and give the information to the Reporter.[3]

A court also has the power to refer a case to the Reporter, if during relevant proceedings[4] it is satisfied that one (or more) of the grounds for referral for a compulsory supervision order[5] – other than the commission by the child of an offence – exists.[6] Where criminal proceedings are not to be proceeded with against a child who has been detained in a place of safety, a police constable must inform the Reporter who can direct that the child be released from the place of safety or that the child remain there until the Reporter determines whether or not the child requires a compulsory supervision order.[7]

Under s 12(1A) of the Antisocial Behaviour etc (Scotland) Act 2004, if the sheriff makes an antisocial behaviour order and considers that a ground for referral – other than the offence ground – has been established, the sheriff can require the Principal Reporter to arrange a children's hearing.[8] Where a child or another person has pled guilty or been found guilty of a criminal offence, the court can remit the case to the Principal Reporter to arrange for the disposal of the case by a children's hearing.[9]

1 Children's Hearings (Scotland) Act 2011, s 64.
2 CH(S)A 2011, s 61.
3 CH(S)A 2011, s 60. This could involve the application for a child assessment order: for discussion, see para **14.5**.
4 CH(S)A 2011, s 62(5). That is actions for divorce, separation, declarator of marriage, declarator of nullity of marriage, dissolution of a civil partnership, separation of civil partners, nullity of a civil partnership, declarator of parentage, declarator of non-parentage, proceedings in relation to parental responsibilities and parental rights, applications for adoption orders or permanence orders, proceedings in relation to offences under the Education (Scotland) Act 1980 and an application for a forced marriage protection order under the Forced Marriage etc (Protection and Jurisdiction) (Scotland) Act 2011.
5 On these grounds, see para **15.7**.
6 CH(S)A 2011, s 62(1).
7 CH(S)A 2011, s 65. The Lord Advocate may direct that in any specified case or class of case that evidence lawfully obtained in the investigation of a crime or suspected crime be given to the Principal Reporter: CH(S)A 2011, s 63.
8 CH(S)A 2011, s 70. For the purposes of the children's hearing the ground is to be taken as established.
9 Criminal Procedure (Scotland) Act 1995, s 49. For the purposes of the children's hearing this is to be taken as conclusive evidence that the offence was committed by the child or the other person: CH(S)A 2011, s 71.

The role of the Reporter

15.4 When a child has entered the system by the routes described above, the decision whether or not to refer the case to a children's hearing is that of the Reporter. The Reporter (an officer of the Scottish Children's Reporter Administration) acts independently.[1] The Reporter, who need not have a legal background, has the right of audience before a sheriff, the Sheriff Principal or Sheriff Appeal Court.[2]

After having received the information, if it appears to the Reporter that a child might be in need of protection, guidance, treatment or control, the Reporter must determine whether grounds for referral exist and, if so, whether it is necessary for a compulsory supervision order to be made.[3] If the Reporter takes the view that no ground for referral exists or it is not necessary for a compulsory supervision order to be made, the Reporter must inform the child, each relevant person, the relevant local authority, any person specified in a child protection order and the persons who provided the information, of the decision not to proceed.[4] But note that this does not include persons who are entitled to request that information under s 179A(3) of the 2011 Act.[5] If the Reporter considers that the family may be able to benefit from social work support, the Reporter can refer the case to the relevant local authority to provide advice, guidance and assistance to the child and the family.[6] If the child is being kept in a place of safety, the Reporter must arrange for the child's release.[7]

However, if the Reporter feels that the child is in need of a compulsory supervision order, it is the Reporter's duty to arrange a children's hearing to consider the case[8] and to call upon the local authority for a report on the child and the child's social background. As we shall see, the Reporter has important powers and duties in relation to the conduct of the children's hearing and subsequent proceedings. The Reporter is, in effect, the lynchpin of the whole system and the importance of the role cannot be over-emphasised.

1 Children's Hearings (Scotland) Act 2011, s 22.
2 CH(S)A 2011, s 19.
3 CH(S)A 2011, s 66.
4 CH(S)A 2011, s 68(3) and (4).
5 See CH(S)A 2011, s 179A(4) for the persons to whom the Reporter may not provide information.
6 CH(S)A 2011, s 68(5).
7 CH(S)A 2011, s 68(2).
8 CH(S)A 2011, s 69(2). Note that, if the Reporter receives information under s 53 of the Criminal Justice (Scotland) Act 2016 and the child is being kept in a place of safety, then the Reporter must arrange a children's hearing no later than the third day after the Reporter receives such information: CH(S)A 2011, s 69(3).

The child and relevant persons

15.5 A 'child' is a person who is under the age of 16 (or between the ages of 16 and 18 if already subject to a compulsory supervision order).[1] The child must be present in Scotland at the date of the referral.[2]

A 'relevant person' includes:[3]

(a) A parent or guardian having parental responsibilities or parental rights in relation to the child. However, it is expressly provided that a parent does not have parental responsibilities or parental rights for this purpose merely by virtue of having a contact order or a specific issue order under ss 11(2)(d) or (e) of the Children (Scotland) Act 1995.[4] Read literally, this means that a father of a child is not a relevant person under this provision unless he has parental responsibilities and parental rights. Nor does he qualify as a relevant person under this provision even if he has a contact order in his favour. However, in *Principal Reporter v K*,[5] the Supreme Court held that where an unmarried father had established family life with the child, to deny him the status of a relevant person amounted to a breach of his European Convention on Human Rights, Article 8 right to respect for private and family life. Therefore, to avoid any incompatibility with the ECHR, the UK Supreme Court used s 3 of the Human Rights Act 1998 to construe the definition of a relevant person in s 93(2)(b) of the Children (Scotland) Act 1995 – which was the relevant legislation at that time – in such a way as to include, as a relevant person, a father who had established family life with his child.

In order to avoid a breach of Article 8 of ECHR, the Scottish Ministers provided in regulations[6] that all parents are within the definition of relevant persons (except those whose parental responsibilities and parental rights have been removed by court order).[7]

(b) A person in whom parental responsibilities or parental rights are vested under s 11(2)(b) of the Children (Scotland) Act 1995, *viz*, an order imposing parental responsibilities on a person and giving parental rights. This is the way that a child's relative, for example the child's grandparent, should proceed.

(c) A person having parental responsibilities or parental rights by virtue of s 11(12) of the Children (Scotland) Act 1995, *viz*, a person who has relevant responsibilities and rights by virtue of a residence order under s11(2)(c).

(d) A person in whom parental responsibilities or parental rights are vested by virtue of a permanence order.[8]

(e) Any other person specified by order made by Scottish Ministers.

A specific issue order cannot be made for the purpose of enabling a person to qualify as a relevant person.

A person who is not a relevant person by virtue of the above provisions, *must be deemed* to be a relevant person if a pre-hearing panel[9] considers that that person 'has (or has recently had) a significant involvement in the upbringing of the child'.[10] In *AG v Principal* Reporter,[11] the sheriff observed: 'Note the use of the word "must". The pre-hearing panel has no discretion once it is considered that there is or has recently been a significant involvement in the upbringing of the child or children.'[12] The children's hearing is not concerned with whether it is in the best interests of the child to deem the individual to be a relevant person. The test is purely factual rather than judgmental.[13] Nevertheless, it is not sufficient that the person has had *some* involvement in the child's upbringing: the involvement must have been significant so that the person's views are important when considering the welfare of the child.[14]

The matter of whether an individual should be deemed to be a relevant person must be referred to the pre-hearing panel by the Principal Reporter at the request of the individual making the request, the child or a relevant person in relation to the child.[15] The Principal Reporter also can refer the matter to the pre-hearing panel on his or her own initiative.[16] So, for example, the child's grandparent may be deemed to be a relevant person by a pre-hearing panel if he or she is playing a significant part in the upbringing of the child. If a person is deemed to be a relevant person, that person will have the right and duty to participate in subsequent hearings. There is a right of appeal to the sheriff from the pre-hearing panel's decision whether or not an individual should be deemed to be a relevant person.[17]

The case can be referred back to the pre-hearing panel to consider whether a person should no longer be deemed to be a relevant person. In *CF v MF and GF*[18] a 14-year-old girl requested that a pre-hearing panel consider removing deemed relevant person status from her grandparents on the basis that she had very little contact with her grandparents for several years, nor had they had any significant involvement in the child's upbringing.

---

1 Children's Hearings (Scotland) Act 2011, s 199. In relation to failure to attend school, a child includes a person over 16 who is not over 'school age': see s 31 of the Education (Scotland) Act 1980. Where the case has been remitted to the Principal Reporter under s 49 of the Criminal Procedure (Scotland) Act 1995, a child is any person 'over the age of 16 and not within six months of attaining the age of 18': s 49(6) of CP(S)A 1995.

2 See: *Principal Reporter v LZ* 2017 SLT 961 in which the nine-month-old child was removed from the mother's care while visiting the UK from their habitual residence in Poland.

3 CH(S)A 2011, s 200(1). Also included are parents and persons having parental responsibility under the Children Act 1989 and the Adoption and Children Act 2002.

4 CH(S)A 2011, s 200(2).

5 [2010] UKSC 56; [2011]1 WLR 18.

6 The Children's Hearings (Review of Contact Directions and Definition of Relevant Persons) Order 2013, para 3.

7 Ibid, para 3(2)(a)(ii).

8 See: s 80(2) of the Adoption and Children (Scotland) Act 2007.

9 The panel (or pre-hearing panel) consists of three members of the Children's Panel selected by the National Convener. See CH(S)A 2011, s 4 and Sch 2

10 CH(S)A 2011, s 81(3). See: *F and F v Principal Reporter*, Sheriff S F Murphy QC at Glasgow, 25th April 2014: 2014 FLB, 2014(Sept), 5–7 in which grandparents successfully appealed against a refusal of a children's hearing not to grant deemed relevant person status. The grandparents had visited, fed, cared for and made arrangements for the child to live with them after discharge from hospital. This was held to be sufficient to meet the conditions necessary for deemed relevant person status.

11 2013 SLT (Sh Ct) 125 (Foster carers deemed to be relevant persons).

12 Ibid, at para 3.

13 See: *CC v Locality Reporter* [2016] SAC (Civ) 13 in which it is re-stated that the welfare principle does not apply – the decision is purely factual.

14 See: *M, Appellant* 2014 Fam LR 55.

15 CH(S)A 2011, s 79(2)(a).

16 CH(S)A 2011, s 79(2)(b). See also: *AG v Principal Reporter* 2013 SLT (Sh Ct) 125.

17 CH(S)A 2011, s 160(2).

18 [2017] CSIH 44.

The children's hearing

15.6 Whether a child is in need of a compulsory supervision order and, if so, what steps should be taken to promote the child's welfare, are *prima facie* issues for a children's hearing. The National Convener of Children's Hearings Scotland is an independent officer who selects members of the children's hearing from the Children's Panel whose members have, in turn, been appointed by the National Convener and includes persons from all local authority areas.[1] The children's hearing consists of three members of the Children's Panel and the National Convener must ensure that it includes both male and female members and, so far as practicable, consists only of members who live and work in the local authority which is relevant for the child concerned in the hearing.[2] The National Convener may select one of the members of the children's hearing to chair the hearing.[3]

The National Convener may provide advice to the children's hearings about any matter in connection with carrying out their functions, for example, advice on the law,[4] procedural matters, the consequences of their decisions and how they are to be implemented. However, neither the National Convener nor the Principal Reporter can direct or guide the hearings on how they carry out their functions in a particular case.[5] In other words, the children's hearing is independent.

The members of the Children's Panel are ordinary members of the public who have an interest in helping children in need of care and support. The National Convener makes arrangements for the training of panel members and potential panel members. The training should involve persons under the age of 25 who have had experience of a children's hearing. In particular, the training must have regard to how panel members can best elicit the views of children. The performance of panel members may be monitored by the National Convener.[6]

A children's hearing was not intended to be a court. Its proceedings were intended to be relatively informal and conducted in private with the Reporter, the child and any relevant person present. Despite this original intention, persons taking part in children's hearings have the right to appeal to the sheriff against a relevant decision of a children's hearing or a pre-hearing panel. This often will involve the engagement of legal representation for the parties.[7] Children's legal aid may be available to parties.[8] In certain circumstances,[9] children's legal aid will be automatically available. It is worth noting that, in *S v Miller*,[10] the children's hearings system was challenged on the ground that it was incompatible with Article 6 of the European Convention on Human Rights.[11] The Inner House held that where the ground of referral[12] was that the child had committed an offence,[13] the child was *not* being charged with an offence. Consequently, the mandatory protections of Article 6(3) did not apply. But the court held that in every referral a child is entitled to a fair hearing under Article 6(1) of the European Convention. To avoid a violation of Article 6(1), the Lord President (Rodger) considered that the child was entitled to legal representation (and legal aid) at the hearing if:

(a) the child might be held in secure accommodation;[14]

(b) the case involved difficult issues of fact and law;

(c) because of his or her age or intelligence, it was difficult for the child to understand the issues involved; or

(d) the child could not present an effective case and therefore was unable to exercise his or her right of access to justice.

A children's hearing[15] or a sheriff[16] may appoint a safeguarder[17]where, for example, a case is considered particularly complex or where relationships between the family and the local authority have broken down. The duty of a safeguarder is to 'safeguard the interests of the child to whom the children's hearing relates'.[18] Where a safeguarder is required to provide a report to a children's hearing or to a sheriff in which a recommendation is made which assists in determining the matter, 'the safeguarder must, so far as is practicable and taking account of the age and maturity of the child: (a) give the child an opportunity to express his or her views; (b) have regard to any views expressed by the child; and (c) include the views of the child, and the means by which the child's views were obtained, in any report prepared for the children's hearing or the sheriff'.[19] A safeguarder has the right to appeal against a relevant decision of a children's hearing in relation to a child.[20]

Section 122 of the Children's Hearing (Scotland) Act 2011 introduced children's advocacy services to provide a child with support and representation for the purpose of assisting a child's involvement in a children's hearing.[21] It is the duty of the chairing member of a children's hearing to inform the child of the availability of the children's advocacy services.[22]

There is no doubt that, while the Kilbrandon principles and ethos remain in place, the children's hearings system is a far cry from that first envisaged by Lord Kilbrandon and now involves a much greater degree of legal formality. This is necessary to ensure conformity with the European Convention on Human Rights.

---

1 Children's Hearings (Scotland) Act 2011, ss 1, 2, 4, 6(2) and Sch 2.

2 CH(S)A 2011, ss 5 and 6(3)(a) and (b). The relevant local authority is the local authority where the child predominantly resides or where the child does not predominantly live in the area of a particular local authority, the local authority with which the child has the closest connection: CH(S)A 2011, s 201(1)(a) and (b).

3 CH(S)A 2011, s 6(4).

4 See *JS v Decision of a Children's Hearing* [2021] SC EDIN 1, in which the appellant successfully appealed against the decision of the children's hearing not to include measures that would allow a DNA test to be carried out to determine paternity. The panel sought the advice of the National Convenor (CH(S)A 2011, s 8) who advised that the test to be applied was one of 'necessity'. The hearing followed this advice and concluded that the DNA test was not necessary for the child's best interests. On appeal, the sheriff held that the advice given by the National Convenor was 'plainly wrong in law' and that, by following it, the hearing had also erred in law.

5 CH(S)A 2011, ss 8 and 9.

6 CH(S)A 2011, Sch 2 para 3.

7 For example, the child, a relevant person or a safeguarder can appeal against a decision of a children's hearing: CH(S)A 2011, s 154.

8 Children's legal aid is dealt with in s 28B–28F of the Legal Aid (Scotland) Act 1986. It is a complex process and its process and complexities are outwith the scope of this book.

9 LA(S)A 1986, s 28C.

10 2001 SLT 531. See also *S v Miller (No 2)* 2001 SLT 1304.

11 The text of Article 6 is to be found at para **14.1**.

12 Note that the CH(S)A 2011 uses the term 'ground *for* referral'.

13 See para **15.7**.

14 On secure accommodation, see para **15.10**.

15 CH(S)A 2011, s 30, and Part 4, generally.

16 CH(S)A 2011, s 31. The duty to safeguard the interests of the child applies also where the safeguarder is appointed by a sheriff: CH(S)A 2011, s 31(4).

17 For the role of the safeguarder, see Children's Hearings (Scotland) Act 2011 (Safeguarders: Further Provisions) Regulations 2012 (SSI 2012/336), para 8. For information about the training and tenure of safeguarders, see Children's Hearings (Scotland) Act 2011 (Safeguarders Panel) Amendments Regulations 2016 (SSI 2016/61).

18 CH(S)A 2011, s 30(1).

19 CH(S)A 2011(S:FP) Regulations 2012, para 7.

20 CH(S)A 2011, s 154.

21 CH(S)A 2011, s 122.
22 CH(S)A 2011, s 122(2).

The grounds for referral

15.7 Before a child will be considered to be in need of a compulsory supervision order, the Reporter must be satisfied that one or more grounds for referral exist. But even if there is a ground for referral, the Reporter is not obliged to refer the case to a children's hearing unless the Reporter takes the view that it is necessary that a compulsory supervision order be made.[1] The grounds for referral are listed in the 2011 Act, s 67(2):

(a) the child is likely to suffer unnecessarily, or the health or development of the child is likely to be seriously impaired, due to a lack of parental care.

This ground for referral is the most common ground on which a child is referred to the Reporter. 'A lack of parental care' includes care given by a person who is not the child's parent, but who has care or control of the child. The reasons for the lack of parental care are irrelevant; it is sufficient justification that the child is likely[2] to suffer unnecessarily without intervention. The standard that is applied to parental care is an objective one.[3] It is not necessary for the child actually to have suffered from a lack of parental care to give rise to this ground.

(b) a Schedule 1 offence has been committed in respect of the child.[4]

This ground applies if, on the balance of probabilities, an offence was committed against the child.[5] It is now considered proper to identify the perpetrator of the offence.[6] Even if the alleged perpetrator is identified, the balance of probabilities is still the correct standard of proof. It is irrelevant that the alleged perpetrator is ultimately acquitted of the offence in criminal proceedings.[7]

(c) the child has, or is likely to have, a close connection with a person who has committed a Schedule 1 offence.

For these purposes[8] a child is to be taken to have a close connection with a person: (a) if the child is a member of the same household as the person; or (b) the child is not a member of the same household as the person but the child has significant contact with the person.[9] Household has a wide meaning which is discussed below.

(d) the child is, or is likely to become, a member of the same household as a child in respect of whom a Schedule 1 offence has been committed.

Being a member of the same household is included in having a 'close connection'. In *Cunningham v M*,[10] the Sheriff Principal held that: 'the question of whether people are members of the same household is a question of fact and degree; the concept of "household" is of a group of persons and not the location in which they live; the fact that persons are living for the time being in separate houses is not decisive of the question whether they are members of the same household; the important question is whether the ties of affection and regular contact which hold the parties together as a group still continue; the criterion is that of relationship rather than locality'.[11] In *M v Locality Reporter*,[12] the Sheriff Appeal Court held that the child was not a member of the same household as the father. The mother and father did not cohabit; the willingness of the mother sporadically to supervise contact between the father and the child was not enough to create a tie of affection to hold the mother, the father and the child together a group.[13]

(e) the child is being, or is likely to be, exposed to persons whose conduct is (or has been) such that it is likely that:

(i) the child will be abused or harmed, or

(ii) the child's health, safety, or development will be seriously adversely affected.

'Persons' is not limited to adults and can include the child's own peer group. Also, the 'person' need not be a member of the same household as the child, or have a close connection with the child.

(f) the child has, or is likely to have, a close connection with a person who has carried out domestic abuse.

There is no definition of 'domestic abuse' in the 2011 Act. However, s 1 of the Domestic Abuse (Scotland) Act 2018 sets out behaviour towards a partner or ex-partner[14] that constitutes 'abusive behaviour'. Section 5 of the DA(S)A 2018 creates an aggravation to a s 1 offence where, at the time of the commission of the offence the abusive behaviour is directed at the child or the abuser makes use of the child in directing the behaviour to his or her partner or ex-partner. The offence of domestic abuse is also aggravated if the child sees, hears or is present during an incident of domestic abuse.[15] This ground applies where the child has, or is likely to have, a close connection with the person who is known to have carried out domestic abuse.[16]

(g) the child has, or is likely to have, a close connection with a person who has committed an offence under Parts 1, 4 or 5 of the Sexual Offences (Scotland) Act 2009.

This ground for referral gives the child further protection that goes beyond the s 67(2)(c) ground for referral ('the child has, or is likely to have, a close connection with a person who has committed a schedule 1 offence') by extending the protection to include offences under Parts 1, 4 or 5 of the Sexual Offences (Scotland) Act 2009. Offences under these Parts of the 2009 Act include offences where the victims are not children.

(h) the child is being provided with accommodation by a local authority under s 25 of the Children (Scotland) Act 1995[17] and special measures are needed to support the child.

'Special measures' is taken to mean those additional supports required by the child to enable 'protection, guidance, treatment or control'.

(i) a permanence order[18] is in force in respect of the child and special measures are needed to support the child.

(j) the child has committed an offence.

The Children's Hearings (Scotland) Act 2011 proceeds on the basis that when a child commits a criminal offence this is merely symptomatic often of the dysfunction of the child's upbringing and family life. In keeping with the Kilbrandon principles, the child who commits an offence is therefore in need of care and protection, not punishment.[19]

The age of criminal responsibility was increased in December 2021 from age 8 to age 12.[20] This means that a child under the age of 12 cannot be referred to a children's hearing under the s 67(2)(j) ground for referral.[21] Where the Reporter receives information that a child under the age of 12 may have been involved in behaviour which would, ordinarily, amount to a crime, and it appears to the Reporter that he child might be in need of protection, guidance, treatment or control,[22] it will be for the Reporter to decide which s 67(2) ground for referral (other than s 67(2)(j)) is most relevant to the child.[23]

Where a child aged 12 and over is brought before a children's hearing on the criminal offence ground for referral, the ground must be established to the standard of proof which applies in criminal proceedings, namely, 'beyond reasonable doubt'.[24]

(k) the child has misused alcohol;

(l) the child has misused a drug, whether or not a controlled drug within the meaning of the Misuse of Drugs Act 1971.

This includes the child misusing medicinal drugs for non-medicinal purposes.

(m) the child's conduct has had, or is likely to have, a serious adverse effect on the health, safety or development of the child or another person.

This may include, for example, the child becoming involved in risk-taking behaviour that might include sexual behaviour, self-harm, drug-taking, bullying.

(n) the child is beyond the control of a relevant person.

The reason that a child may be beyond the control of a relevant person can be a consequence of poor parenting that results, for example, in the child being exposed to risk or danger. It may also arise where a child has needs, the care of which, goes beyond the normal ability of the parent, for example, autism, a medical condition or behavioural needs that require specialist intervention. It is not necessary for a failure or lack of parenting skills for a child to be referred to the Reporter under this ground for referral. The referral will be based on the needs of the child.

(o) the child has failed to attend school regularly without reasonable excuse.

This ground applies only to children of school age.[25]

In the absence of an allegation of misconduct on the child's part, it has been held that an order excluding the child from school is a reasonable excuse for non-attendance.

(p) the child –

(i) has been, or is likely to be, subject to physical, emotional or other pressure to enter into a civil partnership, or

(ii) is, or is likely to become, a member of the same household as such a child.[26]

A person is not eligible to enter a civil partnership until he or she reaches the age of 16,[27] at which age, the young person cannot be referred to a children's hearing.[28] However, s 67(2)(p)(ii) will facilitate the protection of a child who may be, or may become, a member of the same household where pressure was exacted on a person to enter a civil partnership.

(q) the child –

(i) has been, or is being or is likely to be forced into a marriage (that expression being construed in accordance with s 1 of the Forced Marriage etc, (Protection and Jurisdiction) (Scotland) Act 2011), or

(ii) is, or is likely to become, a member of the same household as such a child.

The word 'force' is defined in s 1(6) of the FM(P&J)(S) A 2011.[29] While persons cannot marry in Scotland until age 16,[30] situations may arise where a child is forced to agree to enter a marriage on reaching adulthood. It may be that a child – female or male – is sent furth of Scotland with the intention that a forced marriage take place elsewhere.[31] A referral under s 67(2)(q) will be appropriate where information is passed to the Reporter in relation to a child who may be the victim of pressure to marry against his or her wishes or who is, or is likely to become, a member of the same household where a forced marriage has already taken place, perhaps a sibling of the child. Note that a 'protected person'[32] or a local authority[33] can make an application to the sheriff for a Forced Marriage Protection Order to protect the person from being forced into a marriage or from any attempt to force the person into a marriage or to protect a person who has been forced into a marriage.[34]

---

1 Children's Hearings (Scotland) Act 2011, s 66(2).
2 See: *M v McClafferty* [2007] CSIH 88, in which it was stated that 'likely' was 'not probably' or 'more likely than not' but 'there was a significant or substantial risk of the events … occurring in the future'. See also: *KH v Children's Reporter* [2016] SC GLA 18; [2016] 3 WLUK 142.
3 See: *M v McGregor* 1982 SLT 41, at p 43, in which the Inner House stated that the standard applied to 'lack of parental care' was an objective one: 'namely whether a reasonable person looking to the circumstances of the particular case would consider that this child is likely to be caused unnecessary suffering or serious impairment to [his or her] health or development through lack of parental care on the part of the [parent]'.
4 That is an offence listed in Schedule 1 to the Criminal Procedure (Scotland) Act 1995, which lists offences against children under the age of 17 years. Offences include physical and sexual abuse of a child, actual, or the risk of, female genital mutilation, and taking indecent photographs of children under 17.
5 *S v Kennedy* 1987 SLT 667. See also: *AW v Principal Reporter* 2022 Fam LR 13.
6 *AW v Principal Reporter* 2022 Fam LR 13, at para [23], the Sheriff Appeal Court stated: 'In our opinion, in the modern context it is both competent and appropriate that in applications for grounds of referral in terms of section 67(2)(b) sheriffs identify the perpetrator of criminal conduct in referral proceedings, at least where he or she is named in the supporting facts.'
7 *Harris v F* 1991 SLT 242. See also *H v HM Advocate* 2019 SLT 943 and *U v Locality Reporter Manager* [2021] CSIH 65.
8 And grounds (f) and (g).
9 CH(S)A 2011, s 67(3).
10 2005 SLT (Sh Ct) 73.
11 Ibid, para [26]. See also *McGregor v H* 1983 SLT 626, *A v Kennedy* 1993 SLT 1188.
12 [2016] SAC (Civ) 16.
13 Ibid, para [13].
14 Domestic Abuse (Scotland) Act 2018 s 11. 'Partner' is a spouse, civil partner or cohabitant.
15 DA(S)A 2018, s 5(1), (2), (3).
16 See the discussion on 'close connection' for ground for referral 67(2)(d) (above), and *M v Locality Reporter* [2016] SAC (Civ) 16.
17 On Children (Scotland) Act 1995, s 25, see para **14.2**.
18 On permanence orders, see paras **13.13** and **14.7**.
19 See generally *Report on Children and Young Persons* (the Kilbrandon Report) Cmnd 2306 upon which the Social Work (Scotland) Act 1968 was based and which, in this

respect, continues to be followed in the CH(S)A 2011. In *S v Miller* 2001 SLT 531, the Inner House held that where a referral was brought on this ground the child was not being charged with a criminal offence for the purposes of Article 6(3) of the European Convention on Human Rights; for text of Article 6 see para **14.1**.

20 Criminal Procedure (Scotland) Act 1995, s 41.

21 Age of Criminal Responsibility (Scotland) Act 2019, s 3. This section came into force in November 2019.

22 CH(S)A 2011, s 66(1) and s 69(1) and (2).

23 A concerning consequence of this is that, where a child under 12 has engaged in criminal activity and is brought before a hearing on a ground for referral other than s 67(2)(j), it is within the remit of the Reporter to prove that the child's activity amounts to criminal behaviour, yet the standard of proof to be applied is the civil standard, namely, on the balance of probabilities, and not the criminal standard of beyond reasonable doubt, thus denying the child the fundamental protections expected by an accused. For a full discussion, see: Mark Allison, *The Age of Criminal Responsibility (Scotland) Act 2019 – The present, the future and a cautionary note*, Fam LB 2022, 175, 1–4.

24 CH(S)A 2011, s 102(3). See Lord President Rodger judgment in *Constanda v M* 1997 STL 1396, at 1398.

25 Education (Scotland) Act 1980, s 31. Note that, even where a pupil has attained the age of 16, he or she may not be eligible to leave school until the 'summer leaving date' (last day of May) or the 'winter leaving date' (appropriate date in December) and, as such, will remain of school age until such dates. This means that a referral may be made under s 67(2)(o) for a pupil (who is not already subject to a compulsory supervision order: s 199(6) and (7)) who has attained the age of 16 but has not yet reached school leaving age. But see: *O v Rae* 1993 SLT 570.

26 On marriages or civil partnerships entered into under duress, see para **2.18**.

27 Civil Partnership Act 2004, s 86(c).

28 Unless that young person is already subject to a compulsory supervision order: CH(S)A 2011, s 199(6) and (7).

29 See also Marriage (Scotland) Act 1977, s 20A where a marriage entered into by reason only of duress is void.

30 M(S)A 1980, s 1(1).

31 For discussion on forced marriage, see para **2.18.**

32 FM(P&J)(S)A 2011, s 1(1)

33 Or the Lord Advocate, or a person specified by Scottish Ministers: FM(P&J)(S)A 2011, s 3(1) and (7).

34 See *City of Edinburgh Council v S* 2015 SLT (Sh Ct) 69. See also *C v T* [2021] 5 WLUK 395.

Procedure in referrals

15.8 Where a case is referred by the Reporter to a children's hearing, the child has the right to attend all stages of the hearing[1] and is obliged to do so.[2] However, the child can be excused from attending all or part of the hearing if the children's hearing is satisfied that:

(a) the hearing relates to the ground mentioned in s 67(2)(b), (c), (d) or (g) and the attendance of the child at the hearing, or that part of the hearing, is not necessary for a fair hearing; or

(b) attendance of the child at the hearing, or that part of the hearing, would place the child's physical, mental or moral welfare at risk; or

(c) taking account of the child's age and maturity, the child would not be capable of understanding what happens at the hearing or that part of the hearing.[3]

The question whether the child's attendance should be excused can be determined by a pre-hearing panel. It is the Reporter's responsibility to secure the attendance of a child whose attendance at the hearing has not been excused. If such a child fails to attend, the Reporter can apply to a children's hearing which on cause shown can grant a warrant to secure the child's attendance at the hearing.[4] The warrant authorises a police officer to apprehend the child, take the child to a place of safety and bring the child to the hearing.[5] Whether or not a warrant to secure attendance is granted, the grounds hearing[6] may, where the child has failed to attend, require the Reporter to arrange another grounds hearing.[7] Because the child has a statutory right to be present, the child can insist on attending, even where the child has been excused from attending.[8]

Where a children's hearing is considering a child's case, a relevant person has the right to attend all stages of the hearing[9] and is obliged to do so.[10] Where a relevant person is required to attend a hearing and fails to do so, this is a criminal offence.[11] But if it is appropriate to do so the hearing can proceed in the relevant person's absence. However, a relevant person's attendance may be excused if the children's hearing is satisfied that it would be unreasonable to require that person's attendance or that person's attendance is unnecessary for the proper consideration of the matter before the hearing.[12] The question whether a relevant person's attendance should be excused can be determined by a pre-hearing panel.[13]

The children's hearing can exclude a relevant person (and his or her representative) from any part(s) of the hearing for so long as it is necessary in the interests of the child where the hearing is satisfied that it must do so in order to obtain the child's views or because the presence of the relevant person is causing, or is likely to cause, significant distress to the child.[14] After the relevant person (or representative) has returned, the chairing member of the hearing must explain to the relevant person what has taken place during the excluded person's absence.[15]

The Reporter is under a duty to prepare a statement of the grounds for referral which the Reporter believes apply to the case and the supporting facts on which that belief is based.[16] A children's hearing is then arranged. This first hearing is known as a grounds hearing. When the child and the relevant persons appear, it is the chairing member's duty to explain to them the ground(s) for referral and the supporting facts in relation to the ground(s). The chairing member then asks them whether they accept that each ground applies in relation to the child and that they accept each of the supporting facts.[17] If the relevant person(s) and the child accept each ground for referral, the hearing will then consider how best to dispose of the case.[18] The hearing can also dispose of the case if at least one of the grounds is accepted and the hearing considers it appropriate to consider making a compulsory supervision order on the basis of the ground(s) that was accepted.[19]

The hearing can defer a decision on whether or not to make a compulsory supervision order until a subsequent children's hearing.[20] Notwithstanding, if the grounds hearing considers that the nature of the child's circumstances is such that for the protection, guidance, treatment or control of the child it is necessary as a matter of urgency that a compulsory supervision order be made, the hearing can make an interim compulsory supervision order.[21] The interim order comes to an end at the next hearing arranged for the child or the expiry of 22 days beginning with the date the interim order was made, whichever is earlier.[22] But before the expiry of the interim order, the Reporter can apply to a sheriff for an extension of the interim compulsory supervision order which in turn can be further extended by the sheriff.[23] The extended order expires 22 days after the order was extended unless it is further extended.[24]

If the grounds hearing considers that it is necessary to do so for the purpose of obtaining any further information or carrying out any further investigation that is needed before the subsequent children's hearing, the grounds hearing can make a medical examination order.[25] This can contain the following measures:[26]

(a) a requirement that the child attend or reside at a specified clinic, hospital or other establishment;

(b) a requirement that a specified local authority arrange a specified medical examination of the child. But if the child has capacity under s 2(4) of the Age of Legal Capacity (Scotland) Act 1991,[27] the child can refuse consent;[28]

(c) a prohibition on the disclosure of the place specified in (a);

(d) a secure accommodation authorisation;[29]

(e) a direction regulating contact between the child and a specified person or class of person;

(f) any other specified condition appearing to the children's hearing to be appropriate for the purposes of ensuring that the child complies with the order.

If the grounds hearing decides not to defer making a decision, it must make a compulsory supervision order if satisfied that it is necessary to do so for the protection, guidance, treatment or control of the child. If it is not so satisfied, the children's hearing must discharge the referral.[30]

If either the child or a relevant person does not accept the ground(s) for referral,[31] unless they are prepared to discharge the referral, the hearing must direct the Reporter to make an application to the sheriff for a determination on whether each ground not accepted by the child or relevant person is established.[32] The chairing member must explain to the child and the relevant person the purpose of the application and inform the child that he or she must attend the hearing before the sheriff unless the sheriff excuses the child's attendance.[33] If it considers that it is necessary to do so, the hearing can make an interim compulsory supervision order.[34] If, before the disposal of the application to the sheriff, the interim compulsory supervision order ceases to have effect, the Reporter may arrange a children's hearing or to consider whether a further interim compulsory supervision order should be made.[35] The children's hearing can make the further order if it is necessary to do so unless it would be the third such order in consequence of the original interim compulsory supervision order.[36]

Where the child is not capable of understanding or has not understood the explanation of the ground(s) for referral, then the hearing must direct the Reporter to make an application to the sheriff[37] to determine whether the ground(s) is established or to discharge the referral in relation to the ground(s).[38] Again, if it is necessary to do so, an interim compulsory supervision order can be made.[39]

The application by the Reporter must be heard by the sheriff within 28 days of being lodged.[40] Unless excused, the child has a duty to attend.[41] The sheriff can release the child from the obligation to attend where:

(a) the hearing relates to a ground mentioned in s 67(2)(b), (c), (d) or (g) and the child's attendance is not necessary for a fair hearing of the application;

(b) the attendance of the child at the hearing, or a part of the hearing, would place the child's physical, mental or moral welfare at risk; or

(c) taking account of the child's age and maturity, the child would not be capable of understanding what happens at the hearing or part of the hearing.[42]

If the child fails to attend, the sheriff may grant a warrant to secure the child's attendance.[43] The child and the relevant persons have the right to be represented.[44]

The onus lies with the Reporter to establish by evidence that the ground(s) for referral exist. The sheriff can dispense with hearing evidence if:

(i) the child and the relevant persons accept the ground(s) before the application is determined;[45] or

(ii) the application has been brought because of the child's incapacity to understand the explanation of the grounds and the relevant persons accept the grounds.[46]

In these circumstances the grounds for referral are deemed to have been established.

The standard of proof normally required is that on the balance of probabilities the ground(s) exist.[47] There is no need for corroboration.[48] There is an important exception. When the ground for referral is that the *child* has committed an offence, the standard of proof is the criminal standard, ie, it must be proved to the sheriff beyond reasonable doubt that the child committed the offence and corroboration is required.[49]

If the sheriff decides that none of the grounds for referral is established, the sheriff must dismiss the application and discharge the referral.[50] If a ground for referral is established (or deemed to be established), the sheriff must remit the case to the Reporter to arrange a children's hearing to consider and determine the case.[51] The sheriff can make an interim compulsory supervision order if it is necessary to do so.[52]

Where the sheriff makes a determination that a ground(s) for referral has been established – a grounds determination – the child or a relevant person has the right to apply to a sheriff for a review of the grounds determination.[53]

---

1 Children's Hearings (Scotland) Act 2011, s 78(1)(a).
2 CH(S)A 2011, s 73(2).
3 CH(S)A 2011, s 73(3). Where the children's hearing is a grounds hearing, the child can only be excused from attending the hearing to hear the grounds explained if the child is incapable of understanding the explanation: CH(S)A 2011, s 73(4). If the child is able to attend hearings or parts of hearings then he or she should be encouraged to do so. Section 73(3)(b) should not be invoked in situations where it is more convenient that the child does not attend. The criteria in this section should underpin the reason for the child's non-attendance.
4 CH(S)A 2011, s 123.
5 CH(S)A 2011, s 88(1). A warrant may include a secure accommodation authorisation: s 88(2). The warrant expires seven days after the child has been first detained or the beginning of the hearing if earlier: s 88(4). In *Martin v N* 2004 SC 358 the Inner House of the Court of Session held that the child's detention under the parallel provisions under the previous law was not in breach of Article 5 of the European Convention (right to liberty and security) because it fell within the proviso in Article 5(d) *viz* 'the detention of a minor by lawful order for the purpose of educational supervision or his lawful detention for the purpose of bringing him before the competent legal authority'.
6 CH(S)A 2011, s 202(1) and s 90.
7 CH(S)A 2011, s 95. The grounds hearing can make an interim compulsory supervision order if it is necessary as a matter of urgency for the protection, guidance, treatment or control of the child.
8 CH(S)A 2011, s 78(1)(a).
9 CH(S)A 2011, s 78(1)(c). Unlike the child's right to attend, the relevant person's right is expressly subject to the children's hearing's power to exclude a relevant person under s 76(2).
10 CH(S)A 2011, s 74(2).

11 CH(S)A 2011, s 74(4).
12 CH(S)A 2011, s 74(3).
13 CH(S)A 2011, s 79(3).
14 CH(S)A 2011, s 76(1) and (2) and s 77(1) and (2).
15 CH(S)A 2011, s 76(3) and s 77(3). This may satisfy any potential breach of Articles 6 and 8 of the European Convention on Human Rights: *McMichael v United Kingdom* 51/1993/446/525.
16 CH(S)A 2011, s 89.
17 CH(S)A 2011, s 90(1) and (1A). The chairing member must ask the child whether the documentation accurately reflects any views the child expressed before the hearing; CH(S)A 2011, s 121.
18 CH(S)A 2011, s 91(1)(a).
19 CH(S)A 2011, s 91(1)(b).
20 CH(S)A 2011, s 91(2). For example, the hearing may wish to appoint a safeguarder.
21 CH(S)A 2011, s 92(2).
22 CH(S)A 2011, s 86(3)(a) and (d).
23 CH(S)A 2011, ss 98 and 99.
24 CH(S)A 2011, s 86(3)(e).
25 CH(S)A2011, s 92(3).
26 CH(S)A 2011, s 87(2).
27 Discussed at para **10.2**.
28 CH(S)A 2011, s 186.
29 Discussed at para **15.10**.
30 CH(S)A 2011, s 91(3).
31 Or where at least one of the grounds has been accepted but the hearing does not consider it appropriate to make a compulsory supervision order on the basis of the ground(s) that has been accepted.
32 CH(S)A 2011, s 93(2).
33 CH(S)A 2011, s 93(4).
34 CH(S)A 2011, s 93(5).
35 CH(S)A 2011, s 96(3).
36 CH(S)A 2011, s 96(4). Before the expiry of the 66 days, if a further extension of the interim compulsory supervision order is necessary, the Reporter can apply to a sheriff for the further extension of the interim order. The sheriff can then further extend the interim orders as necessary: CH(S)A 2011, ss 98 and 99.
37 Unless the hearing discharges the case.
38 CH(S)A 2011, s 94(1) and (2).
39 CH(S)A 2011, s 94(5).
40 CH(S)A 2011, s 101(2).
41 CH(S)A 2011, s 103(2).
42 CH(S)A 2011, s 103(3).
43 CH(S)A 2011, s 103(5).
44 CH(S)A 2011, s 104(2) and (3). The person representing the child or relevant person at the hearing need not be a solicitor or advocate: CH(S)A 2011, s 104(4).
45 CH(S)A 2011, s 105.

46 CH(S)A 2011, s 106(1). However, the child, relevant person, a safeguarder and the Reporter can request that a hearing be held and the sheriff may consider that it is not appropriate to determine the application without a hearing: CH(S)A 2011, s 106(3) and (4).
47 *Harris v F* 1991 SLT 242.
48 Civil Evidence (Scotland) Act 1988, s 1(1).
49 CH(S)A 2011, s 102(3). If the offence cannot be proved beyond reasonable doubt, the child's alleged criminal act cannot *per se* establish the existence of another ground on the balance of probabilities test: *Constanda v M* 1997 SC 217.
50 CH(S)A 2011, s 108(3).
51 C(S)A 2011, s 108(2).
52 CH(S)A 2011, s 109(3).
53 CH(S)A 2011, ss 110–117.

Disposal of the case

15.9 If the child and the relevant persons accept the ground(s) for referral or if the ground(s) for referral have been established in proceedings before the sheriff, the children's hearing will then consider whether a compulsory supervision order should be made in respect of the child.[1] The hearing will have the social work report and any other relevant information. If the hearing considers that further investigation is necessary into the child's circumstances, the case can be deferred.[2] If the children's hearing decides to defer the children's hearing (held in accordance with s 119) and it considers that the nature of the child's circumstances is such that for the protection, guidance treatment or control of the child it is necessary to make an interim compulsory supervision order or a medical examination order, it can do so.[3]

1 Children's Hearing's (Scotland) Act 2011, s 119(3). This is also the situation where the case has been referred to the Reporter by a court which is satisfied in relevant proceedings that a ground for referral exists.
2 C(S)A 2011, s 119(2).
3 CH(S)A 2011, s 120.

Children in need of compulsory supervision orders

15.10 The children's hearing must proceed on the course which, in its view, is in the best interests of the child: the welfare of the child throughout the child's childhood is the paramount consideration.[1] The child's views must be taken into account.[2] Where the children's hearing is satisifed that no further action is required, it must discharge the referral.[3] However if the hearing is satisfied that it is necessary for the protection, guidance, treatment or control of the child to make a compulsory supervision order it must do so.[4] In doing so, the hearing is under a duty to consult the child and must be satisfied that it is better for the child to make a compulsory supervision order than that none be made at all.[5]

The compulsory supervision order contains measures which the hearing considers necessary to safeguard and promote the child's welfare.[6] The same measures can be made in interim compulsory supervision orders.[7] It also specifies the local authority which is to be responsible for giving effect to the measures included in the order (the implementation authority).[8] The measures include:

(i) a requirement that the child reside at a specified place,[9] for example with kinship carers or foster carers; or within residential care or secure accommodation. A direction can be made authorising the person in charge of the establishment in which the child is to reside to restrict the child's liberty as that person considers appropriate having regard to the measures included in the order, for example to ensure that the child receives counselling at a particular time and place.[10] Disclosure of the place where the child resides can be prohibited.[11]

(ii) a movement restriction condition. This restricts the child's movements and may require the child to comply with arrangements specified in the condition for monitoring the child's compliance with the restriction.[12] A movement restriction condition can only be made if (a) the child had previously absconded and is likely to abscond again and, if the child were to abscond it is likely that the child's physical, mental or moral welfare would be at risk, or (b) the child is likely to engage in self-harming conduct, or (c) the child is likely to cause injury to another person and the children's hearing is satisfied that it is necessary to include a movement restriction order.[13] If the hearing considers the movement restriction condition is necessary to protect members of the public from serious harm, the welfare of the child is not the paramount consideration but remains a primary consideration.[14]

(iii) a secure accommodation authorisation. This requires the child to reside at a residential establishment which contains secure and not secure accommodation.[15] The authorisation allows the child to be placed and kept in secure accommodation within the establishment.[16] An authorisation can only be made if (a) the child has previously absconded and is likely to abscond again and, if the child were to abscond, it is likely that the child's physical, mental or moral welfare would be at risk or (b) the child is likely to engage in self-harming conduct or (c) the child is likely to cause injury to another person and, having considered the other options available – including a movement restriction condition – the children's hearing is satisfied that it is necessary to include a secure accommodation authorisation.[17] If the hearing considers that a secure accommodation authorisation is necessary to protect the public from serious harm, the welfare of the child is not the paramount consideration but remains a primary consideration.[18] The chief social worker can only implement the secure accommodation authorisation with the consent of the person in charge of the residential establishment containing the secure accommodation.[19] There is an appeal to the sheriff in respect of any decision to implement the authorisation.[20]

(iv) a requirement that the implementation authority arrange a medical (or other) examination of, or treatment for, the child;[21] but if the child has capacity under s 2(4) of the Age of Legal Capacity (Scotland) Act 1991,[22] the child can refuse to consent.[23]

(v) a direction regulating contact between the child and a specified person or class of person, for example the child's parents and family. The hearing must consider whether a contact requirement should be made.[24] It should be noted that new subsections (3), (4) and (5) were added to s 29A of the CH(S)A 2011[25] and came into force in July 2021. These impose a duty on a children's hearing[26] when making, varying or continuing a compulsory supervision order[27] in relation to a child, to consider whether to include a measure directing contact between the child and another person. That duty is to consider the inclusion of a measure regulating contact between the child and a person with whom the child does not reside, for example, a relevant person, a sibling[28] or any other person with whom the child has resided and with whom the child has an ongoing relationship with the character of a relationship between siblings, eg, a peer member(s) of a foster family in which the child has resided and with whom the child has built up a sibling-like relationship.

(vi) a requirement that the child comply with any other specified condition, for example to receive counselling or psychiatric support.[29]

(vii) a requirement that the implementation authority carry out specified duties in relation to the child.[30]

A compulsory supervision order ceases to have effect on the day one year after it was made unless it has been continued. If it has been continued, it ends on the day one year after it was last continued. The order will automatically come to an end on the day the child attains age 18.[31]

However, the compulsory supervision order should not continue any longer than is necessary in the interests of the child. The Reporter must initiate a review of a compulsory supervision order by a children's hearing if the order will expire within three months and it would not otherwise be reviewed before it expires.[32] The implementation authority must by notice to the Reporter require a review if it considers that the order should be terminated or varied or is not being complied with, or that the child should be subject to a permanence order or be placed for adoption.[33] Moreover, and perhaps even more importantly, the child, any relevant person or any person afforded the opportunity to participate in the hearing have the right to require a review of the compulsory supervision order by giving notice to the Reporter to have the order reviewed by a children's hearing.[34] A person not afforded the opportunity to participate in the most recent hearing that made a decision in respect of a compulsory supervision order, may also require a review if they meet the required conditions.[35] A requirement to review a compulsory supervision order may not be made during the three months beginning with the day on which the order is made.[36] On review, the children's hearing may continue the order, vary the order, or terminate it.

The child or relevant person or the appointed safeguarder may appeal to the sheriff against any decision of the children's hearing.[37] The appeal must be made before the expiry of 21 days beginning with the day on which the decision was made.[38] An appeal is competent not only in relation to the making of the compulsory supervision order itself but also as to any of the measures it contains.[39] The sheriff may hear evidence from the child, a relevant person, a report writer, the Reporter, the person in charge of the specified secure accommodation, social work and any other person who may give material additional evidence.[40]

If the sheriff is satisfied that the decision of the children's hearing is justified, the sheriff must confirm the decision. If the circumstances of the child have changed since the decision was made, the sheriff may take steps[41] to: (a) require the Reporter to arrange a further children's hearing; (b) continue, vary or terminate the order, interim variation of the order, or warrant; (c) discharge the child from attending further hearings in relation to which the order was made;[42] (d) make an interim compulsory supervision order or interim variation of a compulsory supervision order; or (e) grant a warrant to secure attendance.

If the sheriff is satisfied that the decision of the children's hearing is not justified the sheriff must: recall any warrant to secure attendance; and, if in place, terminate any interim compulsory supervision order or medical examination order.[43] The sheriff may also take one or more of the steps in s 156(3) and (3A) (see above).

If satisfied that the appeal was frivolous or vexatious the sheriff can order that for a period of 12 months from the date of the order the person who appealed must obtain leave from the sheriff before making another appeal.[44]

There can be further appeals from the sheriff to the Sheriff Appeal Court[45] and the Court of Session.[45]

Such appeals are restricted to points of law or any procedural irregularity.[46]

The implementation authority must give effect to the compulsory supervision order.[47] This includes securing or facilitating the provision of services for the child.[48] The child is regarded as being looked after by the local authority.[49] Consequently the principles in s 17 of the Children (Scotland) Act 1995 Act which determine how a local authority is to look after the child apply. Where the child is residing with the child's own family, the implementation authority must from time investigate whether any conditions imposed by the order are being complied with while the child is living there.[50]

If it appears to a children's hearing that the implementation authority is in breach of these duties, the hearing may direct the National Convener to give notice to the authority of an intended application by the Convener to enforce the authority's duty.[51] The Convener's notice must set out the respects in which the authority is in breach and state that if the authority does not perform the duty within 21 days, the National Convener at the direction of the hearing will make an application for the enforcement of the duty.[52] At the same time the National Convener sends a copy of the notice to the child and each relevant person.[53] If the hearing gives such direction, it must require a further review of the order and if on that further review it appears that the authority is still in breach of its duty, the hearing can direct the National Convener to make the application.[54] In determining whether to direct the National Convener to make an application, the hearing must *not* take into account the adequacy of the means available to the local authority to enable it to comply with the duty.[55] The National Convener makes the application to the Sheriff Principal who can order the implementation authority to carry out its duties in respect of the compulsory supervision order.[56]

---

1 Children's Hearings (Scotland) Act 2011, s 25(2).
2 CH(S)A 2011, s 27. Note that, at the time of writing (July 2022), s 27(3) and (4) of CH(S)A 2011 remain in force but will be repealed and replaced with s 27(3), (4) and (4A) on the coming into force of s 3 of Children (Scotland) Act 2022. The main gist of the updated law is that the child will be given the opportunity to express his or her views 'in a manner that the child prefers' and that 'the child is presumed to be capable of forming a view unless the contrary is shown'.
3 CH(S)A 2011, s 119(3)(b).
4 CH(S)A 2011, s 119(3)(a).
5 CH(S)A 2011, s 28(2).
6 CH(S)A 2011, s 83(1)(a).
7 CH(S)A 2011, s 86(1)(a).
8 CH(S)A 2011, s 83(1)(b).
9 CH(S)A 2011, s 83(2)(a).
10 CH(S)A 2011, s 83(2)(b).
11 CH(S)A 2011, s 83(2)(c).
12 CH(S)A 2011, ss 83(2)(d) and s 84.
13 CH(S)A 2011, s 83(4) and (6).
14 CH(S)A 2011, s 26.

15 Or two establishments one of which is not secure accommodation.
16 CH(S)A 2011, s 83(2)(e) and s 85.
17 CH(S)A 2011, s 83(5) and (6).
18 CH(S)A 2011, s 26.
19 CH(S)A 2011, s 151(3). See also: CH(S)A 2011, s 135, s 136 and ss 151–153. The implementation of secure accommodation authorisation is the subject of detailed regulations. See the Children's Hearings (Scotland) Act 2011 (Rules of Procedure in Children's Hearings) Rules 2013 (SSI 2013/194), rr 94, 95 and 96.
20 CH(S)A 2011, s 162.
21 CH(S)A 2011, s 83(2)(f).
22 Discussed at para **10.2**.
23 CH(S)A 2011, s 186.
24 CH(S)A 2011, s 83(2)(g).
25 Sections 29A(3), (4) and (5) were added into the CH(S)A 2011 by s 14 of the Children (Scotland) Act 2020. See: *ABC v Principal Reporter* 2020 [UKSC] 26. This is a very important case in relation to the status of siblings in children's hearings.
26 The duty under s 29A(3), (4) and (5) also apply to cases before a sheriff. See: *Locality Reporter Manager v AM* [2017] SAC (Civ) 36.
27 This includes an interim compulsory supervision order: CH(S)A 2011, s 86(1)(a).
28 CH(S)A 2011, s 29A(5). See also C(S)A 1995, s 17(1A) and (1B).
29 CH(S)A 2011, s 83(2)(h).
30 CH(S)A 2011, s 83(2)(i).
31 CH(S)A 2011, s 83(7).
32 CH(S)A 2011, s 133.
33 CH(S)A 2011, s 131.
34 CH(S)A 2011, s 132(2), (3), (3A) and (6). See CH(S)A 2011, s 79(2)(ba), s 132(8)(a) and s 79(5ZA)s for the criteria to be 'afforded an opportunity to participate' in the hearing.
35 CH(S)A 2011, s 132A. The required conditions are set out in s 132A(3) and (4).
36 If the order was continued or varied, then a requirement to review may not be made during the period of three months beginning with the day on which the order was continued or varied.
37 CH(S)A 2011, s 154(1): the appeal must be made within 21 days beginning with the day the decision was made by the children's hearing.
38 CH(S)A 2011, s 154(5).
39 CH(S)A 2011, s 154(3).
40 CH(S)A 2011, s 155(5).
41 CH(S)A 2011, s 156(4).
42 CH(S)A 2011, s 156(1), (3) and (3A).
43 CH(S)A 2011, s 156(2).
44 CH(S)A 2011, s 159. See *CM, Appellant* [2017] 9 WLUK 178, *B v Locality Reporter* [2017] SAC (Civ) 10.
45 All references to 'Sheriff Principal' (including the section headings in ss 163, 164, 165 and 167) will change to 'Sheriff Appeal Court'. See Children (Scotland) Act 2020, s 27 (not yet in force at time of writing (July 2022)).

46 CH(S)A 2011, ss 163(9), 164(5), 165(5), 167(5). See: *L v Children's Reporter* [2020] 8 WLUK 288, *M v Scottish Children's Reporter Administration* [2019] CSIH 37, *X & Y v Principal Reporter* [2022] CSOH 32.
47 CH(S)A 2011, s 144(1).
48 CH(S)A 2011, s 144(3).
49 Children (Scotland) Act 1995, s 17(6)(b).
50 CH(S)A 2011, s 145.
51 CH(S)A 2011, s 146(1) and (2).
52 CH(S)A 2011, s 146(3).
53 CH(S)A 2011, s 146(4).
54 CH(S)A 2011, s 146(5) and (6).
55 CH(S)A 2011, s 146(7).
56 CH(S)A 2011, ss 147 and 148.

The effect of a compulsory supervision order

15.11 Parents do not lose their parental responsibilities and parental rights in respect of a child who is subject to a compulsory supervision order. Not only does a court have jurisdiction to regulate residence or contact in relation to such children but the parent retains title to sue.[1] In deciding whether to make any order under s 11(1) of the Children (Scotland) Act 1995, the court has a duty to consider the overarching principles in s 11(7) of the Act.[2] However, the making of an order in cases where a compulsory supervision order is in place may be of little value to the parent where the compulsory supervision order contains measures, for example, that the child resides at a specified place[3] or includes a direction regulating the child's contact with the parent.[4] Therefore, although the parent has parental responsibilities and parental rights, he or she cannot *exercise* those responsibilities and rights if it would be incompatible with the compulsory supervision order and any measures it contains. As a relevant person, the parent could seek a review and ask the children's hearing to vary the condition in relation to contact.

The reason why parental responsibilities and parental rights do not automatically cease when a compulsory supervision order is made is because, in many cases, it is desirable that the child should continue to live, or at least, retain links, with his or her family. A local authority has a duty to take steps to promote personal relations and direct contact between the child and any person with parental responsibilities and parental rights where it is practical and appropriate to do so and where, in the exercise of its decision-making, the child's welfare is the paramount concern.[5] Where a local authority takes the view that in order to safeguard and promote the welfare of a child (who is the subject of a compulsory supervision order) it is necessary that the child should no longer be part of his or her family, the local authority may apply for a permanence order.[6] Before doing so, the local authority must refer the case to the Reporter who must arrange a children's hearing to review the case.[7] If the children's hearing agrees that it is in the best interests of the child to do so, it can vary the compulsory supervision order to allow the local authority to proceed.

1 This principle was established in the case of *P v P* 2000 SLT 781, in which a grandmother and the father of a child successfully appealed against the decision of the sheriff to dismiss their actions seeking parental responsibilities and parental rights over the child. The fact that a supervision requirement was in place did not fetter the court's discretion to make any order under s 11(1) of the Children (Scotland) Act 1995.

2 On the C(S)A 1995, s 11, see **Ch 12**. Note the impending changes to ss 11(7)–(7E) of the C(S)A 1995 when ss 1(3) and (4) of the Children (Scotland) Act 2020 come into force.

3 Children's Hearings (Scotland) Act 2011, s 83(2)(a).

4 CH(S)A 2011, s 83(2)(g).

5 C(S)A 1995, s 17.

6 Discussed at para **14.7**.

7 CH(S)A 2011, s 131(2).

CONCLUSION

15.12 The children's hearings system introduced a welfare-based approach to address the problem of children who commit criminal offences and children who are in need of care and protection. All children who come before a children's hearing have in common the background of a dysfunction within the family. The children's hearings system provides personnel with expertise, experience and commitment to make decisions that are in the best interests of children. It could be argued that the danger of such interventionist legislation is that insufficient weight is given to the rights of children and their families. However, by insisting that a hearing cannot proceed unless the child and relevant person(s) accept the grounds for referral or, where they do not, that the grounds must be established to the satisfaction of a sheriff, the present system recognises the importance of family autonomy. By imposing a duty to consult the child at all the important procedural stages, the Children's Hearings (Scotland) Act 2011 also places emphasis on children's rights. Nevertheless, the procedures will continue to be scrutinised to ensure they do not violate Articles 5, 6 and 8 of the European Convention on Human Rights.

On the other hand, the responsibility for implementing the compulsory supervision orders rests on local authorities. Many local authorities simply do not have the resources – particularly social workers – to discharge this obligation. It will be interesting to see how the procedure to force local authorities effectively to fulfil their duties towards children who are subject to compulsory supervision orders will operate in practice at this time of increasingly severe cuts in public spending.

Index

[All references are to paragraph number]